TEST
PILOTS

The Frontiersmen of Flight

RICHARD P. HALLION

TEST PILOTS

The Frontiersmen of Flight

Revised Edition

Smithsonian Institution Press
Washington, D.C.
London

Library of Congress Cataloging-in-Publication Data

Hallion, Richard.
    Test pilots.

    Bibliography: p.
    Includes index.
    1. Airplanes—Flight testing—History.   I. Title.
TL671.7.H288   1987   629.134'53'09   87-28846
ISBN 0-87474-549-7 (pbk.)

British Library Cataloging in Publication Data is available

The paper in this book meets the guidelines for permanence and durability of the Committee
on Production Guidelines for Book Longevity of the Council on Library Resources.

For
Mike Swann
Dick Gray
Cecil Snyder
Doug Benefield
Chuck Sewell
Harvey Victor
and all the rest who have died . . .

Flight testing of new concepts, designs, and systems is fundamental to aeronautics. Laboratory data alone, and theories based on these data, cannot give all the important answers. . . . Each time a new aircraft flies, a "moment of truth" arrives for the designer as he discovers whether a group of individually satisfactory elements add together to make a satisfactory whole or whether their unexpected interactions result in a major deficiency. Flight research plays the essential role in assuring that all the elements of an aircraft can be integrated into a satisfactory system.

—James E. Webb, NASA Administrator, in testimony before the Senate Committee on Aeronautical and Space Science, 1967.

CONTENTS

FOREWORD

Michael Collins

"Through these portals pass the world's finest pilots," read the sign above the entrance to the Air Force Test Pilot School. It was 1960, I was a student there, and I fervently believed that sign. Today I still do. Test pilots are a select group within a select group. That fact has remained constant since the early days of aviation. On the other hand, the machines themselves have changed radically, and so have the methods and techniques used in perfecting them. Dick Hallion has done a masterful job of tracing this evolution, and the vital and occasionally deadly relationship between pilots and some of the most complex machines ever created.

Today our craft fly so well that the public's main concern is that airliners will bump into each other in the crowded skies. In 1903, on the world's first powered flight, Orville Wright discovered that because of poor elevator design ". . . the machine would rise suddenly to about ten feet, and then as suddenly dart for the ground." This original flight test report describes a problem in the area that engineers call "stability and control." The other major area of flight testing is "performance," examining the speed and altitude regime ("flight envelope") of a new design. Between the Wright Flyer and today's docile airliners, there have been some weird and wild machines, many of them darting for the ground and some, unfortunately, making it there with the pilot still strapped in the cockpit. The laws of aerodynamics are unforgiving, and the ground is hard.

In a profession such as this, especially in the early days, when danger lurked in every new maneuver, the people attracted to this work could legitimately be called "dare devils." Yet those who survived and became successful were basically shrewd risk assessors. They organized their flights to build methodically on what they already knew about their planes, and introduced unknown elements slowly and carefully. They advanced in a series of stair steps. As instrumentation improved, engineers on the ground could assist them mightily in measuring what was taking place minute by minute in flight, and the test pilot learned to confer long and often with this ground support team. It became more and more common for the test pilot to be an engineer himself. Instead of listening to the wind in the wires, he was more apt to spend his time poring over graphs and equations. Jimmy Doolittle's career probably represents the epitome of the transition from white-scarf "flying fools" to pragmatic engineers. Jimmy was both a daring race pilot and the holder of a doctorate from the Massachusetts Institute of Technology.

The advent of the simulator also changed the test flying business. It was now possible to insert mathematical equations into a computer and thereby predict the performance, stability, and control characteristics of an airplane not yet off the drawing board. Most test pilots would rather fly an airplane than a box on the ground, but, hey, why not discover—and correct—as many mistakes as possible before committing your little pink body to the real sky.

At about this stage in the evolution of flight testing, the space program came along. All the early astronauts were test pilots, and they brought with them the caution as well as the daring of their profession. They were involved in the layout of their spacecraft (which were designed by aeronautical engineers), and they recommended many changes to make them more like the airplanes they knew instead of alien machines built to explore an entirely new environment. They also used simulators to great advantage, as engineering tools to assess designs and as a method of ground training that closely replicated flight conditions.

But one thing was different about space. It was not possible to stairstep into orbit, to test the craft by making a long series of flights, each with a small incremental increase in performance. It tended to be all or nothing, zooming out to the four corners of the envelope on the first try. Frank Borman's Apollo 8 moon crew, for example, took the third Saturn V—the first manned Saturn V—all the way to escape velocity (25,000 miles per hour), over 7,000 miles an hour faster than anyone had ever traveled before.

In space with no wind buffet, traditional airplane stability and control rules are modified somewhat, but basically the same yardsticks of flight testing apply. Every last bit of performance is demanded, as evidenced by the fact that Neil Armstrong landed *Eagle* on the moon with less than thirty seconds of fuel in his tanks. The average airline pilot starts squirming in his seat when fuel remaining drops to the half-hour range.

Yet test pilots Borman and Armstrong would be the first to explain that they really weren't doing anything more difficult or demanding than their predecessors had done in putting a tricky new airplane through its paces. On the first lunar landing flight, Apollo 11, the most intricate piloting task assigned to me was docking my command module *Columbia* with *Eagle*, the landing craft flown by Armstrong and Buzz Aldrin. It was a completely manual operation, without help from Mission Control, and involved my manipulating pitch, yaw, and roll controls with my right hand while working a three-axis throttle with my left. A delicate touch was required, and certainly a great deal was riding on the outcome of this one maneuver, but the precision involved was no greater than in some rolling pull-outs I had done at 750 knots in an F-104 Starfighter a couple of years earlier at Edwards Air Force Base.

I was born in 1930, exactly the right time to fly in the Gemini and Apollo programs. My first squadron flying was in early jets, the F-80 Shooting Star and the F-86 Sabre, and later I progressed through the Century Series of Air Force fighters and even got a ride in some of today's super performers such as the F-14, F-15, and F-16. I wouldn't trade these experiences for anything, but I feel that I came in just as Act II of a great play was beginning. I grew up with visions of the Granville brothers' Gee Bee racer, all engine and fat fuselage, an unstable bumblebee. I dreamed of soaring high in a Spitfire or lumbering along with Howard Hughes in the Spruce Goose. I marveled at Igor Sikorsky's first ungainly helicopter. I listened raptly at my flying school graduation while Roscoe Turner described his varied career. He flew with a waxed mustache and a pet lion named Gilmore. I was stuck with a computer.

Yes, I missed Act I, but one of the great pleasures of this book is that Dick Hallion has not. It's all here, even the story of Brother Eilmar, the flying (?) Monk of Malmesbury Abbey, who attempted to soar nine hundred years before the Wright brothers. Then the pace picks up, sixty-six years from first powered flight to first lunar landing, on to the Shuttle, and now, who knows what next?

Dick Hallion is a brilliant young historian, and this book is an accurate, lucid, and fascinating exposition of the real role of the test pilot, from Kitty Hawk to the moon.

PREFACE

It is 4 A.M. The buildings and runways at Palmdale Airport's Air Force Plant 42 are still cloaked in pre-dawn darkness when an Air Force-Lockheed test team sets to work, readying a SR-71 Blackbird strategic reconnaissance aircraft for flight testing at Mach 3: three times the speed of sound. Overhead, the moon is a huge glowing orb and the stars of the desert night gleam jewel-like; there is no hint that the brisk chill of the Mojave night will give way to the pleasant warmth of a California summer morning, or the Saharan heat of midday.

Out on the ramp at Palmdale, snuggled close to the Lockheed complex at Site 2, stands a rakish black SR-71A, with its distinctive blended wing-body, angular fins and inlets, and, above all, its reptilian look and massive turboramjet engines dramatically illuminated by high-intensity lighting. It is a sight out of science fiction; in contrast, parked nearby is a small white Northrop T-38A trainer that will chase the Blackbird as it takes off and begins its climbout to Mach 3. Only subtle signs reveal that these are flight test aircraft, not from the "operational" world. A saucy skunk peers perkily from the vertical fins of the Blackbird, the symbol of Lockheed designer Kelly Johnson's famed "Skunkworks." The T-38 is devoid of any markings except for a Blackbird silhouette on its own fin and a natty blue fuselage stripe. Connected to the Blackbird are some umbilical lifelines of aerospace technology, including air hoses to start the engines and instrumentation monitoring systems. The two cockpits, one for the test pilot and the other for the flight test navigator, are open with technicians checking under the raised canopies.

The day before, "Det 6" (as the Air Force's SR-71A test detachment is known) had coordinated final arrangements for the flight with the nearby Air Force Flight Test Center at Edwards Air Force Base, and had held its last test briefing and flight readiness review. Some preparations took longer; scheduling a special Boeing KC-135Q tanker loaded with exotic JP-7 fuel from Beale Air Force Base had been completed a full two weeks earlier. Traffic controllers from the Federal Aviation Administration were briefed on what they needed to know about the mission, for the flight will take the Blackbird on a gigantic circuit of the western United States, across several air route traffic control zones, including time out for a midair pitstop for refueling from the tanker.

It is getting lighter; the moon and stars are dimming, and the shadows cast by surrounding ridges are shortening. Pink and gold highlights brush some high cirrus over the desert, and then, suddenly, the sun pops over Saddleback Butte. It gives a dull luster to the Blackbird's flanks, and illuminates the support equipment and crewmen as they work. Electrically, the SR-71A is alive, and already technicians within the Lockheed center are monitoring the performance of the plane's on-board instrumentation system. It is nearly 7 A.M.; over at Rockwell's facility, a row of dark new B-1B bombers pick up faint traces of color from the sun as they patiently squat lizard-like awaiting equipment installation and final flight checks before delivery to the Strategic Air Command.

The test crew arrive for work a few minutes apart, edging their automobiles into the employee parking area, past a fenced-in storage area where rest dismembered and cocooned examples of the Blackbird family's predecessors: the single-seat Lockheed A-12, and the YF-12C; already a quarter-century has passed since these first probed the Mach 3 frontier. The crewmen are not the reckless daredevils of popular imagination, possessing some indefinable and mythical "right stuff," hung-over from the night before and weaving their way to work, tattered silk scarves waving jauntily in the breeze. Rather, they are thoroughgoing aerospace professionals. The test pilot has thousands of hours in operational and experimental aircraft ranging from transports and fighters to the SR-71 and its subsonic predecessors the U-2 and WB-57F. The flight test navigator flew a combat tour as a reconnaissance systems operator in RF-4C Phantoms over Southeast Asia, has flight test experience in a wide range of airplanes, and, coincidentally, is an aerospace historian. Both are family men with young children. In a curious twist from what one might expect, the test pilot, a Texan, is a Civil War buff, while the navigator, a Virginian, runs a small ranch. Both men are graduates of the Air Force Test Pilot School at Edwards: the famed "Schoolhouse" where test pilots, flight test engineers, and flight test navigators are minted before entering the ranks of an aerospace elite.

After arriving, the pilot and navigator go over any remaining details with the engineers and technical staff, then go downstairs in the main building to begin the laborious process of suiting-up in the cumbersome pressure suits that will save their lives in the event that something happens and they lose cockpit pressurization while cruising above 80,000 feet. First come inner garments and liners and then, finally, the outer suit. As technicians assist them, they put on their suits, boots, helmets, and gloves, hooking up to portable air-conditioning units, and checking out communications. No detail is too insignificant to overlook. Special attention is paid to glove and helmet seals; should one fail, its wearer could die in seconds. The oxygen system is checked. At last all is ready, and a van from the physiological support unit at Edwards pulls up outside the building. The two men waddle awkwardly over to it, entering and settling in for the short ride of several hundred feet to the waiting airplane. The van lurches off and soon wheels into position beside the Blackbird, and the two men disembark. As they make their way up the tall gantry beside the cockpit, technicians carry their portable air conditioners and, for a minute, the image of knights assisted by trusty squires comes to mind. It is 8:15 as the crew enters the airplane.

For what seems an interminable length of time they proceed through a series of careful checks. Outside, a group of technicians huddle around the cockpit and under the airplane, ignoring dripping JP-7 fuel that dribbles from the wings and fuselage to puddle and pool on the ramp beneath the Blackbird. Like much about the Blackbird, even this is not what it first appears; instead of a flight-cancelling safety hazard it is, instead, an accepted fact of Blackbird life. The sleek Blackbird's structure is designed to withstand the thermal expansion of flight at speeds above Mach 3, and thus, the fuel tanks, at normal temperatures, leak profusely so that its undersides and flanks often glisten with moisture. But so high is the flash point of the Blackbird's special fuel that it is immune to ignition from ordinary flame and, instead, requires a squirt of an unholy substance called tetraethylborane—a substance so unstable that it explodes in the mere presence of air—to detonate the fuel-air mixture in the engines. All is set and the crew signals for engine start. With a soaring whine, a high-pressure air hose kicks over the compressor section of the left engine. Air mixes with fuel, a shot of "TEB" is added to the mixture, and there is an almost invisible green flash in the exhaust as the engine ignites. In the cockpit, engine rpm rises and fuel flow and exhaust temperatures stabilize. A shimmering exhaust wave washes the ground aft of the plane, sending a warm torrent of heated air over the edge of the field's security perimeter.

Next, the right engine lights off; still the technicians work around and under the plane, and even between the exhausts, as if choreographed for a technological ballet.

Functional checks continue, and, next to the Blackbird, others are readying the T-38A for flight. On other mornings, fuel lines have sprung leaks, instrumentation has turned sour, hydraulic systems have proven recalcitrant, and flights have been scrubbed. Multimillion dollar airplanes can be replaced—but not the crews. Flight researchers at Det 6—like flight researchers around the world—simply don't take irresponsible chances with their lives or the lives of others. It is nearly forty minutes since the pilot and navigator have strapped in, nearly twenty minutes since the engines fired up. As onlookers observe with a critical eye, the pilot cycles the controls: the massive all-moving vertical fins, the elevons on the wing's trailing edge, the inlet spikes of each engine nacelle. All is set: the Blackbird is on internal power; all hoses and wires have been unplugged; the canopies are closed; the gantry ladder has been pulled away, as has any remaining ground equipment; already the tanker is aloft, on its way to the refueling track to await the SR-71. The T-38, crewed by another SR-71 pilot and navigator, taxies noisily out, heading up the ramp toward the bright sun and the east end of Palmdale's Runway 25. Palmdale tower gives the blessing for taxi, and, moments later, the Blackbird pilot advances the throttles. The Blackbird begins to roll, turns onto the taxiway, and bobs slightly on its stalky landing gear as it follows the chase plane to the end of the runway.

A Lockheed C-141B Starlifter transport from Norton Air Force Base is on final approach to Runway 25, on the last of several touch-and-goes. A Lockheed technician and Air Force NCO critically observe the "trash-hauler's" landing, watching as the big but graceful airplane takes off, climbing out to the south. They are there for a "FOD check": to examine the runway for any debris that might endanger the Blackbird's tires and engines. Bolts, rocks, and even lost tools—nothing surprises a FOD crew, and they scan the runway and its shoulders carefully. Today, as they drive slowly down the length of the strip, they note with satisfaction that the runway is clean. They turn off at the end of the runway to await the takeoff. A small safety team has given the T-38A a "last-chance" once-over, and now, as the SR-71A rolls up, they pronounce the T-38 set and turn their attention to the Blackbird. The SR-71 is healthy as well. It is now 8:57 and the mission is scheduled to commence.

Palmdale tower clears the T-38A to launch; it turns onto the runway, goes to full power as the crew makes a final instrument check, and then into afterburner. For a second it quivers against its brakes until the pilot liberates it, allowing the small white dart to scoot down the runway and into the air, turning to the right to commence a closed traffic pattern. The SR-71A taxies to the end of the runway and is cleared for takeoff; its crew makes its own last minute instrument checks, and the Blackbird pilot, noting that the T-38 pilot is directly abeam of the SR-71A, calls "thirty seconds." Thirty seconds from now—at precisely 9:00 A.M.—he will go to full power and brake release, committing the Blackbird to flight. It is the duty of the T-38 pilot to position his chase plane close off the left wing of the Blackbird so that he and his backseater can observe its takeoff and climbout, when rapid life-or-death decisions might have to be reached. Exactly thirty seconds after the call the Blackbird goes into full afterburner, twin bolts of shockwave-studded light rocketing back from its exhausts. With a shattering roar drowning out the T-38's puny engines, the Blackbird lunges forward; three quarters of the distance down the runway the SR-71A "unsticks" and noses into the air, its afterburners glaring a golden orange, and the T-38 tucked in right in position beside it. Both flash over the railroad tracks at the end of the runway by Sierra Highway, over the waiting camera-laden onlookers parked along Avenue N (who always seem to know when a Blackbird will fly), and accelerate toward the western boundary of the Antelope Valley, curving gently northward. It is 9:02, the T-38A will soon return, and the SR-71A will shortly be at altitudes and speeds undreamed of a few short decades ago.

Every time a weekend pilot goes aloft in a light airplane, every time a military pilot slams into afterburner, every time a businessman or a tourist relaxes in an airline seat, every time an oil rigger flies out to a drilling platform—in short, every time any of us fly as flight crew or passengers, we follow in the wake of the test pilot and flight test engineers who have gone that way before. They have acquired the detailed scientific knowledge that designers have put to use in building the aircraft upon which we rely. They have spent thousands of hours proving out the vehicles we fly in, so that we may fly with confidence. They have chosen to verify the expectations of the engineers and to furnish the manual writers with the information pilots and flight crews need to know about their aircraft. Above all, they have demonstrated the products of the drawing board aloft, in actual flight, away from the static conditions of the laboratory. And they follow in the trappings of a long and noble tradition, for flight testing of new aircraft, systems, and concepts is as old as flight itself.

Periodically, the popular press predicts the imminent passage of the test pilot and flight researcher. They will be replaced by remotely controlled models, by ground-based computer simulation, by more exacting paper studies and analysis—just a matter of time. And every time, the obituary notice is premature, for so long as humans fly, there will be a need for manned flight testing. Otto Lilienthal, the great German gliding pioneer, and Wilbur Wright, codeveloper of the world's first successful airplane, expressed it best. In 1896 Lilienthal wrote, "One can get a proper insight into the practice of flying only by actual flying experiments."[1] Wright compared the testing of an airplane to riding a fractious horse: "If you are looking for perfect safety you will do well to sit on a fence and watch the birds, but if you really wish to learn you must mount a machine and become acquainted with its tricks by actual trial."[2] Both statements are as true today—and for the future—as they were in the past.

So flight research and flight testing are a vital component of aviation. But what of the test pilots, the flight researchers themselves? What are the qualifications, the attributes, the qualities they must possess? The answer is complex, for, as with most professionals, test pilots blend both "made" and "born" characteristics. It is perhaps best to describe what the test pilot is *not:* an unthinking, reckless daredevil who will do anything at least once in an airplane. Unfortunately, it is this image that all too often pervades the popular media, a stereotypical holdover from the days of Clark Gable and the motion picture *Test Pilot.* Having set aside the "show me the stick and I'll fly it" myth, one can approach more clearly what constitutes the successful test pilot.

A typical successful test pilot is an individual who possessess advanced training in a scientific or technical field and who has excellent basic aircraft handling skills. He is a graduate of a recognized test pilot school such as the Air Force or Navy test pilot school, or the Empire Test Pilots' School, in Great Britain. He is imbued with a sense of adventure, highly motivated and self-disciplined, thoroughly familiar with the craft he will fly and with whatever mission he is called upon to perform. Flight testing, like most activities, requires close cooperation and teamwork among many individuals, expecially between the designers and the test pilot. (Cyril Uwins, the great British test pilot, once stated, "The designer must have faith in the pilot's ability to locate faults, the pilot must believe in the designer's ability to produce good aeroplanes and engines.")[3] It is critically important that a test pilot never succumb to the temptation to do too much too soon, for that path leads but to the grave. He must adopt a conservative approach, emphasizing wariness and caution, not placing absolute trust in the machine and the predictions of its creators until it has proved itself by actual trial. Finally, after taking all reasonable precautions, after studying, practicing, planning, the test pilot is ready to go aloft to confront whatever challenge he faces with confidence in his abilities and with courage.

The close bonds between flight researchers that form during the testing process set test pilots and flight test engineers apart from others in the aeronautical community. Because they are the pioneers, the frontiersmen of flight, there is an unspoken *esprit* that draws them together. They have recognized their professionalism by creating worldwide organizations— The Society of Experimental Test Pilots, The Society of Flight Test Engineers. But it is more than their training and background that distingiush them. It is an attitude, a philosophical approach, a quality. Writing of French test pilots for the journal *Document* in 1939, Antoine de Saint-Exupéry alluded to this quality when he stated:

> I still believe in Coupet, Lasne or Détroyat, for whom an airplane is not merely a collection of parameters, but an organism that you examine. They land; they discreetly take a look around the plane. With the tips of their fingers they touch the fuselage and pat the wing. They do not calculate, they meditate. Then they turn to the engineer and simply say: "The fixed surface must be shortened."
>
> I admire science, but I also admire wisdom.[4]

The story of American test pilots and their flight research is a long one, a story of challenges confronted and overcome. It is a story laced with courage and sacrifice, the story of aviation itself. It is, finally, a story without end, for the frontiers of the sky can only be pushed back, and are never closed.

Richard P. Hallion

Wright-Patterson Air Force Base
1 June 1987

CHAPTER 1

HARBINGERS

The desire to fly has always been one of humanity's strongest aspirations. The prehistory of human flight, running up to 1783 and the invention of the balloon, offers ample proof that peoples around the world dreamed and sought to fly with almost innate unanimity. Sigmund Freud found dreams of flight and flying so common as to be a definable human characteristic—an impulse rooted deep in our collective unconscious. All the world's major religions had greater and lesser deities—both "good" and "bad"—that could fly, typified by the flying bulls of ancient Assyria and the angels of Judeo-Christian tradition. The Greeks gave the world the legend of Daedalus and Icarus. According to the Second Century B.C. Athenian scholar Apollodorus, Daedalus, the Greek architect who had planned the Labyrinth on Crete for the Minotaur, was imprisoned in his own creation, together with his son Icarus, by King Minos. Escape by land or sea was impossible. So the father constructed wings for himself and his son, fashioned from feathers and held on the body by wax. Despite Daedalus' shouted warnings, Icarus flew too close to the sun, which melted his wings. He plunged into the sea, while his heartbroken father continued onward to Sicily. In today's terms, Icarus had exceeded his craft's thermal limits, inducing structural failure with subsequent loss of control.

THE TOWER JUMPERS: LEAPING WITH WINGS AND A PRAYER

In fact, the actual history of flight is full of examples of individuals who tried to fly, often with disastrous results. These individuals, usually termed "tower jumpers," wrapped themselves in cloaks and enthusiastically leapt into the air to emulate the birds, usually jumping to their doom. There is the popular medieval legend of Simon Magus, whose fatal attempt at flight was allegedly quashed by the prayers of St. Peter; the fatal plunge, at least, quite possibly took place. The first demonstrable human flight was that of a Moorish physician and inventor (as well as a "rather bad poet," in the words of historian Lynn White), Abu'l-Qasim 'Abbās b. Firnās, of Cordova, in Andalusia. Ibn Firnās, like the legendary Greeks, attached feathers to his body, together with wings, and leapt from a high spot. According to the Moroccan historian al-Maqqarī, Ibn Firnās glided for a considerable distance but landed heavily, severely injuring his back. Al-Maqqarī attributed the accident to Ibn Firnās's lack of tail surfaces. And so, as with so many other aspects of science and technology, it was the sweeping tide of Islam that introduced flight to the West.

However, it is to medieval England that we turn for evidence of the first proto-test pilot. It is not known whether word of Ibn Firnās's flight had reached England; given the growing progressive views of English culture at the time, would-be English airmen did not need foreign inspiration to get started. About the year 1000, over a century after Ibn Firnās's flight, a remarkable event took place in the abbey town of Malmesbury, near the banks of the Avon, in Wiltshire.

The architect of this particular event was a Benedictine monk at Malmesbury Abbey, Eilmer by name. Then a young man, probably in his early twenties, Eilmer was interested in science and wrote treatises on astrology and geometry. He became convinced that if he attached wings to his hands and feet, he could leap from the West Tower of the Abbey and glide for a considerable distance. According to a subsequent account by the twelfth-century historian William of Malmesbury, Eilmer fashioned the wings, climbed up the tower, and then dived off, gliding for a distance greater than six hundred feet. However, "agitated by the violence of the wind and the swirling of air, as well as by awareness of his rashness, he fell, broke his legs, and was lame ever after." After his accident, he is alleged to have stated "that the cause of his failure was his forgetting to put a tail on the back part." Another source credits him with wishing to try again, "but the Abbot of the day refused to allow it." Eilmer retired from aviation, remaining as a monk at the Abbey, and witnessing Halley's comet in 1066 and the subsequent Norman invasion.[1]

Imagine what it must have been like: Malmesbury Abbey was a wonder in its time, though not as impressive as it later was or even as its remains are today. Situated in the extreme Northwest of Wiltshire, the Abbey had originated about 600, when Maildulph, a Celtic monk, built a small hermit's cell on the present site of the Abbey. His pupil and successor, Aldhelm, enlarged upon his efforts, really starting the Abbey, which prospered under the rule of the Saxon king Athelstan. The Abbey and town suffered the usual vicissitudes of medieval life, being all but destroyed by Danish raiders at one point. It was an unusual site for the first occidental flight. Brother Eilmer would probably have chosen a gray, windy spring day for his flight, with the winds blowing out of Salisbury Plain, and trudged to the top of the West Tower, his fellow monks helping him with the wings—early churchmen, contrary to myth, were fascinated with both temporal and spiritual flight—lugging them up the tower and then helping fasten them to his body. Of the wings, we know —and can surmise—little. Almost certainly they were of cloth, and of considerable size. A mere cloak-parachute sort of device could not have produced the flight that William of Malmesbury describes. They would be braced with wooden spars, perhaps attached to a shoulder yoke. He probably planned to flap them but recognized that they should be fixed so that they would not fold upward, but, rather, would stay extended, enabling him to soar.

Finally all was ready. As a rising gust sprang up, Brother Eilmer spread the wings and, with a deep breath and last Pater Noster on his lips, leapt from the tower. Almost immediately, the force of air under the wing prevented him from flapping; up loomed the rolling Wiltshire countryside; the gust blew violently, rolling him. Now, perhaps, he managed to attempt to flap, and in the final seconds he lost lift and fell to earth, braced for the impending crash and cursing his own rashness and presumption upon divine mercy. Then the bone-cracking impact; the rush of running monks and townsfolk; the head-shaking abbot; the groaning test pilot. And finally, the stretcher carrying him off to a long convalescence. His self-analysis is all we need to rank Eilmer as the ancestor—one is tempted to say patron saint—of the modern-day test pilot. He had made a test flight. Low-altitude gustiness combined with pilot error had caused him to crash. From his statement, via William of Malmesbury, it would seem that he intuitively grasped that the addition of tail surfaces might possibly have given him adequate longitudinal stability. His critical analysis of the flight and his actions are in the best tradition of the engineering test pilot, as is his alleged willingness to try again, presumably with the necessary design modifications. It is fitting that Malmesbury Abbey, as it is today, has a stained-glass window in the vestry showing Brother Eilmer holding a glider (the actual configuration of his is, of course, unknown). He is wearing, appropriately enough, a cloak in hues similar to today's Royal Air Force blue. The town boasts a pub named The Flying Monk, and on town celebration days, the RAF reenact Brother Eilmer's flight with a pilot dressed as a monk sliding down cables to the ground, to be carried off on a stretcher by other pilot-monks! Eilmer, it can be safely presumed, would take his greatest delight in knowing that a few miles away is Wiltshire's contribution to modern aeronautics: the Aeroplane and Armament Experimental Establishment (A&AEE), RAF Boscombe Down. There, at the Empire Test Pilots' School, Eilmer's modern-day equivalents learn their trade before proceeding to test the finest aircraft that Britain's industry can produce. Its motto, "Learn to Test, Test to Learn," is one Eilmer would have endorsed and taken to heart nearly a thousand years before.

In the centuries following Eilmer, countless others attempted flight in the same way. Some of these individuals were inspired by accounts passed down of Eilmer's experiment at Malmesbury. Most, however, were simply working alone, on their own, without knowledge of what had gone on before. A partial catalog of these early tower-jumping "flights" is most depressing reading:

c. 1008: Al-Jauharī leaps to his death from the mosque of Hishapur, in Khorosan.

1162: An unnamed Saracen is fatally injured after leaping from a column in the Hippodrome of Constantinople with a voluminous cloak fitted with stiffeners.

1496: An old cantor of Nuremberg breaks his arms and legs while trying to fly.

1503: Giovanni Danti, an Italian mathematician, is seriously injured in a tower jump at Perugia.

1507: Giovanni Damiani (John Damian, Abbot of Tungland), breaks a leg while attempting to fly off a wall of Stirling Castle.

1536: Bolori, an Italian clockmaker, is killed in a flight attempt from the Cathedral of Troyes in France.

1628: The painter Guidotti makes an unsuccessful attempt at flight at Lucca.

c. 1660: Allard, a French gymnast, is seriously injured while attempting a flight before King Louis XIV at Saint Germain.

1673: Bernoin, a citizen of Frankfort-am-Main, breaks his neck and his legs while attempting to fly.

1678: Besnier, a French locksmith, completes a floundering descent (probably just from a rooftop), without injury.

c. 1690: Canon Oger of Rosoy Abbey is saved from serious injury when he falls into a bush while attempting a flight. At about the same time, a priest of Peronne is killed when he falls into a moat. A Russian peasant survives an unsuccessful flight attempt about this time but is whipped for his failure!

c. 1742: The Marquis de Bacqueville attempts to fly the river Seine by fixing wings to his legs and arms; his flight is cut short when he crashes into a barge, breaking his legs.

1772: The Canon Desforges, of Étampes, jumps from a tower at Guinette with an ornithopterlike contraption. Its huge fabric canopy enables him to survive the attempt with but minor injuries.

1781: Karl Friedrich Meerwein, architect to the prince of Baden, constructs a primitive glider that enables him to make one or two short glides, without injury. His vehicle resembles a flying wing.

And so, on the rather upbeat note of Karl Meerwein, the era of the tower jumpers came to an end, just on the eve of practical human flight via balloons. As tower jumpers progressed, their schemes became more complex, and they had experimented with various types of machinery, the most popular of which were ornithopters—flapping-wing devices designed to emulate the birds, and powered by human muscle. Toward the end of the seventeenth century, Giovanni Borelli, an Italian mathematician, published *De motu animalium*, which demonstrated that humans lacked sufficient muscle power to operate ornithopterlike craft. (Additionally, until the work of George Cayley, Ferdinand d'Esterno, and Otto Lilienthal, the actual method by which birds flew was shrouded in mystery.) It is sad that tower jumpers continued, determined to flap their way into history, long after Borelli's work became known; no worthy descendants of Eilmer, these! He would not have flown in the face of reason and scientific fact, once that information became available. Likewise, the test pilot of today is always careful never to exceed his own capabilities or those of his equipment: the penalty for violating this common-sense rule is all too often death. The unlucky tower jumper never survived; the lucky tower jumper faced, in the words of aviation historian Charles Gibbs-Smith, "those survivals and maimings with which fortune favoured a few."

Oddly, little attention, save for written accounts, was devoted to the kite. The kite, the earliest-known fixed-wing surface and the basis for modern aircraft design, appeared in China about 1000 B.C. Europe became aware of the kite through the writings of Marco Polo, who described how thirteenth-century East Asian society actually flew man-carrying kites from merchant ships. Apparently, however, Eastern society viewed flying as skeptically as did the West. Polo relates how, when all is ready for a flight, the ship's crew "will find some fool or drunkard and lash him to the frame, since no one in his right mind or with his wits about him would expose himself to that peril." Such attitudes did little to encourage the development of manned aviation. And just when the kite *did* begin attracting serious attention, the Jesuit Francesco de Lana-Terzi conceptualized the balloon. Though impractical (he proposed using evacuated copper spheres), his general concept led to both the hot-air and hydrogen balloons of a century later, distracting advocates of lifting (i.e., winged) flight until the advent of George Cayley.

By the mid-eighteenth century, the dawn of practical flight was nearly at hand. It is paradoxical that humanity had sought to fly for centuries and yet it took so long for humans to actually attain flight. The glider flights of Lilienthal could just as easily have been made in antiquity, since all the basic elements were there: wood, cloth, leather thongs for bindings, small copper or iron fittings, observers studying birds. Equally odd is the absence of hot-air balloons. The rising of smoke and hot gases from a fire was well known, especially to medieval technologists. By the end of the fifteenth century, in fact, some European cooks were using small turbines in chimney flues to rotate spits, the hot gases of the fire spinning the turbines, which drove the spits via gears and shafts. Yet, until the eighteenth century, little if any thought seems to have been given to enclosing these gases and using them to produce lift. Or was it? Who can say definitely that, even before Eilmer, some enterprising technologist-test pilot living in the Han Dynasty, or along the Indus, or in Hellenistic Greece, or perhaps a citizen of Rome did not indeed develop some practical glider or some primitive balloon? The technology was there and required little more than trial-and-error development and flight testing. But if such happened, we do not know of it, nor did it change subsequent history. As romantically appealing as such hypotheses are, they are ahistorical. Reality dictates that it is unlikely. We only know what has come down to us through recorded history, and that history is clear: practical human flight began with the balloon, invented in France, the land of Diderot and Voltaire, during the eighteenth century, the fabled "Age of Reason." It is curious that this revolution in technology took place in a society beset by contradictions, a society at once backward and progressive, feudal and liberal, and on the verge of its own violent social upheaval.

THE BALLOONISTS

The balloon gave the world its first aeronauts, and these courageous individuals, many of whom were motivated by scientific and technological curiosity and not merely a desire for acclaim or adventure, can rightly be considered forerunners of modern test pilots and flight researchers. There is some evidence that, at the beginning of the eighteenth century, a Brazilian cleric residing in Portugal, Father Laurenço de Gusmão, built a small hot-air balloon. The next figures in ballooning, however, are indisputably the fathers of lighter-than-air flight: the brothers Joseph and Étienne Montgolfier, who were papermakers residing in the French town of Annonay. Joseph, who first became interested in flight, began experiments with steam-filled paper balloons. His work attracted the interest of his brother, and the two men collaborated on further studies. They abandoned steam in favor of balloons filled with hot air generated by the burning of wool and moist straw. In November and December of 1782, they experimented with free-flying taffeta balloons, one of which rose to 985 feet. In June 1783, the brothers built a large balloon which rose to 460 feet during a demonstration before members of the Académie des Sciences. The French Academy next asked that the brothers demonstrate their balloon in Paris. The brothers built a very beautiful and ornate balloon over 74 feet high, but a storm destroyed it before it could be launched. Their next balloon, built in haste for the royal demonstration before the ill-fated Louis XVI and his court, was more successful but flew only after physicist Jacques Alexandre César Charles had demonstrated a small unmanned hydrogen-filled balloon before throngs of Parisians on August 27, 1783. The lifting potential of hydrogen had been known as a result of the work of Henry Cavendish, Joseph Black, and Tiberius Cavallo. (The hydrogen gas for Charles's balloon was produced by pouring sulfuric acid over iron filings.) Nevertheless, the Montgolfier brothers pressed on, despite Charles's success with the more practical hydrogen-filled balloon, and they eventually flew their balloon at Versailles on September 19, 1783. The balloon, named the *Martial*, lifted off from the courtyard of Versailles, swathed in noxious smoke and carrying three passengers: a sheep, a duck, and a rooster! As Louis and his queen, Marie Antoinette, watched, the colorful balloon, radiant in blue and gold, drifted along for over two and a half miles before landing in Vaucresson Forest eight minutes after lift-off, its barnyard animals dazed but safe. Next, the Montgolfiers realized, would come trials with human aeronauts—and Paris watched as both the Montgolfier brothers and Charles worked toward the goal of human flight.

The honors went to the Montgolfiers. Before the end of the year, the brothers had built a very large balloon, having an internal volume of more than 56,000 cubic feet. The aeronaut could feed a small fire in a pan placed in the open neck of the balloon to replenish the supply of hot air and keep the balloon aloft. As with a flight test program today, the brothers and their aeronauts moved in cautious, incremental steps. It had been suggested that condemned criminals should have the dubious honor of first flying in the Montgolfier balloon, but a young French professor of physics and chemistry, Jean François Pilâtre de Rozier, protested vehemently, persuading Louis XVI that the honor for the flight should be granted to a free man. On October 15, 1783, Pilâtre de Rozier rose 50 feet into the air in the balloon, which was firmly tied to the ground. He repeated the flight two days later, and on October 19 made yet another captive flight to a height of 340 feet, with Giroud de Vilette and later, an infantry captain, François Laurent, the Marquis d'Arlandes, as passengers. With the concept proved and with confidence in free-flight trials bolstered, the brothers and Pilâtre de Rozier moved the balloon to the Château de la Muette, in the Parisian suburb of Bois de Boulogne. There, on November 21, 1783, Pilâtre and the Marquis d'Arlandes became the first humans to make a free balloon flight, flying from the Château to Butte-aux-Cailles, the present-day Place d'Italie.

Then as now, flying a balloon required enormous preparation. Early in the morning, Pilâtre, the Montgolfier brothers, and d'Arlandes inspected the balloon. A strong wind gust damaged the balloon slightly and delayed the flight, to the annoyance of the large and growing crowd. Finally, seamstresses repaired the damage, and at 1:54 P.M. the aeronauts cast off. A subsequent report prepared the same day for the *Journal de Paris* by the Duc de Polignac and other distinguished luminaries including the American minister to France, Benjamin Franklin, stated that it left

in a most majestic fashion and when it reached about 250 feet above the ground, the intrepid travellers, taking off their hats, bowed to the spectators. At that moment one experienced a feeling of fear mingled with admiration.

Soon the aerial navigators were lost from view, but the machine, floating on the horizon and displaying a most beautiful shape, climbed to at least 3,000 feet at which height it was still visible; it crossed the Seine below the gate of la Conférence and, passing between the Military Academy and the Hôtel des Invalides, it was borne to a position where it could be seen by all Paris.

When the travellers were satisfied with this experiment, not wishing to make a longer journey, they agreed to descend; but realizing that the wind was bearing them down upon the houses of the Rue de Seve [Sèvres], in the Faubourg Saint-Germain, they retained their calm and, increasing the production of gas, rose once more and continued on their way through the sky until they had passed over the outskirts of Paris.

They made a gentle descent into a field beyond the new boulevard, opposite the Croulebarge mill, without suffering the slightest discomfort, with two-thirds of their supplies still intact; so they could, if they had wanted to, have journeyed three times as far. Their voyage had taken them 20 to 25 minutes over a distance of 4–5,000 fathoms.[2]

It had been a remarkable flight. A letter sent after the flight by the Marquis d'Arlandes reveals that the two men had experienced their share of unsettling moments. When d'Arlandes, who was charged with refueling the fire pan, paused to admire the bends in the Seine, Pilâtre de Rozier testily blurted, "If you look at the river in that fashion you will be likely to bathe in it soon. Some fire, my dear friend, some fire!"[3] Later, the fire pan's hot embers burned some minute holes in the balloon cloth, and several of the bracing cords supporting the basket broke. These two worthies, test pilots before the phrase existed, were the talk of Paris, and their portraits appeared throughout France. Unlike many later balloonists, they were not merely daredevils or barnstormers. Rather, like the test pilots of today, they were educated professionals seeking to verify and demonstrate the potential of a new form of transportation.

The next stage belonged to Charles. Working with the brothers Robert, he developed a 26-foot-diameter balloon, and on December 1, 1783, took off from the Tuileries Gardens with the eldest Robert brother, Marie Noël. The two men completed an uneventful flight—the first manned flight of a hydrogen balloon—from Paris to Nesles, over twenty miles away. Then Charles, after disembarking his passenger, took off alone before sunset, climbing to an altitude of 9,000 feet within ten minutes. He made various scientific observations, saw the sun set for the second time that day, and then, cold and not a little frightened, developed an earache so annoying that he valved off gas and landed, his second flight having lasted but thirty minutes. Curiously, Charles never flew again, though he subsequently wrote, "Nothing can approach the joy that possessed me." Through him, the hydrogen balloon had become a practical reality.

It is no wonder that historians have referred to 1783 as "The Astonishing Year." Within the space of a few months, humanity had gained the ability to fly with relative safety. True, the balloon was still far from a routine apparatus, and one was at the mercy of the elements; nevertheless, humanity had, for the first time, ventured untethered into the air, courtesy of Messrs. Montgolfier, Charles, Pilâtre, d'Arlandes, and Robert. They were, by any standards, remarkable men, and by their example they influenced their successors. Within a year, budding aeronauts had made free balloon flights in Italy, Sweden, America, and England. In the United States, on June 24, 1784, Edward Warren, a lad of thirteen, became the first to pilot a balloon, flying in one built by Maryland lawyer Peter Carnes. The balloon was too heavy to carry Carnes (or vice versa), and so young Warren went aloft, behaving, as *The Maryland Gazette* reported, "with the fortitude of an old voyager." (Sadly, we do not know what became of Edward Warren after this interesting flight.) On January 7, 1785, Jean Pierre Blanchard and Dr. John Jeffries (an American physician who served with British forces during the Revolution) flew a balloon across the Straits of Dover to a crash landing in the forest of Felmores near Calais. But these triumphs were marred by tragedy when, on June 15, 1785, Pilâtre de Rozier and Pierre Romain died in the crash of an experimental combined hot-air-*and*-hydrogen balloon during an attempted crossing of the Channel from France to England. Shortly after lift-off, As Pilâtre was releasing gas, a spark ignited the hydrogen, and the hydrogen portion of the combined balloon exploded violently. The remains of the balloon plunged to the ground; Pilâtre died instantly, but his companion lingered on for ten minutes. Pilâtre de Rozier, acclaimed throughout France as the world's *premier navigateur aérien*, was just thirty-one.

Less well known today than his other, more famous contemporaries is aeronaut Jacques Garnerin. This courageous French balloonist began his career with a balloon ascent at Metz in 1787. Fighting between revolutionary France and Austria interrupted his activities, and he spent three years as a prisoner of the Austrians. Upon his release, he decided to flight-test an unusual device, one that eventually contributed greatly to the safety of aircrews: the parachute. Sketches of parachutes had appeared as early as Leonardo da Vinci and Fausto Veranzio in the fifteenth and sixteenth centuries. The French balloonist Jean Pierre Blanchard actually dropped animals with parachutes from his balloon in 1785 to entertain watching crowds, something the Society for the Prevention of Cruelty to Animals would certainly not condone today! Garnerin, perhaps inspired by this limited demonstration of safety, developed a parasol-like parachute having a diameter of about 40 feet. He closed it and suspended it below a conventional hydrogen balloon. The pilot himself stood in a small gondola attached to the parachute. On October 22, 1797, his green-and-orange "launch vehicle" rose from the park of Monceau, in Paris. At an altitude of approximately 2,300 feet, Garnerin severed the attachment lines connecting the balloon to the parachute, and the parachute and gondola dropped away, the parachute opening quickly and oscillating downward to earth, Garnerin safely on board. The balloon, for some reason, lunged upward and then exploded! Garnerin landed safely in the park, to the delirious cheers of the onlookers. It was, as French aviation historian and balloonist Charles Dollfus has aptly stated, "one of the great acts of heroism in human history." Garnerin had conceptualized the kind of parachute he should require, had deliberately conducted a proof-of-concept flight test (at his own risk), and then gone on to further refine his creation. On a later jump, over London, he leapt safely from nearly 10,000 feet. On the way down, however, the parachute oscillated so violently that the plucky airman became violently ill, and he was badly bruised upon landing. Subsequently, at the suggestion of friends, he cut a hole in the top of the device to relieve the air pressure under the canopy. Thereafter, parachute descents were so commonplace that they became a standard showstopper at balloon ascents and public festivals. Indeed, Garnerin, a showman like many of the early aeronauts, was joined by his wife and his niece as parachutists. His wife completed the first parachute descent by a woman, and his niece, Élisa Garnerin, became the first professional woman parachutist. Garnerin himself became the French Government's official aeronaut, with the title "balloonist to public festivals."

Unfortunately, though the French had pioneered in the use of balloons for military observation, the revolutionary committees and even Napoleon himself failed to recognize their tactical worth, relegating balloons to the realm of entertainment and celebration. Though balloons appeared most successfully in military roles during the American Civil War and the Franco-Prussian War, and though many high-altitude flights were made by balloonists, including one to over 30,000 feet as early as 1894, the focus of flight research turned back to winged flight, away from flying with "a cloud enclosed in a bag." As the nineteenth century dawned, a century that would see the steam railroad, the steel ship, and the automobile, there was already a small coterie of individuals thinking about winged flight. Some were visionaries, others mere tinkerers. But one man above all others stood out—a Yorkshire baronet named Sir George Cayley. Through his efforts, the dream of winged flight edged dramatically closer to the awakening of reality.

CAYLEY AND THE FIRST WINGED EXPERIMENTERS

George Cayley was a young man when he first became intrigued with aviation. Born in 1773, his boyish awakening to the development of the balloon caused him to devote prodigious amounts of time to the study of aeronautics. At the age of twenty-three, he developed a helicopter model that flew with great success. In another three years—by 1799—he had accurately dissected the problem of flying, recognizing the separate forces of lift, thrust, and drag. That same year, he postulated the shape of the modern airplane: a configuration having a fixed main wing, a control car for the pilot, and cruciform tail surfaces. Anachronistically, the craft also had paddles for propulsion, rather than propellers. One could criticize him for the latter retrogression, as well as for a predeliction for ornithopters and wing-flapping devices. Nevertheless, such criticisms would be, on the whole, unjust: it was Cayley who introduced scientific methods to the development of flight technology. (He recognized, for example, the importance of model testing, using such devices as whirling-arm test rigs, with a model mounted on the end of the whirling arm.) He also understood that the problem of *control* was just as important as the problems of lift and propulsion, something too few prospective airmen would later accord sufficient respect. He recognized that a curved, or cambered, surface generated greater lift than a flat surface, and appreciated the existence of a low-pressure region above the wing. He studied the shift in the center of pressure as a wing varied its angle of attack, was the first to accurately understand how a bird flies, appreciated the importance of streamlining (he studied the body lines of fish and then designed streamlined, finned artillery projectiles), and recognized that successful aircraft would require the development of practical internal-combustion engines (which was not achieved until work later in the century by Nicholas Otto and Carl Benz). For all these reasons and many others, Sir George Cayley has been hailed as the father of the modern airplane and the science of aerodynamics.

Less well known, however, is Cayley's pervasive interest in flight testing and flight research, using both unmanned and manned flight test aircraft. In 1804, following tests of an airfoil cross section using a whirling-arm test rig, Cayley built a small model having a kite-like wing fixed upon a wooden pole "fuselage" and a cruciform tail section attached to the pole via a universal joint. Cayley could vary the center of gravity by moving an adjustable weight. He flew the glider at his estate at Brompton Hall, near Scarborough, and later recalled:

> It was very pretty to see it sail down a steep hill, and it gave the idea that a larger instrument would be a better and a safer conveyance down the Alps than even the sure-footed mule, let him meditate his track ever so intensely. The least inclination of the tail towards the right or left made it shape its course like a ship by the rudder.[4]

In 1809, after further aerodynamic studies, including studies of longitudinal and lateral stability, Cayley constructed a full-size glider having a wing area of 200 square feet and flew it successfully both unmanned and piloted by a small boy (whose name is, regrettably, lost to history). That same year, he published his monumental treatise *On Aerial Navigation*, one of the most important works ever written on aviation. In 1849, he built a triplane glider, flying it on the end of a ground tow with a small boy on board, another adventurous child-airman who is unknown to posterity. Three years later, he constructed an improved version of this machine and persuaded his coachman to fly it across a small valley! Perhaps apocryphally, the coachman is alleged to have said after his flight, "Please, Sir George, I wish to give notice. I was hired to drive, and not to fly!" Sir George Cayley died in 1857 and so failed to witness the revolution in aviation over the next half century. It is curious to wonder if this unusual member of the English gentry could have fully appreciated before his death just how much he had contributed to the advancement of aeronautics.[5]*

As it is now known, modern flight testing began with that towering figure of the late nineteenth century Otto Lilienthal. But between Cayley and Lilienthal were a host of other experimenters and enthusiasts, many of whom contributed bit by bit to the development of aeronautics. In the 1840s, William Henson and John Stringfellow drew up plans for a fixed-wing, propeller-driven airplane, the first design of its kind in aviation history. They called it the Aerial Steam Carriage, and drawings of this remarkable-looking craft appeared in journals all over Europe. Surprisingly, the public seized upon it, and although it remained merely a paper conception, it helped make airplane enthusiasts respectable; to a society just getting used to steam-powered ships and trains, the notion of a steam-powered airplane seemed only a little more fantastic and, hence, perhaps quite possible. Flying models appeared as well: first Félix du Temple's clockwork-driven airplane of the 1850s and then Alphonse Penaud's *Planophore*—the ancestor of the modern rubber-driven model —in 1871. And with modeling came further interest in aerodynamics. In 1864, Count Ferdinand d'Esterno published *Du vol des Oiseaux* (The Flight of Birds), drawing the first distinction between *soaring* and *gliding*. He also drew plans for actual aircraft, publishing a drawing of a proposed glider. It is believed d'Esterno greatly influenced Lilienthal; the count's work preceded another detailed examination of bird flight by Louis P. Mouillard (a French émigré living in Algeria and Egypt who experimented without success with gliders) in Mouillard's own book *L'Empire de l'Air* (The Empire of the Air), published in 1881 and translated for English-language readers by the Smithsonian Institution in 1893. In this fashion, Mouillard's work became known to Octave Chanute and the Wright brothers.

The wind tunnel made its appearance between Cayley and Lilienthal. Cayley had relied on a primitive whirling-arm test rig to test the lift of models. In 1871, Francis Wenham, one of the founders of the Aeronau-

* In 1971, the well-known British soaring and test pilot John Sproule built an exact replica of an 1853 Cayley glider design, then test-flew it at Brompton Hall. The verdict: the glider exhibited excellent flying characteristics, constituting (in Sproule's words) "splendid proof of Sir George Cayley's aeronautical theories."

tical Society of Great Britain (now the Royal Aeronautical Society), built the world's first wind tunnel, in conjunction with John Browning. Crude in the extreme—as were all such early tunnels—it nevertheless enabled researchers to conduct limited testing of airfoils to verify such hypotheses as Wenham's own conception that airfoils produce most of their lift forward of the mid-chord position (i.e., forward of a position halfway between a wing's leading and trailing edges) and that broad (high-aspect-ratio) wings produce lift more efficiently than short-span (low-aspect-ratio) ones. By the mid-1890s, wind tunnels existed in such nations as Russia, Austria, and the United States, as well as in Great Britain; the scientific study of the problems of flight had clearly begun.

The wind tunnel spurred greater interest in actual flying trials—and so dawned the age of the powered "hopper." There had always been those who followed in the tradition of the tower jumpers. Now, however, individuals were willing to fly on the basis of scientific belief. Indeed, the era of gliding had already begun when, in 1857, a French sea captain, Jean Marie le Bris, built a piloted glider shaped like an albatross and launched it from a drawn cart; he successfully completed a short gliding flight, but broke his leg on a second attempt. (Far less successful was the flight attempt of Vincent de Groof, a Belgian shoemaker, who plunged to his death over London in 1874 in a parachutelike ornithopter, tragic proof—if any were still needed—that this craft was a fatal delusion.) The first of the powered hoppers was the indefatigable Du Temple, who, in the same year De Groof met his violent end, built a powered full-size machine (the particulars of the engine are unknown) and persuaded a young sailor to ride it down a ramp and into the air. It was certainly not a controlled or sustained flight, and it relied on a healthy "gravity assist" for takeoff, but it did mark the start of powered flight trials of piloted aircraft. Similarly intriguing but unsuccessful was the ramp-launched steam-powered airplane of czarist naval officer Alexander Mozhaisky, tested at Krasnoye Selo by "pilot" I. N. Golubev in 1884. In 1890, the French electrical engineer Clément Ader made a short hop off the ground at Armainvilliers in a steam-powered bat-like craft named, appropriately, the Éole. Ader's Éole managed to stagger aloft under its own power in a level takeoff and hurtle about 165 feet before coming to earth, neither a sustained nor a controlled flight. (In 1897, he unsuccessfully attempted to fly another craft, the Avion III, at Satory.) A much more ambitious craft—an example of "thinking big" if, unfortunately, thinking unwisely—was the gigantic test rig of Britain's Sir Hiram Maxim. With a three-man crew and a loaded weight of 8,000 pounds, the Maxim rig was gargantuan by the standards of the day. Powered by two 180-horsepower steam engines and designed to run along a straight section of railroad track, the test rig succeeded in becoming briefly airborne in July 1894, though it was designed with an outrigger wheel system to prevent it from achieving free flight. Despite Maxim's energetic nature, he did not pursue aeronautics seriously, and aside from this brief and expensive foray (and a later and even more lackadaisical effort with another machine in 1910), Maxim left aviation to others. Across the Atlantic, in the United States, the secretary of the Smithsonian Institution, Samuel P. Langley, was embarking upon his experiments with "Aerodromes," even as Maxim's efforts ended in failure—as Langley's eventually would too. But it was not Ader or Mozhaisky or Maxim or even Langley who captured the imagination of the public as the century drew to a close. Rather, it was the "German Darius Green," the "Winged Prussian," Otto Lilienthal, the first great test pilot.

LILIENTHAL AND THE BIRTH OF MODERN FLIGHT RESEARCH

To a degree far greater than any of his predecessors, Otto Lilienthal symbolized the new wave in aeronautics: the wedding of the professional engineer with the enthusiastic visionary. It is entirely fitting that this revolutionary figure, a native of Anklam, Pomerania, was born in that year of great revolutions, 1848. From watching storks in flight, Lilienthal and his younger brother Gustav developed a lifelong interest in flight—but, for Otto, it became an obsession. When Otto was fourteen, he and his brother built an unsuccessful ornithopter model, the first of three such failures. He recognized that a successful aircraft would depend upon a strong base of aerodynamic knowledge—and that birds held the keys to that knowledge. He received a solid technical education from various schools, including the Berlin technical academy, from which he graduated as a mechanical engineer in 1870, just in time to take part in the siege of Paris during the Franco-Prussian War, which marked the emergence of modern Germany. Following wartime service, Lilienthal worked for a number of engineering firms, designing steam machinery, but he also immediately resumed his interest in heavier-than-air flight. Although he remained fascinated by ornithopters to the end of his life— and undoubtedly would have been frustrated and unsuccessful had he pursued them actively—he believed that one should first construct fixed-wing gliders based upon knowledge of how birds fly. Lilienthal was convinced, as he phrased it, that a prospective airman must get on "intimate terms with the wind." His endorsement of actual flying trials and his undertaking of such tests mark him as the father of modern flight testing. Shortly before his death, Lilienthal wrote:

One can get a proper insight into the practice of flying only by actual flying experiments. . . . The manner in which we have to meet the irregularities of the wind, when soaring in the air, can only be learnt by being in the air itself. . . . The only way which leads us to a quick development in human flight is a systematic and energetic practice in actual flying experiments.[6]

But first one had to have a proper data base from which to work. After studying the design and construction of birds' wings with a view to applying his results to human flight, Lilienthal set out to quantify available airfoil data, and he published tables giving the lifting values for various airfoil cross sections. While he was extremely influential on such later pioneers as the Wrights, these later figures found it necessary to correct some of the data; this in no way casts doubt upon the ability and contributions of Lilienthal, who may be said to have pioneered the scientific study of flight. He published his research results in 1889, with a book entitled *Der Vogelflug als Grundlage der Fliegerkunst* (The Flight of Birds as the Basis of the Art of Flying). Within five years, through the efforts of such enthusiasts as Octave Chanute and James Means, Lilienthal's data were available for others to use in both Europe and America. Having methodically set forth the principles of bird flight, Lilienthal felt confident to embark on systematic flight trials of fixed-wing gliders.

His first two designs, in 1889 and 1890, were failures. Undeterred, Lilienthal pressed on with the development of another, the "No. 3," of 1891. As with most of his gliders, it had a cloth-covered batlike wing, with a fixed horizontal tailplane and a fixed vertical rudder. Very similar to today's hang gliders, the craft had a batlike appearance. Lilienthal began his flight tests with this machine at Derwitz, running down the slope of a hill and leaping into the air. He controlled the attitude of the craft by shifting his body weight. The No. 3 glider flew reasonably well, and Lilienthal embarked on the design of another glider—and so on, until, by the time of his death, in 1896, he had built a total of eighteen types, including one, the No. 11, which was in "production"! By 1894, Lilienthal had moved the site of his test flights to the lovely and ideal Stöllner Hills, near Rhinow, although he also built an artificial hill at Lichterfelde, a suburb of Berlin.

Lilienthal recognized that flight testing could be risky business, even for those who understood the risks and methodically prepared to meet them. He often remarked that, if progress was to be achieved in aviation, *"Opfer müssen gebracht werden"* (Sacrifices must be made). To prevent serious injury should he crash during his flight trials, Lilienthal shrewdly added a curved willow hoop, which he termed a *Prellbügel* (rebound-bow) to the front of the glider. Such a device saved his life when, during a flight in 1895, one of the gliders stalled, flipped over, and dived into the ground, splintering the hoop. Widespread publicity surrounding the accident influenced the Wright brothers to place the horizontal stabilizer of their aircraft ahead of the wing, thus giving the historic Wright Flyers a "canard" ("tail first") configuration. Lilienthal's own account of the accident stated:

> During a gliding flight taken from a great height this was the cause of my coming into a position with my arms outstretched, in which the center of gravity lay too much to the back; at the same time I was unable—owing to fatigue—to draw the upper part of my body again towards the front. As I was then sailing at the height of about 65 feet with a velocity of about 35 miles per hour, the apparatus, overloaded in the rear, rose more and more, and finally shot, by means of its *vis viva*, vertically upwards. I gripped tight hold, seeing nothing but the blue sky and little white clouds above me, and so awaited the moment when the apparatus would capsize backwards, possibly ending my sailing attempts forever. Suddenly, however, the apparatus stopped in its ascent, and, going backward again in a downward direction, described a short circle and steered with the rear part again upwards, owing to the horizontal tail which had an upward slant; then the machine turned bottom upwards and rushed with me vertically towards the earth from a height of about 65 feet. With my senses quite clear, my arms and my head forward, still holding the apparatus firmly with my hands, I fell towards the greensward, a shock, a crash, and I lay with the apparatus on the ground.[7]

By mid-1896, Lilienthal had made over twenty-five hundred gliding flights. His exploits were reported all over Europe, and his fame had spread to America. His example inspired a host of imitators, including the Wrights. Sundays witnessed curious crowds journeying forth from Berlin and Potsdam to Lichterfelde to see Lilienthal sail through the air. His No. 11 Normal Segelapparat (standard sailing craft) proved so successful that he built at least eight, selling them to other enthusiasts and supporters including physicist George Francis Fitzgerald, of Dublin's Trinity College, and American newspaper magnate William Randolph Hearst. Under proper conditions, the No. 11 glider could sail more than a thousand feet. Curiously, Lilienthal paid little attention to using control surfaces to change the attitude and flight path of his gliders. Up to his death, he concentrated on shifting body weight, although some notes that he left indicate that he was turning his thoughts toward providing his future gliders with rudimentary pivoting control surfaces. He experimented with three successful biplane gliders. He built two experimental powered aircraft using carbonic gas engine propulsion, the No. 16 and the No. 17, but these craft, equipped with moving "flippers" on the wingtips—in direct imitation of birds—would have been totally unsuccessful (they were tested, but only as gliders). He designed another glider, the No. 18, which was, it is believed, built but certainly not flown. Then came Sunday, August 9, 1896.

That day, a typically beautiful summer's day, Lilienthal was flying from the Gollenberg, in the Stöllner Hills, in one of his No. 11 gliders; the glider did not have the safety *Prellbügel* installed. Conditions were windy, with sharp gusts. He leapt into the air and glided forward. Then, as alarmed witnesses watched, a rising gust brought the glider to a standstill, and its nose started to rise. Lilienthal shifted his body as far forward as he could, but the nose continued to rise, and then, abruptly, the glider stalled. Before the horrified gaze of onlookers, the glider dropped off on its right wing and slipped to the ground, crumpling the wing. It was a tragic accident; the material damage was slight, and undoubtedly the *Prellbügel*, had it been present, would have saved Lilienthal from serious injury. Unfortunately, however, the crash broke his back. Rushed to the Bergmann Clinic, in Berlin, Lilienthal lingered until the next day, then died, having himself made the ultimate sacrifice to further the cause of aviation. Lilienthal is buried in the Lichterfelde cemetery. The Lilienthal memorial on the site of his artificial hill commemorates the great contributions and greater sacrifice of this early aviator.

Too often, advances in technology have been achieved only with the accompaniment of death; this has, unfortunately, been all too common in the history of aviation. The death of Lilienthal gave aviation its first great martyr, an individual who served as an inspiration and motivation for those who sought to follow in his steps. His technical work was painstaking and thorough; his influence (in the words of aviation historian Charles Gibbs-Smith) "was universal and profound"; his popularity, the photographs of him in flight, all served to promote the cause of aviation, and to convince the public that, at long last, perhaps humanity was on the verge of a transportation breakthrough. Would Lilienthal have contributed seriously to powered flight had he lived? Once more, the rigorous confines of historical judgment dictate a cautious answer that he might have done so. Of Lilienthal's influence there can be no doubt: he influenced Octave Chanute and the Wrights. That alone would be enough. But his influence spread throughout Europe as well—to Ferdinand Ferber of France, to Percy Pilcher (who was likewise tragically killed, in 1899) in Scotland, and to George Francis Fitzgerald in Ireland. After Lilienthal, aviation would never be quite the same, for he had given the world a vision of the future, in physical terms that lent credence to the poetic visions of Tennyson's *Locksley Hall:* the repeated sight of a man confidently gliding through the air with swiftness and skill, in a vehicle of his own making.

A devoted band of followers and fellow enthusiasts took up Lilienthal's quest. In the United States, Octave Chanute was ready to embark upon his own flying experiments. Langley still toyed with his Aerodromes. The Wrights were still studying, their youthful interest reawakened and reenforced by Lilienthal's example, plodding determinedly toward their eventual triumph at Kitty Hawk. It is curious, then, why so many individuals who otherwise should have known better still refused to recognize the revolution that was about to occur. Men of science, of proven accomplishment, remained convinced that the *ancien régime*, the status quo, would remain intact. They saw in Lilienthal's death not the reaffirmation of the pioneering spirit but, rather, proof positive that humanity could not fly with wings. Yet this attitude, so prevalent in both Europe and America, represented essentially a denial of the Industrial Revolution and its consequences, for if the airplane was developed, it would be only slightly more revolutionary than the steam engine or the locomotive. In December 1896, a scant four months after Lilienthal's death, Major B. F. S. Baden-Powell, of the Aeronautical Society of Great Britain, invited Lord Kelvin, president of the Royal Society, distinguished physicist and mathematician, to membership. In his crushing reply, he wrote, "I have not the smallest molecule of faith in aerial navigation other than ballooning, or of expectation of good results from any of the trials we hear of. So you will understand that I would not care to be a member of the Aeronautical Society."[8] Such a pronouncement coming from so esteemed a critic did much to stifle British aviation in the years that followed. Curiously, such attitudes often are expressed on the eve of revolutions, both political and technological, by individuals who cannot break away from the familiar. As with the political conservatives of 1789 and 1848, Kelvin and others like him could not have foreseen the tidal wave about to break upon the shores of established scientific doubt. It was a revolution whose origins stretched to the prehistory of humanity, back into the hidden recesses of the mind, a revolution that Eilmer, the Montgolfiers, Cayley, Lilienthal, and all the other flight researchers had helped shape. Now the responsibility for bringing it to fruition passed to another society with a revolutionary tradition, across the Atlantic from Europe to America.

CHAPTER 2

THE AWAKENING

The most respected of late-nineteenth-century American engineers was, without a doubt, Octave Chanute. Born in Paris in 1832, into a family steeped in intellectual and academic traditions, young Chanute came to America with his parents in 1838. He displayed a talent for mathematics at an early age and, by seventeen, had decided to embark upon a career as a mechanical engineer. He started out, in traditional fashion, by apprenticing himself to a railroad survey crew. From then on, he moved from triumph to triumph. By the 1860s, Chanute was chief engineer supervising the track-laying operations of several major railroads. He followed this by a stunning series of architectural and civil engineering projects including the Kansas City Bridge; the first span over the Missouri River, at St. Charles; the Kinzua Creek bridge, in Pennsylvania; and finally, the massive Chicago Union Stockyards complex. Appointed chief engineer of the Erie Railroad in 1873, Chanute actively practiced engineering professionally until his retirement in 1890. Now with time on his hands, he busied himself by working as a consultant specializing in the preservation of wood—and by thinking about aeronautics.

As early as 1875, Chanute, with keen engineering insight, had studied applying his knowledge of stress analysis and structures to aviation. He began lecturing to professional societies and organizations concerning flight. Always fearful of ridicule, this dapper pioneer with the distinct appearance of a Parisian *boulevardier* proceeded cautiously. At the urging of like-minded friends, Chanute wrote twenty-seven articles on aviation for the *Railroad and Engineering Journal*, the first of which appeared in 1891. In 1894, these articles were reprinted in a single work entitled *Progress in Flying Machines*, a monumental tome covering the history of aviation, the theory of flight, and the state of contemporary aeronautics. Two years after the publication of this book, Chanute began his own gliding experiments on the shores of Lake Michigan. He was already past sixty.

Chanute set up a small experimental camp on the sand-dune shores of Lake Michigan, near Miller, Indiana; there, with a few fellow enthusiasts including William Avery, Augustus Herring, Paul Butusov, and Dr. James Ricketts—the latter a physician "with a slack practice and a taste for aeronautics"—he undertook the flight testing of experimental hang gliders. Initially, results were disappointing. Tests of a Lilienthal-type glider built by Herring and a very large glider built by Butusov were unsuccessful. The group next concentrated on gliders of Chanute's own design. Chanute favored multiwing gliders, having as many as six wings, and constructed one such glider (with four wings), known as the *Katydid*, in 1896. The upper wings of the craft could move backward to compensate for changes in the aerodynamic center of pressure, for Chanute firmly believed that any airplane should be inherently stable (or, as he termed it, have "automatic stability in the wind"). His major contribution, however, was an excellent biplane glider built in conjunction with Herring. Reflecting Chanute's engineering expertise and bridge-building background, the biplane glider, first flown in 1896, had its wings and struts constructed in the layout of a Pratt bridge truss. The wing spars and ribs were set at right angles. The upper and lower wings were attached to one another by uniformly spaced vertical struts mounted at the leading and trailing edges of the wings. The pilot hung well below the wings, adding to the craft's stability by his pendulum position, and the craft also had a pivoting cruciform tail held in position by rubber cords that acted as a gust damper. Here, indeed, was a major advance over Lilienthal's own gliders, and the Chanute-Herring biplane glider must be considered the most successful glider developed up to the time of the Wrights themselves. It weighed a mere 23 pounds and made over seven hundred flights, safely covering distances up to 350 feet.

Chanute's wedding of the airplane and the Pratt truss constituted his most important contribution to the technology of flight and set the standards for the structural design of future biplane aircraft. However, by acting as an aeronautical clearing house of information, Chanute exerted a far more significant impact. Here was a man who was in touch with all the major pioneers—and most of the minor ones as well—working toward solving the problem of heavier-than-air flight in Europe and

America. In 1900, at the age of sixty-eight, he met the Wrights, the beginning of a fruitful partnership that included personal visits, exchange of ideas, and even an offer by Chanute—gracefully declined—to provide the struggling brothers with financial support. His generous and supportive nature makes him one of aviation's most appealing figures; indeed, of Chanute, Wilbur Wright wrote that "few men were more universally respected and loved." He died in 1910, having seen the fulfillment of mechanical flight.

THE SAD TALE OF THE LANGLEY AERODROME

Between Chanute and the Wrights, however, stands that most enigmatic figure, Samuel Pierpont Langley, the secretary of the Smithsonian Institution. If ever anyone deserved to be the first to fly a powered aircraft successfully, it was Langley, but despite this tragic figure's persistent efforts, success eluded him and his flight tests ended in disastrous failure. Langley, unlike Chanute, totally rejected the idea of flying manned gliders, preferring to proceed directly from small powered models to a full-size aircraft.

Langley was a largely self-taught physicist, the developer of the bolometer (a device to determine the intensity of solar radiation) and the founder of what eventually became the Smithsonian Astrophysical Observatory. Born in 1834 and a native of Massachusetts, Langley had first worked as an engineer and an architect before becoming an assistant at the Harvard Observatory in the last year of the Civil War. He served as a professor of mathematics at the Naval Academy, as a professor of astronomy and physics at the Western University of Pennsylvania, and then as director of Pittsburgh's Allegheny Observatory. In 1887, already the nation's senior scientist, Langley became the Smithsonian's third secretary. The previous year, he had attended a lecture on aeronautics that had intrigued him, and in 1887, the same year as his appointment to the Smithsonian, he began his own study of flight. First, following Cayley's example, he built a whirling-arm test rig. He quickly concluded that manned flight was possible. Skeptics influenced his next step, a decision to prove his theories by model tests. Between 1887 and 1891, he built and flew nearly a hundred different (and largely unsuccessful) models powered by rubber-band motors. In 1892 he decided to fly larger models powered by small, lightweight, yet powerful steam engines, and having wingspans up to fourteen feet. These he dubbed "Aerodromes," in a mistaken application of Greek (aerodrome can only mean a place where aircraft are flown from, not an aircraft itself). Supported by Smithsonian funding, Langley constructed two of these large models, Aerodromes 5 and 6, and successfully flew them in 1896. They were catapult-launched from a houseboat moored in the Potomac. Aerodrome 5 flew for over a minute and a half, covering a distance of half a mile before its steam engine ran out of fuel. Aerodrome 6 flew a total distance of 4,300 feet. They were excellent accomplishments in modeling.

The outbreak of the Spanish-American War prompted then Assistant Secretary of the Navy Theodore Roosevelt to support Langley's work for military purposes: observation and reconnaissance. Learning of Langley's efforts from Charles Walcott, director of the U. S. Geological Survey and later secretary of the Smithsonian himself, Roosevelt helped Langley receive a $50,000 grant from the War Department's Board of Ordnance and Fortification, the world's first military R&D funding for a heavier-than-air vehicle. The money could not have come at a more critical time, for Langley was at the end of his Smithsonian support. Over the next six years, Langley devoted his energies to developing what he termed the "Great Aerodrome," a man-carrying craft four times the size of the original models.

Langley's vision, however, far exceeded his technical grasp—or, for that matter, understanding. He failed to recognize that one simply cannot scale up a vehicle without drastically redesigning its structure to take the greater loads expected of it. He placed little emphasis on the study of flight control systems, continued to pursue the awkward—and dangerous—practice of catapult launchings from a houseboat, and was too firmly wedded to the theory of inherent stability. In short, even if his final efforts had met with success, they would have proved little. In August 1903, he successfully tested a quarter-scale model powered by a petroleum-fueled engine, the first petroleum-fueled model to fly. Recognizing that the "Great Aerodrome" required a light but very powerful engine for propulsion, Langley turned to Stephen Balzer, who developed a disappointing 8-horsepower air-cooled rotary engine. Charles Manly, Langley's technical assistant, redesigned the Balzer engine so that it could produce the then-phenomenal figure of 52.4 horsepower (the Balzer-Manly engine was one of the few good features on the aircraft). Finally, by the fall of 1903, all was ready; the "Great Aerodrome" was complete. It had a wingspan of 48 feet and a wing area of over one thousand square feet. High quality and expensive workmanship had produced a beautiful, impressive, yet flawed machine. Its two large wings were of equal span, with pronounced dihedral (up sweep). The pilot (if one can call him that) sat in a small "aviator's car" underneath the forward wing. The engine rested athwartships, driving two pusher propellers via shafts and linkages. At the rear of the craft was a cruciform "Pénaud tail." (Like much about the Langley machine, this, too, was not as it seemed; Alphonse Pénaud had never used or conceptualized such a device.) A small rudder underneath the fuselage framework provided limited steering. Langley installed the "Great Aerodrome" on its houseboat, setting off down the Potomac for flight trials.

On October 7, 1903, Langley's faithful assistant-pilot, Charles Manly, got into the craft and fired up its engine as waiting reporters watched from small boats. One observer, from the Washington *Post*, wrote:

> Manly looked down and smiled. Then his face hardened as he braced himself for the flight, which might have in store for him fame or death. The propeller wheels, a foot from his head, whirred around him one thousand times to the minute. A man forward fired two sky rockets. There came an answered "toot, toot," from the tugs. A mechanic stooped, cut the cable holding the catapult; there was a roaring, grinding noise—and the Langley airship tumbled over the edge of the houseboat and disappeared in the river, sixteen feet below. It simply slid into the water like a handful of mortar. . . .[1]

A pin in the launching mechanism had failed to release properly and snagged one of the front wing's bracing wires. Manly clambered out of the water, wet but unhurt. Langley, disappointed, recovered and repaired the craft; slowly at first, the public ridicule that greeted his subsequent efforts began to build up.

The next attempt came two months later, on December 8. Again launch preparations went forward; again the revolutionary engine spun up the two pusher propellers. Once more Manly readied himself for the flight, wearing a union suit covered with a cork-lined jacket. It was late afternoon, after four-thirty, and already twilight was darkening the sky. Cold, wintry gusts shook the "Great Aerodrome" and its houseboat, and the Potomac was dotted with floating ice. It was inhospitable, bleak, and the prospect of a flight was nothing short of ludicrous. But Manly and Langley were convinced that not to fly this day would postpone their efforts for months. And so, the final act was to be played out. At 4:45 P.M., Manly signaled for release. The spring catapult fired, and the roaring Aerodrome raced down the track and into the air. With a violent snap, the Aerodrome's after wings failed, most probably simply because their insufficient structure could not withstand the flight loads. The Aerodrome pitched nose up, paused for a moment, its propellers racing and Manly hanging on for dear life, then simply tumbled down into the water.

Somehow, amid the tangle of wreckage, with the immense wings and the maze of bracing wires, Manly was able to swim clear, though only after stripping off his cork jacket when it caught on a projection. An ice block prevented him from getting to the surface, and he dived below it, finally coming to surface in clear water. A workman, thinking Manly was still with the Aerodrome, dived in to save him. Waiting boats quickly pulled both men from the frigid waters; Manly had to have his frozen clothing cut from his body. Then, fortified with a shot of whiskey, the lucky pilot delivered a "most voluble series of blasphemies." The "Great Aerodrome" was finished, as was Langley. Congressional critics ridiculed the craft, which newspapermen dubbed the "Mud Duck." Critic Ambrose Bierce caustically penned, "I don't know how much larger Professor Langley's machine is than his flying model was—about large enough, I think, to require an atmosphere a little denser than the intelligence of one scientist and not quite so dense as that of two."[2] In the face of this harsh criticism, Langley gave up. He died, brokenhearted, in 1906; as a man who had briefly given flying the sanction of scientific respectability, Langley deserved a kinder fate.

After the Langley fiasco had run its course, the War Department, $50,000 poorer, issued a statement on human flight, concluding, "We are still far from the ultimate goal. . . ." Yet, at this darkest moment, the two brothers from Dayton, Ohio, were even then readying for flight what would become the world's first powered aircraft capable of making a sustained and controlled flight. They had come a long way from their initial conceptions about what an airplane would look like, and they possessed two important characteristics lacking in all who preceded them: experience aloft and confidence born of that experience. But two more unlikely figures could not have been imagined to succeed where so many others had failed.

TRIUMPH AT KITTY HAWK

Wilbur and Orville Wright, ages thirty-six and thirty-two, respectively, in 1903, were the sons of a minister. They lacked formal training in engineering or science. They were small-business men; Orville had started a local newspaper, and in 1892 the two brothers had opened up a bicycle shop, following this up by starting a small magazine. Far from being in touch with the major intellectual currents of the day, the Wright brothers were the stuff of Sinclair Lewis. Their interest in flight was sparked by an article, in *McClure's Magazine*, on Otto Lilienthal. Following his death, the brothers embarked upon the study of flight with almost zealous fervor. But what separated these two somber and reclusive researchers from their unsuccessful compatriots was their methodical, scientific analysis of the problems of flight, and their engineering answers to these problems and challenges. Most important, however, was their immediate assumption that the only way to study flight was by making flying experiments. The Wright brothers were intuitive engineers of Promethean proportions, and the first major figures in American flight testing.

Though the Wrights seemed indistinguishable from their fellow small-town Midwesterners, there were some significant differences. Their father had invented a form of early typewriter. Their mother held a degree in mathematics and encouraged her sons' experiments. Fiddling with machinery all their lives, the Wrights were appreciative of the mechanical requirements of flying machines. Experienced bicycle riders and manufacturers, they also recognized that *control* and *stability* were the critical problems in aeronautics, and not just the obvious ones of generating enough power and lift. And they knew where to write for assistance: to Chanute, to the Smithsonian and Langley. They also knew what to reject, and after studying Langley's approach, they recognized the seeds of inevitable failure. As with all their predecessors, the Wrights started by studying birds and by reading voraciously. They were especially concerned with "lateral balance" (what we would later term "roll stability" and "roll control"), because (as a result of their bicycle experience) they recognized that controlling an aircraft would be like controlling a bicycle: one would have to lean into the turn. Flat turns, a la automobiles, were out. So, besides providing pitch control and directional control, they realized one would have to provide some means for dipping and raising the wings. Their answer, gleaned from flexing a shoebox and studying birds, was the principle of wing-warping. By changing the camber of the wing, one would change its lifting characteristics, and hence the unequal lift would roll the airplane about its longitudinal axis. The concept of wing-warping, which Wilbur Wright conceived in July 1899, was tested by the brothers on a five-foot biplane kite that same month. This rudimentary start of their flight testing was successful; convinced the problem of lateral control was within their ability to solve, they moved on to their first manned trials.

In 1900, the brothers built a manned kite-glider and shipped it to Kitty Hawk, North Carolina, for testing. They had selected the wind-swept dunes of Kitty Hawk on the advice of the U. S. Weather Bureau, yet another example of their cautious, leave-nothing-to-chance approach. (They were not the first explorers to grace its dunes: in 1524, as historian Samuel Eliot Morison has related, the great Italian navigator Giovanni da Verrazano had stopped there on his historic exploration of the Atlantic coast.) Their kite-glider had a 17-foot wingspread, a Chanute-like biplane structure, and a horizontal elevator (which they termed a "front rudder") in front of the lower wing. They placed the elevator

forward, so that, like Lilienthal's *Prellbügel*, it could protect them in case
of a crash, as well as give the pilot a convenient reference to the flight
path of the craft. During October 1900, the brothers flew their first
glider at Kitty Hawk. Mostly, they flew it as a kite, but a few piloted
flights were made as well. Then they left for Dayton and further work.
In the summer of 1901, the brothers returned to Kitty Hawk, moved
their camp four miles south to the Kill Devil Hills, and tested their second glider during July and August, with Octave Chanute watching some
of the trials. But the trials were disappointing; in a fit of despair, Wilbur,
always the leader, stated, "Nobody will fly for a thousand years!" The
second Wright glider had shown an alarming tendency to slew out of
control during wing-warping, and sideslip to the ground. Troubled, the
brothers returned to Dayton.

Gradually they realized that the data from which they had designed
the machine—Lilienthal's pressure-distribution tables—were in error.
They were on their own. Initial despair set aside, the brothers tenaciously tackled the problem of generating reliable aerodynamic data. At
first they built a small lift-and-drag balance and mounted it on a bicycle.
Then, and most important, they built a small wind tunnel and tested over
two hundred airfoil shapes. The tests, concluded in December 1901,
proved that, indeed, the Lilienthal tables were in error. But, more
significantly, the brothers now had the data they needed to proceed with
their own designs. The result of this intensive blending of flight and
ground research was the Wright 1902 glider, a major advance. A biplane
spanning 32 feet, it had a canard elevator, wing-warping, and a fixed
double-surface vertical rudder to improve stability in turns. Flown at
Kitty Hawk in September and October 1902, this glider convinced the
brothers that they had proceeded far enough to contemplate the construction of a powered machine. During flight testing, the original fixed-
rudder configuration had not prevented a tendency of the machine to
spin, owing to unequal drag produced by wing-warping. Accordingly,
the Wrights made the rudder movable and linked it to the wing-warping
mechanism, which was controlled by a hip cradle. When the prone pilot
moved the cradle, the wings twisted, and the rudder automatically assumed the proper position for the desired turn. The Wrights made hundreds of glides in the 1902 glider, which was capable of being fully controlled. In late October 1902, they returned to Dayton and immediately
set about designing and constructing the famous Kitty Hawk Flyer, the
world's first successful aircraft.

The Wrights completed the fabrication of the Flyer over the summer
of 1903. In late September, they left with the craft for Kitty Hawk. Like
the gliders, it was a biplane, spanning just over 40 feet, with a biplane
front elevator and a movable double rudder aft of the wing linked to the

wing-warping controls. The craft used landing skids, and the brothers planned to launch it in the face of the wind, from a 60-foot wooden monorail launching track, using a small yoke under the craft. Most significantly, the 1903 Flyer had a reliable petroleum-fueled engine designed and built by the Wrights themselves with the assistance of Charles Taylor, a machinist. It was cast from iron, with four cylinders, and could generate just over 12 horsepower at 1,090 rpm. It drove two counterrotating pusher propellers via chains and long shafts, but unlike the awkward paddles of Langley or his predecessors, these propellers were true rotating airfoils, carefully crafted as a result of the Wrights' wind-tunnel research.

The Wrights were well aware of Langley's efforts, and viewed his first failure with matter-of-fact calm. Writing to his sister Katharine, Orville stated:

> I suppose you have read in the papers the account of the failure of Langley's big machine. He started from a point 60 feet in the air and landed 300 feet away. . . . We are able, from this same height, to make from 400 to 600 feet without any motor at all, so that I think his surfaces must be very inefficient. They found they had no control of the machine whatever, though the wind blew but 5 miles an hour at time of the test. That is the point where we have a great advantage. We have been in the air hundreds and hundreds of times, and have pretty well worked out the problem of control.[3]

During their first few months at Kitty Hawk, the brothers readied the Flyer for flight. Problems with the propeller shafts delayed flight testing, and indeed Orville was on his way back to the Outer Banks with replacement shafts the morning after Langley's second flight attempt had ended wetly in the ice-filled Potomac. Five days later, on December 14, the brothers were ready for their first flight trials. A coin toss resulted in Wilbur's having the first crack at the machine. The track was placed on a small incline, facing downhill, and as brother Orville and a small band of witnesses watched, the machine roared down the track and into the air. Wilbur nosed up too steeply, however, and the machine stalled and landed heavily, sustaining minor damage. Repairs kept it grounded for the next two days, until December 17, when it was Orville's turn to fly.

That morning was fiercely cold and windy, a 27-mile-an-hour wind blowing across the hills from the north. At 10 o'clock, the two brothers decided to make the flight attempt, signaled volunteers from a life-saving station at Kill Devil Hills for assistance, took out the aircraft, and prepared for flight. Five volunteers and visitors arrived, and two others watched the flight effort through telescopes from the life-saving station at Kill Devil Hills and another station, four miles away, at Kitty Hawk.

At 10:30, they started the engine. The brothers shook hands, and Orville
lay down upon the lower wings, in the hip cradle, his left hand controlling the front elevator lever and his right controlling the engine. John
Daniels, one of the life guards, set up a camera. At 10:35, Orville released
the tether holding the aircraft back, and it began to move along the rail
into the wind. As Orville recollected later:

> Wilbur ran at the side of the machine, holding the wing to balance it
> on the track. Unlike the start on the 14th, made in a calm, the machine,
> facing a 27-mile wind, started very slowly. Wilbur was able to stay with
> it till it lifted from the track after a forty-foot run. . . .
>   The course of the flight up and down was exceedingly erratic, partly
> due to the irregularity of the air, and partly to lack of experience in han-
> dling this machine. The control of the front rudder was difficult on ac-
> count of its being balanced too near the center. This gave it a tendency
> to turn itself when started; so that it turned too far on one side and then
> too far on the other. As a result the machine would rise suddenly to
> about ten feet, and then as suddenly dart for the ground. A sudden dart
> when a little over a hundred feet from the end of the track, or a little
> over 120 feet from the point at which it rose into the air, ended the
> flight. . . . This flight lasted only 12 seconds, but it was nevertheless the
> first in the history of the world in which a machine carrying a man had
> raised itself by its own power into the air in full flight, had sailed for-
> ward without reduction of speed, and had finally landed at a point as
> high as that from which it started.[4]

John Daniels's remarkable photograph of that event shows the Wright
Flyer in full flight, with brother Wilbur, visibly tense with excitement,
poised in a dynamic stance, watching the Flyer soar along. The photograph caught a pivotal moment in the history of technology: the birth of
a new form of transportation that changed forever the world in which
humanity lives. After the Flyer landed, the volunteers jubilantly returned
the aircraft to its launching rail, and after a short break, Wilbur made
the next flight. Then Orville flew it again. Finally, at noon, in the fourth
and final trial, Wilbur flew for 852 feet in 59 seconds. After it landed,
the crew again brought it back to camp, but further flight plans evapo-
rated when an errant wind gust caught the craft and rolled it over and
over, causing extensive damage. The volunteers moved the wreckage into
the hangar and then ran off to tell the world, one of them yelling, "They
did it! They did it! Damned if they didn't fly!"[5] Following a triumphant
lunch, the Wrights walked through the cold and blustery wind up to
Kitty Hawk and telegraphed the news to their father, concluding, "inform Press home Christmas."[6] But aside from a garbled account that appeared and was ignored and forgotten quickly, the outside world did not

learn of the flight, for the press did not give it credence. After all, if the eminent Langley had failed with the support and resources of the U. S. Government behind him, how could two private individuals such as the Wrights possibly succeed? Quietly the Wrights went home to Dayton, there to continue their work.

FLEXING FLEDGLING WINGS

In 1904, the Wrights returned to the air. Instead of flying at Kitty Hawk, the brothers selected an eighty-seven-acre pasture, Huffman Prairie, for their tests. Situated eight miles east of Dayton, Huffman Prairie became the center of Wright flight test activities. There they flew their 1904 machine, the first to complete a circling flight, and later, their 1905 craft, generally heralded as the first practical airplane capable of repeated use. With the 1905 machine, the brothers disconnected the wing-warping mechanism from the rudder control, making it, like most future airplanes, a three-control aircraft. On October 5, 1905, it set an endurance record of 38 minutes. Jubilant, the brothers confidently wrote to the Secretary of War offering (for the second time) to furnish the Army with a scouting airplane. But, later that month, the Bureau of Ordnance and Fortification—still smarting from the Langley fiasco—declined politely. Stung by this rebuff, the two brothers sought foreign buyers for their aircraft, and perfected their own Flyer, deriving what is commonly referred to as the Wright Model A. Finally, cognizant of its errors, the U. S. Signal Corps issued Specification No. 486 on December 23, 1907, tailored to fit the Wright proposal. The craft had to be capable of being carried in a wagon, fly at 40 mph, and carry a crew of two. The Wrights applied, the Signal Corps responded with a contract on February 10, 1908, and the result was the famed and ill-fated 1908 Wright Military Flyer. That August, Orville Wright delivered the Military Flyer to Fort Myer, Virginia, just across the Potomac River from Washington, D.C., for testing. Simultaneously, Wilbur was in Europe, demonstrating the Wright machine in France.

It is hard, in this age of moon landings and routine supersonic commercial air transportation, to re-create the atmosphere that permeated these early flights by the Wrights. In 1906 the dapper and tormented Brazilian expatriate Alberto Santos-Dumont had hopped off the ground in his ungainly *14-bis* box-kite biplane, at Bagatelle, near Paris. For the next two years, other European aviators tried with varying success to emulate his modest feat. As for the Wrights, they were regarded as mere *bluffeurs*. All this changed dramatically on August 8, 1908, when Wilbur

Wright made his first European flight, at the small racecourse of Hunaudières, five miles south of Le Mans. He took off, circled, and demonstrated complete, practical mastery of the air. Stunned, French aviator René Gasnier commented wonderingly, "Who can now doubt that the Wrights have done all they claimed? We are as children compared with the Wrights."[7] And so it was. But sometimes it pays to be a fast second—and the Europeans were not slow in catching up and (for a time) surpassing the United States in the field of aviation technology. Meanwhile, back in the United States, Orville readied the Military Flyer for flight. After preparations were complete, Orville began the Army trials on September 3. To the crowds that flocked to the parade grounds at Fort Myer, the sight of Orville, cap placed jauntily on his head, wheeling and pirouetting in the air above, was no less astounding than it had been to the French watching Wilbur less than a month before. The tests went well, and Orville flew one flight with Major George O. Squier, soon to become chief of the Signal Corps. On September 17, Orville agreed to fly with Lieutenant Thomas Selfridge, an aviation enthusiast (he was a member of Alexander Graham Bell's Aerial Experiment Association). During the flight, the right pusher propeller cracked, setting up a vibration that caused it to strike and sever one of the rudder's bracing wires. Orville felt a light tapping, then "two big thumps, which gave the machine a terrible shaking."[8] It plunged out of control from 150 feet, virtually in a vertical dive. Orville tried desperately to raise the nose, and in fact the Flyer was just beginning to recover when it hit the ground, seriously injuring Orville and inflicting a skull fracture on the unfortunate passenger, who died shortly afterward, the first victim of a powered airplane accident. The crash brought the Army trials to an end but did not spell the end of official interest in the Wright machine. In less than a year, Orville would return to Fort Myer, successfully demonstrating the 1909 Military Flyer, a modified Type A machine, to the Army. The service bought the craft, and after pioneering American military aviation, it was sent to the Smithsonian Institution. It is now on exhibit at the National Air and Space Museum—together with the original Wright Flyer and a later Wright Model EX—the oldest military aircraft in the world. That same year, Wilbur and Orville flew in France, Italy, and Germany, then returned to the United States and made flights witnessed by millions of New Yorkers. But by 1909, there were a number of aviators flying, both in the Americas and in Europe. It was 1908 that had marked the public's recognition that, as with the balloon, humanity now possessed the capability of flying with mechanical wings. Truly, as Charles Gibbs-Smith has written, "The year 1908 was an *annus mirabilis* in aviation history."

The Wright brothers, in retrospect, were model flight researchers. There can be no doubt that, had their interest in aviation not included a recognition of the importance of airborne experimentation, they would have failed as miserably as their predecessors. Yet, like the engineering test pilot of today, the brothers recognized that their machines had to incorporate the highest standards of engineering reasoning and insight, and to this end their work on the ground was fully as impressive as their work aloft. And like today's test pilots, both were "good sticks." Wilbur, an accomplished pilot, died at the age of forty-five from typhoid, ending (as his father sadly wrote) "a short life, full of consequences." In 1918, Orville retired from piloting airplanes. For the rest of his life, until his death in 1948 at the age of seventy-six, he remained the doyen of American aeronautical pioneers, busying himself in such organizations as The Daniel Guggenheim Fund for the Promotion of Aeronautics and the National Advisory Committee for Aeronautics. But the instincts of an old pro remained. In 1944, during a demonstration flight of a Lockheed C-69 Constellation, Orville Wright took the controls and smoothly piloted the elegant four-engine airplane from the right seat; the pilot reported that the younger Wright had a nice touch. Fittingly, the flight took place at Wright Field, outside Dayton, in the skies above Huffman Prairie; the airfield, known to flight researchers around the country as simply "the Field," had been dedicated in honor of the brothers in October 1927. By 1910, the Wrights had completed their major work; the world would never be the same as it was in the time before Kitty Hawk.

Next to the brothers Wright, the most notable name in early American aviation was that of Glenn H. Curtiss. Like the Wrights, Curtiss, born in 1878, established himself by repairing and later building bicycles. By nature a daredevil, he had graduated to motorcycles, manufacturing both the cycles and lightweight yet powerful air-cooled engines for them. In 1903, Curtiss built a special engine for airship pioneer Thomas Scott Baldwin. Then, in 1907, he set a world's speed record—and became the world's fastest human—by guiding a powerful, eight-cylinder motorcycle over a measured mile at an average speed of 136.3 mph. Self-confident, an accomplished technologist, possessed of an adventurous streak—all attributes common to a test pilot—Curtiss became involved with aviation naturally.

Curtiss's future changed when telephone pioneer Dr. Alexander Graham Bell invited the young engine manufacturer to build engines that Bell could use in his aerial experimentation at Beinn Breagh, near Baddeck, Nova Scotia. Bell, a Smithsonian Institution regent, was fully committed to studying the possibilities of human flight. Curtiss's first engine was a failure, being too heavy for its power. A second was more successful, and Bell asked Curtiss if he would come to Nova Scotia to assist Bell and a small group of associates in their experiments. Curtiss agreed. Bell's group consisted of Curtiss, Canadians J. A. D. McCurdy and Frederick W. ("Casey") Baldwin, and Lieutenant Thomas Selfridge, on temporary assignment from the U. S. War Department to observe the work of the Bell group. At the suggestion of Bell's wife, the group banded together as the Aerial Experiment Association in September 1907; Curtiss served as director of experimental research. The AEA was one of the world's first aeronautical research and development establishments, and while it was short-lived, its activities were impressive. In contrast to laboratories in other countries—such as that of the great Ludwig Prandtl at Göttingen, or Nikolai Riabouchinsky's research establishment at Koutchino, in Russia—the AEA was not content merely to study aviation in the clinical isolation of the laboratory. Bell recognized that full-scale flight testing would have to complement the theoretical work on the ground and model testing, to validate or disprove the research being undertaken. Eventually each member of the group agreed to direct development of an airplane, to be built in Glenn Curtiss's shop at Hammondsport, New York. At first, however, the members gained tentative flight experience by flying a Chanute-type hang glider. The AEA's first airplane, designed by Selfridge, was the *Red Wing* (so-called because of the color of its fabric), flown once by Baldwin in March 1907 at Hammondsport. A very primitive craft (it did not have provisions for lateral control), it rolled wildly and crashed on its first flight. It was superseded by the *White Wing*, designed by Baldwin and tested by the group in May 1908. Curtiss developed the AEA's next craft, the *June Bug*, and on July 4, 1908, flew over a mile, winning the Scientific American Trophy. All this and more, of course, had been accomplished earlier by the Wrights, but the members of the AEA were learning for themselves, in that manner of near isolation that often accompanies the development of a new technology.

The AEA's decline began in September 1908, with the death of Thomas Selfridge at Fort Myer. With money from Bell's wife, the group continued work into 1909; Curtiss modified the *June Bug* with two floats and renamed it the *Loon*. It failed to leave the water, and finally sank following damage to one of its floats. McCurdy completed the AEA's fourth and last airplane, the *Silver Dart*. In February 1909, with McCurdy at the controls, this craft completed the first flight made by a British subject anywhere in the British Commonwealth. Bell continued his own work on gigantic tetrahedral kites, without great success. In March 1909, by mutual consent, the group amicably disbanded and the

AEA ceased to exist. Curtiss returned to Hammondsport to continue his work.

By the end of 1909, Curtiss was a public figure ranking with the Wrights. He had flown from Albany to New York City, winning a $10,000 prize offered by the New York *World;* his trim pusher airplanes, with a ruggedly functional appearance, became as familiar to Americans as the distinctive Wright canard designs. Like the Wrights, Curtiss established an exhibition team to demonstrate the firm's aircraft; daring public exhibitions, such as the epochal Belmont Meet of 1910, enabled the average citizen to examine these new contraptions at close range and watch company pilots perform daring stunts. Not all of this early barnstorming activity was good for the image of aviation. Aircraft, simply stated, were not in any sense reliable. As historian Roger Bilstein has written,

> As romantic as the flying machine might seem to poets and enthusiastic crowds, the airplane was still a tricky thing to fly. The early products of the Wrights and others were controllable but unstable, and pilots preferred to go aloft early in the morning or late in the afternoon when the air was at its calmest. Even then, they were carefully watching flags and smoke plumes, and anxiously sticking wet fingers above their heads to test the breeze.[9]

Fatalities rose sharply, and the image of the "unsafe airplane" became firmly rooted in the public mind. Responsible spokesmen and interested manufacturers consciously sought to reverse this trend, but with indifferent results. In part, the problem stemmed from pilots themselves. In truth, many of the exhibition pilots, such as Lincoln Beachey and Casey Jones, were risk takers. Naval aviation pioneer George van Deurs has written:

> Most of the professional pilots knew little about the "why" of their machines. They had been parachute jumpers, balloonists, racing drivers, or circus stunt men. Few of them ever formally learned how to fly. They took off by luck, superstition, and rule of thumb, and then landed by sheer audacity and agility. They would try anything for publicity and big money. These men were the mainstays of the exhibition teams, but they bored thoughtful men like the Wrights and Curtiss. Capt. Washington Irving Chambers of the U. S. Navy found them uninteresting because they could only discuss flying in terms of muscular exercises and sensations.[10]

Another group of aviators were often working quietly and carefully: those professional airmen who flew for the companies and, after 1909, for the military services to develop the airplane into a reliable vehicle. These men, already imbued with the highest standards of professionalism, were true test pilots, in fact if not in name.

THE MILITARY TAKES TO THE AIR

As part of the agreement whereby the Army purchased the Wright 1909 Military Flyer, the brothers agreed to train the first Army pilots. The Wrights had never liked flying at Fort Myer, because the grounds were too small for safety. Following a survey by Lieutenant Frank Lahm, the Army selected a field on the outskirts of the Maryland Agricultural College (now the University of Maryland), near the then tiny community of College Park. The 160-acre site was bordered by marsh and scrub forest, and on its western edge by a railroad; this modest field, within a dozen miles of the U. S. Capital, became the Army's first aeronautical training, research, and development center. The Wrights began flight operations at College Park in October 1909, and by the end of the month, Lieutenant Lahm and Lieutenant Frederick Humphreys had soloed, qualifying as the service's first pilots. In November, the Military Flyer was badly damaged when the left wing snagged the ground during a low-altitude turn, and because of increasing bad weather, the Army set up flying quarters at Fort Sam Houston, in Texas, and did not return to College Park until 1911. While in Texas, Lieutenant Benjamin Foulois (later chief of the U. S. Army Air Corps) checked out in the craft—often corresponding with Wilbur and Orville Wright for instruction!—and discovered the problems of in-flight turbulence. On one flight, turbulence bounced the Military Flyer around so badly that Foulois was nearly thrown from it; upon landing, he arranged for installation of a seat restraint strap. The strap kept him in the plane during his next turbulence encounter, when he inadvertently flew into a "dust devil" rising off the parade ground of the fort. The little twister threw the Flyer out of control, and Foulois desperately lowered the nose to regain control; before he could completely recover, however, the plane force-landed heavily, sustaining major damage and dazing its pilot. Gradually the service was learning how to master its new beast.

In early 1911, the Army assigned two other aviators to train in Dayton on the Wright machines: Lieutenant Henry H. "Hap" Arnold, who later rose to command the Army Air Forces during the Second World War, and Lieutenant Thomas Milling. In those early days of flight, the prospective pilots were then expected to go forth, train others, and themselves serve as research and evaluation pilots, determining the military capabilities and suitabilities of aircraft. Arnold and Milling reported to the old Wright factory outside Dayton, and following a thorough ground school, began their flight training. Al Welsh, the Wrights' chief test pilot, took Arnold aside before his first flight and pointed out an ominous figure sitting in a wagon parked on the edge of the field. "That's the local undertaker," Welsh confided. "He comes out every day and drives back empty. Let's keep it that way."[11] Fortunately, everything went smoothly; Arnold and Milling won their wings and then reported back to College Park, where they were soon buzzing over the local countryside. By today's standards, their flights were unremarkable, even trivial—but that simply serves to reemphasize just how far aviation has advanced in the years since Kitty Hawk. For example, on one of Arnold's early proving flights, he had to fly a triangular course from College Park to Washington Barracks, in the District of Columbia, fly on to Fort Myer, locate a troop of cavalry, and return to College Park, all in a demonstration of the craft's usefulness as a reconnaissance vehicle.

Though a 1910 report, in the *Journal of United States Artillery*, by Lieutenant Fred Humphreys had concluded that aircraft were virtually incapable of damaging ships or fortifications and that their "first and probably the greatest use will be found in reconnaissance," the pilots at College Park thought otherwise. Over the summer of 1911, the airmen tested a bombsight developed by Riley E. Scott, dropping 18-pound "bombs" from a height of 400 feet while sighting through the instrument. On the best run, both bombs landed within a 10-foot radius of a 4 × 5-foot target. Army Headquarters was not enthusiastic over these tests, nor with later ones in 1912 when the airmen fired a machine gun from an airplane at ground targets: the official mission of the airplane was reconnaissance, not armed combat. (Yet, within a few months, Italy, engaged in a war with Turkey over the possession of Tripoli, undertook limited bombing operations using hand-dropped bombs flung from German-built Rumpler Taube monoplanes. The handwriting was clearly visible to those willing to see it.)

In August 1911, the Army undertook its first long cross-country flight, sending two aircraft from College Park to Frederick, Maryland, a distance of just over forty miles. One plane force-landed almost immediately because of engine trouble, without injuring its crew. The other, flown by Hap Arnold and Captain Charles De F. Chandler, reached Frederick safely. On the return trip, however, ground haze and winds disoriented them, and they landed to ask directions; on takeoff, the plane stalled and crashed, and Arnold and Chandler returned to College Park by train. Later that year, Tom Milling completed the Army's first night flights, landing at College Park in the glare of two acetylene searchlights. Arnold undertook a series of altitude flights, finally climbing to 6,540 feet on June 1, 1912, then a world's record. But then, as before and since, the progress being made demanded sacrifices. On June 11, 1912, Wright test pilot Al Welsh and Army pilot Lieutenant Leighton Hazelhurst were killed when their Wright Type C Scout failed to pull out of a dive. Three months later, another Wright Flyer crashed, killing Lieutenant Lewis Rockwell and Corporal Frank Scott under almost identical circumstances. Then, in November, the Army closed down its College Park operations, transferring flight testing and training to the Southwest, where weather conditions were generally more favorable. Though this action terminated the Army's involvement at College Park, it did not bring the flight test activities of this field to an end, as will subsequently be seen.

The Army, of course, was not alone in operating a fledgling air service. The Navy, too, had begun the slow process that would lead to the development of the aircraft carrier and the demise of the battleship—a result hardly any aviation advocate, no matter how enthusiastic, could have predicted. During 1910, at the direction of the Navy Department, Captain Washington Irving Chambers, a line officer (Annapolis, 1876) and former captain of the battleship *Louisiana*, attended aviation meets and studied aeronautics in order to advise the Navy about aviation matters. The more he saw, heard, and read, the more enthusiastic this archetypical deck officer became. Chambers was particularly impressed with the planned Curtiss "Hydroaeroplane," a float-equipped Curtiss "pusher" that seemed ideal for the Navy's needs, and with one of the Curtiss test pilots, Eugene Ely. Eugene Ely, a pleasant young man, was a self-taught aviator who, in contrast to most of the exhibition pilots flying for the Wright and Curtiss companies, was seriously interested in aviation technology and the mechanics of flight. In late October 1910, during the Belmont Park flying exhibition, Chambers had asked Wilbur Wright if the Wright company would be willing to fly a plane from a ship. Wright declined, insisting it was too dangerous. Now, less than a month later, in early November, during the Halethorpe Field flying exhibition, outside Baltimore, Chambers mentioned the idea to Gene Ely. Without hesitation, Ely volunteered, offering to fly his own plane free. Chambers and Ely, together with other supporters of the scheme, had to apply intensive lobbying to the Secretary of the Navy to win approval of the scheme; their efforts succeeded, and the Navy authorized a test from the four-stack cruiser *Birmingham* at Norfolk, Virginia. An 83-foot sloping ramp was installed on the forward deck of the cruiser, from the bridge to the bow; its edge was a scant 37 feet above the water. And Ely prepared his aircraft.

The actual flight attempt came on November 14, 1910, less than two weeks after Chambers had first broached the subject to Ely at Baltimore. On the appointed day of the trial, the small Curtiss pusher sat forward of the bridge, 57 feet of available ramp space before it. Ely busied himself with the plane as the *Birmingham,* ropes of black smoke curling from its stacks, steamed toward Old Point Comfort, amid squalls. In time, the cruiser reached its destination and anchored off the point, and Ely waited for the weather to clear. It had been planned for the *Birmingham* to steam into the wind, assisting Ely's takeoff. But the weather remained marginal, and Ely, fearing that the trials would be postponed, decided to take off while the ship remained at anchor. At 3:16 P.M., with the sky darkening from an impending squall, Ely—who could not swim and who, indeed, feared the water—added full power to the engine and gave the release signal. A mechanic released the plane from its hold-back on the ramp, and the pusher, engine roaring, slowly rolled down the ramp and dropped over the bow. For a moment the plane was lost to view. Then, ominously, observers saw a curtain of water rise in front of the ship; during the descent from the bow, the plane had dropped nose high, semi-stalled, and in fact, had brushed the water, splintering the propeller's tips. The plucky pilot recovered; the plane scooted low above the murky sound, vibrating badly. Hastily, Ely landed as soon as he crossed over the shoreline, on Willoughby Spit. Discouraged that he had hit the water and then failed to reach his goal, the Norfolk Navy Yard, Ely was surprised that Chambers and other air-minded naval officials were delighted with the flight. Traditionalists, though, argued that the modifications necessary for the pusher to be launched from the cruiser had robbed the cruiser of its ability to fight at sea; foreign reporters, however, speculated that the United States would rapidly move to construct special aircraft-carrying ships. But first, Chambers and Ely wanted to demonstrate that an airplane could operate both *from* and *to* a ship.

Ely's Norfolk flight had made aviation a little more respectable to the individuals running the Navy Department, but only just. Once again, Chambers and Ely were really on their own, when it came to arranging for a flight to and from another vessel. Since Ely would be taking part in an aviation meet at San Francisco in January 1911, Chambers arranged for the trials to be made from the armored cruiser *Pennsylvania,* then assigned to the Pacific fleet. A 120-foot wooden platform was built on the quarterdeck of the cruiser, with a 14-foot overhang above the stern. The platform sloped gently forward over the after gun turret, and canvas barriers and a timber backstop would prevent the plane, should it still be moving, from crashing into the mainmast. Cable lines, with 50-pound sandbags on each end, were stretched across the platform at three-foot intervals, designed to snag hooks Ely had installed on the underside of the plane—a scheme remarkably similar to modern carrier arresting gear. Though Chambers wanted to have the ship steaming into the wind during the landing approach, Ely preferred landing with the ship at anchor.

In mid-January, the *Pennsylvania* left the Mare Island Navy Yard in heavy fog, steamed into San Francisco Bay, and anchored off Goat Island. For over a week, weather prevented any flight attempt, and even Glenn Curtiss hoped that Ely would abandon the plan to land aboard ship. Weather conditions improved on January 17, and Ely announced plans to make the flight on the eighteenth, taking off from Tanforan (near San Bruno) and then flying out to the ship. The next morning, the weather was clear, with high clouds. Ely took off at 10:48 A.M., climbed over San Bruno, turned out over the bay, and droned steadily toward Goat Island. At 400 feet, Ely approached the ships at anchor, then descended to mast height. He flew up the *Pennsylvania*'s starboard side, turned, flew down the port side, banked around, throttled back the engine, and lazily approached the stern platform. Fifty feet from the stern, he cut the engine entirely, and the plane sank toward the deck, propeller whirring. Just before touchdown, a gust lifted the machine; Ely jammed the nose down, and the hooks under the aircraft snagged the weighted lines stretching across the deck, stopping the plane smartly. The ship's captain declared the landing the most significant since the dove flew back to Noah's Ark, then ordered some ship's crewmen to "respot" the craft for launch—the first use of this now common naval aviation term. In the captain's own cabin, guests—including Ely's wife, Mabel—toasted the pilot and the "birth of naval aviation." Then Ely went topside, and just before noon, took off uneventfully from the cruiser, the plane climbing in a wide spiral, then heading back to Tanforan, where it landed 13 minutes later. With this flight, Ely passed into the annals of naval aviation. Within the year he was dead, killed during an exhibition flight in Georgia.

The next steps in naval aviation belonged to Curtiss and the "Hydroaeroplane." Two weeks after Ely's epochal San Francisco flight, Curtiss was at long last able to demonstrate a successful takeoff from water in the float-equipped Curtiss pusher at North Island, San Diego. He was assisted by the first naval officer assigned to train under Curtiss, Lieutenant Theodore G. ("Spuds") Ellyson, a submariner. Curtiss grew to like the mechanically adept and gregarious Ellyson, who proved an apt pupil and a good pilot.

Bureaucratic stalling within the Navy Department again stymied those who were pushing for rapid acquisition of aircraft; in congressional testimony, the Secretary of the Navy was asked about the military potential of airplanes. "That they will be used as fighting machines is very doubtful," he replied. Eventually, however, Chambers's persistent lobbying

THE FRONTIERSMEN OF FLIGHT

resulted in the Navy's purchasing its first airplane: a Curtiss Hydroaero-plane dubbed the "Triad" (because it could operate from land with re-tractable wheels and from water with floats, and flew in the air), which received the official designation A-1. Its testing did not proceed without incident. Curtiss himself wrecked it on landing, owing to a leaky pontoon (the plane was rebuilt), and Ellyson flew the rebuilt airplane on one oc-casion when the wooden propeller fractured, miraculously missing the struts and wires supporting the tail, and he had to glide down to land powerless. Such experiences became commonplace, because it seemed that nearly every flight resulted in an emergency landing from some form of engine trouble.

So far, naval aviation—if it could be said to exist—had managed to function without a permanent base of operations. Chambers, however, recognized that a permanent site was required, especially since the serv-ice had reluctantly acquired other aircraft, an underpowered Curtiss pusher landplane designated the A-2, and a rival Wright Type B-1. The logical site was one close to the nation's capital, and of course, this from the start made the selection of Annapolis an almost forgone conclusion. At Chambers's urging, the Navy established a small flying field on Greenbury Point, across the Severn River from the Naval Academy it-self.

In September 1911, Ellyson and the second and third Navy pilots, John Rodgers (a cousin of aviation pioneer Calbraith Perry Rodgers) and John Towers arrived at Annapolis to activate the fledgling air station, discovering that their mission was low on the Navy's list of priori-ties and that, indeed, they had more in common with their comrades-in-arms at the Army station at College Park than they did with the tradi-tionalist officers running Annapolis. Their early flights involved much hard work, frustrating mechanical problems, and occasional heartbreak, punctuated by frequent forced landings. During one flight on a chilly November day, a wind gust stalled the A-1, which dived out of control into the icy water; pilot Towers, injured in the crash, had to lash himself to the plane's float and wait nearly an hour for rescue. The Wright B-1, equipped with floats, flew badly, taking off at 32 knots and having a max-imum level flight speed of only 33 knots! Needless to say, pilot Rodgers cracked it up on its first flight, stalling during a turn. The A-1 and B-1 continued this way for months, being rebuilt, flown, crashed, and rebuilt.

Nevertheless, at Annapolis and San Diego, the Navy's first aviators kept at it. In 1912, they conducted practice exercises with the fleet, in-cluding wireless telegraphy. (The Army at the same time was experi-menting with aircraft as spotters for artillery fire, corrections being sig-naled to firing batteries by wireless and dropped notes.) The nagging problems of launching from ship remained; the wooden platforms *were* awkward for line vessels, and short of constructing special deck-landing ships, the catapult appeared as a useful alternative. Accordingly, the Navy's Bureau of Ordnance set up a compressed-air catapult at the Naval Academy's Santee dock. The catapult was anything but subtle, and in its first tests, on July 31, 1912, the abrupt acceleration threw the Curtiss A-1 into a stall as Ellyson tried vainly to control the craft. It nosed into the water and turned turtle; Ellyson gamely said, "A little bump like that should never bother a good aviator,"[12] as he was fished from the Severn River. The Navy redesigned the catapult, and on November 12, during tests on the Anacostia River from a barge anchored at the Washington Navy Yard, Ellyson successfully flew a new Curtiss Hydroaeroplane, the A-3, off the catapult, and followed this up with the heavier Curtiss C-1 flying boat. Flight testing had validated the concept of the catapult launch, which eventually became an accepted facet of naval aviation worldwide.

These early military aircraft, of both the Army and the Navy, were extraordinarily light and thus extremely gust-responsive. The Curtiss A-1, for example, had a wing area of 286 square feet and a gross weight of only 1,500 pounds. With their low flight speeds—on the order of 60 mph—and built-in control lag, they were certainly not refined flying machines. The pusher configuration likewise generated special problems; sometimes, if a gust caused the craft to dive, the dynamic characteristics of the aircraft under power would cause it to plunge earthward; the pilot, sitting exposed over the front frames of the craft, might nervously pull back too far on the elevator controls, inadvertently stalling the craft, which would then continue its deadly descent into the ground.

Eventually the bad safety record of pusher aircraft caused both the Army and the Navy to phase them out in favor of more modern tractor designs such as the Martin trainer and the early Curtiss "Jenny." Until then, however, they continued to take a toll of the unwary and unfortunate. During a flight of the Wright B-2 floatplane at Annapolis, a gust upset the craft, hurling its pilot, Ensign W. D. Billingsley, to his death. John Rodgers, along for the ride as a passenger, just managed to hold on as the stricken plane dived into the water off Kent Island; he survived with injuries. After the Navy moved its flight training activities to the old navy yard at Pensacola, Florida, a similar accident was averted when the pilot managed to hang on to a strut as he was nearly thrown from the plane. This second incident led to the introduction of lap belts on all Navy airplanes, though mistrust of the older pushers continued.

One notable flight research endeavor aimed at improving the safety of airplanes was Lawrence Sperry's demonstration of a practical airplane autopilot during testing at the Navy's North Island airfield, climaxed by a spectacular public demonstration at Bezons, France, in June 1914.

Lawrence Sperry, dubbed "Gyro" by his fellow pilots, is one of those brilliant, tragic figures who dot the landscape of aviation history. The handsome eldest son of inventor Elmer Sperry, he did not live comfortably in the shadow of his father's impressive reputation. On his own, Lawrence contributed significantly to the development of aviation during his brief career, cut short in a fatal accident in 1923.

Sperry had joined forces with Glenn Curtiss at North Island in 1913, at the age of twenty. There he worked to perfect a gyroscopic stabilizer consisting of two gyros, one vertical and one horizontal, to prevent an aircraft's flight path from deviating in roll, pitch, and yaw. The gyros would be connected to servomotors linked to cables attached to the plane's control lines. The Navy, watching the project with interest, appointed Lieutenant Patrick Bellinger as project test pilot, but Lawrence himself undertook many of the often hazardous trial flights. During previous tests of Sperry gyros to control roll and pitch, one plane had crashed with a Sperry "lateral stabilizer," seriously injuring its pilot. Later another Army plane testing a pitch-control device developed by Sperry crashed on landing, killing a passenger. The tests of the three-axis autopilot for the Navy went much more smoothly, however, and Bellinger completed fifty-two test flights in a modified Curtiss C-2 flying boat equipped with the experimental device, Sperry riding along as a flight test engineer.

Sperry remained convinced, however, that the autopilot had yet to be demonstrated conclusively. Early one Sunday morning in November 1913, he went aloft by himself in the hydroplane. The noise of the plane awakened puzzled onlookers, including Glenn Curtiss himself, who saw the plane buzzing around, seemingly without a pilot. He immediately surmised the truth: that Lawrence was in the hull, bent over his autopilot, forcing the plane off course and then studying the gyros as they brought it back in line. This impressive demonstration encouraged Sperry and Curtiss to enter the device and the plane in an international safety competition sponsored by the Aéro Club de France and the French Ministry of War.

During the Aéro Club trials, in June 1914, Sperry astounded his international audience by standing in the cockpit of the smoothly flying machine, his hands clearly not on the controls. Émil Cachin, his French mechanic, went further, and actually stepped out on the lower wing, the plane momentarily dipping and then automatically righting itself without Sperry's touching the controls. It was inevitable that Sperry would win the 50,000-franc first prize of the competition. Without question, much research work remained to be done before the autopilot could be considered ready for widespread commercial and military service. Nevertheless, the first steps had been taken—and flight testing, as before and since, had validated the concept.

By 1914, American military aviation, though rudimentary, was ready for its first operational tests. In April of that year, the Navy's service chiefs were confident enough of their new air arm that they detailed two aircraft to take part in the naval landing at Veracruz, following tension between the American and Mexican governments. During this active combat evaluation, Pat Bellinger flew scouting missions for the fleet, his C-3 floatplane being lowered overboard from the battleship U.S.S. *Mississippi* for takeoff. During Bellinger's flights, it was actually holed by Mexican sharpshooters. Naval aviation had undergone its combat baptism; the Army would receive its own in two years, when Benny Foulois would take the 1st Aero Squadron south to assist "Black Jack" Pershing in his futile search for Pancho Villa, whose bandits had murdered American citizens both in Mexico and the United States.

The American military establishment was just in the midst of assimilating its recent experience in Mexico when word came that Serbian terrorists had murdered the Austro-Hungarian heir apparent, Franz Ferdinand, and his wife. Within weeks, a crisis in the Balkans, fueled by decades of national jealousies and inept diplomacy, erupted into appalling war, on a scale no one could have believed possible. The old order—political, social, cultural, technological—was at once swept away, relegated to the past. In the war Americans thought they could avoid, four weapons would emerge to shatter previous doctrine and relegate hallowed strategies to the dustbin of military history: the machine gun, the tank, the submarine, and the airplane.

The airplane came of age over the battlefields of Europe. It had been made possible by the Wrights, but it had been the Europeans—the "fast seconds" who forged it into a useful weapon in the opening weeks of the war. In the United States, a nation uncertainly pursuing a policy of neutrality, observers of the aviation scene were discovering with unpleasant shock just how much catching up American aviation had to do.

CHAPTER 3

THE GREAT WAR

The airplane with which the European nations went to war in 1914 bore little resemblance to the kitelike craft that first sputtered aloft from the sands of Kitty Hawk. While bureaucratic inertia and official disinterest had hampered European aviation as well, the malaise afflicting American aeronautics was far more pervasive. Without question, by 1914, American aviation lagged badly behind that of Europe, due in part to the skepticism and hostility of critics of the airplane, as well as the prisonlike confines of established military thought and doctrine. And sadly, the great Wright-Curtiss patent-infringement controversy, which the Wrights brought against Curtiss, also hampered the development of American aviation technology. Still, however, American designers had made small gains, and thoughtful test pilots staked their lives—and their companies' futures—on the products of the engineers.

By 1914, Europe had already established a firm laboratory tradition in aeronautics with (for example) the creation of aeronautical research facilities at Britain's National Physical Laboratory (equivalent to the American Bureau of Standards) and Farnborough, and at Göttingen, in Germany. The United States did not match these efforts (aside from a brief attempt to reopen the "Langley Aerodynamical Laboratory" at the Smithsonian Institution) until Congress, rudely confronted with blatant American inferiority, authorized the National Advisory Committee for Aeronautics (the predecessor of today's NASA), in March 1915. The

Army and the Navy eventually organized their own research centers, such as McCook Field and Anacostia. Until the test and research facilities of these centers became available, however, aircraft design and research rested largely in the hands of a not-always-too-conscientious-and-careful "industry."

By 1914, certain trends in aeronautics were already well established. The open-framework pusher biplane, as typified by the prewar Wright, Farman, Curtiss, and Voisin designs, had already given way to much shapelier and efficient configurations having an enclosed framework fuselage, the pilot and crew (if any) sitting in tandem open cockpits. Ahead of the crew nestled the fuel tank (sometimes placed in the center section of the upper wing) and then the engine. Relatively reliable and powerful liquid-cooled engines and the air-cooled "rotary" engine (a distant relative of the later, radial engine) typified by the universally popular Gnôme, developed in France by the Seguin brothers, replaced the crude air-cooled and liquid-cooled engines of the early pioneers. Already, designers had built multiengine airplanes—the impressive Sikorsky Le Grand, a four-engine design, being a particularly striking example. The strange and often inefficient propeller designs that had appeared on earlier craft disappeared, replaced by scientifically crafted shapes designed for maximum aerodynamic performance. Wing-warping, though still used on some machines, was disappearing in favor of the aileron. The profusion of flight control levers (a hallmark of early planes) also disappeared, in favor of the simple "joystick" for pitch and roll control, and rudder bars or pedals for directional control.

Pointing the direction of future flight were such outstanding craft as the Deperdussin "Monocoque Racer," which, in 1912, had introduced the revolutionary concept of *monocoque*, or "single shell," construction to aircraft design. This configuration used a thin plywood shell internally stiffened by wooden rings to carry the flight loads of the craft; it gave the plane a smooth external shape, which the designers added to by enclosing the engine in a cowling (more because radial engines belched great gouts of lubricating oils than because of aerodynamics) and a propeller having a massive spinner. Significantly, the "Monocoque Racer" was a monoplane, like the Blériot (which had crossed the Straits of Dover in 1909) and such other early aircraft as the Antoinette and Demoiselle. The wing remained externally braced. The monoplane would not become universally popular for many more years, and because of demanding manufacturing conditions, neither would the wooden monocoque fuselage shape. Nevertheless it influenced the design of the sharklike and elegant German Albatros fighter and some other aircraft, and presaged the appearance of the all-metal "stressed skin" monoplane over a decade later.

The same general staffs whose muddled thinking so greatly influenced the tragic road from Sarajevo to war, who, for the most part, dismissed the significance of the machine gun and massed artillery, who spoke of massed infantry advances in terms of parade-ground-like marches, who thought only of *élan vital* and the "will to conquer," not unexpectedly dismissed the airplane as having little consequence to the bloody conflict already raging. They were, for the most part, men conditioned by studying the tactics of Blücher, or Wellington, or Napoleon; they had fought at Sedan or in the colonial wars; they thought of Kitchener's resolute squares against the Mahdi. In short, they were ready to refight Waterloo or Austerlitz; they were not ready for the Western Front of 1914.

The pilots went to war as airborne cavalry, filling the cavalry's traditional role as scouts. Soon, far sooner than its strongest proponents could have forecast, the airplane proved of crucial importance. In the opening weeks of the war, Allied pilots had detected Von Kluck's fatal wheeling movement away from Paris prior to the battle of the Marne, enabling hard-pressed British and French troops to end the German advance at the gates of the City of Light. German airmen had kept Von Hindenburg accurately informed as to the location and strength of Russian units during the battle of Tannenberg, enabling his units to pick their points of attack and crush the Russian force, which had, to that time, operated with singular and unexpected success during its drive from the east. Very quickly, then, ground commanders discovered they had to cope with another problem not considered by prewar infantry manuals: how to shield their units from the prying eyes of airborne enemy scouts. The camaraderie of opposing airmen passing in flight with a casual wave or waggling of wings soon dissolved amid the sharp crack of a rifle or carbine. By mid-1915, the machine gun had made its appearance in the air. When Dutch-born airplane manufacturer Anthony Fokker introduced the machine-gun-carrying *Eindecker* (monoplane) equipped with an interrupter mechanism to prevent the pilot from shooting off his own propeller, the age of the fighter airplane (then called "fighting scout" or "pursuit") had arrived. By 1917, over the Somme, specialized fighters were clashing in large numbers to deny opposing forces control of the air; their names—such as Albatros, Sopwith Pup, Nieuport, S.P.A.D.—have become symbols of an overromanticized era of savage and merciless combat. In this constant dialectic of challenge and response, the quest for technical supremacy took on tremendous significance. Designers and engineers sought to extract the maximum performance from these new and evocative flying craft. Test pilots evaluated their performance before sending them to the fronts.

FARNBOROUGH AND MARTLESHAM: BIRTH OF A TRADITION

By the war years, flight testing was an emerging specialty already cloaked in the first trappings of scientific professionalism, due to the efforts of a distinguished group of British pilots whose influence extended far beyond their native land. The first of these individuals who made a major impact on the development of flight testing was Edward "Teddy" Busk, holder of an honors degree from Cambridge and employed as assistant engineer physicist at the Royal Aircraft Factory, Farnborough. In the years immediately prior to the First World War, Farnborough, situated in the midst of Laffan's Plain, in Hampshire, had a reputation comparable to that of Edwards today: the recognized center of advanced flight research and flight testing. Busk, the professional engineer, had qualifications that ideally suited his becoming an engineering test pilot. In 1912, he had started flying lessons at Hendon, then studied aerodynamics at the National Physical Laboratory before joining the technical staff at Farnborough.

The heady atmosphere of the Royal Aircraft Factory whetted Busk's interest in flying, and he convinced Mervyn O'Gorman, the director of the factory, to let him continue his flying lessons. He flew as a pupil of pioneer Geoffrey de Havilland, and by mid-1913, was test-flying De Havilland's R.E. 1 and the B.E. 2 biplanes. Busk was particularly intrigued by the field of aircraft stability and control, especially the concept of "inherent" stability, and his ideas were incorporated in later models of the B.E. 2 (notably in the B.E. 2c, with which the Royal Flying Corps went to war in 1914), capable of being flown "hands off."

In 1914, however, despite the efforts of a Busk (the test pilot who, in fact, introduced scientific flight testing methods to British aeronautics), aviation still involved considerable risk and chance-taking that would not be tolerated today. The early B.E. 2 airplanes often flew drenched in gasoline, because the pilot had to use a hand pump to supply the craft's forward fuel tank and the plane lacked a fuel gauge to indicate when the tank was full—so the preoccupied pilot would often overfill it. When that happened, the raw gasoline would overflow and cover the floor of the cockpit, often—unbelievably—to a depth of an inch or more. And so it was that this defect led to the death of Teddy Busk. On November 5, 1914, before horrified witnesses including "D.H." himself, Busk's airplane burst into flames during a test flight and descended in a gentle glide, crashing in the dusky twilight.

Busk's example lived on, however, for this supremely capable young man—he was only twenty-eight when he died—had impressed all who knew him. As a result, O'Gorman hired more trained scientists and technologists to assist in the flight test process, men such as William Farren, George Thomson, Frederick Lindemann, Henry Tizard, Bennett Jones, and Herman Glauert. Eventually, some of these persuaded their supervisors to train them as pilots. Lindemann, for example, together with Tizard and Keith Lucas, underwent flight training in 1916. The unfortunate Lucas perished in a training accident, but Lindemann and Tizard graduated, despite the fact that both men had weak vision. Indeed, Lindemann was nearly blind in one eye and had to bluff his way past the RFC's medical examiners! Lindemann, who later became Winston Churchill's scientific adviser (and later Lord Cherwell), conducted a major mathematical and experimental study of airplane spinning, in response to rising casualties among British pilots then flying the treacherous R.E. 8 reconnaissance aircraft.

In addition to the flying at Farnborough, the RFC had established a test site at Martlesham Heath, in Suffolk. There Henry Tizard undertook pioneering flights to the then-high altitude of twenty thousand feet, in freezing cold, with lungs starved from lack of oxygen. He also evaluated aircraft performance with a view to developing standardized criteria for test evaluation. Tizard recognized the critical importance of having well-trained, scientifically inclined pilots evaluating the latest aircraft, and sought to impart such values to the other pilots attached to the testing squadron at Martlesham. As Constance Babington-Smith has written, "A Martlesham pilot was, by definition, one who could turn his hand to testing any variety of aeroplane, and a Martlesham report meant a report that included an analysis of unprecedented detail and comprehensiveness."[1] And when, in 1917, the United States finally entered the war, the U. S. Army Signal Corps recognized this by sending some of its best pilots to Martlesham to be trained in British test flight methods. One of these was Eddie Allen, who stayed on at Martlesham as a test pilot and then returned to McCook Field to join their flight testing staff.

Without question, Busk, Lindemann, and Tizard placed flight testing on a firm scientific footing, drawing upon the earlier heritage of such individuals as Lilienthal and the Wrights. It is unfortunate that Busk perished at so early an age—and that Tizard and Lindemann's later years were consumed by a professional acrimony that left both men embittered enemies.

. . . MEANWHILE, ACROSS THE ATLANTIC . . .

Despite the clamoring of such enthusiasts as the Army's George Squier, the Navy's Washington Chambers, and the Smithsonian's Charles Walcott, the United States lagged badly behind the European nations in the technical development of aviation; indeed, the United States generally remained so throughout the war and into the 1920s, when finally, because of the work of such organizations as the National Advisory Committee for Aeronautics and The Daniel Guggenheim Fund for the Promotion of Aeronautics, America drew equal to—and in some cases surpassed—the rest of the world. Nevertheless, the trends that had appeared in European aviation prior to the war remained valid for the American experience as well. A host of new designs emerged reflecting these changes in design philosophy, and in one field—that of large flying boats—the United States led the world. Typical of this gradual progress were the new generation of tractor trainers such as the Martin TT and the Curtiss JN "Jenny," which quickly eclipsed the older, pusher aircraft.

The Martin TT in particular constituted what was a significant design. This trim biplane spanned nearly 40 feet and was powered by a 90-hp Curtiss engine. Its designer, Glenn Luther Martin, had been the first to fly in California—though not to the universal acclaim of all who knew him. Indeed, the family doctor had written to Martin's mother in 1910, "For Heaven's sake, if you have any influence with that *wild-eyed, Hallucinated, Visionary* young man, *call him off* before he is killed. Have him devote his energies to *substantial, feasible* and *profitable* pursuits, leaving *dreaming* to the professional dreamers."[2] Fortunately, the *wild-eyed, Hallucinated* youth had ignored the well-meaning advice, and had proceeded to develop a pusher biplane along Curtiss lines. He turned from this to the tractor configuration, however, and won a government contract for seventeen of the Model TT trainers. The increasing accident rate of pushers, which had strange handling characteristics and whose engine installation meant certain death for the pilot in event of a diving crash, had forced the Army to buy the newer craft; at the Army field at San Diego, for example, eight out of fourteen licensed Army pilots had been killed in pusher accidents. After the service switched to the Model TT, the field recorded only one death out of twenty-nine student pilots, and that with greatly increased utilization of the planes for training purposes. The Navy, likewise, was forced to abandon its older aircraft because of a series of accidents that invariably claimed the lives of skilled and neophyte aviators alike. That service replaced its pushers with early models of the one aircraft that came, more than any other, to symbolize America's aeronautical contribution to the First World War: the Curtiss JN trainer.

Immediately dubbed "Jenny," the Curtiss JN trainer occupies a position of great importance in American aviation history, being the airplane that trained thousands of pilots, introduced postwar barnstorming to a curious nation, first flew the airmail, and indeed, served as the nation's first major flight research testbed with the National Advisory Committee for Aeronautics (NACA). This maid-of-all-work, in fact, launched American general aviation. Despite its glamour, it was not a very good airplane: it was slow, underpowered, with little useful load. The journalists who waxed eloquent that "Jenny was too much a lady" to take part in overseas combat preferred to ignore that this docile and unimpressive craft simply could not have survived in the skies over Europe. This was well recognized in military aviation circles, however, and the services set out to develop some combat-worthy aircraft of their own.

In April 1917, the United States, succumbing to interventionist pressures, declared war on Imperial Germany, adding an unprecedented sense of urgency to attempts to improve the combat potential of the American air services. But the United States did not become an armed aeronautical camp overnight. Great questions and disputes raged between the military services, the industry, and Congress. Should, for example, the United States build its own designs or rely on foreign types such as the De Havilland D.H. 4 or Bristol Fighter? Eventually, the country proceeded in both directions, though building foreign designs received first priority. This did not always work to the nation's advantage: Glenn Martin once approached the Army with an offer to build aircraft for the service. The officer who met with him rejected his offer perfunctorily, stating that the service preferred to rely on *automobile* companies (expecting the car companies to produce one hundred thousand planes within two years!) and that the service had decided to concentrate on the production of the British D.H. 4. Martin, glowering, stalked out of the office, the plans of the future "Glenn Martin Bomber," which eventually proved a brilliant design, still locked up in his briefcase. The idea of such a rejection—discouraging a manufacturer eager to work, whose design staff included such already promising future luminaries as Larry Bell, Donald Douglas, and "Dutch" Kindleberger—seems ludicrous in retrospect but was typical of the tragicomic way in which America attempted to expand its military air forces. Exasperated by ineptness, the Army finally moved in the right direction in early 1918, authorizing a number of American firms, including Martin, Vought, Loening, and Thomas-Morse, to proceed with the development of various bomber, pursuit, and training aircraft. American production of American designs built up, encouraged by the formation of the Manufacturers Aircraft Association, which, created at the behest of the NACA, reached an agreement ending the debilitating effects of the lingering Wright-Curtiss patent suits. In contrast, American production of foreign designs did not proceed smoothly at all; it was a case of too little, too late. Had the war continued into 1919, American forces would have been well represented by combat airplanes of indigenous manufacture and designs that were the equal of any country's. Such, however, was not to be. Overall, America's wartime aero production effort must be judged as, at best, a disappointment and, at worst (in the words of manufacturer Grover Loening), a "most shameful misuse of American talent."[3]

But if America's wartime aircraft mixed bright promise with dismal failure, the record of the nation's flight researchers was one of singular accomplishment. American test pilots developed their skills apace with the development of new and often exciting aircraft. The need for specialized flight test sites led to the creation of three experimental fields: Langley Field, outside Norfolk and Hampton, Virginia (for the Army and the NACA), Anacostia (for the Navy), and in Ohio the complex of Wilbur Wright Field and McCook Field (for the Army), both of which eventually spawned the great research and development center of Wright Field, known for years as simply "the Field," so general was its reputation for excellence.

Out in industry, too, the test pilot soon came to occupy a position of great importance. Designers soon recognized that it was not merely sufficient to choose a good pilot, a good "stick-and-rudder man," but, rather, a pilot who could work with and talk the language of the engineer: a good stick-and-rudder man with solid technical credentials.

Organizationally, three groups of test pilots quickly emerged: the research pilot, the corporate test pilot, and the service test pilot. The research pilot, typical of the individuals who flew for the National Advisory Committee for Aeronautics, was a pilot who acquired data and information useful to the entire aeronautical field and not related simply to one particular airplane. He flew to acquire knowledge, not to demonstrate meeting a contract specification or design requirement. The second type, the corporate test pilot, flew as a company test pilot, testing the new creations generated by the firm's engineering design staffs. Today, the corporate test pilot is one element in an organization of many thousands of individuals. In the First World War, however, when a design team often could be counted on the fingers of one hand, the corporate test pilot was frequently far closer to the actual design process than he could hope to be today. The service test pilot was a professional military pilot, familiar with the needs and requirements of his service branch. He assessed the aircraft for its compliance with military specification and its ability to fulfill a useful military mission. These three interests in the flight research and flight testing process were evident in the backgrounds of pilots of the time; many NACA pilots, for example, were credentialed technologists. Most corporate test pilots, while perhaps lacking formal engineering training, were at least accomplished technicians and thus able to comprehend the intricacies of the aircraft design process. Many service test pilots had strong backgrounds in military flying (especially, as time went by, combat experience), this being deemed of equal, if not greater, importance than any technical skills they might have.

Given this group structure, there were three general fields within flight testing that these various pilots specialized in. Some test pilots were excellent at demonstrations, showing how an airplane could meet the requirements of a specification such as landing over a 50-foot obstacle and coming to rest in a certain distance. Others excelled in handling and flying qualities and were true engineering test pilots, capable of analyzing aircraft behavior from a stability and control standpoint. Still others specialized in performance, mapping out the performance envelope of an airplane during, for example, a "sawtooth" climb or a steady cruise. And then there were the usual pilot preferences: those who liked to fly nimble pursuits, those who liked to fly seaplanes, those who preferred multiengine designs. (One must add that, in those early days of American flight testing, test pilots were often jacks-of-all-trades and would go from testing a pursuit one day to flying some monstrosity the next.)

Standard test pilot rating scales such as the present-day Cooper-Harper system for evaluating aircraft performance did not exist. In those days, before formal test pilot training programs, test pilots learned by having to, in the manner of the Wrights, "mount a machine and become acquainted with its tricks by actual trial." For the most part, quantification itself was a thing of the future. Harold R. Harris, one of the most distinguished of the early band of Army test pilots, has remarked that pilots were not overly concerned with precisely evaluating aircraft handling qualities. Rather, as he recalled, they viewed flying in nearly philosophical terms: "Airplanes took off, they flew around, they landed—it was an accomplishment."[4]

It would be a while before the budding scientific methods of Martlesham Heath and NACA Langley became a routine part of flight test operations. Nevertheless, as reflected in testing manuals from that time, engineers stipulated a variety of tests for new airplanes. First would be a static test on the ground, loading the airplane with sandbags to determine the strength of its structure. Then would come flight tests, usually consisting of a maneuverability test, a visibility test, an "accessibility test" to determine "ease of replacement of damaged parts in the field," and then the all-important performance tests to determine the plane's rate of climb at various altitudes, the maximum ceiling of the airplane, and its maximum speed at altitude, as well as such matters as fuel economy. In order for such tests to be meaningful, however, it was necessary to relate the airplane's performance to certain standard conditions, and for these reasons, then and now, flight researchers rely extensively on standard atmosphere tables when analyzing the performance of airplanes undergoing testing.

As undertaken in 1918, a typical flight test program for an experimental airplane might be as follows: A test pilot would fly the airplane on two or three flights to accustom himself to its handling qualities. Then engineers would equip the airplane with test instrumentation (such as recording barographs), and the pilot would next make two or three flights to ensure that the instrumentation was calibrated and operating properly. He would follow this with a preliminary performance flight, consisting of a climb to the plane's apparent performance ceiling, followed by a series of maximum-speed runs at various altitudes. He would follow these flights with a flight test report (sent to the manufacturer), any changes deemed necessary would be made, and then the official performance tests would be conducted. These consisted of determining the best climbing speeds for the plane, followed by flights to the absolute ceiling of the plane, and to the service ceiling of the plane (where its rate of climb dropped to 100 feet per minute). During the descent, at intervals of two or three thousand feet, the test pilot would make level speed runs to determine its performance at various altitudes. Engineers made certain, through various continuous checks, that recording instrumentation functioned within tolerances and that the engine's power output remained uniform.

Of paramount importance, of course, was flight safety, and despite the popular "reckless" image of the early test pilot, the emphasis, then and now, was on absolute caution and thorough planning. As one early test manual, written by Army flight test engineer George Patterson warned,

> As practically all performance testing is done on experimental machines of new types, the greatest care must be exercised by performance pilots to avoid damaging the planes due to forced landings away from the airdrome. This is especially important as the plane under test is usually the only one of its type and any delay due to damages in forced landing will greatly hinder development and production of the airplane. Pilots should be extremely careful to keep within gliding distance of the field at all altitudes and to bear in mind while flying at very high altitude the direction of the airdrome. Under no circumstances should any test flights

be made above clouds. If clouds begin to form beneath the plane during a test, discontinue the test at once. It will be found that the pilots can keep track of the direction of the airdrome very much better by arranging their flights so as to stay on the side of the field toward the sun, as it is very much easier to see long distances when facing away from the sun. . . .

The duties of an observer in performance tests are to relieve the pilot of as much work as possible. The observer should take the readings of as many instruments as he can see and keep track of the direction of the airdrome. . . .

Above all things, the OBSERVER MUST KEEP TRACK OF THE WHEREABOUTS OF THE AIRDROME DURING HIGH ALTITUDE FLYING. It is very easy to become lost while making climb and speed tests, particularly if there are clouds, or where the atmosphere is hazy, because the pilot has his entire attention centered on the accurate flying of the airplane. It should be borne in mind that with modern airplanes a level flight at full speed of five or six minutes may mean a distance covered of twelve to fifteen miles, and that constant watchfulness on the part of the observer is necessary to prevent the pilot from becoming lost and landing away from the airdrome.

When possible, the recording instruments should be placed in such a position that the observer can watch their action and see whether the ink is flowing properly from the pens and that the clockwork mechanism is functioning. . . .

In addition to a pencil tied to the data board, the observer should carry two or three pencils in an outside pocket of his flying suit. Fountain pens should not be used as the ink will freeze at high altitudes.[5]

A special memorandum, stipulating regulations to be followed when testing aircraft and issued a few months after the Armistice by the commandant of the Army's Technical Division at McCook Field, clearly reflects the great concern with safety that has become one of the major traits of flight testing:

HEADQUARTERS TECHNICAL DIVISION
BUREAU OF AIRCRAFT PRODUCTION

Dayton, Ohio, February 5, 1919

SPECIAL MEMORANDUM
NO. 27.

1. Test flights have priority over all other flying. All test flights will be under the direction of Major Schroeder. He will designate the pilot to fly the test, the time at which the test will be flown, and he will give

all instructions covering the flying of the test. The Planes & Engines Maintenance Department will furnish the machine and the crew.

2. Pilot will inspect machine before taking it up.

3. Pilots will make sure that they thoroughly understand the operation of all controls, especially the motor controls, before taking off.

4. Be certain that the air pressure, the oil pressure, and the temperature are right before leaving the ground.

5. Taxy machines slowly, well away from the hangars before taking off in order not to blow a cloud of dust and dirt into the hangars.

6. Take full advantage of the wind and the size of the field in getting away.

7. Never leave the ground with a missing motor or if anything else is wrong.

8. Pilots will remain within gliding distance of McCook Field at all times. There is no excuse for forced landings outside the field.

9. Whenever possible land into the wind.

10. No stunting will be done below 2,000 feet.

11. Report any trouble that may develop during flight, or anything else that is wrong with motor or machine, no matter how slight, to the crew chief immediately upon landing.

12. Owing to the small number of machines available and the large number of Officers desiring flights, no machines will be flown to Wilbur Wright Field or to other outside fields, except on important official business that can not be handled otherwise. This rule will be strictly observed.

13. Certain parts of the field have recently been graded and seeded. These spots are soft in wet weather. In order not to cut up the field, avoid these spots when field is in a muddy condition.

14. Whenever the field is muddy and the wind is from the right direction, take off and land on the runway.

15. All flying, except important tests that cannot be delayed will stop at 4:00 P.M. from Monday to Friday, and at 11:00 A.M. on Saturday, and all machines will be at the hangars by that time.

16. Except on test flights, flying will be limited to one hour per day per man.

> T. H. BANE
> Col., A.S.A.
> Chief of Division
>
> By
>
> DELOS C. EMMONS
> Lt. Col., A.S.A.
> Business & Military
> Executive[6]

More poetic but no less emphasized was a large sign visible to all who flew from McCook in those early days:

THIS FIELD IS SMALL, SO USE IT ALL

McCOOK FIELD DAYS

The hub of American military aviation during the First World War was, fittingly enough, Dayton, Ohio. Here sprawled McCook Field, the first and greatest of America's early flight test sites, which earned the sobriquet "the crucible of aviation technology." Military aviation had come to Dayton before the First World War, when the Wrights had trained the first Army airmen. In May 1917, however, as a result of pressure brought by local citizens, the Signal Corps assumed a lease of 2,075 acres of land near Fairfield, outside Dayton, including the historic Huffman Prairie tract, for use as a training field. Two months later, the first Standard SJ and Curtiss JN trainers could be seen and heard bobbing about the traffic pattern of this base, known as Wilbur Wright Field (it eventually became Patterson Field, and is now part of the giant Wright-Patterson AFB complex). On August 7, 1917, the War Department established another "temporary" field near Dayton just for experimental flight research. The Army planned to fly from this site only until the service completed a national flight research center at Langley Field; as with most temporary projects, however, this site continued in use until 1927, long after Langley had started operations! This special experimental center, a little over a mile from the heart of Dayton's downtown area, opened on December 4, 1917, consisting of a small sod flying field of 254 total acres, a single 1,000-foot, macadam-and-cinder runway, and some Spartan buildings. The Army named it McCook Field, in honor of Civil War General Anson McCook and his seven sons, Ohio's famed "Fighting McCooks." Headquartered at this field, the American equivalent of England's Martlesham, was the Army's Airplane Engineering Department, which itself evolved into the near-legendary McCook Engineering Division.

For once, the service provided technologists and flight researchers at McCook with the funding, material, and manpower support they required, and by the end of the war, the site had expanded to include sixty-nine buildings, a civilian and military staff numbering over twenty-three hundred, laboratories, hangars, a hospital, an engine test stand, a static testing laboratory (for loading the structure of aircraft with sandbags), and a small wind tunnel. Under the leadership of the tempestuous Virginius E. Clark and then the gifted (and tragically short-lived) Thurman Bane, the McCook center employed a number of outstanding engineers who would make their mark upon American aviation, including the mercurial Alexander Klemin, propeller expert Frank Caldwell, Lawrence Kerber (who later attained recognition worldwide as an expert on flight test procedures), and such gifted engineers as Samuel D. Heron and J. G. Vincent, and airframe designers Jean Roché, I. M. Laddon, Donovan Berlin, and Alfred Verville. By mid-1918, the center buzzed with activity ranging from engine tests to gunnery trials and that most dramatic of all aspects of flight research, experimental flight testing of new and unproven aircraft. Tests of American-built copies of foreign designs did not go well, either at McCook or elsewhere. McCook pilots and engineers closely monitored testing of Curtiss-built copies of the versatile Bristol F.2B twin-seat fighter. These "Curtiss Bristols" were powered by the excellent American-designed Liberty 12 engine, but the engine and airplane were a poor match, and poor engineering production control plagued the copies as well. Over the spring and summer of 1918, three experimental Curtiss Bristols crashed near the Curtiss plant, two seriously injuring or killing their crews. Tragedy again struck, this time at McCook on June 19, 1918, when an American-built D.H. 4 piloted by Lieutenants Frank Patterson and Leroy Swan crashed during gunnery trials. The synchronization mechanism, which prevented the fuselage guns from hitting the propeller, failed, and the stream of bullets shattered the propeller, which flew off and damaged the wings of the plane. Patterson and Swan died in the crash that followed, and later, Patterson Field was named in honor of the test pilot, the first, and sadly not the last, to lose his life at McCook. The Bristol Fighter never did work out for the Army, even after the Engineering Division tried its hand with a copy. The "DH" did, however, though not in time to greatly influence America's role in the air war. Eventually, the United States produced a total of more than three thousand; by the Armistice, 196 American D.H. 4's were at the front, and the type became a mainstay for the postwar air service and airmail.

A far more promising aircraft tested at McCook, however, was the Packard-Le Père LUSAC-11, which, aside from Curtiss flying boats, became the only indigenous American combat aircraft to be sent overseas before the end of hostilities. Captain G. Le Père, of the French Aviation Mission, had designed the LUSAC-11 for the U. S. Army. Powered by a 360-hp Liberty engine, the LUSAC-11 was a strikingly handsome aircraft possessed of a vaguely Bristol Fighter look: sturdy and purposeful. A two-seat fighter, the LUSAC-11 had provisions for two Marlin guns firing forward and two Lewis guns mounted on a Scarf ring and operated by the observer. The Army constructed the prototypes of this fine airplane on site at McCook, but eventually Packard produced a batch of twenty-five, two of which arrived in France prior to the Armistice; French researchers tested these two against their own types. The Armistice, of course, immediately resulted in the cutback of further production; the great pity is that the United States wasted so much time on so many mediocre airplanes and expended so little time on such machines as the LUSAC-11.

McCook completed the first LUSAC-11 over the summer of 1918 and undertook its initial trials in mid-August. It completed its first flight on August 13 and made two others over the next three days. The diligent McCook flight test personnel wrote up a meticulous (for the time) summary report of thirty-one pages, including graphs, charts, and performance curves and tables, and summarized the first three flights as follows:

LOG OF LE PERE FIGHTER, S.C. NO. 42128
EQUIPPED WITH
LIBERTY ENGINE NO. 19004

Aug. 13th. Altitude climb test by Lieutenant De Marmier, French Army. Engine stopped at 8,000 feet owing to pilot running on reserve tank only. Dead stick landing blew both tires.

Aug. 15th. Altitude climb and speed at high altitude by Captain Schroeder, propeller No. 3012 S.C.60370, designed and built at McCook Field. The results of this test are incorporated in this report. The propeller is evidently a speed propeller as the performance falls off very considerably at high altitude; although results near the ground are excellent. Calibration test of airspeed record made in the evening over three miles speed course. Maximum ground speed 136 miles per hour.

Aug. 16th. Charavay propeller tried on 25 minute flight by Lieutenant De Marmier. Bad landing wiped off landing gear and otherwise damaged plane. No further tests.[7]

The report, classified Secret, included a critical evaluation of the LUSAC-11's flying qualities submitted by test pilot Captain Rudolph "Shorty" Schroeder, and it is a typical example of a flight test report from that early era:

RESULTS OF TRIALS OF FLYING QUALITIES

HOUR-9:00 A.M.   AUGUST 15, 1918
EQUIPMENT-Not Equipped   PILOT-Capt. R. W. Schroeder

EFFICIENCY OF CONTROLS

The elevators, ailerons and rudder respond very readily in climbing, diving, banking and in horizontal flight.

PRESSURE OF THE CONTROLS

The pressure exerted on the controls for the movement of the elevators is normal; for ailerons and rudder, light; in climbing, diving, banking and in horizontal flight.

REMARKS ON STABILITY

The longitudinal, lateral and directional stability of this machine is good.

The machine has a tendency to climb to the left when pilot turns the controls loose while flying horizontally. The pilot experienced no tiring tendencies in driving this machine.

No adjustment of the stabilizer is necessary.

REMARKS ON STARTING

The machine taxies properly and leaves the ground quickly.

REMARKS ON LANDING

Is it easy to hold the machine off the ground? Yes. How far does the machine roll after wheels touch the ground in a ten mile wind or less? If flying speed is killed in the air, I would estimate about 300 to 400 feet. Does the machine turn over easily? Which way and why? I do not believe this will happen, if care is used at all.

GENERAL REMARKS

How does the machine behave in the following movements?

1. Vertical Bank. In one complete turn no altitude is lost. Due to continuous spinning a little altitude is lost on each turn.

2. Tail Spin. The left spin is very fast and recovers very well. A right hand turn is quite slow and recovers very well.

3. Nose Dive. This ship dives and recovers with very little effort, either on the part of the pilot or the ship.

4. Half Loop. This can be done with full control.

5. Side Slip. This can be done with full control.

RANGE OF VISION

The range of vision is very good as compared with other fighters. I would say it is superior.

INSTALLATION OF CONTROLS AND INSTRUMENTS

The controls are very well placed and require very little effort to operate. I am over six feet tall and I will say that I am not crowded in any way.

The instruments are so arranged that the Pilot need only move his eyes. They are well placed.

R. W. SCHROEDER
Captain, A.S.M.A.[8]

By today's standards, this is a most cursory document, typified by its lack of explicitness and quantification. Back in the days of Shorty Schroeder, engineers relied on a few recording instruments (such as an altitude barograph having an ink pen tracing on a rotating paper drum), and most important, on the pilot's ever-present kneeboard notes. So much a part of the test pilot's accouterments was the kneeboard with its test card that a test pilot would no more fly without one than he would without a flight suit. However primitive, flight engineers and test pilots were looking for the answers to the right questions: handling qualities, control forces, stability, takeoff and landing performance, and the plane's behavior during maneuvering flight.

Despite the initial accidents with the LUSAC-11, it soon proved a highly reliable airplane, and although it did not win any large production orders, the LUSACs that were built flew on for years in a variety of research activities, including trials with early superchargers. Shorty Schroeder's first flight in the LUSAC began a long association between the lanky airman and the rugged plane, and both gained fame for their pioneering research on supercharger performance and high-altitude flight. Inspired to a career in aviation by the 1910 Gordon Bennett race, held in his hometown of Chicago, Schroeder was a skilled mechanic whose formal education had been cut short by the untimely death of his father; young Schroeder gave up school to support his mother and a younger brother. He worked for aviation pioneer Otto Brodie and enlisted in the Aviation Section of the Signal Corps as a private in 1916. Two years later, a careful and methodical pilot, Schroeder was a captain, making major just at the Armistice. Schroeder had a natural flair for flight testing, and eventually the Army appointed him chief of the flight test section at McCook. The nagging accidents caused by thoughtlessness and carelessness that occasionally marred operations at the field annoyed the safety-conscious pilot and caused him to create a special trophy, "The Cup of Good Beginnings and Bad Endings" (inscribed to read, "We Crashed Not Because We Ran Out of Gas, but Because We Ran Out of Knowledge"), which he duly awarded to any test pilot unfortunate enough to crack up one of the field's airplanes. (The trophy became a McCook Field tradition, and others, such as the Alibi Trophy, the Bonehead Trophy, and the Flying Ass Trophy, eventually joined it.)

A mere month after the LUSAC-11's first flight, Shorty Schroeder attempted to set a world's altitude record in the craft. This involved flying over five miles high; the rigors of such altitude flights in those early days to win (as Schroeder termed it) "the icicle crown" cannot be overestimated. Pilots relied on thick fur-lined flying suits, face masks, and primitive oxygen systems consisting of little more than a rubber tube from an oxygen bottle clenched between the teeth. On the second of two practice ascents in the LUSAC-11, he reached 27,000 feet. Finally, on September 18, 1918, he took off on the actual record attempt. The trim biplane, not yet fitted with a turbocharger, labored through the thin air above 20,000 feet. Schroeder's goggles frosted, and he could read the plane's instruments only with difficulty. Incredibly, he did not activate his oxygen supply until he reached 25,000 feet, when he noticed the onset of anoxia: the engine seemed quiet, and the sun grew dim, and the pilot's thoughts began to wander. "As soon as I started to inhale the oxygen the sun grew bright again," Schroeder wrote later. "My motor began to exhaust so loud that it seemed something must be wrong with it. I was no longer hungry and the day seemed to be a most beautiful one."[9] Onward the Le Père droned, climbing slowly above the Ohio countryside. Nearing 29,000 feet, Schroeder again experienced the symptoms of oxygen deficiency, stubbornly refusing to believe even the horizon's indication that the plane was flying a ragged course. He had been flying for so long that he was running out of both oxygen and fuel. Suddenly the Liberty spluttered to a stop; the plane's maximum altitude, as recorded by the on-board Hué barograph, then being 28,900 feet, a world's record. The chilled pilot promptly lowered the nose of the biplane and began a dead-stick descent to earth. The flight had placed the plane far from McCook, and Schroeder could not locate Dayton; he had to make a rough-field landing. Like the pro he was, he set up an approach and touched down; the Le Père slowed, rose on its nose, and broke the propeller, being otherwise undamaged. Schroeder, the new icicle king, was not finished with altitude flights, however, as will be seen.

The Le Père LUSAC program was one of many that put the Army firmly into aeronautical research and development, and it constituted a major step forward in the development of American flight test methods and research. Meanwhile, burgeoning aircraft manufacturers approached the military services with possible designs. The military services expressed the most concern over the lack of suitable pursuit, or *chasse*, aircraft similar to the single-seat scouts then tangling in the skies over the Western Front. In response to this requirement, Thomas-Morse built the abortive MB-1 (which broke up while taxiing prior to its first flight!) and the MB-2, forerunners of the delightful Thomas-Morse/Boeing MB-3A, of the 1920s. Grover Loening, looking ahead, tried his hand at a trim monoplane, the M-8. The Standard Aircraft Corporation developed the obsolescent but pleasant-flying Standard M-Defense scout. There were eccentric designs as well: James V. Martin championed a *45 hp* proposed high-altitude fighter, the diminutive Martin K-3 Kitten, and William Christmas, M.D., undertook design of the ill-fated Christmas Bullet. (The Christmas Bullet, in fact, is an interesting case study in how far one could go in receiving official support in those days for an obviously deadly design. With drooping, understrength wings attached to a robust fuselage and a powerful government-furnished Liberty engine in the nose, the Bullet truly was an accident waiting to happen. Predictably, on its first flight the Bullet shed its wings, killing its pilot. The equally unairworthy second prototype also crashed. No self-respecting professional test pilot would ever have granted the plane the courtesy of occupying its cockpit; Dean Smith, one of many ex-Army pilots looking for aviation jobs at war's end, recollected, "If you were really desperate, I learned . . . you could get on as test pilot for Doctor Christmas, flying the Christmas Bullet."[10]) The government directly sponsored several others, including the Orenco Model B, the Pomilio FVL-8, and the Engineering Division VCP-1, the latter a very excellent design by Alfred Verville and Virginius Clark. Yet, on balance, the most significant fighter designs industry proposed during the First World War came from the drawing boards of Curtiss—and their development involved considerable flight research.

ROLAND ROHLFS AND THE SAGA OF THE FIRST CURTISS FIGHTERS

The first American airplane that could lay claim to being a fighter was the experimental Curtiss S-3, of 1916, a trim but underpowered triplane. Curtiss built four of the pleasant-flying machines, and they inspired the firm's continued presence in the field. The firm next became involved in the misbegotten attempt to copy the Bristol Fighter; along with this fiasco, Curtiss undertook development of an American equivalent to the Bristol, the abortive Curtiss CB "Battleplane," but this, too, crashed while undergoing testing. Curtiss had little better luck with their next indigenous product, the Navy-designed Curtiss HA "Dunkirk Fighter."

The Navy-Curtiss HA gives the lie to the often-held myth that the Navy never seriously considered developing fighter aircraft until the advent of the aircraft carrier. Indeed, Navy-sponsored Curtiss designs inspired derivatives manufactured to Army requirements. In mid-1917, the Navy drew up a specification and design for a two-seat heavy fighter to operate on floats. The Navy hoped to place the craft in service quickly enough so that it could achieve air superiority for the Allies over the Dunkirk area by late 1918. Thus the HA (for Hydro Aeroplane) quickly became known more popularly as the "Dunkirk Fighter." Curtiss received the go-ahead to manufacture the craft. As finally built, the HA had a portly fuselage, dihedral on the top wing, an equal amount of anhedral (droop) on the lower, and an awkward, four-bladed propeller with a massive spinner. The Dunkirk Fighter thus resembled a bloated S.P.A.D. that had come out the worse for wear from a high-speed dive. Curtiss completed the first HA prototype and invited representatives of the Navy to witness its first flight, on March 21, 1918. Curtiss had selected company test pilot Roland Rohlfs to make the all-important first flight, accompanied by Lieutenant B. L. Smith of the U. S. Marine Corps, the plane's designer, from the picturesque waters off Port Washington, Long Island.

In many respects, Roland Rohlfs typified the corporate experimental test pilots of the era. Then twenty-six, Rohlfs had attended schools in the Buffalo area, graduating from the Buffalo Technical High School. A New York native, his father was a Buffalo furniture manufacturer and his mother, Anna Katherine Rohlfs, a noted novelist. Like Glenn Curtiss himself, the tall pilot, whose serious demeanor masked a ready wit, had designed and built racing motorcycles, then worked as an assistant chemist for the Lumen Bearing Company. In 1914, Curtiss decided to expand from Hammondsport to Buffalo, and the company advertised for skilled technicians and mechanics. Rohlfs joined Curtiss as a mechanic in December 1914; within the year, Curtiss, impressed with the talented Rohlfs, offered him the opportunity to take flying lessons. A quick study, Rohlfs learned to fly from Victor Carlstrom and Phil Rader, two outstanding Curtiss test pilots. (Rader died in the crash of one of the ill-fated Curtiss Bristols, which broke up during a test flight.) On April 25, 1917, he received his pilot's license; the prolonged instruction period reflected Rohlfs's heavy schedule, for he had to fit in flying lessons along with his other technical duties, and did not imply in any way slowness or lack of aptitude. That Curtiss felt fully confident in Rohlfs's abilities is apparent from his decision, later in 1917, to appoint Rohlfs a full-fledged experimental test pilot following the death of the Swedish-born Carlstrom in a training accident at Newport News. Thus Rohlfs gained the flight test position so recently occupied by his former flight instructor. In early 1918, Curtiss sent him to the company's newly formed Engineering & Experimental Development Division, at Garden City, where Curtiss workers were even then constructing the first of the HA's.

It fell to Rohlfs to discover the many vices the Dunkirk Fighter possessed. On its first flight, Rohlfs fired up the massive Liberty, and the floatplane accelerated across the water under the critical eyes of the official test observers. It pleasantly surprised onlookers with the quickness of its leap into the air; they did not realize the frightening drama being played out in the front cockpit. As Rohlfs edged toward lift-off speed, the plane suddenly pitched into the air, avoiding a stall but then wallowing along, distinctly tail-heavy, rocking its wings as well. With a massive Dutch-roll oscillation, and obvious control-system lag letting the pilot get behind or ahead of the pitching motions, the violently unstable HA roared onward, its motions pitching designer Smith around in the after cockpit. "We were like nothing more than birdshot in a wash boiler,"[11] Rohlfs recollected. He climbed to 1,000 feet and turned into the wind to set up an immediate landing approach. The bucking machine smoothed out when he retarded the throttle, pitched up, then down, and as it accelerated in the dive, its violent motions reasserted themselves. Rohlfs used judicious application of the control stick and the throttle to maintain some semblance of control and made a heavy but serviceable landing in Hempstead Harbor.

Curtiss returned the vicious airplane to Garden City for design alterations, where technicians discovered that an engineering error had resulted in the center of lift being a foot too far forward on the wing. Curtiss also enlarged the size of the vertical fin to improve directional stability, and thus modified, the plane embarked on its second flight, which went worse than the first. Rohlfs took off with project engineer Joe Meade in the after cockpit on a planned 10-minute test flight. The big Liberty gradually overheated because of poor cowling design, misfired, and a telltale puff of smoke entered the cockpit. Rohlfs immediately closed the throttle and started a dive, passing through 2,000 feet. Suddenly, long thin jets of orange flame shot through screw holes in the engine firewall into the cockpit; gasoline in the carburetor had caught fire. Rohlfs could not stand the intense heat and edged back out of the cockpit onto the fairing behind it, straddling the fuselage. The stricken HA assumed a near-vertical dive, and Rohlfs, eager to get back down on the water, let it continue. Finally, he judged that the plane was low enough, and he hooked a foot around the control stick and jerked it back; the abrupt pullout almost overstressed the biplane, and it pitched up. Rohlfs poked at the control stick, and the smoking plane entered a gradual glide, touching down roughly on the water. As the fire raged, Rohlfs and Meade dived overboard into the water and swam to a nearby boat, where they watched the Navy's first fighter burn to destruction.

Curtiss continued to fiddle with the HA, even developing a landplane version for the airmail service (in one of which, in fact, Rohlfs had yet another emergency, this one with Glenn Curtiss's half brother as a passenger), though the plane was clearly a disappointment. But Curtiss was learning.

In 1917, Curtiss engineers had, on their own, built three experimental triplane floatplanes for the Navy as fighter trainers. The design gave the Curtiss company considerable experience, and the following year, the company embarked on development of a combat-worthy two-seat fighter triplane for the Navy, the Curtiss 18-T, known popularly as the Curtiss Wasp Triplane or the "Kirkham Fighter," in recognition of its principal designer, Charles Kirkham. The Wasp, a landplane, featured a wooden monocoque fuselage and a triplane wing arrangement. Powered by the excellent 400-hp Kirkham K-12 engine (the forerunner of the very influential Curtiss D-12, of the next decade), the 18-T possessed every quality the tubby HA lacked, as Rohlfs quickly demonstrated during its flight test program. Flight testing on the first of two built began on July 5, 1918, and apart from having to sweep the wings aft 5 degrees for better balance, the testing went smoothly. The triplane attracted Army interest, and the service briefly evaluated it at McCook Field, where Rohlfs attained a then-phenomenal speed of 163 mph with full military load. Dubbed "Whistling Rufus" because of the distinctive screech of air around its wires and struts during flight, the Wasp Triplane underwent stringent official Navy trials at Curtiss Field, Mineola, Long Island, in the first week of September, 1918. Again it repeatedly demonstrated a maximum speed in excess of 160 mph, making it the fastest fighter flown during the First World War by any of the combatant nations. The Army, suitably impressed, ordered two Wasp Triplanes, delivered in early 1919, as well as two biplane versions, designated by Curtiss as the 18-B Hornet. Like many ventures, however, the Armistice effectively ended their development, and neither the 18-T nor the 18-B entered quantity service with the Army or Navy, though the 18-T flew on into the 1920s in racing guise.

A RECKONING

In retrospect, the Army's Le Père LUSAC and the Navy's Wasp Triplane demonstrate that by the end of the First World War, the United States was capable of matching the latest in foreign aircraft technology. Likewise, the evident benefits of careful flight testing had caused industry and the government to place emphasis on thorough evaluation of new prototypes. The European laboratory movement helped spawn an American equivalent, the National Advisory Committee for Aeronautics, an organization implicitly concerned with both ground and flight research. As has been seen, McCook opened in December 1917 and was thereafter busy until the Army Air Service transferred its operations to the new Wright Field, in 1927. The United States Navy, which had experimented with aircraft at Annapolis, Pensacola, and the Washington Navy Yard, received its own flight test center with the creation of Anacostia Naval Air Station. As a result of joint Army-Navy planning, the War and Navy departments had opened an airfield on the drained swampland of Anacostia Flats, across the Anacostia River and within sight of the nation's capital, in November 1917. In January 1918, the Chief of Naval Operations authorized the field to be used as "a base from which to make short test flights . . . to afford the opportunity for the various bureaus concerned to send representatives to examine new types of seaplanes in order to study questions of improvements and to become thoroughly familiar with the construction of seaplanes."[12] Thus was born the Navy's equivalent to McCook, the ancestor of the modern Naval Air Test Center, at Patuxent River, Maryland. By the war's end, planning for the National Advisory Committee for Aeronautics' first flight test and ground-research center occupied the agency full time, with construction underway at Langley Field. With the growing coordination of aeronautical research activities by the federal government, it came as no accident that Anacostia and Langley were relatively close to the District of Columbia, just as Edwards would eventually spring up from Muroc, encouraged by the close proximity of the West Coast aircraft industry. American aviation in the years after 1918 would receive great stimulus from McCook, Langley, and Anacostia, and their spinoffs, such as Wright, Edwards, and Patuxent River.

On November 11, 1918, the war ground to a halt. In the uncertain weeks that followed, America slowly demobilized, thousands of airmen returning home and turning to other endeavors, or trying to exist as barnstormers. Some joined the airmail service. Some simply went back to prewar careers. A few remained in the service. And some, who had flown as test pilots during the war, continued advancing the frontiers of flight. The First World War had taught many lessons in aviation. For the United States, it had revealed great weaknesses in the national aeronautical situation, though at great cost. The United States had managed, against all odds, to bring aviation technology further in the year and a half of American participation in the "war to end all wars" than the nation had gone in the preceding decade. When the war began, in 1914, the United States lacked, in a practical sense, any aircraft industry. In 1917, the year America went to war, the nation had a great deal of catching up to do. In November 1918, the nation had assembled a network of manufacturers beginning to work in close cooperation with the government and the academic community. These trends would continue.

By the end of the First World War, highly specialized and efficient combat aircraft capable of bombing, strafing, antisubmarine patrol, and air fighting had replaced the slow observation planes of 1914. The Zeppelin, the dread "city-destroyer" of prewar apocalyptic literature, had been unmasked as a short-lived menace that disappeared amid a holocaust of erupting hydrogen gas when attacked by rudimentary interceptors firing explosive and incendiary bullets. Flying Gotha and other large bombers, Germany had launched a mini-Blitz against London and the southern English coast, a frightening vision of the future. Britain and France had responded with development of excellent long-range bomber airplanes such as the Handley Page o/400 and the Vickers Vimy (too late for service); in Czarist Russia, Igor Sikorsky, drawing upon his prewar work, had developed a series of four-engine bombers that the Imperial Russian Air Service had used to good effect until revolution tore the country apart.

In Germany, Tony Fokker and his chief engineer, Reinhold Platz, had produced perhaps the finest operational fighter of the war, the Fokker D VII. This superlative aircraft featured a welded steel tube fuselage, an efficient high-lift wing, minimal bracing, and excellent flying qualities. Platz, at war's end, had gone a step further with the Fokker D VIII, a trim monoplane having an internally braced wing, though crashes and groundings caused by poor quality control saved Allied pilots from encountering this "Flying Razor" in quantity. Hugo Junkers had already test-flown the first practical cantilever all-metal monoplane, the Junkers J-1, and by war's end had placed both an all-metal monoplane fighter and attack aircraft in service, starting the tradition of Junkers corrugated metal monoplanes that would persist right through the Junkers Ju-52 trimotor.

At McCook Field, Frank Caldwell was busily thinking about variable-pitch propellers to extract maximum available horsepower from aircraft engines, as S. D. Heron pondered using a sodium-filled exhaust valve to make piston engines more reliable, and Sanford Moss, of General Electric, prepared for the first trials of his turbosupercharger for high-altitude flight.

In England, Frederick Handley Page contemplated cutting slots in the leading edge of a wing to improve a plane's low-speed performance and reduce the danger of stall, as did Gustav Lachmann, a German pilot recuperating from a crash. They would consolidate their efforts and develop the practical wing slot and slat. At the same time, other designers were examining ways of raising aircraft performance by using flaps for landing, changing the camber (curve) of wings, and retracting the landing gear. And unexpected problems faced them; for example, as planes droned along at more than 100 mph, their propeller tips often exceeded 650 mph, and propeller efficiency dropped markedly. Researchers investigating this problem could perhaps little realize that the fruits of their research would mature nearly three decades later, when Chuck Yeager first exceeded the speed of sound, another triumph of flight research. Some visionaries spoke of flying without propellers, using high-velocity jets—and a Clark University professor, Robert Goddard, even postulated a rocket going to the moon! But was that any less visionary than the dreamers who spoke of passengers *flying* across the oceans? Enough speculation existed for advocates and skeptics alike. Only one thing was certain: if past is truly prologue, the wartime advance of aviation would not be slowed in the years ahead.

CHAPTER 4

FLIGHT TESTING
IN THE JAZZ AGE

As 1919 dawned, the promise of aviation glowed brightly even as the hopes of lasting peace in the world dimmed. Shortly, the great powers again squabbled among themselves, while little wars raged in Europe and Asia. But, within a year, aviation startled the world with no fewer than four flights across the North Atlantic, two by airplanes (the Navy's NC boats and Alcock and Brown in a modified Vimy) and two by a British dirigible, the R-34. Of more practical value were experiments in civil air commerce that have resulted in historians' calling 1919 the first year of air transport. In February 1919, Germany opened air service between Berlin, Weimar, and Leipzig, and in August the first postwar passenger Zeppelins took to the air. France and England opened air service between London and Paris. The United States again trailed behind Europe, not really catching up until the Guggenheim Fund sponsored an experimental air service by Western Air Express using American-built Fokker F-10 Trimotors. The airmail service, begun in 1918 using Curtiss Jennies and later modified D.H. 4's, kept American air transport alive. And in the United States, flight technology was alive and, indeed, flourishing.

THE NACA TAKES TO THE AIR

The year 1919 marked the emergence of the National Advisory Committee for Aeronautics as a major national research resource. Created by a rider attached to the Naval Appropriations Act of 1915, the NACA had been chartered

> to supervise and direct the scientific study of the problems of flight, with a view to their practical solution, and to determine the problems which should be experimentally attacked, and to discuss their solution and their application to practical questions. In the event of a laboratory or laboratories, either in whole or in part, being placed under the direction of the committee, the committee may direct and conduct research and experiment in aeronautics. . . .[1]

The structure and organization of European laboratories directly influenced the structure and organization of the NACA; in fact, excerpts from the enabling legislation directly copied the language used by Britain's Parliament in creating the aeronautical research branch of its National Physical Laboratory. The committee first convened in April 1915, and after surveying the ground and flight research facilities available to the United States, concluded that the agency should have a laboratory with wind tunnels for model research, as well as a flying field where full-scale flight experimentation could be undertaken. It was critically important (and it still is today), for example, to relate data taken from the testing of models in a wind tunnel to data taken from the full-size aircraft in flight. After consulting with the Army and the Navy, the NACA decided to build a suitable research center north of Hampton, what eventually became Langley Field. Appropriately, the laboratory became the Langley Memorial Aeronautical Laboratory, the ancestor of the modern NASA Langley Research Center. Construction started in July 1917, and in early 1919, the NACA pronounced Langley ready for its first flight tests, even though the ground facilities were still under construction, including a wind tunnel.

Directing flight research for the NACA at this time was Edward P. Warner, an accomplished mathematician, a graduate of both Harvard and MIT. Warner, who later became the first Assistant Secretary of the Navy for Aeronautics, supervised flight trials of the agency's first research airplanes, two Curtiss JN-4H Jennies. The agency's first two test pilots were Thomas Carroll, a graduate of law school and a veteran pilot, and Edmund T. "Eddie" Allen, who became the most outstanding American test pilot of his generation. Born in 1896, Allen had served at

Martlesham Heath as a test pilot studying Tizard's methods before returning to the United States and test flying at McCook Field. After the Armistice, he returned to school, first at the University of Illinois and then at MIT, all the while spending his summers as a test pilot with the NACA! So it fell to Allen, assisted by other pilots and flight test observers, to undertake the initial NACA flight experiments.

The first flight research project NACA embarked upon involved flying the Jennies to determine how their actual flight behavior differed from that predicted by wind-tunnel tests of models. A secondary goal was determining the control forces required to keep the plane in longitudinal trim. The trials were, to say the least, interesting. Edward Warner and his assistants discovered that, although nominally alike, the two Jennies differed greatly from each other and from published official drawings! One airplane had a badly warped propeller; the wings lacked uniform camber and failed to follow reference drawings. Exasperated, Warner and F. H. Norton noted:

> The discrepancy between the actual form of the wing section and the curve on which it was supposed to be based points a dual lesson. In the first place, it draws attention to the need of making wind-tunnel models to represent the airplane as it is actually built, or to be built. . . . Secondly, these measurements should serve to remind experimenters engaged in the design of wing sections of the futility of drawing forms which it is impossible to construct by ordinary methods . . . otherwise . . . the drawing, the model, and the full-sized wing are likely ultimately to be of three quite different forms.[2]

In what would become a hallmark of NACA testing, the test aircraft were thoroughly prepared for their research missions, carefully measured, and on-board test instrumentation—consisting of an altimeter, tachometer, and airspeed indicator—were carefully calibrated, both on the ground and also during calibration flights over a measured course. Then the agency flew the actual flight tests, the Jenny, usually with Allen piloting and Lieutenant H. M. Cronk as test observer, droning over the hot marshland of southern Virginia. The final document, NACA Report No. 70, "Preliminary Report on Free Flight Tests," issued in 1919, analyzed the trials in detail, giving the rationale for the tests, the ground preparation, the flight test procedure, description of test equipment, performance curves, and analysis of results. Warner and Norton were well aware that meaningful flight research involved serious engineering study. They also recognized the vital importance of competent and cooperative test pilots, and their admiration of Allen and his fellow pilots and observers is evident in their description of the tests:

The tests were carried out at altitudes varying from 1,500 to 4,000 feet. It was not considered safe, in view of the danger of falling into a spin when flying at large angles [of attack] and of the possibility of a forced landing, to work below the former altitude. The altitude chosen on any particular day depends chiefly on air conditions, the climb being continued far enough to escape the "bumps" frequently found near the ground. Each "run" continued for from 1 to 2 minutes, the pilot being instructed to fly level (using the statoscope to detect changes in altitude) and at a constant airspeed during that period. The observer read and recorded the readings of the airspeed meter, the inclinometer and the tachometer every 10 seconds, and noted the altimeter reading and the air temperature at the beginning of each run. The pilot's task was a very difficult one, for he had constantly to watch the statoscope and airspeed meter, in addition to holding the machine steady laterally and watching out for other airplanes. Besides all this, when flying over the speed course to calibrate the meter the pilot had to steer a straight course over the ground between the two observing stations. *Test flying is a very highly specialized branch of work, the difficulties of which are not generally appreciated, and there is no type of flying in which a difference between the abilities of pilots thoroughly competent in ordinary flying becomes more quickly apparent.*[3] (Emphasis added)

Having established the baseline characteristics of their test aircraft, Eddie Allen and F. T. Norton embarked on a study of the structural loads experienced by a Jenny during maneuvering flight. This study, undertaken at the request of the Navy, involved taking readings on an automatically recording accelerometer during takeoff, landing, loops, abrupt control pulses (such as suddenly pulling the stick back, then immediately releasing it), rolls, spirals, and spins. At times, Allen would deliberately pound the airplane down on the ground during landing; during one landing, the faithful JN-4H groaned through a 5.25 g impact. Abrupt 3 g spins and 4 g rolls were commonplace. These flight trials generated baseline data the agency considered useful in deriving criteria for aircraft structural strength and also verified the value of the recording accelerometer. The next year, the agency went further and added 110 pressure orifices to the fabric tail surfaces of the Jenny, connected them to a series of glass-tube manometers (pressure recorders), and added a camera system, all to acquire pressure-distribution data that might be useful in the design of new airplanes. By 1921, the NACA's flight test section was off and running. The two Jennies had been joined by a third, as well as a Vought VE-7 trainer and a perky Thomas-Morse MB-3 pursuit. The next year, the agency added a British-designed S.E. 5A, a captured Fokker D VII, a French S.P.A.D. VII, a De Havilland D.H. 4, and a De Havilland D.H. 9. Over the next few years, the NACA continued its studies of stability and control, seeking to define meaningful criteria upon which to judge maneuverability. Soon the agency had established such a solid reputation in the field that the Army and the Navy, despite having their own flight test establishments, asked the NACA to evaluate their aircraft from a scientific standpoint, a trend that continued for years.

THE DRIVE FOR ALTITUDE

Aside from the pioneering transatlantic flights of 1919, the greatest attention-getters immediately after the Armistice were the continued forays to high altitude. Here, Roland Rohlfs and Shorty Schroeder again played major roles, together with new pioneers, in modifications of those wartime favorites the LUSAC-11 and the Wasp Triplane. During test flights at McCook by Roland Rohlfs in 1918, the Wasp Triplane had flown to an altitude of 26,300 feet with a full military load. Curtiss engineers realized that the plane could certainly attain a new American altitude record (breaking the U.S. record of 28,900 feet so recently set by Shorty Schroeder). At the Navy's behest, Curtiss increased the Triplane's span from 31 to over 40 feet, redesignating the modified craft as the 18-T-2. On July 25, 1919, Rohlfs climbed to an American record of 31,100 feet, then extended this, on September 19, to an unofficial world's altitude record of 34,610 feet, during tests at Roosevelt Field, Long Island. The tests did not go without incident; he burned out three engines during earlier flights (the unsupercharged K-12 had to labor mightily during the nearly two-hour climb to altitude), and on one flight he passed out from lack of oxygen (the equipment had frozen), and came to in a howling vertical descent, having lost 10,000 feet in altitude! The flights constituted the apex of the 18-T story; afterward, the Navy flew the two aircraft as racers, losing the first (equipped with floats) in 1922, and the second, a conventional landplane, the following year.

By 1920, most farseeing engineers and propulsion experts realized that contemporary conventional engines could not endow airplanes with acceptable high-altitude performance. Rather, the engines, starved of air, performed less and less efficiently, often overheating and seizing up, while the planes themselves wobbled about, on the knife-edge of a stall. Clearly, if the high-altitude performance of piston engines could be boosted, practical high-altitude flight might become a reality. The answer, fortunately, was readily at hand: the supercharger. Superchargers consist of two types: gear-driven (operating off the engine by a geared mechanism) and turbo-driven (using a rotating high-speed turbine placed in the engine exhaust). In each case, the rotating gears or the rotating turbine wheel drives a compressor (the supercharger impeller), which feeds the engine compressed air, enabling it to perform with lower-altitude efficiency even in flight far above 30,000 feet. The large inertial forces of a rotating impeller (often moving at 20,000 to 30,000 rpm), plagued gear-driven superchargers, which tended to frequent breakdown, especially when attached to the long crankshafts of in-line piston engines.

A Swiss engineer, A. J. Buchi, had first suggested using turbosuperchargers for aircraft, and Auguste Rateau, a French engineer, successfully bench-tested such a device during the First World War. The NACA immediately transmitted information on Rateau's work to American industry, asking the General Electric Company, in cooperation with the technical staff of McCook Field, to develop an American turbosupercharger for use with the Liberty engine. General Electric, with a strong reputation in the field of steam turbines, was the natural choice, as was its chief turbine expert, Dr. Sanford A. Moss, who had developed a turbine wheel driven by the products of combustion as early as 1903, while at Cornell. GE produced this first Moss-designed turbosupercharger at Lynn, Massachusetts, and delivered it to McCook in May 1918 for sea-level testing. It passed with flying colors, and GE next trucked it to the top of Pikes Peak in August, an altitude of 14,109 feet. At that altitude, an unsupercharged Liberty, by actual test, generated only 230 hp (the same engine produced 350 hp at Dayton). But with the supercharger functioning, the Liberty produced 356 hp at the top of Pikes Peak, a clear indication of the value of such a device. Now GE turned to installing it on a suitable airplane for flight tests; the handy LUSAC-11 was the logical choice.

In September 1918, Shorty Schroeder began test flights in the modified LUSAC, flying with Lieutenant George Elsey as test observer. On September 24, the two men flew to 30,900 feet, close to the record set by Roland Rohlfs less than a week before. Numerous small problems required solution; finally, in early February 1920, Schroeder felt confident to attempt a solo flight to break the official world's altitude record. On February 6, 1920, he took off in the LUSAC-11 and began his climb droning along in the Ohio sky. Over an hour and a half later, he reached 30,000 feet. He had realized that the greatest danger he faced would be from oxygen failure and had thought over and over again, to impress it upon his mind, "In case of darkness, a sure sign of unconsciousness, oxygen failure, pull into a spin." Now, suddenly, he realized he had trouble: his eyesight was failing; his oxygen system was not working. In his oxygen-starved state, he could not find the throttle; he instinctively pulled on the control stick and passed out. He came to gradually, aware of a whirling sensation, then realized it was Dayton passing

in and out of view. The plane had entered a spin directly over the town
—and instead of pulling on the control stick, he was pulling, with all his
strength, on his left foot! His next solo attempt came on February 27.
This time, he carried two oxygen supplies, one connected to a regulator,
the other an emergency canister with an ordinary rubber tube. Dressed
in an electrically heated flying suit lined with dog fur, the tall pilot took
off for altitude. An hour and 47 minutes after takeoff, he reached a record 36,130 feet, the trim LUSAC-11 streaming a contrail (which ground
observers mistook for a comet) buffeted by —60-degree F. winds. Then
his main oxygen supply failed; Schroeder, aware of the onset of anoxia,
fumbled around for the emergency supply, but, in his befuddled state,
could not locate it. He lifted his goggles, then gave up and reached for
the control stick in an attempt to spin the plane. His mind now played a
trick on him, and he mumbled to himself, "Put in *dive*"—and shoved the
stick forward before passing out. Under full power from the turbocharged Liberty, the LUSAC nosed over and dived earthward. The
onboard recording barograph registered an almost vertical descent of
over 33,100 feet. The abrupt pressure change accompanying the dive severely stressed the pilot's heart and internal organs, and the chill wind
blast froze his eyes. Of its own accord, less than a mile above the earth,
the LUSAC pulled out and nosed upward. Schroeder gradually recovered consciousness and limited vision. In a feat of outstanding airmanship, he managed to complete a successful landing at McCook. The
rapid fall, at times over 300 mph by actual record, had crushed three of
the plane's four fuel tanks from pressure differences. After weeks in the
hospital, Shorty Schroeder made a complete recovery, briefly resuming
Army test flying before leaving for private industry.

During the 1920s, following Schroeder's lead, altitude flights by turbocharged aircraft became frequent occurrences. French test pilot Sadi-
Lecointe reached over 36,567 feet in a Nieuport-Delage 29 C 1 in 1923,
and then, on January 29, 1926, Army test pilot John Macready reached
38,704 in the experimental Army Engineering Division XCO-5A. Writing later that year for *The National Geographic Magazine*, Macready
stated:

> In practically all extreme altitude attempts, the plane reaches its limit
> about the time the pilot grits his teeth in anticipation of pushing further
> upward. One isn't thinking as clearly as usual at this height, and it takes
> some time to convince oneself that the plane's ceiling has actually been
> reached. . . . The plane wallows about in a trough, but will not lift its
> nose an additional foot.[4]

Without question, high-altitude flight in the 1920s—and for some time to
come—was quite hazardous. Under the best of circumstances, flight

crews toiled in uncomfortable conditions, chilled to the bone, operating in a low-pressure environment, absolutely miserable. The ideal solution, of course, would be an enclosed, pressurized cabin, where flight crews could function, if not in a "shirt-sleeve" environment, then certainly in a flight-suit one. The practical pressurized cabin would only emerge in the next decade, with the Lockheed XC-35 testbed.

One early attempt at pressurization, in the 1920s, was pure comedy. In 1921, the Engineering Division at McCook Field modified a USD-9A biplane (essentially an American version of the British De Havilland D.H. 9 equipped with a Liberty engine), replacing the cockpit section for the pilot and observer with an experimental cylindrical pressure tank for a pilot. The tank had a small entrance door on its right side that the pilot would close in flight before beginning pressurization tests, and a small propeller-driven supercharger mounted on the leading edge of the left wing fed pressurized air into the test cabin. Designers anticipated great leakage around control lines and runs into the cabin, despite careful packing of all ports, and so boosted the performance of the air induction system. In June 1921, Art Smith, a civilian test pilot employed by the Army at McCook Field, attempted the first tests, but his small stature gave him poor leverage, and he could not place the cabin door in position and secure it. He landed after this unsuccessful attempt, and Lieutenant Harold R. Harris, who had succeeded Shorty Schroeder as chief of the flight test section, decided to fly the plane himself.

Harris, a genial man more closely resembling an account executive than the public image of the test pilot, took off in the plane, peering through its tiny portholes at the instruments mounted just outside the tank on a special board. The modified USD-9A climbed to 3,000 feet, and Harris lifted the door into place and locked it. "Immediately," he recollected, "things began to happen." And they were not good. Tank internal pressure rose precipitously, and the altimeter inside the tank registered an equivalent pressure of 3,000 feet *below* sea level, while the altimeter outside the tank registered 3,000 feet *above*. Harris immediately opened a ceiling dump valve, but the small port of the valve made hardly any difference. Opening the door against the internal pressure sealing it in place was, of course, impossible. And he had nothing to break the thick viewing ports with. Like many test pilots, Harris wore tennis shoes to provide better feel of the controls, and thus he lacked even a shoe to pound open some port. As he later stated,

> The only thing left to do then was to assume as slow speed a glide as I dared, and land as quickly as possible. At no time, from shortly after closing the door until after the plane came to a stop, was the cabin pressure above 3,000 feet below sea level.

There was no possible escape from this ever-increasing pressure. I do not recall any particular area of discomfort although it has been reported that I complained of pain in my ears. The air in the tank was uncomfortably warm from the action of the compressor, and I was wringing wet from perspiration on landing. However, this was probably due in some degree to my anxiety about the outcome of this test, and irritation with myself for having gotten into such a situation without having intelligently considered the possible difficulties and taken the necessary precautions.[5]

Despite safety modifications, including installation of an emergency hammer inside the cockpit so that the pilot could break open a port if necessary, the plane apparently never flew again.

McCook's pilots had many such episodes in the field's early days, flights that began with grave concern but then progressed to unexpected humor. Two extracts from McCook's official chronology for May 1920 illustrate the sometimes zany touches that added color to the field's reputation:

> *May 4*—Capt. L. L. Snow brought his Liberty-powered Fokker into the shallow Miami River when his engine failed. He climbed up the tail, lighted a cigarette, and waited for a rowboat to rescue him.
> *May 6*—Lt. Louis Meister, testing a Nieuport, landed it in a tree to break the fall, when his engine failed. The plane burned and the pilot's life was despaired of until those who rushed to the scene found Meister on the ground calmly looking for his goggles which he'd thrown overboard before the crash.[6]

A clear measure of the growth of American air power and the advance of American flight technology came in a month after Harris's pressure cabin fiasco with the bombing trials off the Virginia Capes during which Billy Mitchell's handful of bombers, including the impressive Martin MB-2, sank three captured German warships, including the battleship *Ostfriesland,* which had survived a pounding at Jutland. In a bid to fully exploit the capabilities of Army bombers, McCook modified one of the Martins with Moss-type turbosuperchargers. On one test flight, on December 7, 1921, a test observer passed out, resulting in the test pilot, Lieutenant Leigh Wade (later one of the Army's "Around the World Flyers" in the Douglas World Cruisers) aborting the flight at an altitude of 20,000 feet. The next day, however, Wade and a test crew reached an altitude of 25,600 feet. Eventually, as a result of further development work, the Army procured a number of turbocharged Martins for service at Langley Field. While these early "boosted" bombers had numerous teething troubles, they did point the way to the eventual development of powerful high-altitude bombers such as the later B-17, B-24, and B-29.

RESEARCH FOR SAFER DESIGNS: CHALLENGE AND RESPONSE

One of the greatest hazards faced in aeronautics in the early 1920s was the danger of structural failure in the air. New high-performance fighters, capable of attaining well over 200 mph in dives, sometimes having novel construction methods, often experienced some form of structural failure, usually with fatal results. Once, in mid-1921, Lieutenant John Macready, one of the Army's finest test pilots (he later completed the first nonstop coast-to-coast flight with Oakley Kelly in the Army Fokker T-2), took off in an experimental Thomas-Morse MB-3 single-engine fighter. The little "Tommy Morse" had performed satisfactorily in early trials, and all remaining was a test of its behavior in a high-speed dive. Macready climbed to over 10,000 feet, nosed over, and dived under full power. Suddenly the fighter shuddered and bucked, there was a cracking sound, and Macready, startled, noted that the entire top surface of the upper wing had ripped away, exposing a network of partially destroyed struts, ribs, and spars. Unable to place the machine in a glide, Macready seemed doomed until, at 1,500 feet, with the pilot coolly holding the control stick full aft, the MB-3 slowly raised its nose and mushed earthward nose-high, crunched into the ground, and rolled over. Macready walked away from the accident, shaken but unhurt. Asked if he had been frightened, the dapper pilot replied, "No. I was thinking so hard and fast I didn't have time to get frightened until later."[7]

Clearly, in such situations, a parachute could spell the difference between life and death. Unfortunately, there seems to have been little sense of urgency attached to wearing them, until the death of a young Army test pilot at McCook, Lieutenant Frederick W. Niedermeyer, on March 13, 1922. That day, Niedermeyer went aloft on an air combat maneuvering test in a Fokker PW-5, a parasol monoplane with a cantilever wooden wing, resembling a cross between Fokker's wartime D VII and D VIII fighters. Fokker's wooden monoplanes had always had a bad reputation for structural failures. The wartime D VIII had not reached the front in large numbers because of problems with its wooden wing—and indeed, the later crash of a Fokker wooden-wing F-10 trimotor from structural failure would cause a national uproar: one of the passengers was fabled football coach Knute Rockne. Niedermeyer had taken off without a parachute. During the flight, he engaged fellow test pilot John Macready in a mock dogfight, then performed a series of aerobatics, concluding with a roll on the top of a loop, followed by a steep dive. Suddenly a spar failed, and the PW-5 shed its starboard wing, diving into the ground. Shaken, observers realized that if Niedermeyer had had one of the new free-fall parachutes recently approved for Air Service use, he might have lived. As it was, he had no chance. A new sign went up in the McCook operations room: "Don't forget your parachute. If you need it and haven't got it, you'll never need it again."[8]

Thus, on October 20, 1922, Harold Harris strapped on a parachute as he prepared for a test flight in a Loening PW-2A pursuit monoplane equipped with experimental ailerons. Like Niedermeyer before him, Harris planned on flying a mock combat with Muir Fairchild in another aircraft. Tempted to leave the parachute behind because of a tight harness, Harris decided to wear it anyway. Fairchild and Harris took off, and the two planes climbed to 2,500 feet. After maneuvering about, Harris followed Fairchild through a gentle left turn at about 150 mph. Suddenly the little fighter started violently shaking, as if in an earthquake. The Loening snapped from side to side, a victim of the then-not-completely understood phenomenon of aileron flutter. The control stick whipped back and forth, smashing into Harris's thighs at close to 1,000 cycles per minute. Harris throttled back, but there was no way that the skilled pilot could have prevented the violent motion from destroying the wing structure; the flutter had reached catastrophic proportions almost instantly. Harris later said:

> I knew it was impossible to regain control of the airplane. There was only one thing to do to save my life. I had seen a good many airplane crashes. I had helped pick up a good many pilots who had been killed. In a collapse of the sort I was experiencing, if I stayed with the airplane, I would undoubtedly be killed. The next thing for me to do was to leave the airplane and trust my parachute.[9]

And so he leapt, as the PW-2A broke up around him, and after fumbling three times for the ripcord, finally located it and pulled. The chute opened with a crack and deposited the battered pilot in the middle of a grape arbor. Harris, Caterpillar Club member #1, could not walk for days because of bruises from the thrashing control stick.

Sadly, sometimes wearing a parachute was not enough. At low altitudes, an unstable airplane could abruptly "diverge" during a maneuver, immediately overstressing its structure and breaking up. Under these conditions, flight crews rarely had time to escape. McCook test pilot Eugene Barksdale and flight observer Ralph Anderson were once aloft in the unstable XCO-7 biplane on a low-altitude high-speed run above Wilbur Wright Field. Barksdale "pulsed" the control stick (pushed it forward slightly and suddenly released it to induce a longitudinal pitching motion), but the plane perversely nosed over into a full-power dive from only 200 feet; Barksdale immediately pulled back on the stick, the biplane's horizontal tail tore off, and it pitched over on its nose, hurling the pilot out of the plane in spite of his safety belt. Reacting automatically, Barksdale pulled his ripcord, and the white chute blossomed just in time to prevent him from smashing into the ground. Anderson was not so lucky. . . . So structural research, especially on the relationship between maneuvering and structural loads, became increasingly important for reasons of flight safety.

Additionally, structural research played a major role in testing programs of the 1920s because the field of flight structures was advancing rapidly. All-metal structures competed with wooden ones, and a general trend toward the monoplane configuration emerged. (Eventually, with the Lockheed Vega and the later metal Northrop Alpha, flight structures came of age, marking the birth of the practical metal semimonocoque aircraft.) However, the failure modes of flight structures and the effect of maneuvering accelerations upon the structures were not well understood. Both the Army and the NACA conducted extensive research into this area. Jimmy Doolittle, an up-and-coming Army test pilot, made one of the first major contributions of flight research to structural theory with a series of test flights in an experimental Fokker fighter.

James Harold "Jimmy" Doolittle eventually became one of the best-known figures in American aviation, a pilot whose reputation ranked with the Wrights and Charles Lindbergh. Widely regarded as a daredevil because of his spectacular flights in America and abroad, the cautious Doolittle was actually a shrewdly calculating professional airman who ultimately earned one of the first doctorates in aeronautical engineering ever awarded in the United States, from the prestigious Massachusetts Institute of Technology. Short and rugged in stature, the pilot had a ready wit and a gregarious nature, which masked a strong will and an aggressive personality. He showed a marked mechanical aptitude, and enrolled in the University of California, hoping to become a mining engineer. Then along came the First World War. Doolittle, convinced he could become a pilot, enlisted in the Aviation Section of the Signal Corps. He trained on Jennies, then served as an instructor, earning a reputation as a daring and skillful pilot. He participated in Billy Mitchell's bombing tests off the Virginia Capes, flying a D.H. 4, and then, in September 1922, completed a coast-to-coast transcontinental flight in a modified De Havilland D.H. 4B, covering 2,163 miles in 21 hours and 20 minutes flying time, stopping only to gas up the plane before taking off again.

Following this record flight, which brought him national attention, Doolittle transferred to McCook Field, joining the small staff of test pilots and attending the Air Service's Engineering School at the field. Doolittle wanted more than just a service technical education, however. Granted an undergraduate degree by the University of California, he determined to get a master's degree in aeronautical engineering from MIT. At this time, not quite a year since his coast-to-coast flight, the state of American aeronautical engineering education was woefully inadequate. Few programs existed. Indeed, it was only through the farsighted generosity of the Guggenheim family—father Daniel and son Harry (a former aviator)—that highly developed quality programs in aeronautical engineering became generally available. MIT (which later received strong Guggenheim assistance) had one of these early programs, and one of the senior professors in the department happened to be Edward Warner, who had earlier helped create and then direct the flight test activities of the NACA's Langley laboratory. MIT, then, was the place to go for a pilot involved in flight testing and who had an engineering mind. Doolittle, applying the same goal-oriented style he used when flying a plane, worked long and hard during his stay at MIT, receiving his master's in 1924. A good student, Doolittle applied for entry into a doctoral program and was quickly accepted. But while he was a doctoral student, the Army recalled him briefly to McCook to undertake exhaustive and hazardous structural flight tests of a new experimental fighter, the Fokker PW-7.

The Fokker PW-7 featured a broad-span upper wing and a smaller lower one, giving it almost a "sesquiplane" configuration. Its lines looked typically Fokker, the heritage of the wartime D VII being clearly visible. The PW-7's most noteworthy feature was its engine, the famed Curtiss D-12 liquid-cooled in-line, which in fact influenced the subsequent course of American and British in-line engine design. The tapered wing (which influenced later fighter wing design) was fabricated with birch plywood skinning, and like all Fokker fighters to that time, the PW-7 had a steel-tube fuselage structure. It was a trim, workmanlike airplane. Unfortunately, it did not fly spectacularly well, being slow, a touch sluggish, and longitudinally unstable. The manufacturer would have rectified all these minor faults, but in the economy-conscious days of the 1920s the Army could not afford to order such a marginal aircraft when existing fighters, such as the Thomas-Morse/Boeing MB-3A, so nicely served the Army's needs. So, as with so many of the early experimental Army and Navy fighters, the three PW-7's built served only as research airplanes.

McCook flight researchers decided to test the biplane in an attempt to derive data that would permit better understanding of the flight loads experienced by a fighter maneuvering under air combat conditions. Technicians equipped the PW-7 with a recording accelerometer and drew up a research program including loops at various airspeeds, single and multiple barrel rolls, spirals and spins both with and without power, half loops, half rolls, Immelmann turns, inverted flight, dive pullouts at various airspeeds and loadings, level flight, and flying in gust conditions. Obviously, a test pilot engaged in such a program should have a thorough understanding of engineering principles and the potential limits of his aircraft: Doolittle was the natural choice.

He undertook the flight tests of the PW-7 in March 1924. Today, such a program could easily run several months and involve considerable ground support and expense. Back then, it involved flying the airplane to the test conditions stipulated on the pilot's test card, then returning, removing the accelerometer, and checking its records to make certain that the plane was still safely within its performance envelope, before readying the craft for its next flight. The flights were grueling, with abrupt maneuvers generating high g loadings, even by the standards of today. And then, on one flight, came a little tidbit of data that made the whole program worthwhile. Doolittle rolled the PW-7 into a steep dive, accelerated to well over 200 mph, and then pulled sharply back, the plane attaining a punishing 7.8 g, reaching its limit load. The rear wooden surface of the upper wing cracked, fortunately not catastrophically, and Doolittle landed the damaged fighter safely. The discovery of the fracture point refuted the then commonly held belief that wings failed under loads from pullouts by shearing backward toward the tail. (Some pilots had even gone so far as to specially tighten any bracing wires running from the leading edges of the wings to the fuselage in mistaken acceptance of this dangerous belief; their actions, if anything, simply made the chance of failure under load greater, for they prestressed the wing for destruction.) Doolittle received a much-deserved Distinguished Flying Cross for this notable series of flights, the citation praising his "skill, initiative, endurance, and courage of the highest type." The tests resulted in publication of a milestone NACA-Army flight research report, *Accelerations in Flight*, that quickly became a standard reference. Doolittle went back to MIT and received his doctor of science degree in 1925, age twenty-eight, before embarking on even more significant flight research accomplishments.

Doolittle's PW-7 tests had concluded that pilots could withstand high "instantaneous" accelerations without discomfort but that prolonged "g," even as low as 4.5, resulted in "a complete loss of faculties" when continued for any length of time. By the mid-1920s, pursuit biplanes had the capability to maneuver at high g loadings. And so, in addition to the questions engineers had concerning the reliability and safety of flight structures, came physiological questions concerning the capabilities of the pilots themselves. The NACA, building on its earlier research using Jennies and other aircraft, as well as Jimmy Doolittle's PW-7 investigation, decided to embark on a series of flights with a high-performance Navy fighter, the Curtiss F6C-4. The service hoped to determine the maximum loads experienced by the tail surfaces of a fighter during maneuvering, in an attempt to develop reliable design criteria that engineers could use, preventing the sort of failures that had nearly killed Gene Barksdale and had killed his unfortunate flight observer. Accordingly, in 1927, NACA Langley borrowed a Navy F6C-4 Hawk straight from an operational fighter squadron, outfitted it with pressure distribution orifices on the vertical and horizontal surfaces as well as on-board recording manometers, and then assigned test pilot Luke Christopher to fly the airplane in a series of abrupt maneuvers, including spins, rolls, high-speed dives with sudden pullouts, and rudder reversals, while the instrumentation worked away, over a range of speeds and altitudes. The results were alarming: design theory for building tail surfaces on fighters was revealed as clearly inadequate. In some cases, the actual flight loads were twice as high as anticipated by engineering practice. Importantly, the flights were equally revealing about the hazards faced by fighter pilots. During one high-speed level run, at 173 mph, test pilot Christopher had abruptly pulled back on the control column, hitting a peak acceleration of 10.5 g, resulting in an emergency landing and immediate hospitalization for "generalized conjunctivitis of both eyes" plus "a mild cerebral concussion with some generalized cerebral capillary hemorrhage. . . . There was a duty recovery from this condition in about two weeks and a complete recovery in about a month."[10] The nimble Hawk had held together; its pilot had not, and the 10.5 g load remained an unofficial record for many years.

The NACA continued its structural and accelerations research, culminating in a maneuverability investigation of another Navy Hawk in 1930, the first major examination of aircraft handling qualities ever done in the United States. On-board recording instrumentation had provided a precise record of the airplane's behavior during loops, pull-ups, pushdowns, and abrupt rudder maneuvers. The results were then reduced to easily understood data that aircraft designers around the country could put to use in engineering new aircraft. By the late 1920s, then, designers and engineers were learning more about the limitations of their craft from the numerous flight researchers working at McCook (and later Wright Field), Anacostia, Langley, and elsewhere. The acceptable boundaries for both aircraft and human performance were being mapped out, to remain as boundaries until flight technology once again surpassed them and engineers' hopes became realities. There were many other

problems demanding answers, as there always would be. And flight
research continued to point the way.

DOWN TO THE SEA IN PLANES

There was, for example, the whole notion of going down to the sea in
planes, first tackled by the enthusiastic Eugene Ely. To most Americans,
naval aviation, after the First World War, meant the Navy's large flying
boats, such as the NC class, one of which, the NC-4, had managed to fly
in stages across the Atlantic in 1919. In fact, however, the Navy had continued with experiments in launching aircraft from ships. Just after the
war, the Navy had experimented with a number of small foreign biplane
fighters, such as the Sopwith Pup and Camel, the Hanriot HD-1, and
some Nieuport 28's, launching them down small platforms mounted on
the forward gun turrets of battleships while the vessels steamed into the
wind. On March 9, 1919, Navy test pilot E. O. McDonnell made the first
such flight, taking off from a gun platform on board the battleship U.S.S.
Texas at Guantánamo Bay, Cuba. During the war itself, however, the
British had actually operated small fighters from towed platforms—and
from a new class of ships called aircraft carriers. Great Britain's first true
aircraft carrier, H.M.S. *Argus*, appeared just too late for wartime service.
It had a flush landing and takeoff deck running the length of the ship,
with the bridge and funnel structure offset in an amidships "island."
Prodded by its increasingly air-minded junior officers, the U. S. Navy
decided to follow suit, and later in 1919 the Navy authorized the conversion of a collier, the *Jupiter*, to serve as the Navy's first aircraft carrier.
In the meantime, the service, and its affiliated partners in the U. S. Marine Corps, built up experience with landplane fighters. The Navy
acquired modified Vought VE-7 trainers having forward-firing guns
(one of the few times a trainer has spawned a fighter) and then a specialized single-seat model, the VE-7F, with a top speed of 121 mph. The
Marines made do with a mix of surplus British SE-5A's and later some
Thomas-Morse MB-3's. The service completed conversion of the *Jupiter*
in early 1922, and on March 20 of that year formally commissioned it as
the U.S.S. *Langley*, CV-1, the ancestor of all subsequent American carriers. The *Langley* measured just over 530 feet in length and had a dis-
placement of 11,500 tons. Attention turned to conducting the first flying
operations from its deck.

    In preparation for the tests, veteran naval aviator Lieutenant Com-
mander Godfrey "Chevvy" de Chevalier (who had made the first American tests of air-launched torpedoes) assembled a group of fifteen Navy

pilots at Florida and later at Mitchel Field, on Long Island, and trained in landplanes. Later they practiced landing on a mocked-up deck of the carrier installed at the flying field at Philadelphia's Navy Yard. Ready by early fall, this early group of proto-carrier pilots reported aboard the *Langley* at Norfolk. Today the technology of carrier equipment is familiar: the launch catapults, the arresting gear, the tail hook on the aircraft, a landing approach light system. But all these were unknown at the time. Indeed, the landing wires ran fore and aft, not across the deck, and early carrier aircraft (such as the VE-7's) were equipped with a multitude of hooks on their landing-gear struts that, at times, gave them the appearance of garden rakes. At last the Navy gave the go-ahead, and the *Langley* put to sea, its strange shape having resulted in its being christened affectionately the "Covered Wagon." Flying off the carrier's deck proved no problem, but all interest centered on landing. On October 26, 1922, Chevvy de Chevalier took off from Norfolk in an Aeromarine training plane. He rendezvoused with the carrier at sea, and as it steamed into the wind, he approached from astern. The gusty air—far choppier than any encountered in training at Philadelphia—buffeted the little plane, and De Chevalier came across the fantail of the *Langley* a little hot; the plane touched down, rolling fast, and its hooks caught the deck arresting lines. It slowed, and then tipped quickly on its nose, a practical if not graceful landing. The *Langley* had made its first "trap." The Navy's "Ship Plane Division" continued to perfect the techniques of deck landing and launch over the months ahead, and by the end of the 1920s, the *Langley*, in company with its later and larger sisters the *Lexington* and the *Saratoga*, were changing forever the character and strategy of fleet maneuvers. It was something that Chevvy de Chevalier would have liked to witness. Sadly, less than a month after his historic landing aboard the *Langley*, he was dead, killed in a crash at Norfolk.

Bolstered by the *Langley*'s trials, the Navy accelerated its development of high-performance fighters. The cumbersome VE-7's and makeshift warplanes gave way to the first Navy fighter in squadron service, the Curtiss TS-1, also the first American naval fighter designed from the outset for carrier operations. Of about the same technological class as the contemporary Fairey Flycatcher, of Great Britain, the lithe TS-1 disappeared in favor of the Boeing FB series and then the first of the superlative and romantic Curtiss Navy Hawks: the F6C series, equivalent to the Army's own P-1's. In time, these spawned their own successors, and by the end of the decade, an experimental Navy fighter, the Wright F3W-1 Apache, equipped with a NACA supercharger, had reached an altitude of 43,166 feet, flown by test pilot Apollo Soucek. Specialized dive and later torpedo bombers joined the fleet, and the carrier quickly emerged as a full-fledged (if still underestimated) rival to the battleship.

The testing of naval aircraft required, of course, a suitable flight test site. Since January 1918, the Navy had used Anacostia as its flight test center. In the mid-1920s, the center had the services of a distinguished and accomplished reserve pilot, Eddie Rounds. A mechanical engineer from MIT, Edward Rounds had entered the Navy, winning his wings at the end of the war. He joined Anacostia in 1919 as a flying-boat and seaplane test pilot, winning official commendation for completing an emergency landing in an airplane that had experienced difficulty aloft. Rounds introduced the Navy to scientific test flying, assembling a small testing staff at the station in the 1920s. Later he flew as one of the three test pilots selected by the Guggenheim Safe Aircraft Competition, and he subsequently specialized in the testing of commercial airplanes, gaining wide recognition for guidelines he stipulated for the testing of such craft.

Despite the best efforts of engineers such as Eddie Rounds, aircraft occasionally continued to betray their pilots, and as at McCook and elsewhere, Anacostia was not immune from tragedy. The first Navy test pilot lost at Anacostia was Lieutenant George T. Cuddihy, a distinguished test pilot with an excellent record in air racing, who perished in the crash of an experimental British Bristol Bulldog that the Navy had acquired to evaluate its steel construction; during a maximum-speed dive, flutter set in and tore the ailerons away, throwing the plane out of control.

The Navy also evaluated airplanes at the Navy Proving Ground, Dahlgren, Virginia. There Navy test pilots tested bombsights, fired ordnance, and evaluated the performance of dive bombers and fighters under combatlike conditions. The air weapon American naval forces employed during the Second World War was forged in the twenties at such places as Anacostia and Dahlgren and tempered to operational excellence in the war gaming of the thirties. Without the vision of such flight researchers as Eddie Rounds and the sacrifices of test pilots such as De Chevalier and Cuddihy, the victories at Midway and the Marianas would not have been possible.

THE GREAT RACERS

Le Corbusier, the exponent of the modern movement in architecture, once wrote that "the airplane mobilized invention, intelligence, and daring: *imagination* and *cold reason*. It is the same spirit that built the Parthenon."[11] Certainly, the airplane typified the application of Louis Sullivan's dictum "Form ever follows function," and this was especially true in the 1920s, the era of streamlining. Nowhere was it more evident than in the design of the high-performance air racers of the 1920s, aircraft that, more than any other, have come to symbolize "the Golden Age of Flight." At the end of 1918, the Curtiss Wasp Triplane had flown at over 160 mph. Yet, barely more than a decade later, a British racing seaplane, the Supermarine S.6B, had flown at over 400. The incredible difference reflected the explosive growth of flight technology during the 1920s, particularly in the area of high-performance power plants and extensive aerodynamic refinement of design—the latter, in short, being streamlining.

Streamlining could be accomplished in many ways: changing over from an externally braced biplane or monoplane to an internally braced monoplane; making the landing gear retractable; reducing the frontal area of the airplane; cleaning up the engine installation. In fact, all of these—and more—eventually appeared on the aircraft of the 1920s. And flight research had to validate, in every case, the potential advantages claimed for each one.

Generally speaking, there were really only three outstanding groups of aircraft built for racing by the United States, but their influence was considerable: the Dayton-Wright, the Verville-Sperry R-3, and the elegant Curtiss racers of the decade. The first of these, the Dayton-Wright RB Racer, is now at the Ford Museum, in Dearborn. A portly and ugly high-wing monoplane, the RB racer had many noteworthy features for its day, including a variable-camber wing having both leading and trailing edge droop and a retractable landing gear a la later Grumman biplanes. Though it never, in fact, won a single race, its configuration helped influence the future shape of propeller-driven airplanes. The second, the Verville-Sperry R-3, allegedly grew out of a technical inspection trip Alfred Verville and air chief Billy Mitchell made to Europe immediately after the Armistice. Upon their return, Mitchell is said to have fixed the engineer with a baleful stare and ordered, "Verville, I want tomorrow's aeroplane today—and I don't want any squirrel cage."[12] He gave the hapless man a night to come up with a suitable configuration.

Verville toiled all night, and when he delivered his sketch the next morning, Mitchell exclaimed, "Now, that's what I call a modern aeroplane!" It had a low, internally braced wing, a retractable landing gear, smooth external lines, and a closely cowled Wright in-line engine. Sperry, under Army contract, eventually built three of the craft, designated the Verville-Sperry R-3. Inexperience with such a structure nearly led to disaster, for on its first flight, the prototype R-3 exhibited severe vibration bordering on flutter, and after a gingerly but uneventful landing, Sperry directed that the wing be covered with sheet plywood to give it greater rigidity. The remarkable landing gear folded inward into the bottom of the wing, giving the R-3 a decidedly modern appearance well ahead of its time. Disappointingly, the R-3's were plagued by stability and control problems as well as more mundane matters such as engine reliability. Eventually, the Army modified two of the craft with a more reliable Curtiss D-12 engine and built the radiators into the wing surface —a concession to aerodynamics.

The R-3 proved disappointing in the 1923 Pulitzer race, Army test pilot Alex Pearson having problems just keeping the plane under control because of an out-of-balance propeller and spinner. Pearson hoped for better in the 1924 Pulitzer, but, tragically, this fine pilot lost his life when flight testing the Curtiss R-8 racer (formerly a Navy R2C) at Wilbur Wright Field on September 2, 1924. During a high-speed dive, that old problem—flutter—ripped a strut from the racer, which shed a wing and snap-rolled into the ground. The Army substituted test pilot Harry Mills for the luckless Pearson, and at last, the Verville-Sperry R-3 had its chance. On October 4, 1924, Mills won the Pulitzer race with an average speed of 216.554 mph. The victory vindicated the design of the R-3, even though the plane never did live up to its full promise. Had the Army supported it more enthusiastically, the advent of the retractable-gear monoplane fighter might have been pushed forward a decade.

It is the Curtiss racers, however, that are most closely associated in the public mind with the great air race meets of the 1920s, especially the trim, pontoon-equipped biplanes that battled in the 1923, 1925, and 1926 Schneider Trophy competitions against some of the finest aircraft in the world. Aside from flirting with a racing version of the Wasp Triplane, Curtiss had earlier entered the racing field with two horrible airplanes— the "Texas Wildcat" and the "Cactus Kitten"—both developed for the Gordon Bennett races immediately after the First World War. The former nearly killed Roland Rohlfs during a landing accident before the 1920 Gordon Bennett race, held at Étampes, France. The latter, a fast but very dangerous airplane, had a *landing* speed of 95 mph, and test pilot Bert Acosta, more willing to take risks than most airmen, nevertheless refused to fly it again following a harrowing first flight! (It eventually flew, but with other pilots.)

Rather than proceed with more "engines with wings," Curtiss recognized at this time the importance of racing planes having acceptable low-speed performance and handling characteristics. European racers with modest high-speed performance but better all-around capabilities had clearly outperformed their American rivals in the 1920 Gordon Bennett; none of the U.S. aircraft had even finished the race. Accordingly, Curtiss adopted a more conventional approach, and the company's response, which won the 1921 Pulitzer race, was the pioneering Curtiss CR-1 racer, two of which Curtiss built to a Navy order, a slim monocoque wooden aircraft having minimal cross section, two equal-span wings, and nice proportions. Its awkward-appearing canisterlike Lamblin radiators were the only break with the streamline philosophy.

Air racing in the 1920s occupied a position of national importance similar in some respects to the early space shots. Aside from being a mass spectator technosport, its international competitive character eventually caused nations to place the full resources of their governments behind the manufacturers of these noisy, temperamental, and often exotic craft. Most important, however, were its technological aspects: the military viewed air racing as a vital research and development activity. A McCook Field booklet for the public stated that:

> The advantages to be ultimately derived from development are frequently not readily apparent to one viewing its intermediate stages. For instance, there are many who look askance upon airplane racing as a dangerous pastime and a foolish waste of money and effort. Such people overlook the basic idea prompting these races: they are essentially tests; tests of design, endurance and performance for both airplanes and motors upon the results of which further advance in aeronautical achievement is predicated. The racing airplane is in itself useless for any purpose other than that for which it was created, but from the winning airplanes in the Pulitzer trophy races of the past two years, has been developed our present type of pursuit airplane. . . .[13]

In the United States, the test pilots of McCook Field and Anacostia spent time preparing, like the gladiators of old, for these spectacles held year after year, particularly the Pulitzer and Schneider events. That the United States did well is a tribute in great measure to the arduous work of these engineering test pilots, some of whom, unfortunately, lost their lives in attempting to demonstrate national supremacy through racing.

Bert Acosta, the suave, self-assured airman who had succeeded Roland Rohlfs as Curtiss's chief test pilot when Rohlfs left the company to become operations manager for Aeromarine Airways, had completed the maiden flight of the CR-1 racer, a landplane, in August 1921. The first flight ended badly; as Acosta landed, the fuselage cracked open, necessitating reinforcement of the structure. Aside from this, however, the plane had impressive performance, including well-harmonized controls, pleasant flying qualities and good maneuverability, and speed near 200 mph. It easily won the 1921 Pulitzer—with Acosta at the controls—and modified with wing radiators built flush into the wing surface in place of the drag-inducing Lamblins, the two racers (redesignated CR-2) placed third and fourth in the 1922 Pulitzer. They were beaten by another, more refined Curtiss design, the R-6, two of which placed first and second. Curtiss domination of air racing in the 1920s had begun.

Following the success of the Navy-sponsored CR-1, Billy Mitchell had ordered two advanced racers from Curtiss for the 1922 Pulitzer race, which Curtiss constructed under the designation R-6. The R-6 racers, designed from the outset for wing skin radiators, were even smaller than the CR's and had a 25 per cent reduction in cross-sectional area from that of the earlier craft, as well as a generally aerodynamically "cleaned-up" appearance. Army test pilot Lester Maitland reached 223 mph during the R-6's first flight, at Curtiss field, a mark fellow test pilot Russell Maughan exceeded a little later. Maughan subsequently won the 1922 Pulitzer handily, combining expert piloting and the innate qualities of the R-6 in a mix of 7 g pylon turns and 200-mph lap speeds. Curtiss used the lessons learned from the CR and the R-6 when developing the first Curtiss high-speed fighter, the PW-8, one of which, two years later, Maughan would fly coast to coast, from New York to San Francisco, in a single day. The two R-6's raced again, in the 1923 Pulitzer (finishing fifth and sixth) and in the 1924 Pulitzer (won by the Verville-Sperry R-3). In the latter contest, one R-6 finished second, but the other broke up in midair when its wooden propeller disintegrated, killing its pilot, Captain Burt Skeel. Clearly, the era of the laminated wooden prop was coming to a close for high-speed aircraft.

At Navy behest, Curtiss followed the CR and R-6 series with a new derivative, resembling the earlier craft but with many significant differences: the R2C racer. The R2C, of which Curtiss built two, had the now familiar streamlined Curtiss racer shape but with a high-speed-airfoil cross section for the wings, greater wing area, with the top wing faired into the top decking of the fuselage, and a new Reed metal propeller. The Curtiss engine could produce a then remarkable 500 hp. Navy test pilot Harold Brow completed the first flight of the first R2C at Mitchel Field, Long Island, on September 9, 1923, and Curtiss immediately realized they had a winner. Within a few days of testing, the prototype R2C had reached a level speed of over 240 mph, flown by Brow and fellow Navy test pilot Alford "Al" Williams, who had raced the CR-2 for the Navy in the 1922 Pulitzer. Within a month, Williams and Brow took first and second places, respectively, in the 1923 Pulitzer, Williams averaging almost 244 mph. On November 4, Brow established a new world airspeed record, of 265.69 mph, during four passes over a measured course, beating a record Williams had set earlier in the day, of 263.3. Not to be outdone, Williams topped this with a spectacular if hazardous flight at an average of 266.59 mph.

Next, one of the R2C's went back to Curtiss for conversion to a float seaplane. The R2C floatplane never raced but became instead a training plane for the 1926 Schneider. Sadly, it stalled during a practice flight and spun into the Potomac River, killing its Marine test pilot, Harmon Norton. But the R2C design philosophy, as with the CR and R-6 series before it, inspired the ultimate Curtiss racer, the beautiful and alluring R3C, of 1925.

The R3C represented a joint Army-Navy venture, and Curtiss received funding support from both services for the construction of this plane. Externally it differed little from the previous R2C, but it had a powerful Curtiss V-1400 engine capable of generating 560 hp, elegant nose contours, and a robust structure designed for over-12 g flight loads. Designed as both a landplane (the R3C-1) and a seaplane (the R3C-2, with floats that could be added to the craft), the first of four R3C racers were completed in September 1925, and the Navy's Al Williams completed its first flight, being followed on the same day by Jimmy Doolittle, who made the second flight on behalf of the Army. At nearly 300 mph, Doolittle felt the racer develop a wing heaviness, and then noticed to his shock that the left wingtip of the plane's upper wing had started to break up; he quickly slowed the tiny racer and made a successful emergency landing. After repairs, the plane rejoined the test program. Al Williams subsequently reached just over 300 mph during one dive.

Elated, Curtiss, the Army, and the Navy prepared for the Pulitzer contest. When the race was held, on October 12, 1925, at Mitchel Field, Long Island, Curtiss swept all five places. Army pilot Cy Bettis took first place in one of the R3C-1's, averaging 248.975 mph. Second came Al Williams, in the other R3C-1, at 241.695 mph. Third went to a Curtiss P-1 fighter, followed by fourth to a Curtiss PW-8B, and fifth to another Curtiss PW-8B. Next, all attention focused on the upcoming Schneider seaplane race, scheduled two weeks later, on October 26 at Bay Shore Park, near Baltimore, Maryland.

In 1922, the United States had first won the prestigious Schneider seaplane contest when the Navy entered the two CR-3 floatplanes, simply modified versions of the original two CR-1/CR-2 aircraft. That year, Navy pilots David Rittenhouse and Rutledge Irvine had taken first and second places, respectively, with speeds of 177.279 and 173.347 mph. Curtiss had revolutionized the Schneider as well as the Pulitzer. The 1924 Schneider race was cancelled, so attention turned to the 1925 contest. The Navy furnished test pilots George Cuddihy and Ralph Ofstie, and the Army supplied Jimmy Doolittle. The victor's crown went to Doolittle. As meticulous as always, he studied with an engineer's insight the tactics of gaining speed around the pylons. He decided to dive into the turn around each pylon, holding a tight constant-g turn and trading speed gained in the dive for the speed built up on the straightaway, where the R3C's inherent behavior caused it to climb slightly, even with the elevator in neutral position. During the Schneider race, Doolittle outflew both Cuddihy and Ofstie, whose planes eventually suffered engine failures that removed them from the race. Doolittle averaged 232.573 mph; his nearest competitor was British test pilot Hubert Broad, whose pretty but inadequate Gloster III-A averaged only 199.170 mph. Then, the next day, Doolittle set a new world's record, of 245.713 mph, over a straightaway course.

The 1925 Schneider race was the swan song of the biplane Curtiss racers, for the future belonged to the monoplane. Though Curtiss tried vainly in 1926 with the R3C-3 and R3C-4, modified versions of the earlier R3C-2, the era of the biplane racer passed. Eventually, advocacy of racing as an important spur for research and development came to an end. Shortly after mastering that deadliest of all racers, the portly and vicious Gee Bee, Jimmy Doolittle declared that air racing had "outlived its usefulness." Racing, Doolittle stated, "originally did promote safety in aviation through testing of materials used in construction of planes and engines . . . lately it appears that the value received is not commensurate with the personal risk involved."[14]

But the 1920s weren't all devoted to a quest for speed. There were other notable aviation activities as well: demonstrations of aviation technology accompanied by related demonstrations of remarkable human courage, attempts to improve the safety of airplanes and aviation equipment, all accompanied by the increasing professionalization of the test pilot.

CHARLES A. LINDBERGH: TEST PILOT

No other aviation event has galvanized public opinion worldwide so dramatically as did Charles Lindbergh's solo crossing of the North Atlantic in a small, single-engine monoplane. Lindbergh burst upon the aeronautical scene in May 1927 when he suddenly showed up in New York after having crossed the country in record time, and then as suddenly took off for Paris. When word reached America of his successful crossing, the nation went wild, for the genuine, boyish, and heroic former airmail pilot had quickly captured the hearts of most Americans. He became "Lucky Lindy, the Lone Eagle" and even "the Flying Fool," as if his trip had been the most casual and reckless of stunts. In fact, this tall, lanky pilot, known as "Slim" to his fellow airmen, was a careful, methodical planner —and well acquainted with flight testing.

Lindbergh had briefly studied engineering at the University of Wisconsin but abandoned it to become a barnstormer and later an Army aviator. He graduated first in his class, a born pursuit pilot. No stranger to danger, he had to abandon one airplane following a midair collision while on gunnery practice (the other pilot also escaped). His next close scrape came during a test flight of a new experimental single-engine biplane called the "plywood special," at Lambert Field, St. Louis, in June 1925. A short and stubby biplane, it featured an awkward, airflow-disturbing radiator installation above each wing root on the lower wing. Like any test pilot, Lindbergh became familiar with the plane's every detail. Then came the all-important first flight. Lindbergh had planned to climb above 2,000 feet, to have enough height to successfully abandon the airplane should something happen. He climbed to 2,500 feet and checked its handling qualities with power on and power off, at various angles of attack. Then he undertook spin trials. Suddenly the plane whipped into a left-hand spin that quickly degenerated into a flat spin. Varying the controls and engine power had no effect, and the craft did not respond to the controls. There is a time to abandon a faithless airplane, a time many pilots, unfortunately, don't recognize, because of an almost hypnotic fascination with trying to recover, "trying to get the bird back home." Not so with Lindbergh, who calmly tried every procedure he knew and then realized the airplane could not be saved:

> The lunging continued. Fields and houses grew tremendous and the ground terribly close. Fingers snapped open the safety belt. Hands grasped cowlings. Legs shoved and flexed in piston actions. "I"—mind and senses and body as a unit—plunged out beyond the confines of the cockpit. Tug on shoulders—turn of body—harness hugging—canopy billowing, white on blue. I swung like the bob of a pendulum, barely two hundred feet from the bottom of earth's air. Body twists—feet hit ground —parachute drags me with the wind.[15]

At the price of a dislocated shoulder, Lindbergh had saved his life.

Lindbergh next flew the airmail between St. Louis and Chicago, and on two of these flights—always accompanied by danger from mechanical failure, storm, and fog—he had to abandon two more airplanes. During his lonely sojourns between the fog-shrouded earth and the clouded sky, Lindbergh pondered many questions. One his mind kept returning to was the possibility of winning the $25,000 prize offered by Raymond Orteig for the first New York-to-Paris flight. He approached the problem not as a reckless daredevil but as a thoughtful, accomplished pilot used to flying in marginal weather conditions in heavily loaded aircraft. He strove for maximum flight efficiency, rejecting multiengine aircraft on the grounds of complexity, poor aerodynamics, and unreliability, preferring a single-seat, single-engine monoplane. After searching for a suitable manufacturer, he settled upon the Ryan company, of San Diego, makers of a high-performance high-wing monoplane used on the airmail. But the *Spirit of St. Louis*, as Lindbergh eventually named his plane, was far more than a mere adaptation of an existing mail plane. It was an entirely new aircraft, and Lindbergh—unlike other pilots, who depended entirely upon their contractors—participated in its design as a full-fledged member of Donald Hall's design team. He decided to emphasize performance and aerodynamic cleanness, using a retractable side periscope to see ahead, placing the fuselage fuel tank ahead of the cockpit, selecting a new and highly reliable power plant, the 223-hp Wright J5C Whirlwind radial engine with a metal propeller, and a well-equipped cockpit. Indeed, at the time of its Atlantic flight, the *Spirit of St. Louis* had the finest instrumentation display of its day. Finally, in late April 1927, Ryan had the monoplane ready for its first flight.

On the morning of April 28, a bare two months since Lindbergh had placed his order, the tall pilot took off in the attractive silver airplane from Dutch Flats, at San Diego. Quickly he climbed over the factory, noting that the plane had "a huge reserve of power." At 2,000 feet he leveled off, flying across the military complex at North Island. He had no time for sight-seeing, and now Lindbergh the test pilot took command:

There are tests to run, and men waiting anxiously for the reports I'm to bring back. Ailerons ride a bit too high. The fin needs slight adjustment. I note these items down on my data board, and push the stick over to one side. The wing drops rather slowly. The ailerons on the *Spirit of St. Louis* aren't as fast as those on the standard Ryan. But we expected that. Hall made them short to avoid overstraining the wing under full-load conditions, and he gained a little efficiency by not carrying them all the way out to the tip. The response is good enough for a long-range airplane.

I straighten out, pull into a stall, and let go of the stick. The nose drops and has no tendency to come back up. The dive steepens and the right wing slants lower until I force the plane back to level flight again. I take my feet off the rudder, and steer with stick alone. The fuselage veers the opposite way to the ailerons. It's clear that stability isn't a strong point with the *Spirit of St. Louis*. But we didn't design the plane for stability. We decided to use the standard tail surfaces to save construction time, and possibly gain a little extra range.

What top speed can I make? That's one of the crucial tests. If the *Spirit of St. Louis* has enough speed and can take off with enough load, I can fly nonstop to Paris. Otherwise I can't. I drop down to one thousand feet, level off, and open throttle. The indicator starts to climb; 100------115------120------128 miles an hour, jumping up and down over several graduations in turbulent air. A hundred and twenty-eight miles an hour is encouraging too. If time over the measured course checks with the needle, then the speed exceeds Hall's calculations by three and a half miles. I throttle down and head toward the white houses of San Diego. That's enough for the first flight. There's no use doing more until ailerons and fin are adjusted.[16]

On the way back, a Navy Curtiss Hawk from North Island dived by for a look, and Lindbergh playfully banked about, beginning an impromptu mock dogfight that lasted for several minutes before he broke away and resumed course for Dutch Flats. Following "two or three" practice stalls, he brought the *Spirit* in for a perfect landing.

Following modifications, the *Spirit* resumed testing over the next few days. Finally, he hopped the continent to New York. When he took off from Roosevelt Field into aviation history, on May 20, 1927, it was with the full confidence of a test pilot who thoroughly understood the capabilities and limitations of his airplane and equipment—and himself— and certainly not the reckless act of a "Flying Fool." Lindbergh would fly many times in the future as a test pilot, and when, in 1969, the prestigious and exclusive Society of Experimental Test Pilots named him an Honorary Fellow of the SETP, it was a distinction he cherished until his death, and one that could not have been more fitting and appropriate.

THE GUGGENHEIM FUND: A BOLD EXPERIMENT IN FLIGHT RESEARCH

As the end of the decade approached, even the most casual observer of the aeronautical scene would have agreed that aviation had made enormous strides in the 1920s. Yet it is safely arguable that the most notable accomplishment of the 1920s in terms of flight safety was not an undertaking of the government or of some company but, rather, a "blind flying" research project sponsored by a unique aeronautical organization: The Daniel Guggenheim Fund for the Promotion of Aeronautics.

Without question, the Guggenheim Fund constituted the most important single activity influencing American aeronautics during the 1920s. Created in 1926 by Daniel Guggenheim, a then sixty-nine-year-old entrepreneur who had never flown in an airplane (and who had a heart condition so serious that he never would), the Guggenheim Fund sponsored university programs in aeronautical engineering, attempted (quite successfully) to make the American public "air-minded," established a "Model Air Line" on the West Coast that served as a working prototype of what eventually became the nation's coast-to-coast traffic-controlled airways system, and undertook two major flight research programs, one to "solve the problems of fog-flying" and the other to demonstrate the capabilities of what are now termed STOL (short-takeoff-and-landing) aircraft.

One of the major hazards afflicting aviation in the 1920s was bad-weather flying. Because pilots lacked adequate instrumentation to fly completely without ground or horizon references, casualties rose to often

fearful levels, especially over such fog-prone and tricky terrain as the airmail's infamous "Hell Stretch" of the Alleghenies between Ohio and
New York. In some instances, even the threat posed by zero visibility
caused pilots to abandon their otherwise functional aircraft. As pioneer
airman John Grierson has written, ". . . when the weather became impossible or the fuel ran out, the Irving parachute was there to be used."[17]
And pilots, as Lindbergh has related, were actually instructed that "A
good pilot doesn't depend on his instruments!"[18] Yet, by the mid-1930s,
all this had changed, and a pilot who flew without relying on his instrumentation was justly held in professional contempt. That this change occurred is due to the activities of the Guggenheim Fund and two distinguished Army test pilots: Jimmy Doolittle and Benjamin Kelsey.

Several problems were interrelated in the quest for a means of flying
blind, without access to external visual references. One concerned point-
to-point long-range navigation. A second involved developing more precise altimeters to avoid the serious built-in instrument lag that rendered
early models nearly useless during a quick descent. A third was the problem of developing a reliable magnetic compass. The fourth necessitated
developing some sort of instrument to provide the pilot with an artificial
horizon reference. With the solution of these problems, aviation safety
could be expected to make a great advance, hastening the day of true
around-the-clock commercial and military aircraft operations.

In late June 1928, Harry Guggenheim, Daniel's son and president of
the Guggenheim Fund (and a former naval aviator), announced that
the Fund would undertake actual technological and scientific research
with special emphasis on meteorology "and the problem of fog-flying."
Within a month, he and the Fund's trustees had decided to purchase
some aircraft and modify them as experimental "fog-flying" research
testbeds. Looking about for a pilot, young Guggenheim approached
Major General James Fechet, the chief of the Air Corps, who supplied
Doolittle, detached on special assignment, and later Ben Kelsey as well.
The Fund purchased two airplanes for research—a Consolidated NY-2
trainer and a powerful Vought O2U-1 Corsair—both two-seat single-engine designs, and using Army-furnished space, set up a "Full Flight Laboratory" at Mitchel Field, Long Island.

Because of Bureau of Standards work, experimental radio installations
already existed that could solve the long-range navigation problem.
Using a two-antenna radio beacon generating an A (·-) and N (-·)
Morse signal, the Bureau of Standards had developed the so-called "four
course" radio range. A pilot could approach an airfield by flying down
the "equisignal," the solid Morse dash (—) formed by the overlapping N
and A signals, where they merged and became one. If equipped with an
aural headset, he could hear the N and A gradually blend into a solid sig-

nal. Otherwise, he could use a visual course indicator consisting of two thin reeds that would vibrate, their apparent length indicating if the plane was to the right or the left of the equisignal, or (if both appeared to have equal length) on the equisignal itself. The Bureau of Standards' Aeronautical Research Division installed test equipment on board a modified De Havilland D.H. 4 and flew it from College Park, Maryland, in mid-1926. By the end of 1927, the Bureau felt confident enough to install experimental radio beacons on the New York to Cleveland airway, and by the beginning of 1928, Bureau test pilots routinely flew their D.H. 4 as far as 130 miles from the beacon, then navigated back to it using a reed indicator in the cockpit.

So, at the time the Guggenheim Fund established the Full Flight Laboratory, the pilot was no longer completely at the mercy of bad weather if he had a receiver and the airfield had a radio range. He could fly down the equisignal (the "beam," to most pilots), reach the "cone of silence" directly over the beacon, and then. . . . Then is when his real problems began. He had to complete a tricky letdown, using only his compass, a turn-and-bank indicator (which could not provide angle-of-attack information), his airspeed indicator, and an often lagging altimeter. And cloud or fog frequently extended right down to ground level. . . . For these reasons, Jerome Hunsaker, one of the nation's outstanding aeronautical engineers, wrote in 1927 that "safe landing in fog is not today possible and no means are in sight to make it so."[19] But in 1928 there was The Daniel Guggenheim Fund for the Promotion of Aeronautics, with its Full Flight Laboratory, at Mitchel Field.

Mitchel Field already had a standard McCook Field-tested 125-mile aural radio range for long-range navigation, and early in 1929, Bureau of Standards engineers installed a shorter-range, 15-mile "localizer" (landing beacon), enabling a pilot to fly right down the center of the field by watching a cockpit indicator having moving reeds to indicate the plane's position relative to the radio transmitter. Technicians installed this landing beacon on the east side of Mitchel Field. On the west side of the field, intersecting the landing beacon's equisignal, they installed an experimental "marker" beacon for Doolittle to use to begin his landing approach (i.e., landing from the west to the east, Doolittle would follow the localizer equisignal until another cockpit reed indicator registered that he had passed over the marker beacon; then he would begin a steady "blind" descent to touchdown). In fact, however, this early marker beacon proved of no use and Doolittle preferred to approach from the east, watching his reed indicator until it registered that he was over the localizer (i.e., in its "cone of silence"). Then he would set up a steady descent, landing to the west.

The Fund received both the NY-2 and the Corsair in late 1928, and

Doolittle flew both to gain proficiency in them. The slow and docile NY-2 was an ideal blind-flying airplane, and the Fund decided to use it for the actual research program, preferring the Corsair as a chase plane and general liaison craft. So slow was the NY-2 that, on one occasion, when Doolittle flew the plane from Mitchel Field to College Park, the flight took a full *five* hours, and the frustrated pilot watched automobiles on the roads below making better time! Finally, at the beginning of 1929, the Fund stood ready for its initial blind-flying research. With the assistance of Professor William Brown, an authority on flight research and Doolittle's former thesis and dissertation adviser at MIT, Doolittle and fellow pilot Ben Kelsey began flying the NY-2 around Long Island. Engineers had installed a closed hood over the rear cockpit of the trainer so that Doolittle, the research pilot, could not see out when undergoing tests. Kelsey rode in the open front cockpit as a safety pilot, a wise precaution in the already crowded skies near New York City.

Very quickly, the remaining three problems manifested themselves. The NY-2's existing altimeter lacked the precision necessary for a pilot to make a descent with confidence over fog- or cloud-shrouded terrain. The plane's magnetic compass also experienced known but nevertheless annoying problems of wandering during turning motions, either lagging behind or leading the airplane. The turn-and-bank indicator, while of course useful, nevertheless only indicated the rate of turn, not the degree of bank, nor did it indicate pitch (angle of attack). These three difficulties required solution if practical blind flying was to become a reality. Above all, one could not rely on "seat of the pants flying."

In 1926, an Air Corps researcher, Major David Myers, had proved beyond question that a pilot could not rely on his senses over his instrumentation. Myers placed veteran pilots in a Jones-Barany revolving chair, with their eyes covered. If he rotated the chair at a constant rate, they could not tell which way the chair was rotating. If he slowed the rotation rate, they invariably thought the rotation had stopped entirely! And finally, when he actually stopped the chair, they now thought it was rotating in the opposite direction! When aeromedical researcher Captain William Ocker added a turn-and-bank indicator and magnetic compass to the chair and then enclosed the pilot and instrumentation before rotating it, most pilots refused to believe their instrumentation, relying on false sensory cues, until they realized with a shock how misled they were.

On the night of March 15, 1929, Doolittle had a brush with danger that brought home forcibly the necessity of solving the blind-flying problem. He had gone to Buffalo on business, flying the Fund's O2U-1 Corsair. He took off on the return flight at night, in fair weather, planning to fly back to Mitchel Field via Albany and then down the Hudson River. After passing Albany, however, he encountered worsening weather conditions; he already had used half of his fuel and did not have enough to return to Buffalo. So he followed the lights of a southbound express train racing down the Hudson River Valley. It disappeared. Doolittle began following the dimly illuminated bank of the river itself. Eventually he reached New York City, but fog blanketed the entire East River area, rendering Mitchel Field inaccessible. Meanwhile, the fog had also closed in behind him, and Doolittle urgently hunted an emergency landing site, as the Corsair's gas gauge rested on empty.

He flew westward, away from populated areas, planning to bail out. Then, near Elizabeth, New Jersey, the pilot spotted a revolving airways beacon and, next to it, swathed in mist and fog, a flat area. He turned on his landing lights and descended for the small patch, flying low to ascertain whether it was suitable for landing; it was. He snagged a treetop with the Corsair's left lower wing, turned around, spotted the plot, and crash-landed, "wrapping the left wing around a tree trunk." "The moral of the story," Doolittle later wrote, "is that with the NY-2 mounting blind landing equipment and the Full Flight Laboratory radio station alerted at Mitchel, this would have been a routine cross-country flight with 'no sweat.' "[20]

This dramatic incident further strengthened the resolve of the Guggenheim test team to develop methods preventing such accidents from happening in the future. With characteristic thoroughness, Doolittle approached the problems of improving altimeters, finding some new form of reliable compass course indicator, and developing some new form of attitude indicator—an "artificial horizon." To develop a suitable altimeter, Doolittle, on the advice of the Bureau of Standards, turned to Paul Kollsman, a German-born instrument maker whose love of precision mechanisms had been nurtured amid the traditions of skilled craftsmen in his native Black Forest. Kollsman turned to Swiss watchmakers for appropriate gearing inside the altimeter, and the resulting instrument was over twenty times as sensitive as a standard service-quality barometric altimeter. Doolittle and Kollsman tested the altimeter in flight, with Kollsman carrying the instrument in his lap in the rear cockpit of the Fund's second Corsair, a more advanced O_2U-2, purchased after the crash of the earlier O_2U-1. The result: complete success. Doolittle had the Kollsman precision altimeter installed in the test cockpit of the NY-2.

For the suitable course indicator and the artificial horizon, Doolittle, quite naturally, turned to the undisputed authority on gyroscopic instrumentation, inventor Elmer Sperry, then age sixty-eight. It was the kind of task that Elmer's son Lawrence "Gyro" Sperry would have relished, but the younger Sperry had, tragically, drowned when his tiny Sperry Messenger biplane had crashed into the English Channel in December

1923. The elder Sperry delegated the task to his other son, Elmer, Jr. Together with Doolittle, young Sperry assembled a design team and set to work. Within months, they had developed an artificial horizon to complement the plane's existing turn-and-bank indicator, using a fixed airplane symbol superimposed over a horizon bar controlled by a gyroscope. This instrument provided the pilot with instant visual clues as to the attitude of the airplane: he could tell if the craft was in a climb, a dive, or banking flight in either a climb or a dive.

Next, Elmer Sperry, Jr., turned to the problem of developing a suitable instrument to complement the magnetic compass. The result was a nonmagnetic instrument, the directional gyrocompass. It consisted of a compass card attached to a gyro-controlled gimbal. The pilot would set it after reading his magnetic compass in straight-and-level (i.e., non-"accelerated" flight). The gyro stabilized the compass card, and a needle indicator would reveal any drift away from the desired course as the pilot maneuvered the plane through banks and turns.

Doolittle and Elmer Sperry, Jr., then went aloft with the experimental "directional gyro," flying over a section of railroad track near Mitchel Field, ascertaining the compass heading, setting the gyro, performing maneuvers, and flying about the countryside, and then returning to the railroad track to see how much the gyro had drifted off its original heading. As a result of these proving flights, Sperry modified the bearings inside to reduce friction and render the instrument less susceptible to drifting.

Finally, convinced that the directional gyro and the artificial horizon were ready for actual blind-flying tests, Doolittle had them installed in the NY-2. That sturdy trainer, equipped with Kollsman's precision altimeter, the directional gyro and artificial horizon, a radio transmitter, and aural and reed-indicator radio navigation receivers, was now the world's most advanced blind-flying research airplane.

Doolittle and his fellow test pilot, Ben Kelsey, now began flying the airplane around Mitchel Field on tests of the experimental equipment. Doolittle would take off in clear weather, Kelsey in the front cockpit as safety pilot, and navigate the airplane "blind," with the rear-cockpit hood closed. By early September, the two men had perfected the operation of the aircraft. All that remained was to demonstrate the craft under actual "fog-flying" conditions. Nature rewarded their patience on September 24, 1929. That morning, Jack Dalton, Doolittle's crew chief, awoke to notice pea-soup fog blanketing the field, perfect for testing an experimental blowtorch heater that inventor E. C. Reader hoped could be used to clear airfields of fog. However, Reader's little burner made scant impression on the thick mist rolling in from Long Island Sound.

Doolittle immediately realized that here was a perfect opportunity to test the NY-2 under actual fog conditions. He ordered the research airplane readied for flight; radio technicians manned the radio navigation equipment, mechanics warmed up the craft's engine, and then Doolittle climbed in, added full throttle, and took off to the west, disappearing from view almost immediately. He did not bother to close the enclosure over the rear cockpit—he did not need to, for visibility was nonexistent. While Elmer Sperry, Jr., and Doolittle's wife, Josephine, waited tensely on the ground, hearing the throbbing sound of the trainer's radial engine, Doolittle intently followed the localizer beam, watching his artificial horizon and directional gyro. He circled over Mitchel Field at an altitude of 500 feet, set up his descent guided by the Kollsman precision altimeter, and then landed, 10 minutes after takeoff. Just then, Harry Guggenheim arrived by auto from his mansion, together with other Fund representatives.

By 11 A.M. the fog was lifting. Guggenheim requested that Doolittle now make an "official" blind flight, this time with the canvas hood shut and with Ben Kelsey as safety pilot riding in the front seat, on the rare chance that the clearing conditions might have tempted another pilot to go aloft. Again Doolittle took off, as Kelsey sat with his hands resting outside the cockpit. The NY-2 climbed away to the west. Five miles out, Doolittle turned around, flew east seven miles, and again turned around, once more heading west, two miles from the field. He began a gradual descent, following the localizer beam until the indicator's reeds stopped vibrating, showing that the NY-2 was directly above the landing beacon. He then began a steady descent at 60 mph and held this until touchdown, fifteen minutes after takeoff. "Actually," the perfectionist test pilot later wrote, "despite previous practice, the final approach and landing were sloppy."[21] The age of instrument flying had arrived. For the first time in history, a pilot had taken off and flown a precise course through to landing, guided only by the instrumentation display within his cockpit. The next day, the New York *Times* commented on the flight, stating that "aviation had perhaps taken its greatest single step in safety."

After Doolittle's flight, blind flying proceeded rapidly. Kollsman and Sperry placed the three instruments developed at the Guggenheim Fund's behest into production, and they became indispensable for blind flying. In mid-1930, the Army added a blind-flying course to its advanced flight training program at Kelly Field. In July 1930, two Marine Corps test pilots, Arthur Page and V. M. Guymon, flew a modified Vought Corsair "blind" from Omaha, Nebraska, to Anacostia, via Chicago and Cleveland. Guymon, the safety pilot, would take control for landings only after Page, flying completely blind in an enclosure, had brought the biplane down to an altitude of 200 feet on final approach. On May 9, 1932, Army test pilot Albert Hegenberger completed the first solo blind flight enclosed "under the hood" without a safety pilot from takeoff to landing, at Wright Field. (Orville Wright, walking to church that Sunday morning, noted with annoyance the noisy airplane and asked an Air Corps officer also on his way to church what the apparently joy-riding aviator was doing flying on Sunday. The officer promised, "Who-ever he is, Mr. Wright, we'll talk to him about it."[22]) Hegenberger used a newly developed radio compass, an aerial direction finder to assist in navigating the plane. He later stated:

> It was tougher flying under the hood than flying in fog. . . . In the thickest weather you feel you've got a chance for a break at any instant and that's consoling. But in that blacked-out cockpit you're really on your own, and God help you if you haven't got faith in those little dials in front of you.[23]

In March 1933, Bureau of Standards test pilot James Kinney piloted an experimental Bellanca monoplane under actual bad-weather conditions from College Park to Newark, carrying two passengers and following a newly developed "glide slope beam" down to a precision landing at Newark in weather conditions that had grounded all other aircraft. Finally, on August 23, 1937, Army test pilots Carl Crane and George Holloman and engineer Raymond Stout flight-tested an old Fokker monoplane modified to have an automatic pilot connected to the craft's radio navigation gear. That day, as Holloman later described the flight,

> We took off and circled the field once. Then we turned on the automatic pilot and tuned in the Indianapolis radio station. We flew for about an hour and found ourselves circling over Indianapolis. Then we changed the station on the radio and tuned in on Dayton, and the plane flew without fault over the same distance, and before we knew it we were back over Wright Field. We then tuned in on the localizer stations, put the radio compass and automatic pilot combination to work and the plane settled itself to a smooth landing. About all we did was sit there with arms folded and pray that everything would function right and it did. That's all there was to it.[24]

And so arrived the age of electronic flight. The passenger in today's jumbo jet, crossing the Atlantic near the speed of sound, gives little thought to the electronic network that keeps his craft on course over an invisible highway in the sky. But the network is there, and while the instrumentation has changed dramatically since those early days of the Guggenheim Fund and Wright Field, it is descended from those first few instruments tested and evaluated by a handful of flight researchers and test pilots, men who ended the era of "seat of the pants" flying.

By the end of the twenties, the state of aircraft design had advanced dramatically. Gone were the largely wooden-framed biplanes and early monoplanes. The wooden Lockheed Vega of the mid-1920s constituted a noteworthy design, for this pretty passenger monoplane had a wooden monocoque fuselage (indeed, it reintroduced the monocoque configuration to the United States), a cantilever (internally braced) wing set above the fuselage, and a similarly constructed tail group. The elegant Vega's sleek shape and smoothly rounded contours embodied the very essence of the streamline doctrine.

Streamlining underwent a major advance with the introduction of the NACA engine cowling, which appeared in 1928. As a result of Navy and industry concern, the NACA had embarked on a study of means whereby the drag of radial engines could be reduced and the cooling characteristics of these engines improved. Engineer Fred Weick (later known for his design of the Ercoupe sports plane) developed a cowling shape that fitted closely around the engine. Hundreds of tests in the NACA's Propeller Research Tunnel, at Langley, followed, and then NACA technicians installed a similar shape on an Army Curtiss AT-5A trainer. NACA flight tests revealed that the cowling not only improved engine cooling by directing a high-velocity airstream around the hot cylinders but that the shape reduced total drag so greatly that the speed of the AT-5A jumped from 118 to 137 mph, equivalent to adding 83 hp to the engine! By 1932, the NACA cowling was *de rigueur* for all new radial engine designs.

As a result of work by propeller researcher Frank Caldwell, the path had been cleared for the advent of the variable-pitch propeller, which enabled an airplane to achieve maximum propulsive efficiency at both low and high speeds over various altitudes and various power settings. (Nevertheless, it is surprising to note that when Britain went to war in 1939, her Hurricane and Spitfire fighters were equipped with fixed-pitch propellers, already well behind the state of the art.)

As a further attempt to improve the high-speed performance of aircraft, researchers at McCook Field tested aircraft with radiator installations using water mixed with ethylene glycol instead of the traditional water for cooling. The water-glycol mix, which soon became standard, enabled engineers to design much smaller radiators, which further reduced the frontal area of airplanes and hence reduced the drag. But as aircraft speeds rose higher and higher, so did landing speeds and low-speed accidents. Designers turned to the other end of the performance spectrum, to safe slow-speed flight.

This interest led to the Guggenheim Safe Aircraft Competition of 1929, a milestone event in the history of STOL (short-takeoff-and-landing) aircraft. As with the blind-flying research program, the impetus for the competition came from flight safety. One of the major accident causes was a low-altitude stall followed by a spin into the ground. Pilots, to avoid stalling, would increase their landing speed, and thus often crash when landing on small fields. The quest to alleviate these problems led to the development of a variety of aircraft and mechanical devices, including the Cierva Autogiro (a distant ancestor of the helicopter), the Westland-Hill Pterodactyl tailless aircraft, and the Handley Page - Gustav Lachmann wing slat, as well as greater reliance on wing flaps and such unconventional ideas as variable-camber wings. Over the summer of 1926, the Fund drew up a series of rules, stipulating, for example, that any aircraft entered in the competition have a landing speed no greater than 30 mph, a maximum landing run of only 100 feet, and a minimum controllable level flight speed of 35 mph. The Guggenheims hoped that the competition would stimulate the creation of influential new designs.

Eventually, the competition got underway at Mitchel Field in the fall of 1929, with a variety of airplanes exhibiting novel features. One, designed by Heraclio Alfaro, had large flaps and spoilers for roll control. "Shorty" Schroeder entered a variable-camber design, but during preliminary flight testing it entered an uncontrolled power-on spiral at 500 feet and crashed into a street, missing a nearby hospital. Schroeder crawled from the wreckage and lamely explained that his lack of injuries demonstrated the safety of the plane. James McDonnell entered a small monoplane called the Doodlebug, the "aerial flivver of the future." During a shallow dive, however, the "aerial flivver" folded up its horizontal tail and pitched nose down. Dreams rapidly shattering, young "Mac" McDonnell unstrapped and prepared to abandon the plane to its fate. Then his Scots heritage overcame basic survival instincts: he wanted to find what caused the tail to fail. As the game test pilot struggled with the controls, the Doodlebug fluttered down to the ground. Spectators pulled the injured pilot from the wreckage, and surgeons later removed one of his spinal discs. McDonnell reluctantly gave up test flying and instead went on to mastermind the creation and eventual evolution of the giant McDonnell Douglas aircraft empire. The Guggenheim Fund's organizers had hoped that a Pterodactyl or an Autogiro might enter the competition, but neither of these interesting vehicles appeared. Rather, the competition quickly narrowed to two airplanes: the Curtiss Tanager and the British Handley Page Gugnunc. Once again, the federal government supported the Fund's activities, supplying test pilots to evaluate the various craft. The Army furnished Stanley Umstead, whose most characteristic trait was an ever-present stogie, and the Navy sent Eddie Rounds up from Anacostia. The Fund also hired Thomas Carroll, who had flown with the NACA. One Fund representative later wrote that all three were "men of exceptional skill and experience and their handling of the various planes with their novel flying features was beyond criticism."[25]

The lithe and attractive Gugnunc had almost a sesquiplane configuration, with a large upper wing having full-span leading-edge slats and broad trailing-edge flaps, as well as full-span flaps on the lower wing. It had an adjustable stabilizer and a long-stroke steel-tube oleo landing gear with wheel brakes. Dapper British test pilot James Cordes had completed its first flight at Cricklewood Aerodrome at the end of April, 1929, and he and fellow test pilot, T. H. England, had further tested it at Martlesham Heath before delivering it to the United States for the Guggenheim competition. The Curtiss Tanager, which finally won the safe-aircraft competition, was a larger and heavier aircraft than the British airplane, with a fully enclosed cabin, full-span flaps and slats on the upper and lower wings, and so-called "floating" ailerons on the tips of the lower wings. Curtiss test pilot Paul Boyd completed its first flight on October 12, 1929, and delivered it to Mitchel Field later in the month. Now the competition began in earnest.

Jim Cordes had demonstrated the Gugnunc on October 3, impressing all who saw it, and later in the day, Stan Umstead and Tom Carroll had also flown it, discovering that they could handle the docile craft almost as skillfully as the British pilot, despite their lack of familiarity with it. Likewise, when Boyd demonstrated the Tanager, a gorgeous scarlet-and-black airplane, all eyes took notice. Both the Tanager and the Gugnunc clearly met the general requirements of the competition, and so detailed evaluation of their flying qualities now began. By early December, the Tanager had surpassed the Gugnunc in two areas: landing in a confined space, and maintaining a gliding speed of not more than 38 mph. The Tanager's structure proved more robust during steep landings, and while the Gugnunc was faster (at 112.4 mph) by .8 mph, the Tanager could fly slower in powered flight, at 30.6 mph compared to 33.4. On January 6, 1930, the Fund presented Curtiss with a check for $100,000, the Tanager having clearly won. Wisely, Fund vice-president Emory Land remarked to assembled representatives of the aircraft industry that "No one in the Fund expected to obtain a 'foolproof' plane. There isn't any such animal. Moving masses cannot be made 'foolproof,' but they can be made safe. Old Man Kinetic Energy can always do damage to a fool."[26]

The Guggenheim Fund's flight testing competition formulated the requirements for STOL aircraft long before many in the aeronautical community recognized a need for them. When the STOL aircraft of the late 1930s appeared, such as the Ryan Dragonfly and the superlative Fieseler Storch, they differed little aerodynamically from the Guggenheim conceptions of a decade earlier. The great increase in engine power gave them better performance, of course, compared to the earlier Tanager and Gugnunc. The competition inspired Otto Koppen, a professor at MIT, and Lynn Bollinger to develop the Koppen Bollinger Helioplane, first flown in a secret test in April 1949. The Helioplane itself inspired more powerful successors as the superlative Helio Courier and Helio Stallion, the outstanding single-engine STOL craft of the 1960s.

TRAINING THE TEST PILOT OF THE TWENTIES

The professionalization of the test pilot kept pace with the rapid advances in aircraft technology. By the end of the 1920s, the military services and private organizations were issuing flight testing guides. One of these, by William Gerhardt and Lawrence Kerber, who had cut their teeth in flight testing at McCook Field, had great subsequent influence on the growth of the flight research profession. Entitled *A Manual of Flight-Test Procedure* and issued in 1927 by the University of Michigan's Department of Engineering Research, this book covered both production testing and research testing, including establishing a research plan, computation and reduction of data, error determination and elimination, aircraft performance testing, evaluation of aircraft components, readying a test aircraft for flight, and installation and calibration of test instruments. Engineers and flight researchers recognized that the training of test pilots was of great significance. Lieutenant Eugene Barksdale, at McCook, one of the Army's finest test pilots, had addressed this question in May 1926 by preparing a course for the training of prospective test pilots. His manual, entitled *Flight Testing of Aircraft*, stated in part that

> The object of this Course is primarily to teach a systematic method of testing aircraft and equipment in flight. It is intended to develop the ability of analyzing the behavior, possibilities, and limitations of aircraft and equipment, as distinguished from performance testing.
>
> Airplanes of various types will be studied as regards their equipment, controls, powerplant, functions, etc. Then a series of flights will be made to observe certain characteristics of the airplane in flight, to determine whether or not it fulfills the functions for which it was designed and to note all other pertinent information. The information required will be noted on a standard tabulated form consisting of seven pages.

REQUIREMENTS

Each officer will complete a flight test of at least one airplane and equipment per month. The first day of the following month a report on this test will be due which will consist of

(a) The completed flight test forms.
(b) Time required and dates for each
part of test.
(c) Remarks, if any.

The articles "Flight Testing at McCook Field" and "Stick Forces" incorporated in this manual, should be thoroughly understood.

Flight tests should be made of the following airplanes, preferably in the order given:

VE-9 (or VE-7)
DH-4B
SE-5
CO-4
CO-6
XO-2
C-1
PW-8 (or PW-9)
DT-2
TA-5
Sperry Messenger
COA-1
PT-1
P-1 [27]

This thorough and intensive flying program further gives the lie to early flight testing's being a haphazard, reckless activity lacking in systematic methods and organization. Sadly, however, flight research has always involved some degree of personal risk, and less than three months after issuing this manual, Gene Barksdale was dead, killed in the crash of an experimental observation plane.

At the end of 1929, from the vantage point of a world just entering the turmoil of the Great Depression, aeronautical observers could note with great satisfaction the progress in aeronautics made during the 1920s: radio navigation, blind-flight instrumentation, passenger airline service, refined high-speed aircraft design, knowledge of flight structures and structural requirements, development of specialized military aircraft including the operation of aircraft from ships at sea. Aviation had come a long way in the Jazz Age, furthered in large measure by the skill, dedication and, sometimes, the sacrifice of test pilots and flight researchers. There were, of course, many challenges ahead: flight in the stratosphere;

development of practical, economical, and reliable airliners and military aircraft; the design of new aerodynamic shapes to meet the demands of high-speed flight on the frontiers of knowledge; and the development of new and powerful propulsion systems. All these would require the continued hard work of engineers, industrialists, researchers, and flight testers. Cyril Uwins, a British test pilot of exceptional ability who flew for Bristol, testing that company's products during a thirty-year career, expressed perfectly the progressive impulse in flight research during a lecture before the Royal Aeronautical Society in May 1929. "Test flying," he said, "has its great attractions and occasionally its anxious moments, but it is the branch of aviation in which one appreciates at first hand how much we *still* have to learn."[28]

THE HERITAGE OF FLIGHT RESEARCH: A PHOTO ESSAY

Unless otherwise listed, illustrations are courtesy
of the National Air and Space Museum,
Smithsonian Institution, Washington, D.C.

The Seven Who Started It All

Modern aviation owes its development to seven individuals who took the dreams of centuries and generated the necessary technological base for the realities of today.

Joseph Montgolfier

Etienne Montgolfier

Joseph and Etienne Montgolfier built the first lighter-than-air vehicles—balloons sent aloft by hot gases generated from burning straw—during 1783, the "Year of Miracles" in pre-revolutionary France.

Sir George Cayley

Sir George Cayley, a noted British inventor considered the father of aerodynamics, derived the modern airplane configuration and undertook notable experiments with small gliders in the early part of the nineteenth century.

Otto Lilienthal

Lilienthal in flight

Otto Lilienthal, a prominent German engineer, gained personal fame and gave aeronautics professional respectability before his untimely death in a hang-gliding accident in 1896. His blending of ground-based and in-flight research furnished a research model that encouraged the activities of subsequent pioneers.

Octave Chanute

Chanute glider in flight

Octave Chanute, the most distinguished of late-nineteenth-century American engineers, served as a "clearinghouse" of technical information for his fellow pioneers, wrote widely and influentially on aviation topics, and developed his own family of research gliders. His contributions in flight structures had profound impact on subsequent aircraft design. Here one of his triplane gliders is shown skimming the dunes of Lake Michigan.

Orville and Wilbur Wright

Ohio brothers Wilbur and Orville Wright (left and right, respectively) worked tenaciously on the problem of heavier-than-air flight, inspired in part by the activities of earlier pioneers such as Lilienthal and Chanute. But the triumph of powered flight was all theirs, thanks to insightful and creative research that blended theory and testing on the ground with flight testing aloft.

Triumph at Kitty Hawk

Recognizing that they needed an unobstructed area having favorable weather conditions for their testing, the Wright brothers selected the windswept dunes of Kitty Hawk, North Carolina, for their flight test site.

Wright 1902 glider

Though they started with kites, the Wright brothers quickly moved on to man-carrying gliders. Here the 1902 glider is launched from the dunes of Kitty Hawk; with this machine, they refined their concept of controllability.

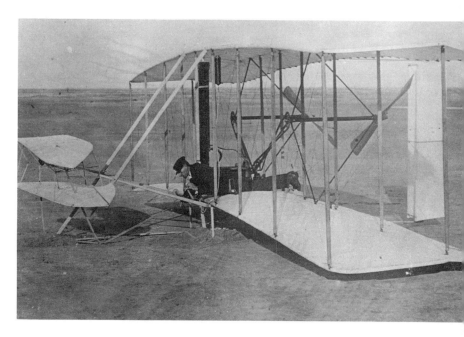

Wright 1903 Flyer on first test

The next step was constructing the powered 1903 Kitty Hawk Flyer. On December 14, 1903, Wilbur Wright attempts the first flight, but over-controls, stalling out and settling heavily to earth, the Flyer sustaining minor damage that necessitates two days of repairs.

Wright 1903 Flyer on first flight

On December 17, 1903, at 10:35 A.M., the era of powered flight dawns as Orville Wright takes off into the face of a 27 mile per hour wind, covers 120 feet, and remains aloft 12 seconds.

Wright 1903 Flyer after last flight

Three more flights that day are made by Orville and Wilbur, the last of which covers 852 feet and lasts 59 seconds. A hard landing by Wilbur inflicts minor damage shown here; but minutes later, rising winds flip the Flyer over and over, damaging it severely and bringing the Wrights' trials for 1903 to an end.

The Legacy of Kitty Hawk

Wright 1905 Flyer

In 1905, the Wrights begin flight tests of a new Flyer at Huffman Prairie, east of Dayton, Ohio, near the banks of the Mad River. The 1905 machine is the first practical powered aircraft possessing full maneuverability and capable of repeated reuse. It inspires all subsequent Flyers.

Wright Flyer in Germany, 1909

In August 1909, Orville demonstrates the Wright Flyer to German dignitaries at Tempelhof and Potsdam; here he passes before a group including the Empress of Germany. The Wrights' European tours in 1908 and 1909 reawakened European aviation which had lain dormant following the death of Lilienthal in 1896 and Percy Pilcher in 1899; the Europeans quickly adopted the Wright approach—and then went rapidly beyond it.

Army Mono Biplane SE 1 (Hallion collection)

At first European efforts are somewhat crude, as with this British S.E. 1 biplane tested at Farnborough . . .

Etrich Taube prototype (Hallion collection)

. . . or this birdlike monoplane built by Igo Etrich in 1911. But such vehicles provide the basis for refined and advanced airplanes such as . . .

Rumpler Taube

. . . the graceful Rumpler *Taube* that typified pre-war German aviation, or

Deperdussin Military Monoplane

. . . the French Deperdussin Military Monoplane, which anticipated the high-speed "fighting scouts" of the First World War.

Deperdussin Monocoque Racer

The French Deperdussin Monocoque Racer, designed by Louis Bechereau, was a true advanced technology demonstrator that introduced shell-type construction techniques and refined aerodynamics, some of which were not fully exploited until the end of the 1920s.

Edward Teshmaker Busk (Royal Aircraft Establishment, Crown Copyright Reserved)

Development of advanced aircraft demanded the equivalent evolution of test pilots thoroughly conversant with science and technology. One of the most influential was Britain's Edward Teshmaker Busk, shown here in the cockpit of a Royal Aircraft Factory R.E. 1, at Farnborough, in autumn of 1913. Busk established traditions of training and professionalism for test pilots and flight test engineers that persist to the present day.

Al Welsh (USAF Photo)

As with England's Busk, early American flight testing took a heavy toll of pioneers. Wright test pilot Al Welsh, shown at the controls of a late model Wright Flyer, perished in a fatal crash at College Park, Maryland, the Army's first flight testing center.

Glenn Curtiss

The best-known early developer of airplanes in the United States, aside from the Wrights, was Glenn Curtiss, who started by working for Alexander Graham Bell's Aerial Experiment Association in Canada. There he had helped pioneer Canadian aviation, working with the first Canadian pilot, J. A. D. McCurdy.

Casey Jones

Adopting the same pusher layout as the Wrights, but using a single propeller and ailerons for roll control in place of the Wrights' wing-warping, Curtiss generated an important and influential design called the "Headless Pusher." Flown by skilled test pilots and demonstration pilots such as C. S. "Casey" Jones, the Curtiss design proved irresistible to military aviators seeking newer and more advanced aircraft.

Eugene Ely flying off *Birmingham*

Modified Curtiss pushers introduced the Navy to flight. Here Curtiss test pilot Eugene Ely flies from the deck of the cruiser *Birmingham* in 1911.

Curtiss Triad

The Curtiss Triad, a "hydroaeroplane," could operate from land or water. Here Glenn Curtiss prepares to demonstrate it to Lt. "Spuds" Ellyson, USN—the first naval aviator.

Lawrence Sperry and French mechanic

Other pioneers worked with Curtiss or made use of Curtiss airplanes for important flight research purposes. Here Lawrence Sperry and mechanic Emil Cachin are shown at Bezons, France, during trials of the Sperry automatic stabilizer in 1914.

The Great War

Of greater significance to military affairs than generally recognized, aviation during the First World War made remarkable strides, thanks in part to the tremendous forcing function of military necessity upon technology. By war's end, America and Great Britain had developed aircraft capable of spanning the Atlantic Ocean—which two did, in 1919. European designers were particularly active in seeking new uses for aircraft and experimenting with new design concepts . . .

Sopwith Camel aircraft

. . . such as this experimental Sopwith Camel "dogfighter" modified with armor and additional machine guns to serve as a ground-attack airplane . . .

Junkers J-7

. . . or the Junkers J-7, the prototype of the world's first all-metal monoplane fighter. Experimental craft such as this benefited from the work of German researchers who had developed a small all-metal wing as early as 1915 . . .

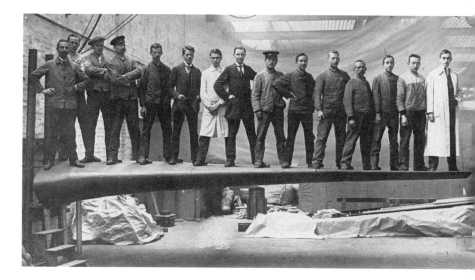

Wing structural test (Hallion collection)

. . . demonstrating its strength in this dramatic fashion .

Fokker D VII (Hallion collection)

American researchers were eager to evaluate the latest European aeronautical technology, welcoming the opportunity, for example, to examine the German Fokker D VII, the finest single-seat fighter of the First World War. Here is a captured Fokker, test flown by the U. S. Army at McCook Field, Ohio, after the war and with an American-built Liberty engine.

During the war, American designers took their cue from European developments—a sad demonstration of how far behind the United States had slipped since the pioneering years of the Wrights and Glenn Curtiss. Designers either copied European designs outright or with some modifications, or else designed aircraft that obviously owed a great deal to European technology.

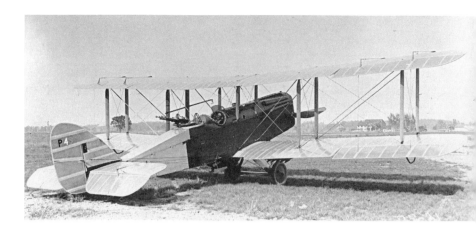

USD-9A (Hallion collection)

One of these European-inspired aircraft was the Army's USD-9A, an American-built version of the de Havilland D.H. 9 bomber, shown here ready for flight testing at McCook Field.

U.S. Bristol Fighter (Hallion collection)

Ironically, the least successful of these copy efforts involved the American attempt to duplicate Great Britain's eminently successful two-seat Bristol Fighter, arguably the finest all-around fighter of the First World War. The USXB-1A, the American copy, was powered by a Liberty engine; one of these ill-fated aircraft is shown here, at McCook Field.

American designers did try their hand at their own designs, with varying degrees of success. Here are two of the most intriguing, from a "what-might-have-been" standpoint:

VCP-1 (Hallion collection)

The Army Engineering Division's VCP-1, designed by Alfred Verville and Virginius Clark, was a rakish and highly advanced fighter prototype . . .

Orenco Model D (Hallion collection)

. . . while the Orenco Model D experimental fighter, also built at McCook Field late in the war, represented a more traditional design approach.

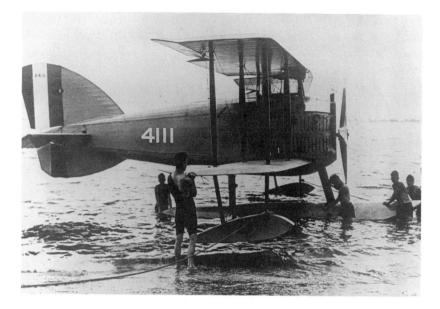

Curtiss HA "Dunkirk Fighter"

It was the Navy-designed Curtiss HA "Dunkirk Fighter," however, that gave rise to perhaps the most dramatic flight test anecdotes surrounding early American fighter development.

Roland Rohlfs

Test pilot Roland Rohlfs managed to survive the HA's wilder antics, thanks to his piloting skill—and not a little luck.

Crucible of Flight: McCook and Wright Fields

During the interwar years, McCook and Wright fields—the predecessors of today's Edwards Air Force Base—were crucibles of aviation technology. Together with the National Advisory Committee for Aeronautics' (NACA) Langley Memorial Research Laboratory, they profoundly shaped the future course of American—and world—aviation.

McCook Field (USAF photo)

This 1922 photograph gives a good idea of the small size of McCook Field, which eventually forced the Army Air Service to move farther east of Dayton, Ohio, to Wright Field in 1927, near the old Huffman Prairie test site of the Wright brothers.

Through the years, McCook and Wright test pilots retained and elaborated upon the quality of excellence that had always characterized their work; the background airplanes might change, but the standards of profession-alism—and courage—remained the same.

Early test pilots (I) (USAF Photo)

Here the McCook Flight Test Branch poses in front of one of the disappointing American Bristol fighters in 1918 (fifth from the left is Rudolph "Shorty" Schroeder).

Early test pilots (II) (USAF photo)

Ten McCook pilots pose with the "Flying Jackass" and "Quacking Duck" trophies awarded for less-than-meritorious flight testing, particularly "quacking up" an airplane: (from left to right; back row) Ralph Lockwood, Harry Johnson, Eugene "Hoy" Barksdale, James Hutchison, Reuben Moffat, and Louis Meister (front row) John Macready, William Amis, George Tourtellot, James "Jimmy" Doolittle.

Early test pilots (III)

A later group of Wright test pilots pose with their Curtiss fighter and commanding officer Capt. James St. Clair Street. Left to right: Lieutenants Berry, Corkille, and Haddon; Captain Street; and Lieutenants Amis, Eubank, and Parker.

Early test pilots (IV) (USAF Photo)

Wright pilots of the late 1930s pose with a gleaming Seversky P-35 fighter. Second from the right is Capt. Stan Umstead, with his ever-present stogie.

LUSAC 11 with Turbocharger (USAF Photo)

The LUSAC 11 two-place fighter was an attractive and robust machine that appeared too late for wartime service. Instead, it flew at McCook Field as a high-altitude research airplane. Modified with an engine turbosupercharger to boost its performance, the LUSAC 11 completed a number of remarkable flights that were as much a testimony to the abilities and stamina of test pilot Shorty Schroeder as they were a tribute to the significance of the turbosupercharger.

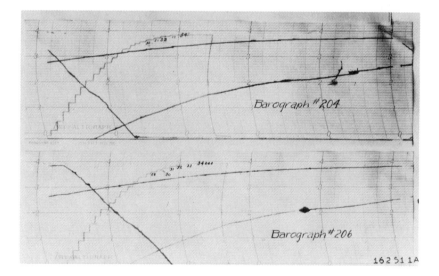

Barograph data strip (USAF Photo)

A sample of the Hué barograph data taken from a LUSAC 11 flight by Schroeder and observer George Elsey during an October 4, 1919, flight to a true altitude of 31,800 feet.

Harold Harris

Harold Harris, a genial individual and one of the Army's earliest test pilots, survived the first emergency bailout (from a disintegrating experimental fighter) and the first attempt to fly a pressurized cabin airplane. Harris typified McCook pilots, who could go from flying a trim fighter . . .

Barling bomber (USAF Photo)

. . . to something as grotesque as the ungainly and unsuccessful Barling Bomber.

Doolittle

James H. "Jimmy" Doolittle became the best known of the McCook and early Wright Field test pilots. In contrast to his daredevil and sensational public image (largely a product of the popular press), Doolittle was a thoroughgoing aeronautical professional, and the first to earn a doctorate of science (from the Massachusetts Institute of Technology) on the basis of flight test research.

Fokker PW-7

Doolittle's reputation rested upon careful, methodical, and cautious flight planning and execution. Typical was his work with the experimental Fokker PW-7, used to derive new structural criteria for aircraft design: if Doolittle had been less cautious, the plane likely would have crashed and killed him.

"NACA Langley"

Curtiss JN-4 Jenny (NASA Photo)

Following creation of the National Advisory Committee for Aeronautics (NACA, predecessor of today's NASA) in 1915, committee leadership moved quickly to establish the Langley Memorial Aeronautical Laboratory at Langley Field, Virginia. Here is a Curtiss JN-4H Jenny operated by the NACA from Langley on the first NACA research flights.

Test pilot and observer (National Archives)

NACA, as its charter demanded, pioneered the "scientific study of the problems of flight." Here test pilot Thomas Carroll and flight test observer John "Gus" Crowley prepare to take off on a test mission.

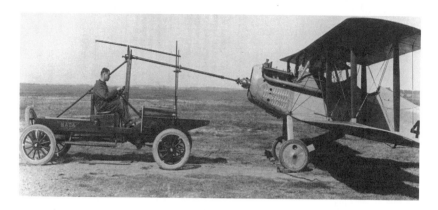

Vought VE-7 and Hucks Starter (National Archives)

As technology advanced, so too did the range of research airplanes used by NACA, such as this Vought VE-7 used for aerodynamic research. Here a NACA mechanic demonstrates starting the Vought's engine by using a Hucks starter gear-and-chain-driven from the engine of a modified Ford truck.

AT-5A on NACA cowl tests (Hallion collection)

Arguably NACA's single most-important flight research program in the late 1920s was the validation of the so-called NACA engine cowling shape. Here is the Curtiss AT-5A trainer used for those tests, shown with the streamlined cowl and side fairings that boosted its speed by 19 mph: equivalent to adding 83 additional horsepower.

Air Racers: Useful Technology Demonstrators

Until the advent of the post–Second World War "X-series" aricraft, air racers constituted a unique group of high-speed flight research airplanes. While their design was sometimes bizarre and they were used for publicity and record-breaking flights more than for pure or applied research (particularly true of later pre–Second World War ones), they nevertheless served a vital function as technology demonstrators and integrators for future generations of high-performance airplanes, much as the Deperdussin Monocoque Racer and Sopwith Tabloid had served before the First World War.

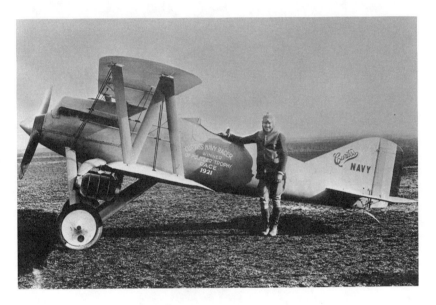

Curtiss CR-1 and Bert Acosta

The Curtiss company dominated world air racing in the mid-1920s with its elegant biplane racers, beginning with the Curtiss CR-1, shown with suave company test pilot Bert Acosta. The shapely CR-1 and later Curtiss racers influenced the design of subsequent American fighters and liquid-cooled engines.

Curtiss R-8 with Alex Pearson (USAF Photo)

Air racers were intolerant of faults or pilot error. In 1924, Alex Pearson, a fine Army test pilot, lost his life in the Curtiss R-8, when aerodynamic flutter set in during a high-speed dive, ripping a strut loose; the plane shed a wing and snap-rolled into the ground.

Curtiss R3C-2 with Jimmy Doolittle

The shapely Curtiss R3C-2 racer was the epitome of biplane racer design. Jimmy Doolittle, shown here with one of them, set a world's speed record of 245.713 mph while flying one of these in 1925.

Verville-Sperry R-3 (USAF Photo)

With the advent of the Verville-Sperry R-3 the future clearly belonged to the high-speed monoplane. The R-3 introduced a retractable landing gear, together with the streamlined, low-wing layout that would dominate fighter aircraft design until the era of the turbojet. First flown in 1923, the R-3 might have hastened the introduction of the "modern" fighter by at least another decade, if designers had paid greater attention to this advanced technology demonstrator.

Charles Augustus Lindbergh

Charles Lindbergh with *Spirit of St. Louis*

Spirit of St. Louis on ground

One of the most remarkable feats of flying during the interwar years was the solo crossing of the North Atlantic, from New York to Paris, by Charles Augustus Lindbergh, a young air-mail pilot, in May 1927 in the *Spirit of St. Louis*, a specially built Ryan long-range monoplane. While the public hailed him as the "Lone Eagle," some dismissed him as "Lucky Lindy," or even "The Flying Fool." In reality, Lindbergh was a highly skilled airman who embodied the classic strengths of a test pilot: careful and methodical planning coupled with courage and resolute execution.

The Guggenheim Fund:
A Bold Experiment in Flight Research

Guggenheim trustees

In 1926, financier Daniel M. Guggenheim and his son Harry F. Guggenheim established a nearly $3 million fund to support the development of aviation. The fund issued grants for education programs at the secondary school, college, and university level, and also undertook a number of actual flight research projects. Here the fund trustees (including Charles Lindbergh, third from the right in the back row, and Orville Wright, second from the right in the front row) pose with founder Daniel Guggenheim and fund president Harry Guggenheim (second from the left, front row, and second from the right, back row, respectively).

Model of NY-2

The fund undertook pioneering research on the problems of blind flight—flight by using cockpit instrumentation alone, without external visual references—using an extensively modified Consolidated NY-2 trainer. (Model by Robert C. Mikesh)

NY-2 cockpit

Using experimental instrumentation including a Sperry gyrocompass, Sperry artificial horizon, Kollsman precision altimeter, and rudimentary radio navigation equipment, project pilot Jimmy Doolittle completed the world's first successful blind flight on September 24, 1929. Here is a photograph of the NY-2's experimental "blind-flying" panel in the plane's aft cockpit.

Curtiss Tanager climbing

The Guggenheim fund extensively studied short-takeoff-and-landing (STOL) aircraft in a comprehensive Safe Aircraft Competition. Here the winning Curtiss Tanager biplane is shown climbing steeply during trials, piloted by Stan Umstead.

Robert Goddard, Harry Guggenheim, and Charles Lindbergh

Guggenheim interest did not end with the airplane. In 1930, the Guggenheims undertook their first grants to support the liquid-fuel rocket experiments of physicist Robert Hutchings Goddard. Here Goddard—the father
of the modern rocket—is shown flanked by Harry Guggenheim and
Guggenheim advisor Charles Lindbergh in front of his test stand in the
New Mexican desert.

The Drive for the "Modern" Airplane

Northrop Alpha

Advances in aerodynamics, structures, and propulsion technology directly led to the advent of the modern monoplane in the early 1930s. An important predecessor was the low-wing all-metal Northrop Alpha of 1930.

Wiley Post

Famed aviator Wiley Post, a one-eyed pilot from Oklahoma, was one of a number of test pilots whose work made possible the modern airplane. Post coupled the showmanship of a barnstormer and aerial adventurer with the shrewd insight and careful calculation of a test pilot. Flying a modified Lockheed Vega named the *Winnie Mae,* he made substantial contributions to the study of high-altitude flight. His fondest wish was to establish an aeronautical research laboratory—a wish that remained unfilled at the time of his death in a flying accident in 1935.

Willis Wells, Eddie Allen, and Dean Smith (Hallion Collection)

Post was one of many important test pilots in the 1930s whose work led to the advent of the modern commercial and military airplane. Another was Edmund T. "Eddie" Allen, a truly legendary test pilot, killed during the Second World War in the crash of an experimental bomber. Here Allen (center) is shown in 1940, flanked by fellow pilots Willis Wells (left) and Dean Smith (right) before the first flight of the Curtiss-Wright CW-20 transport—at the time America's largest twin-engine airliner.

Douglas DC-1

In 1933, the fruition of the intense aeronautical research of the 1920s and early 1930s manifested itself in two new designs: the Boeing 247, and (most eloquently) the experimental Douglas DC-1. Here the DC-1 is readied for its first flight. Douglas wisely decided to regard the DC-1 as a technology demonstrator for later and more capable machines, notably the DC-2 and
. . .

Douglas DC-3

. . . the astonishingly successful Douglas DC-3, which introduced a "DC" revolution in air transport design, thanks in part to exhaustive flight testing of earlier models that had given Douglas the technology base from which to spawn the DC-3, the most successful airliner built to that time.

Boeing Model 299 (Hallion collection)

Ironically, commercial aircraft technology rapidly outstripped that of American military aircraft technology during the early 1930s, a situation redressed in part by the development of the experimental Boeing Model 299 "Flying Fortress," shown taxiing out for a test flight at Boeing Field in 1935, progenitor of a family of bombers that devastated the Axis powers in the Second World War.

Explorer II

High-flying aircraft such as the Boeing B-17 benefited from the intense interest in high-altitude flight that had accompanied aeronautical research in the 1920s and 1930s. Building on the work of "icicle kings" such as Shorty Schroeder and John Macready, the Army sponsored the near-disastrous Explorer I and highly successful Explorer II high-altitude balloon flights of 1934 and 1935. Here Explorer II is readied for launch in South Dakota's famed "Stratobowl" before its epochal flight to 72,395 feet.

Lockheed XC-35 (USAF Photo)

The Lockheed X-35 pioneered the first practical pressurized cabin, and served as a valuable technology demonstrator on the road to subsequent high-altitude transports and bombers.

Carl Greene and Oliver Echols (USAF Photo)

First flown in 1937 by Wright Field test crews such as Carl Greene (left) and Oliver Echols, the XC-35 could maintain a comfortable cabin altitude even as the plane cruised above 30,000 feet.

Boeing 307 (Hallion collection)

Combining the advantages of the supercharger, the technology of the all-metal monoplane (including the retractable landing gear and the potential of the pressurized cabin) led to the long-range high-altitude land-based airliner, shown here with the Boeing 307. Aircraft such as this and the later Douglas DC-4, Lockheed 049 Constellation, and the postwar Douglas DC-6 quickly rendered the long-range flying boat obsolete.

Heinkel He 70 (Hallion collection)

As in the United States, European commercial and military aviation benefited from the revolutions of the 1920s and 1930s; at every step, flight testing proved critically important to generating new capabilities and demonstrating new technology. For example, aviation in Nazi Germany proceeded in a fashion analogous to that of the United States: technology demonstrators (inspired in part by American designs) led to small military and commercial aircraft that gave experience and confidence to proceed with larger and more complex aircraft. Thus the elegant elliptical-wing Heinkel He 70 *Blitz* (Lightning), shown here, served as a technology demonstrator . . .

Heinkel He 111 (Hallion collection)

. . . for the Heinkel He 111B-1 bomber, shown undergoing flight testing at Rechlin, the great German flight testing center, and in turn experience with aircraft of this complexity . . .

Focke-Wulf FW 200 prototype (Hallion collection)

. . . led to designs such as the Focke-Wulf FW 200 long-range transport, the prototype of which is shown undergoing flight testing in 1937. The FW 200 eventually evolved into a highly respected maritime patrol bomber.

The Emergence of the Modern Fighter

Thomas Morse Viper (USAF Photo)

The technological developments of the 1920s and '30s eventually influenced the design of new fighter aircraft—traditionally the most advanced form of warplanes. Interim attempts by designers to blend old and new technology—as exemplified by the Thomas Morse XP-13A Viper—typically proved disappointing or worse; the ungainly Viper caught fire on a test flight, forcing its pilot to abandon it. Even "successful" designs were, in reality, mere transitory machines caught between the older generation of the biplane and the coming generation of the high-performance monoplane.

Brewster XF2A-1 in tunnel (NASA Photo)

The new generation of monoplane fighters demanded careful attention to detail design, and a rigorous blending of flight research and research in laboratories. For example, drag-reduction tests of the actual Brewster XF2A-1 Buffalo fighter prototype in the NACA Langley laboratory's full-size wind tunnel resulted in its speed being increased by 31 mph, a greater than 10 percent improvement over its speed before Brewster had the benefit of NACA data.

Curtiss H-75A-1 Hawk on dive

This remarkable photo shows Curtiss test pilot H. Lloyd Child diving a
Curtiss H-75A-1 Hawk fighter during demonstration tests for the French
government's purchasing mission in January 1939. Child was credited at
the time with reaching 600 mph, though this was in all likelihood due to
instrumentation error, although it is possible he exceeded 500 mph, still a
remarkable figure for the time.

Vought XF4U-1 Corsair

Newer fighter prototypes such as Vought's XF4U-1 Corsair could attain speeds that quickly rendered as unsuitable older forms of flight testing, such as the "zero lift" terminal velocity dive, or the requirement for sustained spinning before initiating spin recovery procedures.

Lockheed XP-38 Lightning

The Lockheed XP-38 of 1939, progenitor of the Lightning fighter of the Second World War, typified the successful application of the advances made in structures, propulsion, and aerodynamics during the 1920s and '30s to a highly streamlined, powerful fighter. With the design of 400 mph propeller-driven aircraft such as this, the next logical frontier constituted applying the gas turbine engine to new experimental airplanes.

Aloft on Rotating Wings:
The Evolution of the Helicopter

One of the major accomplishments of aviation in the interwar years was the emergence of practical rotary-wing aircraft, particularly the development of the first helicopters.

Pitcairn Autogiro (Hallion collection)

Spanish mathematician Juan de La Cierva developed the first successful rotary-wing craft, the autogiro. Numbers of autogiros were built in America and Great Britain; here a Pitcairn Autogiro flown by test pilot J. Paul Lukens and Police Chief Theodore Hallowell demonstrates how an autogiro could prevent criminals from fleeing law-enforcement authorities, by riddling a moving car with machine-gun fire, during tests at Willow Grove, Pennsylvania. This is certainly the progenitor of the helicopter gunship!

Focke-Achgelis FW 61

German designer Heinrich Focke developed the twin-rotor Focke-Achgelis FW 61, a rudimentary helicopter, in 1936. Here it is shown undergoing early flight testing, piloted by Ewald Rohlfs.

Sikorsky VS-300, second configuration (Hallion collection)

It is Igor Sikorsky, however, who is the true inventor of the modern helicopter. During his research, Sikorsky faced control problems as profound as those that confronted the Wright brothers. Here, the experimental VS-300 is shown in the second of its configurations, with a profusion of stabilizing tail rotors.

Sikorsky VS-300, fourth configuration (Hallion collection)

In 1941, Sikorsky succeeded in resolving at last the control problems, flight-testing the control system extensively. Here is the VS-300, with Sikorsky at the controls, in its fourth and final configuration. A milestone technology demonstrator, the VS-300 generated a data base enabling Sikorsky to embark upon the design of the first production helicopter.

Igor Sikorsky and Orville Wright (USAF Photo)

In 1942, Sikorsky accompanied the XR-4, prototype of the world's first production helicopter, to Wright Field. There he met Orville Wright (right), who as a child, had been given a helicopter toy by his father that helped stimulate his interest in flight.

The Second World War

North American B-25

The Second World War greatly accelerated the pace of aeronautical technology and made intense demands upon the flight test community, often to think of new uses for aircraft already in service. The North American B-25B Mitchell bomber, for example, was modified early in 1942 to fly from the deck of an aircraft carrier. A group of B-25's, under the command of test pilot Jimmy Doolittle, raided Tokyo in April 1942 after being launched from the deck of the U.S.S. *Hornet*.

Martin B-26

Flight testing of the Martin B-26 Marauder had given little hint of the problems new pilots had when transitioning into this "hot" airplane from docile trainers. Test pilot Jimmy Doolittle flew to B-26 bases, demonstrating that the craft could be fully maneuvered and flown even on one engine, restoring confidence in its design and dispelling many of the myths that had grown up around it.

Bell P-39

The Bell P-39 Airacobra, a shapely fighter whose configuration, unfortunately, promised greater performance than the plane actually possessed, exhibited strange flying characteristics during certain maneuvers, leading to rumors that it could actually tumble in flight. Here Bell test pilot Bob Stanley prepares for a test flight in a P-39 with a new armament system at the Bell plant in Buffalo, New York.

Lindbergh and F4U (Yale University)

Corporate test pilots served as the backbone of America's industrial flight testing and flight research effort. Charles A. Lindbergh, shown here in the cockpit of a Marine F4U Corsair in the Southwest Pacific, flew on combat missions in P-38's and F4U's to get a better understanding of how to improve the performance of these aircraft. On one such flight he shot down a Japanese Mitsubishi A6M Zero fighter.

Boeing XB-29 Superfortress

Some corporate pilots did not survive the war. The crash of an experimental Boeing XB-29 Superfortress in 1943 killed chief test pilot Eddie Allen—a pilot whose career in flight testing dated to the First World War—and his entire crew.

New Shapes in the Sky

Northrop N1M

The quest for flight efficiency led some designers to develop airplanes differing radically from the norm in aircraft design. Designer Jack Northrop, for example, developed the N1M flying wing, predecessor of a postwar family of propeller and jet-driven experimental bombers.

Vought V-173

Designer Charles Zimmerman developed the Vought V-173, a small technology demonstrator for a proposed fighter that could fly from near-zero forward airspeed to over 500 mph. Actual flight test experience was less encouraging, and the rapid development of the turbojet rendered his proposed fighter obsolete. A prototype of the fighter, the XF5U-1, was broken up for scrap without ever taking to the air.

The Turbojet Revolution

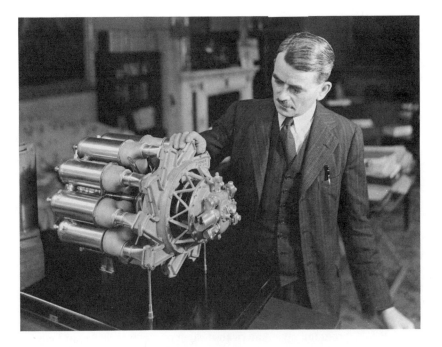

Frank Whittle

Undoubtedly, the turbojet revolution was the single most significant development in aviation history following the success of the Wrights at Kitty Hawk. The British test pilot and engineer Frank Whittle was the most influential and important of early turbojet advocates; he had to fight critics staunchly wedded to the piston engine before securing funding to build prototype jet engines and an actual experimental jet airplane. Here he is shown with a model of his first jet engine.

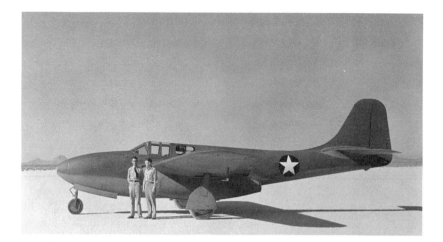

Bell XP-59A Airacomet

In 1941, the United States government arranged for the importation of Whittle engine technology, resulting in the construction of the first American jet engines and the first experimental American jet airplane, the Bell XP-59A Airacomet. Here it is shown following its first flight on October 1, 1942, at Muroc, California (now Edwards Air Force Base), with test pilot Bob Stanley (left) and Colonel Lawrence Craigie (right). The XP-59A program gave American designers the experience and confidence to pursue development of other, more advanced turbojet aircraft.

Dummy prop

To disguise the true nature of the XP-59A, Bell technicians covered the plane in canvas and added a dummy propeller to the nose, lest enemy agents deduce the significance of the top secret project.

Lockheed P-80A Shooting Star

The Lockheed P-80A Shooting Star was the first American jet fighter to enter large-scale production; the one shown here was used by NACA Ames Aeronautical Laboratory as a high-speed aerodynamic research airplane.

McDonnell FD-1 Phantom

The McDonnell XFD-1 Phantom initiated the era of "blowtorch" flying in the Navy, becoming the first jet fighter to "trap" aboard a carrier, and spawning the Phantom and Banshee fighter families.

Examining the Other Team . . .

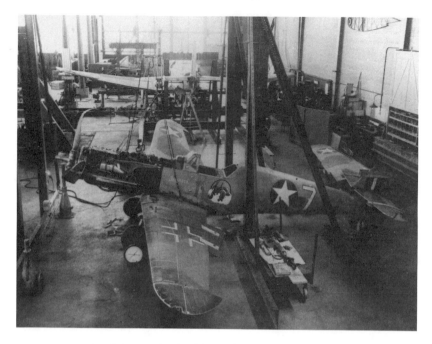

Messerschmitt Bf 109G (USAF Photo)

As in the First World War, testing of captured aircraft afforded Allied engineers and test pilots the opportunity to gain new insight into enemy design practices and capabilities. Here is a Messerschmitt Bf 109G fighter, captured in the Mediterranean theater, undergoing static load testing at Wright Field; notice the bent prop from a landing accident that, in all likelihood, ended the Messerschmitt's flying for good, thus rendering it suitable only for laboratory testing.

Messerschmitt Me 262

After the war, the formidable Messerschmitt Me 262 jet fighter underwent extensive analysis by test pilots at Wright Field and the Naval Air Test Center at Patuxent River, Maryland.

The Supersonic Breakthrough

Republic XF-12

The turbojet revolution quickly rendered obsolete even the most advanced piston-engine propeller-driven aircraft, exemplified here by the elegant Republic XF-12 experimental photo-reconnaissance airplane, the epitome of propeller-aircraft design. The future clearly belonged to the jet.

De Havilland D.H. 108 Swallow (British Aerospace Photo)

The jet's potential, however, seemed threatened by a mysterious region: the "sound barrier," where a plane encountered mixed subsonic and supersonic airflow producing often radical trim changes and dangerous instability. The tiny de Havilland D.H. 108 Swallow seemed well on its way to becoming the first supersonic airplane until it went out of control and crashed in September 1946, killing Geoffrey de Havilland, Jr., son of the firm's founder. Researchers regarded the "sound barrier" with increased wariness.

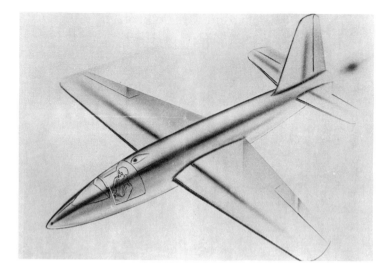

Kotcher "Mach 0.999" study (Hallion collection)

American supersonic aircraft design studies had begun in 1944, with this so-called Mach 0.999 concept (a wry reference to the "impenetrable" sound barrier) for a supersonic research airplane by Army Air Forces (AAF) engineer Ezra Kotcher.

Bell XS-1 and B-29

Kotcher's work, and that of other engineers and researchers within the AAF, NACA, and the Bell Aircraft Corporation, found fruition in the rocket-propelled Bell XS-1 supersonic research airplane, the second of which is shown being carried to launch altitude by a modified Boeing B-29 Superfortress in December 1946 for the type's first powered flight.

Chuck Yeager

On October 14, 1947, Captain Charles E. "Chuck" Yeager became the
first pilot to exceed the speed of sound when he piloted the first XS-1 to
Mach 1.06 (700 mph) at 43,000 feet, over the Mojave desert near Muroc
Dry Lake.

X-series

With the first successful supersonic flights an accomplished fact, designers
conceptualized a whole family of "X-series" research airplanes—a series
that continues even to the present day—to investigate high-speed flight
and the applicability of certain configurations to it. Here is the X-series as
of 1953 (starting clockwise from the top): Bell X-5, Douglas D-558-2
Skyrocket, Northrop X-4, Douglas X-3 (center), Bell X-1A, Douglas D-
558-1 Skystreak, and the Convair XF-92A.

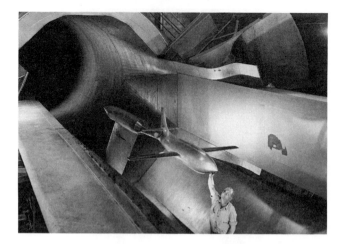

Bell X-1 in tunnel (NASA Photo)

The development of these new aircraft forced improved methods of wind-tunnel testing. Here a model of the Bell X-1 is readied for testing in NACA Langley laboratory's 16-feet transonic tunnel. Comparison of data from flight testing and research in wind tunnels formed a vital part of assembling an accurate data base for supersonic aircraft design.

Northrop YB-49A Flying Wing (USAF Photo)

Designers tried new and unproven configurations for advanced aircraft. The Northrop YB-49A Flying Wing, the largest flying wing built, had eight jet engines. Despite impressive flights, however, it was plagued by operational and stability and control problems that rendered it unsuitable for production. In 1948, test pilot Glen Edwards perished in the crash of this aircraft during stall tests northwest of Muroc Dry Lake. Edwards Air Force Base is named in his honor. Today, in the era of electronic flight controls, the YB-49A's problems could be easily resolved.

Republic XF-91 Thunderceptor

The Republic XF-91 Thunderceptor, an experimental jet-and-rocket-propelled interceptor, incorporated several design innovations, including a wing of reversed taper; despite impressive performance, reliability and maintainability questions mitigated against it seeing service. Here it is shown flying over California's Antelope Valley, piloted by Carl Bellinger.

Convair XP-82 mock-up (Hallion collection)

The Convair XP-92/XF-92A program was one aeronautical oddity that did pay off handsomely. As originally conceived, the angular XP-82 (shown here in mock-up) was a bizarre rocket-and-ramjet-propelled interceptor that would take-off using a rocket-boosted launch cart. The need for reliable information on its then-radical delta wing shape caused Convair . . .

Convair XF-92A

. . . to build the XF-92A, which validated the delta design principle during extensive flight testing over the Mojave. Though the XP-82 rocket-ramjet was canceled, experience gained with the XF-92A was incorporated in Convair's next delta design, the YF-102 interceptor . . .

Convair YF-102A

. . . which itself underwent extensive redesign to incorporate Richard Whitcomb's area rule principle, leading to the revised Convair YF-102A, a genuine supersonic aircraft and progenitor of the F-102A and F-106 interceptor families . . .

Convair B-58

. . . as well as the Convair B-58 Hustler, the first Mach 2 + bomber. The prototype of this important supersonic aircraft is shown at Covair's Ft. Worth, Texas, plant before its first flight.

Fairey Delta 2

The success of American delta-wing aircraft inspired European companion efforts such as the experimental Fairey Delta 2, which set a world's absolute speed record while flown by test pilot Peter Twiss, inspiring in turn French manufacturer Marcel Dassault to pursue the delta configuration for what eventually became the Mirage family of fighters and bombers.

Mel Apt (USAF Photo)

Achieving the expertise to design new aircraft for the high-speed frontier did not come without cost; in September 1956, Air Force test pilot Milburn "Mel" Apt, an outstanding airman, reached Mach 3.2 (2,094 mph) during an ill-conceived test flight in the Bell X-2 rocket-propelled research airplane.

Bell X-2 (NASA Photo)

After Apt achieved his peak speed and began turning back to Edwards, the vicious X-2 tumbled out of control; Apt separated an emergency escape capsule, but was killed before he could parachute from it to safety. The flight dramatically highlighted the need for better understanding of supersonic stability and control—as well as thorough mission planning.

The High-Speed Payoff

Boeing XB-47 Stratojet

The results of intensive high-speed research found fruition in new and more capable aircraft, such as the Boeing B-47 Stratojet atomic bomber. Here the prototype XB-47 is shown during a demonstration flight from Moses Lake, Washington, to Andrews AFB, Maryland, in 1949, high over the snow-covered Washington desert.

Boeing 367-80

The lessons learned from military aircraft such as the B-47 were eventually transferred, in traditional fashion, to the commercial sector. Here the prototype Boeing 367-80, the "Dash 80" progenitor of the 707 airliner family and the military KC-135 cargo and tanker aircraft, is shown on its first flight in 1954, piloted by Tex Johnston and Dix Loesch. The 707 revolutionized air transport in much the same way that the DC-3 had in the late 1930s.

North American F-100 Super Sabre

Early supersonic fighters such as North American's F-100 Super Sabre directly benefited from experience with the X-series aircraft, but often had problems of their own. The "Hun," for example, had pronounced inertial coupling tendencies that led to a devastating series of accidents early in its career, and which required insightful flight testing to resolve.

McDonnell F-101 Voodoo (USAF Photo)

Likewise, McDonnell's sleek F-101 Voodoo had dangerous pitch-up tendencies aggravated by the location of its high "T" tail. Flight testing helped transform it into a valuable reconnaissance and interceptor aircraft.

Lockheed XF-104 Starfighter

Lockheed's F-104 Starfighter, the first Mach 2 airplane, had numerous teething difficulties before it became a worthwhile military aircraft. Here is the prototype XF-104, which used a less-powerful J65 engine replaced in production airplanes by the General Electric J79.

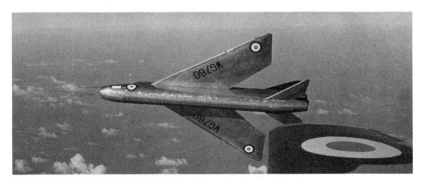

English Electric Lightning

European designers quickly followed American supersonic fighters with their own. Here is the prototype English Electric P.1a Lightning, with a distinctive sweptwing planform, seen on an early test flight from a Meteor chase plane. The Lightning, Great Britain's first supersonic fighter, went on to a lengthy career with the Royal Air Force.

Pioneers of the Supersonic Frontier

Skyrocket pilots

As always, it was the test pilots and flight researchers who probed the supersonic region. Here are three who set new speed and altitude marks in the Douglas D-558-2 Skyrocket (left to right): Douglas test pilot William B. "Bill" Bridgeman, Marine Corps test pilot Marion Carl, and NACA test pilot A. Scott Crossfield, the first pilot to exceed Mach 2.

X-1A and X-2 pilots (Hallion collection)

Three notable Air Force pioneers who set new speed and altitude marks in rocket research airplanes were (left to right): Iven Kincheloe and Frank "Pete" Everest, who set (respectively) altitude records and speed records in the Bell X-2; and Chuck Yeager, supersonic pioneer of the X-1 and the Mach 2 + X-1A. "Kinch" Kincheloe later died ejecting from a stricken F-104 west of Edwards.

Joe Walker (NASA Photo)

NACA/NASA pilot Joseph A. "Joe" Walker flew a wide range of jet and rocket-propelled transonic and supersonic research aircraft, culminating in his setting new speed and altitude records in the hypersonic North American X-15; he died in a mid-air collision between his F-104 and a North American XB-70A in 1966.

Jackie Cochran

Jacqueline Cochran, who earlier had dived past Mach 1 in an experimental model of the F-86 Sabre, followed up on this early supersonic experience by setting a series of speed records culminating in a flight to Mach 2.2 (1,429.297 mph) while piloting the prototype Lockheed F-104G Super Starfighter at Edwards Air Force Base in May 1964.

The X-15: Precursor of Winged Spaceflight

X-15 air-launch (NASA Photo)

In 1959, the North American X-15 began flight testing, air-launched from a modified Boeing B-52 bomber. This ambitious aircraft was designed for hypersonic flight—flight at speeds of Mach 5 and above, on the fringes of space.

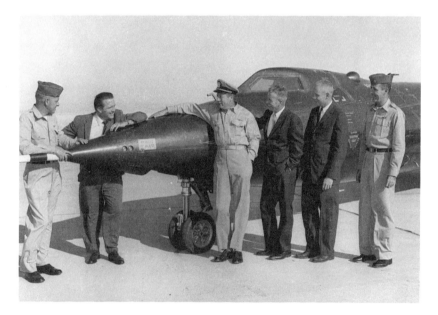

X-15 test pilots (NASA Photo)

A dozen distinguished test pilots shepherded the X-15 through its pioneering flights; here are six of them (left to right): Robert Rushworth, Jack McKay, Forrest Petersen, Joe Walker, Neil Armstrong (subsequently the first man to walk on the moon), and Bob White.

X-15 landing (NASA Photo)

Beginning in 1961, the X-15 routinely exceeded Mach 6 and reached altitudes as high as 67 miles (354,200 feet). Here it is shown landing on the baked clay of Rogers (formerly Muroc) Dry Lake following a research mission. In 1967, a modified X-15, the X-15A-2, reached Mach 6.72 (over 4,520 mph) while piloted by William J. "Pete" Knight. It was the fastest flight by a piloted airplane until the Shuttle reentered from space in 1981.

Through Mach 3 with the Blackbirds

XB-70A (NASA Photo)

During the late 1950s, the United States Air Force began development of the North American XB-70A Valkyrie, an ambitious Mach 3 + strategic bomber. Although two Valkyries eventually flew, changing mission requirements rendered the craft undesirable as a supersonic bomber. Instead it became a research tool supporting development of commercial supersonic transport aircraft.

YF-12A (USAF Photo)

At the same time, however, the Air Force was secretly testing a radical new titanium aircraft that eventually spawned the Lockheed SR-71A Blackbird strategic reconnaissance airplane. Here is the Lockheed YF-12A Blackbird, an experimental interceptor that established a series of records for flight at Mach 3 + at altitudes above 80,000 feet . . .

Blackbird test crew (USAF Photo)

. . . flown by Blackbird test crews such as the legendary test pilot Robert "Silver Fox" Stephens and "back-seater" Daniel Andre. They reached speeds and altitudes routinely that were undreamed of scant years before.

SR-71 (USAF Photo)

The SR-71A Blackbird, the world's premier strategic reconnaissance aircraft, appeared in 1964, and will remain in service well into the twenty-first century. Here an SR-71A of the Blackbird test force is shown on takeoff from Palmdale airport in California's Mojave Desert, piloted by Cal Jewett and Bill Flanagan.

XFY-1

Designing an airplane to take off and land vertically has always been one of the most elusive dreams of aviation. The Convair XFY-1 Pogo, shown taking off while piloted by James "Skeets" Coleman, represented an early and impractical attempt to develop such a craft; lags in the flight and engine control systems made piloting both demanding and difficult.

X-13

The Ryan X-13, shown balancing on jet thrust while flown by project pilot Pete Girard, was another "tail-sitter" vertical take-off-and-landing design. While the pure-jet engine offered a significant improvement over the turboprops of earlier concepts, other difficulties—including the traditional ones of transitioning to conventional wing-borne flight, and then maintaining control while backing down to a landing—mitigated against developing operational aircraft using this concept.

Bedford and P.1127 (Hallion collection)

The British Hawker P.1127, shown hovering while piloted by Bill Bedford, ushered in the era of practical V/STOL flight by winged aircraft, by using a unique system of deflected jet thrust. The P.1127 eventually generated . . .

Kestrel (NASA Photo)

. . . the Kestrel research airplane family, flown extensively in Europe and America; here is one tested at NASA Langley Research Center. The Kestrel eventually evolved into the Harrier fighter, the first combat V/STOL airplane to enter service.

New Directions in Technology

NASA F-8 SCW (NASA Photo)

The increasing interest in improving transonic cruise performance via drag reduction led NASA scientist Richard Whitcomb to conceptualize the so-called Supercritical Wing. Here a modified Vought F-8 Crusader testbed outfitted with a Whitcomb Supercritical Wing cruises high over Edwards Air Force Base. As a result of testing, the Supercritical Wing has come to represent the new standard in transport aircraft wing design, in much the same fashion that the original sweptwing did in the late 1950s.

NASA F-8 DFBW (NASA Photo)

Another modified Vought F-8 flown by NASA pioneered the application of electronic flight controls to aircraft, using equipment originally developed for the Apollo space program. The result of this and other electronic flight control study programs was a technology base enabling the development of new generations of fighters having unparalleled maneuverability and agility . . .

F-14A (NASA Photo)

. . . typified by the Grumman F-14A Tomcat fleet air defense fighter. Here an F-14A flown by NASA on high angle-of-attack flight testing is shown on a research mission, piloted by Einar Enevoldson . . .

F-16 (USAF Photo)

. . . and the extraordinarily nimble General Dynamics F-16 Fighting Falcon, mainstay of the NATO air forces and already a veteran of air combat in the Middle East.

AD-1 (NASA Photo)

Some ideas, such as the oblique wing, or "scissors wing," developed by NASA scientist Robert T. Jones, offer radically new configurations for future aircraft design. Here is the Ames-Dryden AD-1 research airplane, which evaluated the Jones wing in flight. While promising for certain applications, the wing is not likely to see widespread adoption.

X-29 (USAF Photo)

The radical Grumman X-29 technology demonstrator—an aircraft incorporating advanced electronic flight controls, a forward-sweptwing, and extensive use of composite construction materials—exemplified the mastery designers had over both electronic control technology and composite structural materials. Without both, this craft would be impossible to build and fly. The X-29, first flown by Grumman test pilot Chuck Sewell, a superlative airman, demonstrated technology for incorporation in future advanced military and commercial aircraft. Sewell, ironically, was subsequently killed in the crash of a Second World War-vintage Grumman TBF Avenger torpedo bomber.

The Push to Space

NF-104 (USAF Photo)

Flight researchers built on their experience with the X-15 and earlier rocket-propelled airplanes to generate a unique space trainer: the Lockheed NF-104A Starfighter. The NF-104A, a much modified F-104A interceptor, added reaction control thrusters and a rocket engine, enabling student test pilots to fly above 100,000 feet and then complete a precision reentry down to landing, in much the same fashion that an advanced returnable spacecraft might. The NF-104A had vicious characteristics, and of the three built, two crashed, killing one pilot and injuring famed test pilot Chuck Yeager. Here an NF-104A is shown preparatory to ignition of the rocket engine and the climb to altitude.

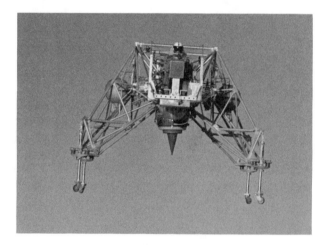

LLRV (NASA Photo)

Researchers at NASA's Flight Research Center and Bell Aerosystems built a unique jet-and-rocket propelled simulator in the mid-1960s to simulate a lunar landing spacecraft operating in the weak gravity environment of the moon. One of the five built is shown here hovering during testing at Edwards. These craft proved vitally important during training for the Apollo lunar landing missions.

M2-F1 (NASA Photo)

NASA researchers at Edwards also built an experimental plywood-and-metal testbed to evaluate the concept of tailoring a modified nosecone shape to create a lifting body configuration that could generate a modest amount of lift during a descent from space. The result was the NASA M2-F1, first flown in 1963 by test pilot Milton "Milt" Thompson.

Lifting Body Family (NASA Photo)

The success of the M2-F1 encouraged development of larger aluminum rocket-propelled supersonic lifting bodies that could assess the low-speed behavior of various configurations that might be suitable for future spacecraft designs. Here are the three lifting bodies built by 1970 (left to right): the Martin X-24A, Northrop M2-F2/3, and the Northrop HL-10.

X-24B (NASA Photo)

Advanced work by the Air Force's Flight Dynamics Laboratory led to development of the X-24B, a new flat-iron lifting body shape gloved around the old X-24A and tested at Edwards in the early 1970s. The X-24B proved an important contributor to the technology base incorporated in the subsequent Space Shuttle. Here the X-24B is shown descending to land at Rogers Dry Lake, piloted by John Manke.

Enterprise (NASA Photo)

In 1977, NASA undertook the first flights of the Space Shuttle, launching it from the back of a modified Boeing 747 jet transport over Rogers Dry Lake. Here the Shuttle *Enterprise* is shown descending to landing piloted by astronauts Joe Engle and Dick Truly, on October 12, 1977, with a dummy engine installation simulating the configuration Shuttle would have during reentry and landing. In the background is the Edwards "ramp" and the installation's famed 15,000-foot runway.

Columbia (NASA Photo)

On April 12, 1981, astronauts John Young and Bob Crippen inaugurated a new era in space transportation with the first orbital flight of the Space Shuttle *Columbia*. Ahead would lay the pain of *Challenger*'s loss in 1986, but *Columbia*'s successful flight—and the many others that followed before *Challenger*—reaffirmed the basic soundness of the Shuttle concept.

Full Circle

Gossamer Condor

On August 23, 1977, at Shafter Airport, California, bicyclist Bryan Allen became a different kind of test pilot—piloting the world's first human-powered, sustained, and controlled flight. Here he is shown in the Gossamer Condor, developed by Paul MacCready: the plane that gave truth to the myth of Daedalus and Icarus.

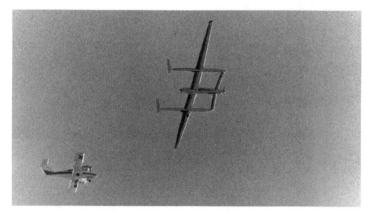

Voyager (USAF Photo)

In December 1986, pilots Dick Rutan and Jeana Yeager completed a monumental journey and aerial adventure: flying nonstop around the world, without being refueled in flight. Here is the Voyager, piloted by Rutan and Yeager, returning to Edwards Air Force Base on the morning of December 23, as brother Burt Rutan (the plane's designer) and team member Mike Melvill fly formation in the project's Beech Duchess chase plane. The flight took nine days, three minutes, and forty seconds, and demonstrated advances in composite structure and piston engine technology applicable to future aircraft.

CHAPTER 5

NEW DIRECTIONS
IN THE THIRTIES

As the decade of the 1930s dawned, the United States found itself in the midst of an international depression brought on by years of poor financial management and stock manipulation. The lively strains of the Jazz Age gave way to the dismal tune of "Brother, Can You Spare a Dime?" Paradoxically, however, the years between 1930 and American entry into the Second World War were particularly fruitful for aeronautics. During the 1920s, an average of six major new prototypes—bombers, transports, fighters—had flown each year. The average number of prototype first flights per year during the 1930s leapt to twelve, a figure unsurpassed for any period since that time, including the hectic years of the Second World War and the 1950s. This explosive growth reflected in its own way the turbulence of the decade. An airmail scandal had erupted, fueled by partisan politics, and had culminated in a presidential order directing the military to fly the airmail. The result, despite subsequent apologetics, cannot be characterized as anything other than disastrous. America's favorite war hero, "Captain Eddie" Rickenbacker, termed the losses in ill-equipped and ill-prepared Army airmen "legalized murder." But, at the same time, these bleak clouds of misery glimmered with the promise of revolutionary new commercial aircraft. After all, Rickenbacker's sensational remarks came just after he and airline pioneer Jack

Frye had crossed the country in the experimental Douglas DC-1 transport flying "blind" and using a newly developed Sperry autopilot to control the aircraft most of the way. The beautiful twin-engine transport had set a new transcontinental crossing record during the trip, of 13 hours 4 minutes.

A REVOLUTION FROM SANTA MONICA

The DC-1 inherited a long tradition of earlier aeronautical research results that had given rise to such major technical developments and innovations as the all-metal semimonocoque "stressed skin" airplane, the controllable-pitch propeller, the NACA cowling, retractable landing gears, and wing flaps, to name just a few. And it in turn became the ancestor of the DC-2 and then that most legendary of all aircraft, the immortal DC-3. With the DC-3, American civil aviation swept past the rest of the world, relegating the trimotors, the ugly biplanes, the open-cockpit "mail planes" obsolete. The age of mass air transportation of people and cargo had arrived.

The story of the DC-3—which is really the story of the first "modern" airliner—begins with the work of Jack Northrop. This insightful engineer, whose name is forever linked to the graceful Flying Wings of the 1940s, had designed the revolutionary Lockheed Vega, a wooden airplane that reintroduced the monocoque tradition of the prewar Déperdussin Racer and the wartime Albatros. Later, in 1929, Northrop had developed the streamlined Northrop Alpha, a low-wing internally braced monoplane, which pioneered the application of all-metal construction to the monocoque configuration. The Alpha first flew later that year but crashed early in its test program after losing its ailerons to flutter, test pilot Steve Shor just managing to escape from the plunging plane. Undeterred, Northrop modified the design and proceeded with production models that quickly demonstrated good performance and ruggedness. The Alpha gave rise to advanced follow-ons, notably the Gamma, and then, because Northrop worked with Douglas, to the DC-1. The direct inspiration for the DC-1, however, was a rival product, Boeing's revolutionary airliner, the 247.

Influenced by the work of German engineer Adolf Rohrbach, Boeing had studied metal airplanes beginning in the mid-1920s and then developed the Model 200 "Monomail," a single-engine all-metal design first flown at Seattle by Eddie Allen, in May 1930. This had led to an abortive Army bomber, the XB-9, but the rival Martin B-10, with slightly more-advanced features, won the Army's favor. Boeing decided to next embark on a twin-engine monoplane transport. They selected a mid-wing layout (resulting in a cramped fuselage), partly cowled radial engines mounted ahead of the wing (in contrast with awkward below-the-wing trimotorlike installations), internally braced wings and tail, an enclosed cockpit, and a retractable landing gear. The result was the 247, a ten-place transport, which first flew on February 8, 1933. Unfortunately for Boeing, Douglas was even then in the process of designing the DC-1 for TWA—and a huge sign in the Douglas plant at Santa Monica showed a cutaway of the rival 247 with the admonishment: DON'T COPY IT! DO IT BETTER! And Douglas did, with greater design refinement (including using wing flaps) and larger passenger capacity.

The DC-1 took to the air five months after the 247, on July 1, 1933, flown by Douglas test pilot Carl Cover. A trim low-wing monoplane having an unobstructed cabin, capacity for twelve passengers (to meet a TWA specification), and powerful Wright Cyclone radial engines enclosed in full NACA cowlings, the sleek and gleaming DC-1 had benefited from extensive testing in Caltech's 200-mph Guggenheim-lab wind tunnel. The morning of the first flight, Carl Cover and copilot Fred Herman fired up the two engines, taxied out to the runway at Santa Monica's Clover Field, ran some high-speed taxi and braking tests, and then opened the throttles to full power and took off. The DC-1 lifted smoothly from the ground and nosed into a climb. And then the left engine quit. The DC-1 nosed earthward, and the engine fired again. Cover nosed upward in a shallow climb and *both* engines quit. Cover, mystified but too busy to be frightened, lowered the nose; the engines came to life. Now he carefully climbed as slowly as he could, babying the sick airplane to 1,000 feet as the engines roared unevenly. Cover wisely decided not to attempt to land back at the airport, but instead chose a large field, set up a landing approach, and touched down without any damage whatsoever. In the Depression economy of 1933, the loss of the DC-1 prototype could have spelled disaster for Douglas.

An investigation revealed that the engine carburetors were at fault; the floats would shut off the gas every time the pilot raised the nose of the airplane. A quick design revision, and the plane resumed flight testing. The rest of the test program went relatively smoothly, as Douglas, TWA, and government pilots wrung out the craft. On one occasion, even the great Eddie Allen lost track of lowering the landing gear, and the DC-1 came to rest on the middle of the runway with a pair of reddening pilots and two bent props amid an embarrassing screeching of scraped metal. Flying out of Winslow, Arizona (elevation 4,500 feet), Allen and pilot D. W. "Tommy" Tomlinson demonstrated that the DC-1 could take off with only one engine—and then flew that way more than 240 miles to Albuquerque. Then Rickenbacker and Jack Frye of TWA flew the craft coast to coast in record time. Without hesitation, impressed TWA officials ordered a slightly more advanced model, which became the DC-2. The DC-1 eventually wound up in war-torn Spain, where it eventually crashed (without injuring anyone) in 1940.

The DC-2 proved a success in its own right. One, a KLM aircraft piloted by an airline crew, placed second in the MacRobertson London-Melbourne Trophy Race of 1934, finishing behind a specially crafted air racer from Great Britain and ahead of an advanced version of the Boeing 247 piloted by Roscoe Turner and Clyde Pangborn. Impressed with the DC-2, American Airlines drew up specifications for a more advanced airplane capable of carrying twenty-one passengers. Essentially, Douglas split the DC-2 down the middle and added a third row, of seven seats. But wind-tunnel tests at Caltech saved the company from possible disaster, by revealing a wallowing instability that required aerodynamic refinement of its wing-and-tail configuration. Equipped with powerful, 1,200-hp Pratt & Whitney engines, the DC-3 made its first flight, fittingly enough, on the thirty-second anniversary of the Wright brothers' first flight, December 17, 1935, piloted by Carl Cover. The DC-3 began American domination of world air commerce. By 1938, 95 per cent of American air commerce flew on DC-3's, roughly thirteen thousand of which were built by Douglas and foreign manufacturers including Japan and the Soviet Union. But first had come the DC-1, which Carl Cover and Fred Herman had so adroitly and fortuitously saved on its maiden flight.

PROBING THE STRATOSPHERE BY
BALLOON

One area of concern to developers of transport airplanes was the problem of high-altitude flight. By the early 1930s, high-altitude flying had changed little from the days of icicle king Shorty Schroeder, and the question of the practicality of pressure cabins remained essentially unanswered, as it had during and after Harold Harris's discouraging flight a decade earlier. Eventually, the 1930s witnessed a three-pronged assault on the problems of high-altitude flight, one by flight research at extreme altitudes using balloons, another by the development of rudimentary pressure-suit pilot protection garments, and a third by the development of practical pressure-cabin-equipped aircraft. Once again, in all areas, American flight researchers led the way.

Flight research at high altitudes certainly did not lack danger. There was the ever-present threat of succumbing to lack of oxygen and the intense and relentless cold. As early as 1901, the German research balloon *Preussen* had risen from the parade ground at Tempelhof, lifting gently to over 34,000 feet. At that altitude, the two crewmen were extremely fatigued, despite breathing oxygen from a crude and inefficient "pipe-stem" mouthpiece. One crew member passed out. The other fortunately opened the balloon's dump valve just before he, too, became unconscious, thus saving both their lives. They recovered, groggy and sick, at lower altitudes in time to dump some ballast and bring the *Preussen* down to a gentle landing. In 1927, Army aeronaut Hawthorne Gray, an experienced balloonist, was less lucky: he reached over 42,000 feet and then died of anoxia, the last victim of open-gondola high-altitude ballooning.

The greatest impetus to high-altitude ballooning came from the scientific community, who saw in the balloon a unique opportunity to raise instrumentation aloft to study such phenomena as cosmic rays. In 1930, August Piccard, a Swiss physicist often hailed as the "Conqueror of the Stratosphere," developed a giant balloon intended for upper-atmosphere cosmic-ray research. Dubbed *FNRS*, for Fond Nationale de la Recherche Scientifique, the balloon featured an enclosed air-tight aluminum gondola of spherical design. An initial flight attempt in 1930 ended in failure, the *FNRS* failing to leave the ground, but with a new balloon envelope, Piccard and assistant Paul Kipfer took off from Augsburg on May 27, 1931, soaring to over 51,000 feet above the Bavarian countryside before settling to earth in the Tyrolean Alps. A year later, accompanied by Max Cosyns, Piccard reached 54,789 feet during a flight from Zürich to Peschiera, Italy. A host of unofficial records now fell before daring high-altitude balloonists. In November 1933, Navy balloonist T. G. W. "Tex" Settle and Marine observer Chester Fordney climbed with a load of scientific instruments to 61,237 feet. Then, in January 1934, a three-man Soviet team rose to 72,178 feet in the balloon *Osoaviakhim*, but the gondola fell from the balloon during the descent, killing the hapless crew. In June 1934, an American team had a narrow escape when the Army - National Geographic Society hydrogen balloon *Explorer I* split its envelope at 60,000 feet. Down the balloon came, its envelope acting like a parachute. In the gondola, aeronauts William Kepner, Albert Stevens, and Orvil Anderson prepared to abandon it if necessary. Then, at 3,000 feet the envelope tore completely apart when its remaining hydrogen gas, mixed with the inrushing air, exploded violently. Anderson, straddling the gondola with his parachute on, immediately dropped off to safety. The other two just barely escaped from the tumbling gondola, parachuting to safety as it smashed into the earth. Then, the next year, came the notable flight of *Explorer II*.

Unlike the ill-fated *Explorer I*, *Explorer II* had a larger and strengthened envelope utilizing helium in place of the unsafe hydrogen, and carried a two- rather than three-man crew. An early flight attempt ended in failure when the envelope ripped during inflation. Following redesign, the next flight was attempted successfully, on November 11, 1935. That morning, Albert Stevens and Orvil Anderson took off from the "Stratobowl," near Rapid City, South Dakota, and set a new world's altitude record of 72,395 feet, a record that lasted until broken by Bill Bridgeman in the Douglas Skyrocket in 1951. Stevens and Anderson spent two hours above 70,000 feet, while on-board recording instrumentation, including infrared cameras and Geiger counters, made thousands of measurements and took thousands of photographs. The crewmen marveled at the view; Stevens later wrote for *The National Geographic Magazine:*

> The earth could be seen plainly underneath through the lower porthole and hundreds of miles in every direction through the side portholes. It was a vast expanse of brown, apparently flat, stretching on and on. Wagon roads and automobile highways were invisible, houses were invisible, and railroads could be recognized only by an occasional cut or fill. The larger farms were discernible as tiny rectangular areas. Occasional streaks of green vegetation showed the presence of streams.
>
> Here and there water could be seen in the form of rivers or lakes, especially if the sun was reflected from the water's surface. No sign of actual life on the earth could be detected. To us it was a foreign and lifeless world. The sun was the one object that commanded our attention; we were temporarily almost divorced from Mother Earth. . . .
>
> The horizon itself was a band of white haze. Above it the sky was light blue, and perhaps 20 or 30 degrees from the horizon it was of the blue color that we are accustomed to. But at the highest angle that we could see it, the sky became very dark. I would not say that it was completely black; it was rather a black with the merest suspicion of very dark blue.[1]

Inside, Stevens and Anderson were comfortable in their sealed gondola, the cabin pressure being equivalent to an altitude of 10,000 feet and the cabin temperature hovering within a few degrees of 40 degrees F. Outside, however, the temperature was as low as —81 degrees F., and indeed, at the balloon's actual altitude, the crewmen would not have survived in an open gondola, for above 63,000 feet, atmospheric pressure equals the vapor pressure of bodily fluids, and they would have died, their blood and bodily fluids literally boiling. Eventually, the crew readied the balloon for descent, and they landed at the end of the over-eight-hour flight midway between Platte and White Lake. It was the greatest of manned balloon flights to its time and was not exceeded until the dramatic *Man High, Excelsior,* and *Strato-Lab* flights of the 1950s and early 1960s.

The pioneering efforts of Piccard and his followers, concluding with the achievement of *Explorer II*, reflected several aspects of flight research. First, these pioneers, test pilots by necessity, recognized that by undertaking specialized flight research programs they could advance the frontiers of knowledge—in this case primarily in the field of atmospheric science and physics. Secondly, the flights clearly validated the concept of the pressurized cabin for high-altitude flight. In contrast to the uncomfortable and often deadly flights of earlier upper-atmosphere explorers, the crews of these gondola-equipped balloons operated in relative comfort and with a great deal more safety. They had attained altitudes unattainable to a human simply relying on oxygen and without some form of pressurized protection garment or cabin. As a result, various nations continued to experiment with prototype pressure-cabin-equipped aircraft. Eventually it was the Army Air Corps, spurred on by the tragic death of Hawthorne Gray, that first demonstrated a practical pressurized aircraft successfully, on the Lockheed XC-35 flying testbed.

But another avenue also beckoned researchers, an approach that advocates thought might, in the long run, prove equally as significant as the pressure cabin (as, in fact, it eventually would). This was, of course, the quest for a practical pressurized suit, a pressure garment that a pilot could simply slip on and wear while flying at high altitudes, a suit that would encase him in the equivalent conditions of the lower atmosphere. And here the pioneering figure is a truly legendary airman: Wiley Post, the one-eyed pilot from Oklahoma.

WILEY POST: PRESSURE-SUITED PIONEER OF THE JET STREAM

Wiley Post is one of the great romantic figures of American aviation. Born in 1898 the fourth child of a Texas farm family, Post was raised from the age of nine in southwestern Oklahoma. In 1913, he saw his first airplane—piloted by the great demonstration pilot Art Smith—a Curtiss pusher biplane that looped and spun over a county fair at Lawton. The pirouetting plane made a profound impact on young Post, who later wrote that from that day onward he dreamed of creating a "Wiley Post Institute of Aeronautical Research." Young Wiley proved adept at working with his hands, and studied engines and radio equipment, then became an oil-field roughneck. During the barnstorming craze immediately after the Armistice, Wiley Post signed on with a barnstorming troupe as a parachutist—an occupation that did not please his father, who at one point confiscated Post's parachute! In two years he made ninety-nine jumps, and also received rudimentary flight instruction on an old Canadian-built Jenny known as a Canuck.

Meanwhile he had proved an adept oil rigger and had risen to directing rigging operations at one facility near Seminole, Oklahoma. There, one day in 1926, a chip thrown from a defective bolt lodged in his left eye, which subsequently became infected, endangering the right eye as well. Doctors had no option but to remove the left eye; it seemed as if the young man's dreams of flying might go with it. But no one had considered the tenacity of Wiley Post. He trained himself as best he could to gauge distance, while recuperating at the home of an uncle living in Texas, and using the $1,800 awarded to him in workmen's compensation, he bought a damaged Canuck for $200, had it repaired for an additional $340, and began to fly! He also married, and embarked on the precarious life of a barnstormer.

One of the first groups to recognize the utility of the "business" airplane was the oil industry. In 1928, Wiley Post went to work as an aerial chauffeur for two oilmen, Powell Briscoe and F. C. Hall, flying a Travel Aire open-cockpit biplane. The company's fortunes prospered, and later in the year, Hall bought a spanking-new streamlined Lockheed Vega. The Vega was a revolutionary aircraft in its time, for in an age of open-cockpit, strut-and-wire-braced biplanes, this exceptional design featured a monocoque wooden fuselage, an enclosed cabin and cockpit, and cantilever wings and tail surfaces. (Later models added NACA cowlings around the radial engines and wheel pants on the landing gear.) Hall named the airplane the *Winnie Mae*, after his daughter, but the stock-market crash of 1929 soon forced the company to sell the airplane; Wiley Post briefly joined Lockheed as a test and demonstration pilot. The next year, Hall again felt confident enough to purchase another airplane, a more advanced Lockheed 5B Vega powered by a 420-hp Pratt & Whitney Wasp radial engine, and Post came back as its pilot.

The new Vega became the second *Winnie Mae*, one of the most famous aircraft of all time. A resplendent white monoplane with purple trim, the Vega looked the part of what it was: one of the highest-performance aircraft in the world. Post demonstrated this by winning the 1930 Los Angeles to Chicago Air Derby when he flew 1,760 miles in 9 hours, 9 minutes, 4 seconds, averaging 192 mph despite having a faulty compass, which cost him 40 minutes! Impressed with this performance, Hall was receptive to Wiley Post's next plan: to use the *Winnie Mae* to fly all the way around the world in record time. In early 1931, Post planned the flight in detail, relying on Harold Gatty, an outstanding navigator, to assist on the flight. The *Winnie Mae* went back to Lockheed for long-range modifications.

By May, all was ready, and Post and Gatty flew the plane, now equipped with additional fuel tankage in the fuselage and a special wind-drift-and-ground-speed indicator developed by Gatty himself, from California to Long Island. There, in the early hours of June 23, 1931, the two men took off from Roosevelt Field on the first leg of their round-the-world journey. They landed back in New York City at Roosevelt Field on July 1, having circled the globe in 8 days, 15 hours, 51 minutes. All the tired pilot could say was, "We had a great time." And indeed they had. Post credited much of the success of the flight to the Vega's blind-flying instruments. They had flown to Newfoundland, England, Germany, Russia, Manchuria, Alaska, Canada, Ohio, and New York. Few flights before and since have so conclusively demonstrated the progress in aeronautics since the time of the Wright brothers. But Post had already set his sight on yet another goal: a solo round-the-world flight with the plane equipped with a newly devised Sperry automatic pilot to ease Post's piloting task as much as possible.

Once again, modifications to the aircraft took time. Finally, the airplane and its automatic pilot (dubbed "Mechanical Mike") were ready. On the morning of July 15, 1933, Post took off from Floyd Bennett Field, on Long Island's Jamaica Bay. This professional airman disdained the riding breeches, leather jacket, and helmet and goggles of his contemporaries, and in fact appeared for the flight that morning dressed in a double-breasted dark gray suit, a white shirt, and a blue necktie, with a tasteful white eye patch (his glass eye had become chilled during the 1931 flight, giving him headaches).

Post flew nonstop from New York to Berlin, covering the 3,942-mile distance at an average speed of 153.5 mph. Then he went on to Moscow, Siberia, Alaska, Canada, and the United States, returning to New York on July 22, having broken his earlier 1931 record with Gatty by flying around the world in 7 days, 18 hours, 49½ minutes. More than fifty thousand enthusiasts greeted Post on his return to Floyd Bennett Field. During the flight, Post actually placed enough faith in the Sperry autopilot that he allowed himself to doze off, trusting the guidance of the plane to the mechanical pilot. And while this flight might have climaxed the flying careers of lesser men, not so with Post. He decided to enter the 1934 MacRobertson race from London, England, to Melbourne, Australia. Here is where Wiley Post enters the story of high-altitude flight.

Aviation science had advanced dramatically since the time of the Vega's first flight, and Post recognized that the aging airplane would be competing with some of the finest aircraft in the world, such as specialized racers and the DC-2 and Boeing 247. He believed, however, that if he could cruise above 30,000 feet he could take advantage of the powerful "jet stream" winds blowing from the west, whose existence was postulated but, as yet, unproved.

Two days after returning from his 1933 round-the-world flight, Post had written in an Oklahoma newspaper:

> The next development for long-distance flying after blind flying and blind landing will be high-altitude flying, flying in the stratosphere. I think that the development of supercharged planes, that is with the cabin as well as the engines kept sufficiently supplied with oxygen in the rarefied atmosphere, will come in the very near future.[2]

Post realized that the wooden *Winnie Mae* was unsuited to installation of a pressure cabin. So he decided to attempt an alternative approach: developing a pressurized pilot-protection suit that he could wear while flying the craft at high altitudes. He turned to Jimmy Doolittle for assistance, and Doolittle suggested that Post contact the B. F. Goodrich Company. There ensued a development program remarkable both for its results and for the short time that it took to achieve them. In April 1934, Post visited the Goodrich plant in Los Angeles and requested that the company develop a rubberized flying suit that could surround the pilot in an equivalent atmosphere of 5,500 feet no matter at what altitude above this the plane was actually flying.

By June, the company had completed the first of an eventual three suits that Post would experiment with. The first suit burst while undergoing a pressure test. The second fitted Post so snugly that he had to be cut out of it, ruining it completely. The third suit, however, worked quite well. It resembled nothing so much as a deep-sea diving suit and could hold an internal absolute pressure of 7 psi; it consisted of a rubber inner suit covered with a three-ply outer suit. The aluminum helmet had a large, circular porthole for visibility that Post could screw in place, and the helmet attached to the suit using butterfly nuts. Post tested the suit in the Army's low-pressure chamber at Wright Field amid great secrecy, both because of his race plans and the value of the suit to military high-altitude flight. High-pressure liquid oxygen boil-off would furnish the pilot both with oxygen and with suitable pressure within the suit.

On September 5, 1934, Post first flew in the *Winnie Mae* with the pressure suit, and the one-eyed pilot reached an altitude of 40,000 feet on this initial test flight, very close to the current world altitude record. (The potential dangers of operating an unpressurized aircraft or not wearing a pressure suit to high altitudes were dramatically illustrated shortly after this flight when, on September 28, Italian test pilot Renato Donati reached an altitude of 47,358 feet in an open-cockpit Caproni 114 biplane. Upon landing, Donati had to be carried from his research plane and hospitalized, remaining in a near coma for twenty-four hours after the flight.) The test flight indicated that the *Winnie Mae* itself required modifications before attempting sustained high-altitude flights; unfortunately, this meant that Post could not possibly finish the modifications in time to enter the MacRobertson race. Instead, Post decided to attempt a coast-to-coast flight through the substratosphere, above 30,000 feet.

Post readied the aircraft for its altitude flights, adding a second supercharger, which enabled the craft's engine to achieve its rated 450 hp up to 35,000 feet and to climb to a maximum altitude of around 50,000 feet—an unbelievable height in the days before the Second World War. To further increase performance, Post had Lockheed design a special lightweight landing gear that he could jettison after takeoff; the *Winnie Mae* would then land at the end of its flight "dead stick" (without power) and on a long belly skid added under the engine cowling and forward fuselage.

In early December 1934, Post, wearing his suit, reached an altitude of 48,000 feet during a test flight from Bartlesville, Oklahoma. Later that month, he may have reached 50,000 feet, but a recording barograph failed to function properly and the record could not be confirmed. Post pressed on, assisted by support from Phillips Petroleum and also from Transcontinental and Western Airlines (the forerunner of the present TWA). TWA later sponsored its own series of high-altitude route-proving flights by airline test pilot "Tommy" Tomlinson, in 1935.

On February 22, 1935, Post took off from the Lockheed plant at Burbank, California, on his proposed coast-to-coast substratosphere flight. He had barely cleared the coastal hills, however, when the engine began throwing oil, and he had no choice but to execute a hazardous dead-stick landing with a full load of fuel. The *Winnie Mae* landed silently on the baked clay of Rogers Dry Lake, by the little desert community of Muroc. Post exited the craft, still wearing his pressure suit, and walked 400 yards to where Muroc native H. E. Mertz was busy working on a wind-powered "sail car." Suddenly aware of Post, Mertz nearly collapsed with fright when he saw the strange, otherworldly apparition that asked him to help unfasten the helmet of the pressure suit! This light moment, however, was the only bright spot in the affair, for Post discovered that a saboteur, working for a jealous and disgruntled pilot, had poured emery dust into the engine just before takeoff, turning it into so much junk.

Three weeks later, however, on March 5, 1935, Post was ready for a second attempt, and he again took off from Burbank, flying nonstop to Cleveland, where he landed, his oxygen supply exhausted. During the flight, Post had cruised over 30,000 feet high at an average speed of *279 miles per hour*, more than 100 mph above the Vega's normal cruising speed and clear evidence that the *Winnie Mae* had received an assist from the powerful jet stream. At times, its ground speed had touched

340 mph, inclining one to speculate that the *Winnie Mae* might well have won the MacRobertson race simply by cruising along at high altitudes in the jet stream; the winning aircraft, after all, was a De Havilland Comet racer that averaged only 171 mph.

Post had conclusively demonstrated the value of the pilot protection suit. Indeed, in this revolutionary suit, we see the ancestor of the present-day full-pressure "space suit" worn by astronauts and cosmonauts on voyages beyond the earth. Wiley Post attempted to fly the country non-stop in the stratosphere twice more after the epochal Burbank-Cleveland flight, but each flight ended from mechanical failure—the faithful Vega was simply too old, too incapable of withstanding the repeated demands for performance being placed upon it. At last, in June 1935, Post retired the airplane, and assisted by a grant authorized by Congress, the Smithsonian Institution added the plane and its historical pressure suit to its national collections.

Post met a crueler fate. He acquired an ill-flying hybrid airplane, the Lockheed Orion-Explorer, constructed of components from various aircraft, including an awkward float installation from a Fokker trimotor. Together with aviation enthusiast and humorist Will Rogers, Post left from Seattle for Alaska. They eventually made their way to a small lake near Point Barrow. The Orion-Explorer had a nasty, unstable flight condition if its engine quit at low speed and low altitude: it would rapidly tuck its nose down, with pronounced nose-heaviness. On August 15, 1935, Post and Rogers took off from a small lake near Point Barrow. Eskimo fishermen heard the plane's engine quit, and saw it suddenly dive into the water, killing both men, a sad end to the lives of a great humorist and a great flight researcher.

The logical conclusion to all this work on high-altitude flight came in 1937, with the development of the first practical pressurized airplane, the experimental Lockheed XC-35 testbed, which historian Douglas Robinson has hailed as "the true ancestor of all modern pressurized airliners." The XC-35 owed its existence largely to one man, Major Carl F. Greene, a former bridge builder and expert on structural design. Greene had gained a great measure of fame as the man who designed the advanced wing used on Martin's revolutionary B-10 bomber. In the early 1930s, he was stationed at the Air Corps development center at Wright Field. The death of balloonist Hawthorne Gray had deeply affected the engineers at McCook and later Wright Field. "We knew we had to operate at high levels," Greene later recalled, "and we knew that it was up to us to find all the answers. It was too easy for men to die the way Gray did."[3] So, early in the 1930s, Greene studied methods of incorporating pressurization into military airplanes. The all-metal monocoque shape, pioneered by John Northrop, seemed ideal for such a structure. Greene proposed that the Army fund development of a fighter prototype having a pressurized pilot's cabin. Instead, the Army decided to go a step further and sponsor development of a transport-size aircraft having a pressurized passenger cabin. Greene and associate John Younger designed a suitable pressurized cabin for use with a modified version of the sleek Lockheed Model 10E Electra, a low-wing twin-engine airplane having two vertical fins. The Lockheed company manufactured the aircraft as the XC-35 and delivered it to Wright Field for testing in late July 1937. The XC-35 had two turbosupercharged radial engines, with compressors for the pressure cabin being driven off the engines. The craft had a service ceiling of 32,000 feet and could carry a crew of five in shirt-sleeve comfort: the pressurized cabin obviated any need for special oxygen-breathing equipment. The internal cabin operated at a pressure of 9.5 psi, actually higher than any operating transport flown up to the time of the jet transports of the 1950s.

It was important that the craft be thoroughly checked before flight. Greene supervised ground tests in which the cabin was pressurized. Then, technicians covered the outside with soap and water to see if there were any leaks. The high-pressure air shrieked out of every aperture with a painfully loud whistle, but at last the gritty technicians had marked every leak and the XC-35 was thoroughly sealed. On its first flight to the fringes of the stratosphere, test pilot Alfred Johnson took a test crew of five up to 28,000 feet, cutting in the superchargers and pressurizing the cabin when he reached 12,000 feet. For the first time, men flew at 30,000 feet in a comfortable cabin atmosphere without recourse to emergency oxygen equipment placed inside the craft.

On subsequent flights up to 33,000 feet, the XC-35 proved an excellent research tool. Numerous unanticipated problems cropped up, enabling researchers to find solutions before having to address these problems on new production aircraft. Aircraft instrumentation malfunctioned because of pressure leakage in the instrument cases, necessitating careful design of instrument casings. Oil and hydraulic lines and equipment dependent on these fluids often operated sluggishly or not at all in the cold, rarefied upper atmosphere. Windows froze over. These problems were all ironed out by the test crews flying from "the Field." Finally the XC-35 was believed ready for a practical demonstration of what a pressure-cabin-equipped airplane could do.

On February 13, 1938, the XC-35 took off at midnight from storm-wracked Chicago in weather conditions that would have grounded any airliner. But the XC-35 did not need to fly at low altitudes in order to keep its VIP passenger comfortable. The crew climbed through the storm and leveled out well above 20,000 feet, flying nonstop to Bolling Field, across from the Capitol, suitably impressing their passenger,

Louis A. Johnson, the Assistant Secretary of War. The American aeronautical community was also impressed: the Air Corps and the XC-35 test team received the Robert J. Collier Trophy, one of aviation's most prestigious awards. And shortly thereafter, a new airliner designed from the outset for a pressurized cabin took to the air: the Boeing 307 Stratoliner. The XC-35 had demonstrated that the age of high-altitude flight by supercharged pressurized aircraft had arrived.

THE NAVY'S FLYING AIRCRAFT CARRIERS

One of the lesser-known yet more intriguing concepts of aviation in the interwar years involved the potential of gigantic dirigibles serving as aerial aircraft carriers. Eventually, though many countries experimented with the concept, only the United States actually introduced such vehicles into operational service, the two greatest American helium-filled zeppelins, the airships *Akron* and *Macon*. Each could carry a small complement of aircraft for scouting purposes, launching and retrieving them in flight from a special hangar in the underside of the airship's hull. In the United States, the concept of flying aircraft from airships had really appeared with the enigmatic John J. Montgomery, an instructor at Santa Clara College, who had launched manned gliders from balloons as early as 1905. But the idea of flying a powered aircraft from an airship and then recovering it back on board the airship in flight was yet another contribution of Lawrence Sperry's fertile mind. The first demonstration of such an aerial "landing" had been made by Army test pilot Clyde Finter over Scott Field, Illinois. During a preliminary test on December 13, 1924, he approached a lowered trapeze, suspended from the Army blimp TC-3, flying a Sperry Messenger biplane equipped with a hook attached to the upper wing. Turbulence tossed the plane against the trapeze, shattering its propeller, and Finter spiraled down to a skillful dead-stick landing. Two days later, however, he succeeded after making several unsuccessful passes. But, five years were to pass before an operational requirement for such a system existed.

In the summer of 1929, Navy test pilot Jake Gorton had flown a Vought OU-1 with a hook onto a trapeze suspended from the Navy's development airship *Los Angeles* (acquired as part of war reparations from Germany), and further refinement of the concept was undertaken by Navy pilot John O'Brien, flying out of Lakehurst, using the same airship, to prove out the air-launch-and-recovery concept before applying it to the two gigantic airships *Akron* and *Macon*, then under development. One critical problem involved flying through the turbulence streaming aft from the airships. Gorton, O'Brien, and other pilots quickly discovered that the secret was to execute a "reverse carrier approach." They would climb slowly at a relatively high angle of attack until the hook rested above the trapeze. Then they would let the plane stall out, the hook settling down onto the trapeze bar. Such approaches, with a noisy airplane seemingly headed in a climb right through the slow airship above it, caused much alarm among *Los Angeles* crewmen until the scheme proved practical and safe. Nevertheless, it required a fine piloting hand and steady nerves.

Building a suitable high-performance aircraft for launch from the *Akron* and *Macon* actually proved the greater challenge, since such a craft had to have acceptable performance and handling qualities and small dimensions. Eventually, the Navy selected a modified version of a plane they had already rejected as being unsuited for operations from a regular aircraft carrier, the tiny Curtiss F9C Sparrowhawk biplane. An attractive airplane, the F9C nevertheless possessed a number of vices: especially dangerous spinning characteristics, poor visibility, and directional instability. Its principal rival for the airship-based fighter role, however, was a Fokker design (the XFA-1) that flew even worse: spin tests at Dahlgren had ended in vicious flat spins from which the plane proved most reluctant to recover. So the Navy settled on the disappointing but small Sparrowhawk.

In September 1931, Navy test pilots Ward Harrigan and Howard "Brigham" Young had hooked onto the *Los Angeles* at night, with the trapeze illuminated by flashlights held by mechanics on board the airship! On October 23, 1931, Harrigan and Young completed the first hook-ons using the XF9C-1 Sparrowhawk prototype; Young had problems getting the little fighter off the trapeze mechanism, and only after an airship crewman physically descended the trapeze structure and knocked the Sparrowhawk's hook free of the trapeze with a wrench could the plane leave the dirigible. A bad moment, that, and one that forced redesign of the trapeze mechanism.

The *Akron*, meantime, had completed its maiden flight on September 23. After six months of proving flights by the airship, it was time for the XF9C-1 in-flight recovery tests, on May 3, 1932. The Sparrowhawk approached the *Akron* from below, climbed slowly toward the extended trapeze, and then connected with its hook at about 70 mph. As it hung by the hook, engine still ticking over, the airship crew raised the trapeze yoke, permitting two other arms to link to attachment points fitted in the upper surface of the Sparrowhawk's wing. With the linkage complete, the trapeze then rose into the bottom of the *Akron*'s open hangar, the pilot shut off the engine, and an overhead trolley transferred the plane from the trapeze to a monorail system so that it could be moved to a resting spot inside the hangar (still suspended by its hook). At this point —in actual operations—another aircraft could be recovered.

Eventually, based on the trials with the XF9C-1 flown by Harrigan and Young, the Navy completed a total of eight Sparrowhawks, planning to have four serve with each airship, and formed a special Heavier-Than-Air (HTA) Unit of picked pilots to fly them. Sparrowhawk operations from the *Akron* became commonplace, and the airship used a modified N2Y trainer for a "running boat," much the same way that today's surface carriers rely on special "COD" (Carrier On-board Delivery) airplanes for logistical support. Then, on April 3, 1933, disaster struck: The *Akron* flew out to sea amid a violent storm that eventually battered it into the waves. It took seventy-three of its seventy-six crewmen down with it, including the chief of the Navy's Bureau of Aeronautics, Admiral William Moffett. Its sister ship, the *Macon*, did not fly until later that month, and the first Sparrowhawk trials with this airship (the most advanced ever flown in the world) did not take place until July. *Macon* subsequently flew on many fleet exercises with its Sparrowhawks, until lost off Point Sur when turbulence ripped off its upper fin, weakened from previous damage. The *Macon* settled onto the Pacific together with all four of its little Sparrowhawks, two of its crew of eighty-three being lost. It was a sad end to the Sparrowhawk program and the intensive research effort that had gone into proving the concept of the lighter-than-air aircraft carrier. So passed the era of the military dirigible. Today only one Sparrowhawk survives, suspended in the Smithsonian Institution.

In part, the concept disappeared because, as British aviation journalist C. G. Grey acidly wrote, "The airships breed like elephants and aeroplanes like rabbits." Airships were expensive, difficult to maintain, and hard to keep in service. Additionally, the Navy really had little conception of how best to use the big airships and their airplanes. Were, for example, the airplanes for the protection of the airship, or for use as scouts? Various tactical opinions existed. Whatever else, however, the airships certainly had great potential as long-range launch platforms for reconnaissance and strike aircraft. The abandonment of the airship-launched airplane seems, at best, to have been premature and, at worst, a serious error. That error, if such it was, however, in no way can detract from the hard work of Navy flight test teams whose efforts demonstrated the practicality of this novel and interesting concept.

Challenge enough existed with the more conventional aircraft of the times. The 1930s constituted a decade in which the American military services sought to develop a variety of new warplanes having capabilities far in advance of the biplanes of the Jazz Age. By the end of the decade, for example, the all-metal monoplane with a streamlined configuration and retractable landing gear was *de rigueur*. Sadly, penny-pinching attitudes still placed American military aviation behind the rest of the world, even though in transports and multiengine technology the United States stood second to none. (A decade later, the shock of Pearl Harbor, coupled with reports from Europe and the growing realization that the United States lagged in the development of turbojet engine technology, would drive the message home emphatically.) Meanwhile, working within the confines of an overly cost-conscious defense policy, industrialists in partnership with the military services still attempted to provide the finest products that they could for national needs.

Sometimes they were not successful. One day in 1931, for example, an Army test pilot took off from Wright Field in a new Lockheed design, the YP-24, which employed the still-novel retractable landing gear. Following completion of the test portion of the flight, the pilot returned to Wright and cycled the landing gear, which stuck partway down. He succeeded in lowering it by violent maneuvering, but ground observers still believed it better for the pilot to take no chances and bail out, rather than risk a fatal crash landing. Communications not being what they are today—the YP-24 lacked a radio—officials on the ground sent up another aircraft with the bailout order *chalked on the side of its fuselage!* The pilot got the message and stepped out of the airplane, and the YP-24 ignominiously dug a hole in the ground.

In another case, Boeing attempted to develop a parasol-wing derivative of the famed F4B and P-12 biplane "Peashooter" family (the result being the XP-15, which vaguely resembled the later Polish PZL fighter), but during a maximum-speed test run at Seattle, the plane threw a propeller blade, and the resulting vibration tore the engine out of the airplane.

The Thomas-Morse company took its final dive when the prototype XP-13A Viper, an awkward-looking metal biplane, caught fire in midair, forcing its test pilot to bail out hurriedly. This old and distinguished pioneer firm could not stand the shock, and collapsed financially.

Sometimes the planes got back on the ground, but just. Lieutenant Ben Kelsey, of Guggenheim fame, won a Distinguished Flying Cross for safely returning a burning Martin B-10 to Wright Field one Christmas Eve after a stuck carburetor caused an engine to quit. Raw gas flooded the engine and poured out over the cowling and wing, igniting when Kelsey attempted a restart. The flaming plane, looking like the Star of Bethlehem in the night sky over Columbus, Ohio, continued on, Kelsey grimly determined to return it safely to earth so that the cause of the engine quitting—a problem plaguing B-10 bombers—could be discovered and also to save Christmas presents he had bought and stored in the back of the plane! The fire continued to burn, melting through the wing skin and causing much of the internal structure to fail. Indeed, only the gas tanks themselves, acting like a heat sink, prevented the heat from weakening the wing spars to the point of failure! Kelsey could have bailed out at any time without coming under the slightest criticism, but he managed to return the craft to earth, battered and burned though it was. An engine inspection revealed that the carburetor's design caused it to malfunction under certain load and gust conditions, and when it was replaced by a more reliable type, the problem disappeared.

Bill McAvoy, one of the greatest of NACA test pilots, once went aloft to test an experimental Martin dive bomber at Anacostia. Richard Rhode, a young NACA structures engineer, had warned the pilot beforehand that the craft's lower-wing leading edge looked understrength, and sure enough, during a high-speed dive, the right lower wing partly failed, nearly sending the plane out of control. McAvoy eased out of the dive with a huge hole in the lower wing—part of the structure and covering had torn away—and kept the plane reasonably in control only with full left aileron deflection and by holding 110 mph. He staggered along, set the biplane down smartly, taxied over to the ashen-faced onlookers, spotted the engineer, and exclaimed, "Hey, Dick! You were right!"

Even relatively routine tests could cause problems. McAvoy once had a NACA cowling come adrift during dive trials on another Navy scout bomber, badly cutting up the wings and tail. Eddie Allen had a similar problem testing an experimental Douglas fighter; the cowling came loose during a dive and started to slide forward into the propeller! Fortunately, the airstream carried it away, damaging the airframe but enabling Allen to return the wounded plane safely to earth.

THE DIVE DECADE

Nothing more typified flight testing in the 1930s than the famed and often misunderstood "terminal-velocity dive." Pulp fiction and a host of motion pictures fixed in the public mind the image of the reckless "daredevil" pilot grimacing as he pulled with all his strength on the control column of some terrible airplane hurtling at fantastic speed toward the ground. The need for such testing, namely to demonstrate that the aircraft could meet some previously agreed-upon load condition (such as pulling 8 or 9 g during a dive recovery) was never made explicit. Author Francis Vivian Drake, for example, wrote of one fictional hero:

> He flung the plane around. Test her, that was the game. Test her to the excited, outraged limit of endurance. Test her until the wires screamed for pity, until the tired body shook and shuddered and the wings clung to a mad eggshell band of safety and the controls stretched

for the cracking point with silent terror. Abuse her some more. Twist and torment and agonize her until she writhed beneath you, but set her down *tested*, foolproof . . . so that some bright young spark in a new uniform could keep his neck safe for the next war.

The pilot did this, Drake wrote, "with cheerful unconcern," for, after all,

That was a test pilot's job. You took them up, untried, flung them around with the pitiless skill of experience, trying in every conceivable way to break them in the air. If you brought everything back in one piece it was a good plane.

At the climax, the power dive, just before pullout, the pilot begins to sweat:

A cold appalling fear seized him like the hand of Death, gripped his stomach, struck along his veins. The stick would mush—he knew it. A few seconds more and he'd be spattered out like paint. . . . *God, get me out of this!* . . .

But the plane does recover, does return the pilot safely to earth, and back in the office he fills out his report:

He drew the report pad across the yellow oak desk. *Type of Machine:* —Pursuit Experimental, F 12c. *Type of Test:*—Mechanically, his pencil filled in, "Routine."[4]

In contrast to this strange fictional portrayal, test pilot Eddie Allen wrote an article for *Aviation* magazine in 1937 in which he commented on the passing of the "Here Goes Nothing!" approach to test flying. There were, he stated, three historical stages in the evolution of test flying. The first, the "Here Goes Nothing!" stage, had been marked by a willingness to take risks bordering on the absurd. However, Allen wrote, "Under the changing conditions of increasing knowledge, fatalistic risk-taking becomes ignorant recklessness." The second stage, therefore, had "brought a demand for the type of test pilot who was bent on reducing his risks, and who was capable of a new investment of thought in planning for every emergency that might occur." Finally, and in Allen's view a hallmark of the 1930s, was the third stage:

At the third stage there definitely emerges a new attitude toward flight testing, away from chance taking altogether and toward a complete analysis of each problem that can be met prior to flight. This stage is the end-product ideally of the progress in the second stage where a compromise had to be effected between the cost of further investigation and the cost of insurance (often exorbitant), against the risks of "trying the thing out in the air." Those who are reaching for this attitude greatly decrease their risks by beginning their "testing" at the inception of the design rather than at the last minute when everyone, from designer to production manager, is so tense that omissions are favored and mistakes difficult to avoid.[5]

Occasionally, however, popular writers came closer to the truth of test flying. Aviation's Homeric poet, Gill Robb Wilson (an individual much respected by both the aviation and flight testing communities), alluded both to the romantic myth and to the practical realities of test flying in general and dive testing in particular when he penned:

> Ten thousand grand for a dozen g's,
> And no one can take thirteen of these,
> And all I do for this princely dough
> Is climb as high as the ship will go,
> And dive until the needle hits the pin
> In the gadget that shows how fast I've been.
> Then throw her in reverse control
> To see if I and the ship stay whole.
> If the wings stay on and the fittings tight,
> And the elevators function right,
> And the ailerons don't flutter away,
> Or pressures buckle where pressures may,
> I climb again with a like intent
> To prove that it wasn't an accident.
> Pick up g's with a spinning fall
> To see if she's weak that way at all.
> I loop for balance and stall for glide
> And whipstall hard with flaps out wide.
> I spin wheels up and spin wheels out
> And spiral and slip and slam about
> In landings rough as the tank can stand
> To prove each step the designer planned.
> Then I taxi into an open ditch
> And don't get paid for the sonofabitch.[6]

In fact, dive testing *was* one of the distinctive hallmarks of 1930s flight testing, especially for high-performance military airplanes. Toward the end of the decade, with truly streamlined aircraft such as the Lockheed P-38, it did become downright dangerous as flight speeds edged upward to the point where aerodynamic trim changes and buffeting occurred from so-called "compressibility" (transonic airflow) effects. Coupled to this was the problem of spinning. An appalling number of prototypes crashed in the 1920s and '30s as a result of losing their wings in dives or simply developing uncontrollable spins. As a result, companies, the NACA, and the military devoted increasing amounts of time to studying load criteria for dive pullouts, and studying the phenomenon of aircraft spinning, first scientifically examined by Lindemann during the First World War. (The changes in aircraft design since the days of Lindemann demanded upgrading and reexamination of spin criteria—as is true today, in the era of the multi-Mach jet.)

The Army undertook a study of spinning at Wright Field, using specially instrumented test aircraft (and as a result of his piloting these hazardous test missions, project pilot H. A. Sutton received a well-earned DFC). So did the NACA, using a variety of airplanes equipped with modified control surfaces and various methods of varying the craft's inertial characteristics and center-of-gravity location, as well as an emergency "spin chute" attached to the craft's vertical fin, which the pilot could deploy to break out of a spin and into a spiral from which a dive recovery could be effected. The intensive nature of these research programs can be measured by a single statistic: during one year of testing, NACA pilot McAvoy estimated that he had spun a grand total of over *three hundred* miles vertically. As a result of this work, however, the mechanism of spin onset and the loads developed during spins and dives were much better understood, in time for these lessons to be incorporated in the generation of aircraft with which America went to war in 1941.

Ed Heinemann, the legendary designer of many Douglas aircraft, was intimately involved with one dramatic series of diving trials while working as a designer for Jack Northrop. Northrop had developed an experimental Navy dive bomber, the XBT-1, a trim monoplane that featured split trailing-edge dive flaps that a pilot could deploy during a dive to slow the airplane and thus improve its effectiveness as a bomber. In the 1930s, it was not at all unusual for a designer to ride along with a test pilot on the proving flights, and though later viewed "as an unnecessary risk," it was condoned for both psychological and technical reasons. So, during the XBT-1's testing, Heinemann would ride along as a test observer in the back seat as test pilot Vance Breese, one of the best in the business, put the plane through its paces, all for the munificent sum of $2,000! Then came trouble. As dive trials got underway, the plane exhibited a dangerous tail-flutter problem when the dive flaps opened. Heinemann decided to go aloft with a Bell and Howell movie camera to photograph the tail. During dive after punishing dive, followed by exhausting 9 g pullouts, Breese and Heinemann explored the flutter problem, bringing back films of the tips of the tortured horizontal tail sur-

faces moving through a vertical arc of about two feet. "This, to be perfectly frank," he honestly recollected years later, "scared the very hell
out of me."[7] Eventually, as a result of the flights and consultations with
the NACA, Northrop and Heinemann decided to cut a series of holes in
the flaps to minimize the disturbed airflow. Back into the air went the
XBT-1 and its dedicated test crew. The perforated "Swiss cheese" flaps
eliminated the problem, at the same time giving the plane a unique appearance. Eventually, the XBT-1 evolved into the famed Douglas SBD
Dauntless, victor of the battles of the Coral Sea and of Midway, the
plane that turned the tide in the war in the Pacific, thanks to a group of
flight researchers who dared to dispense with conventional wisdom and
instead chose to adapt a radical, innovative solution that turned a "dog"
airplane into the progenitor of one of the deadliest antishipping aircraft
ever developed.

No account of 1930s flight testing would be complete, however,
without reference to the tale of Grumman's last and finest fighting
biplane, the F3F, and its test pilot, Jimmy Collins. Its story illustrates the
tenacity that flight researchers often have to possess when confronting a
seemingly insurmountable problem. Grumman is a name that eventually
became synonymous with naval aircraft. Founded in 1929 by Leroy Ran-
dle Grumman, a naval aviator in the First World War and later the general manager of the Loening Aeronautical Corporation, the company
built its first naval fighter, the two-place FF-1, in 1931. A single-seater
having the same basic lines, the F2F, appeared in 1933. All Grumman
fighters built, right up to the wartime Hellcat, tended to have a squat,
tubby appearance (in part because the landing gear retracted into the fuselage), but they were extremely strong and, although the F2F was
tricky to fly, it featured outstanding maneuverability. The 230-mph
speed of the F2F encouraged the Navy and Grumman to proceed with
a generally similar but highly refined version, the F3F. Accordingly, in
early 1935, the Grumman company completed the initial XF3F-1 and, in
the manner of the day, hired a well-known free-lance test pilot, Jimmy
Collins, to test the new ship.

Jimmy Collins was one of the most enigmatic aviators of his time. The
son of a bricklayer, young Collins had held various odd jobs before entering the Army Air Service and graduating from flight training in 1925.
One of his classmates was Charles Lindbergh, and like Lindbergh, Collins
was a fine pilot. A turbulent figure, Collins drifted into socialism and
then communism, contemplated going to China to help establish the Na-
tionalist air force, and finally decided to stay stateside when he received
an offer to dive-test a new Curtiss dive bomber. The tests went
smoothly, and after completion of the contract, Collins found himself in
demand for such dive tests. Collins was unusual in another respect: he

wrote as a reporter for the New York *Daily News,* and also for *The Saturday Evening Post.* And he began working on an autobiography, entitled simply *Test Pilot,* which consisted largely of his articles that had appeared elsewhere. An old friend asked him to write a column on the dive tests for Curtiss that he was then about to fly. He wrote to his sister later:

> I got to thinking it over and thought maybe I wouldn't come back because it was a dangerous job, and then poor Archer would be out of a column. . . . So I playfully wrote one for him in case I did get bumped off.[8]

He kept the column anyway, entitled, "I Am Dead." It is troubling reading, for it reflects a man beset by inner turmoil and uncertainty. Fellow pilots and others recollected later that Collins was emphatic that the Grumman XF3F-1 tests would be his last as a test pilot before he would embark on a career as a full-time writer. "I Am Dead" is also troubling because, in spite of being overwritten, it is a dark mirror of the soul. The novelist William Faulkner, himself an aviator in the "Great War" and (among his many fine works) the author of *Pylon,* an excellent novel of air racing, reviewed Collins's autobiography after it was published, remarking that "I Am Dead"

> should have been a private document, shown you privately by the friend with whom he left it. You are sorry to read it in a book. It should not have been included. It should have been quoted from, at most, quoted not as the document which it is, but for a figure which it contains, the only figure or phrase in the book which suddenly arrests the mind with the fine shock of poetry:
>
> The cold but vibrant fuselage was the last thing to feel my warm and living flesh.[9]

And sadly, so it was to be. Collins completed the first flight on the XF3F-1 at Farmingdale, Long Island, on March 20, 1935, flying two other test missions that same day, including a one-hour flight at full engine power. Two days later, Navy test pilots briefly evaluated the ship on two short flights and then, after lunch, Jimmy Collins embarked on a series of ten high-speed dive tests, which required him to demonstrate a 9 g dive recovery on the final dive. Collins completed nine of the ten dives without incident in the course of five flights. Late in the day, he took off on the sixth flight, for the tenth dive. The stubby biplane climbed noisily to 18,000 feet, and Collins nosed over into the steep dive. For 10,000 feet the plane dropped straight down. Then, at 8,000 feet, before the horrified gaze of the test observers, the biplane abruptly nosed up and disintegrated, its wings and engine separating from the fuselage, which tumbled into Pinelawn Cemetery, outside Farmingdale. The on-board accelerometer recorded that at the moment of pullout, the g loading had been between 11 and 15, well above the plane's acceptable load limit. Collins simply lacked any chance for survival.

The death of this popular and well-known airman shocked New Yorkers and became national news. The posthumous publication of his autobiography, together with the mysterious "I Am Dead" column, further fixed in the public mind the image of the test pilot as a fatalistic risk-taker, a man doomed to a short life, a reckless adventurer. Faulkner himself even baldly stated in *The American Mercury* that the demands of speed would possibly create "a kind of species or race" of airmen:

> They will have to be taken in infancy because the precision pilot of today begins to train in his teens and is through in his thirties. These would be a species and in time a race and in time they would produce a folklore. . . .[10]

What nonsense! Today we recognize it as such. Then, however, it seemed remote yet believable, and millions went to see Clark Gable, Myrna Loy, and Spencer Tracy in a film riding the crest of this sensationalist foolishness, a film not by coincidence entitled *Test Pilot*. (In the film, accidents abound, and Tracy, the loyal mechanic and confidant of the cocksure Gable, bitingly snaps at Myrna Loy, "You little fool! Don't you know it's dangerous even to *look* at an airplane?!") Professional test pilots scorned such cinematographic histrionics.

So Collins was dead and the XF3F-1 destroyed, amid great publicity. The Navy still needed the F3F, and Grumman built a second prototype. Why had Collins crashed? Was it an error of rashness on his part? A mechanical failure? One likely explanation is that the pilot simply overcontrolled the aircraft during the recovery. Even later, production F3F's had such light control-stick forces that the Navy cautioned pilots against inadvertently overstressing the aircraft during recoveries from dives, in which the plane could attain over 400 mph. Collins might simply have pulled back too abruptly, too far, so that the Grumman fighter experienced loads far in excess of its design limit. The Navy's Bureau of Aeronautics, just after the Collins accident, reduced the g load that the next F3F would have to meet, from the fabled 9 down to 7½, a decision that, as might be expected, caused great public sensation.

In early 1935, Grumman sent the second XF3F-1 to Anacostia for tests with company pilot Lee Gehlbach. On May 17, 1935, during a requisite Navy ten-turn right-hand spin demonstration, the plane entered a stable flat spin, and despite Gehlbach's best efforts, he could not recover. He bailed out safely, reporting that the XF3F-1 was directionally unstable. With two down, Grumman built a third, modifying it by adding a short ventral fin to increase the effective vertical tail surface area. The third XF3F-1 passed its trials without incident, piloted by Lee Gehlbach and NACA's Bill McAvoy, the latter a natural choice because of his expertise in both dive and spin testing. Because of the loss of the second prototype, the Navy's Bureau of Aeronautics issued strict guidelines that no manned spinning trials be undertaken in new naval aircraft until the designs had successfully passed tests in the NACA's newly created spin-research tunnel at the Langley laboratory. This effective partnership of ground testing with flight verification aloft went a long way toward preventing the kinds of accidents that plagued the development of new military aircraft in the early 1930s. The third XF3F-1 paved the way for a batch of production F3F fighters, which served with the fleet from 1937 until stricken from active service in 1943, when they had long been relegated to advanced training duties. The F3F brought the era of the Navy's fighter biplanes to a close, and it is recollected with great fondness by its pilots. What must also be remembered, of course, is the sacrifice and determination that flight researchers exhibited in bringing this aircraft from the drawing board to the Navy's fighter squadrons.

One of the most publicized test flights of the 1930s involved a dive demonstration that a Curtiss test pilot performed for a French purchasing commission secretly visiting the United States to buy Curtiss H-75A-1 Hawk fighters and other aircraft for France's Armée de l'Air. The H-75A-1 was an export version of the Curtiss P-36A Hawk entering service with the Army Air Corps. It typified the first generation of modern monoplane fighters, having an enclosed cockpit, a retractable landing gear, internally braced wings and tail surfaces, and a closely cowled radial engine driving a three-bladed controllable-pitch propeller. It flew beautifully, though its 313-mph top speed was already surpassed by the latest European pursuits such as the Supermarine Spitfire and the early Messerschmitt Bf 109.

France's weak interwar governments had effectively reduced that country's military forces to impotency, and as is often the case, the danger of foreign aggression now drove many of the same politicians who had emasculated France's air power to demand instant action. France's demoralized and disorganized aircraft industry could not respond to the rearmament program needed, and so France turned for help to other countries, especially the United States. The nimble and attractive Hawk monoplane, with its excellent handling characteristics, was a natural choice, so the French ordered a batch, but before placing further orders, they had a specific requirement: Could the Hawk maintain a velocity of more than 500 mph for over a mile during a high-speed dive in case it had to catch high-speed bombers? The requirement made sense, for the latest generation of bombers, both German and Russian, had demonstrated a clear ability to outrun opposing fighters during the bloody and callous "proving-ground" war in Spain.

In January 1939, a French military mission arrived at the Curtiss plant in Buffalo, New York, with special instrumentation to be installed in a production Hawk H-75A-1. Curtiss executives selected company test pilot H. Lloyd Child to make the test demonstration. Child had been Curtiss's chief test pilot at Buffalo since 1936 and was no stranger to risk. During one test flight of a Curtiss Falcon in 1934, aileron flutter had set in and ripped the wings from the plane; Child parachuted safely into a plowed field. His brother E. Rushmore Child served as chief of the Curtiss aerodynamics section, and the two worked closely together, though his brother, as Lloyd Child recollected later, "never did approve of my doing dive work."

Curtiss scheduled the flight for January 24, 1939, and that day dawned overcast and murky. By 11 A.M., the weather was clearing to the southwest, and technicians began installing the French instrumentation in the plane. Shortly before noon, Child, wearing a fleece-lined flying suit and boots over ordinary business clothes, strapped into the Hawk, ran up the engine (which had already been prewarmed), and took off, climbing swiftly up to the test altitude of 22,000 feet. The skies were still hazy, and he looked for a clearly identifiable reference spot on the ground that he could sight on during his dive. He finally selected a greenhouse near the Buffalo airport, because sunlight was reflected off its glass. He trimmed the plane nose-heavy, set the propeller blades at very high pitch, rolled the Hawk on its back and pulled through in a partial split S, sighting on the greenhouse and then bringing its bright panes in line with the ring-and-bead gunsight of the Hawk. Down the Hawk whistled, in a dead-vertical dive. He subsequently wrote:

> A pilot's awareness is keyed up during a fast dive! . . . I smelled for gas fumes that would have meant a flooding carburetor. My ears were cocked like a fox terrier's for any whistling or shrieking noise that would tell of a metal plate or piece of cowling being stripped away. With my haunches I tried to feel in the framework any unusual vibration to warn of an impending broken bearing or frozen piston. I watched the wing surfaces for signs of skin wrinkles and the yielding of internal structure that they would denote. I darted glances at the instrument board dials, noting especially whether the oil and fuel pressures were holding up satisfactorily in the vertical position. It is odd to do all this when you know that if anything happened, it would probably be so sudden and final that you could not do anything to stop it, but you do it anyway.[11]

Onward the Hawk dived, with its airspeed indicator climbing toward 500 mph and then going beyond. When Child was certain that the Hawk had attained the requisite figure, he started counting slowly. He had planned to pull out when he reached "eight," but the speeding fighter was flying so smoothly that he decided to continue a little longer: "It was a good opportunity to see what a Hawk could do, if let out a little, and I gave the plane its head." At the count of seventeen, his altimeter registered 5,000 feet, and he eased gently back on the control stick. Even so, the pullout forces reached an estimated 7 g, and when he leveled out, he could plainly see individual windows of houses below—a clear indication that he was below 2,000 feet, lower than he had planned to be. The altimeter, it turned out, had lagged behind the speeding plane by about 1,500 feet, not unusual but potentially dangerous. However, all went well, and the tranquillity of the greenhouse went undisturbed by the whining airplane overhead. Child returned to Buffalo and landed, and the instruments were pulled for examination. With the records being processed, Child took a quick break, then took the Hawk aloft on a few more demonstration tests *and* then went aloft testing a Curtiss dive bomber for the Navy.

By the time he quit flying for the day, the records had been studied. They indicated that the Hawk had not reached merely 500 but had touched 600 mph, at an altitude of about 9,000 feet! A remarkable figure for the day, the "faster than a bullet" dive gained Curtiss and Child great public notice, and the French ordered even more of the Hawks.

Much was made over the precise French recording instrumentation that had registered the 600-mph figure, which corresponds to over eight tenths the speed of sound—Mach 0.813, to be precise—at an altitude of 9,000 feet. That is an amazing speed for a plane having such blunt nose contours and such a thick wing as the H-75A-1 . . . and perhaps can best be explained by recognizing the errors that afflict pressure-sensitive instrumentation when an airplane is flying at transonic speeds. One can have little doubt that the Hawk exceeded 500 mph during the dive—but 600? In tests during and after the Second World War, even such "clean" aircraft as the P-51 Mustang only touched Mach 0.8, and the highest recorded dive Mach number for a piston-engine aircraft was Mach 0.9, reached under very carefully controlled conditions by a modified Spitfire Mark XI at the Royal Aircraft Establishment.

H. Lloyd Child went on to test many other Curtiss aircraft during the war years, and by the time he retired from active test piloting, he had completed forty-one first flights of experimental prototypes, an enviable record and one that helped assure his well-deserved receiving of an honorary fellowship of the Society of Experimental Test Pilots in 1964.

Child's flight was one of the last great dive tests, for the necessity of such testing was fast disappearing. The new generation of aircraft, capable of nudging 400 mph in level flight—such as the Lockheed XP-38 and the Vought XF4U-1 Corsair—could not execute sustained high-speed dives safely, simply because they were too "clean" and accelerated rapidly to speeds above 500 mph. During tests at low altitudes, they could produce undesirably high g forces during recovery. At higher altitudes, they ran into trouble from "compressibility effects" such as trim changes and buffeting that could—and sometimes did—lead to structural failure. So, with these new aircraft emerging off company drawing boards, a lot of the older testing requirements had to be revised.

The early test performance of the Vought Corsair, the first American naval fighter to attain 400 mph in level flight, convinced Bureau of Aeronautics officials to abandon two of the previously hallowed requisite tests for Navy fighters and dive bombers: holding a "zero lift" vertical dive through a 10,000-foot loss of altitude, and demonstrating recovery from a ten-turn spin. Vought test pilot Boone T. Guyton had touched 550 mph during one Corsair dive but suffered a hydraulic failure that caused the XF4U-1's propeller to overspeed, wrecking the engine. Following a perilous low-altitude, high-g pullout, he skillfully swapped airspeed for altitude, then smartly dead-sticked down to a safe landing. During the standard ten-turn spin tests, the angular Corsair developed such control loads that Guyton discovered the forces were too high for him to recover; if the plane had not been equipped with an emergency spin chute, Guyton would have had to abandon it. Flight testing is a dynamic field, and the criteria for yesterday's airplanes are often not sufficient for tomorrow's . . . or even today's. The advanced fighters and bombers of the late 1930s demanded rewriting the test manuals of the 1920s. The high-speed dive would become a thing to be approached with caution, lest the refined subsonic aerodynamics of the day betray one into overextending the airplane into an as yet unknown realm, where the mysteries of transonic flight could tear it apart.

BEYOND THE DC-3 GENERATION

It was in the 1930s that airplanes grew increasingly complex, especially the new multiengine designs just appearing. At the beginning of the decade, the term "multiengine" almost invariably referred to some ungainly biplane, such as a Keystone bomber or a Curtiss Condor. By mid-decade, it conjured up the image of a sleek 247 or DC-2. But, by the end of the decade, the term multiengine, to the American public, brought to mind visions of transoceanic "clippers" and large, four-engine bombers. The transformation had taken place in the early 1930s, when aircraft companies had begun to seriously examine multiengine aircraft having wingspans over 100 feet and usually four-engine layouts. True, there had always been some large aircraft in development, such as the freak Barling Bomber of the 1920s, but these had led nowhere, as the requisite technology to make such large aircraft efficient was lacking.

One of the first large aircraft had been the twin-engine Consolidated P2Y-1 flying boat, test-flown in 1932. It had the then-impressive top speed of 126 mph, and in January 1934 it demonstrated its capabilities to good effect when Navy patrol squadron VP-10 flew six of the big planes to Hawaii for a routine fleet deployment. Consolidated followed this with the graceful XP3Y-1 patrol plane, another twin-engine seaplane, which Bill Wheatley first tested at Norfolk in March 1935—it eventually evolved into the world-famous PBY Catalina, the best-known seaplane of all time.

Igor Sikorsky, who had developed the world's first four-engine airplane in Russia before the First World War, had pointed the way toward commercial four-engine seaplanes with his graceful S-42, which first took to the air (piloted by Sikorsky himself) in early 1934. In August of that year, piloted by Pan American's chief pilot, Ed Musick, Sikorsky test pilot Boris Sergievsky, and Charles Lindbergh, it set eight new world records for seaplanes, adding these to two it had previously set during its early flight testing. Pan Am's Juan Trippe now had an airliner capable of spanning the Atlantic and crossing the Pacific as well.

Glenn Martin, not to be outdone, proceeded with the development of a much more aerodynamically refined four-engine design, the Martin M-130, the first of which—the legendary *China Clipper*—took to the air on December 30, 1934, piloted by Ken Ebel. Sikorsky upped the ante with the not-unattractive VS-44 Excalibur. The greatest of all American flying boats, however, were the beautiful clippers from Boeing. And the story of the Boeing clippers is bound up in the story of this company's development of the first major American four-engine landplanes.

In 1934, the War Department had approved a Wright Field plan for a so-called "Project A": a multiengine bomber capable of carrying 2,000 pounds of bombs 5,000 miles at 200 mph. The Army Air Corps invited Boeing and Martin to submit studies, and Boeing, headed by the farseeing Claire Egtvedt, subsequently received approval to begin development of their entry, the Boeing Model 294, a four-engine airplane spanning 149 feet and weighing over 35 tons when fully loaded. Eventually the Model 294, designated the XB-15, flew in 1937, piloted by Eddie Allen. It proved a disappointment; it could not meet the original Project A specs. (One Boeing executive, asked years later if Boeing had learned any valuable lessons from the XB-15, replied, "Sure—we learned not to build huge underpowered airplanes.") Just as Boeing was mapping out the Project A program, another circular from Wright Field hit the company, this for a multiengine bomber carrying 2,000 pounds 1,020 miles at a required speed of 200 mph and a desired speed of 250. And the Army added that they really would like a range of 2,200 miles. While other companies examined the circular and thought in terms of two engines, Boeing, already working on the Model 294, thought of four. In September 1934, the company directors voted approval to go ahead on a smaller four-engine bomber, the Model 299.

A graceful mid-wing monoplane, the 299 was ready for its first flight by mid-1935. On July 28, Boeing chief test pilot Les Tower took off in the new plane. It handled well. The following August, Tower delivered the new bomber from Seattle to Wright Field, flying the 2,000 miles nonstop at the then-phenomenal average speed of 233 mph. Boeing clearly had a winner. By late October, all talk at "the Field" centered on Boeing's fabulous "Flying Fortress." Then, on the morning of October 30, Army test pilots Ployer "Pete" Hill and Don Putt took off in the 299 for a routine test. Les Tower went along as a test observer, together with some other crewmen. The gleaming bomber raced down the runway and nosed into the air, angling higher, higher, until witnesses on the ground recognized the signs of disaster. The plane, now quite vertical, fell off on one wing and pancaked hard into the ground. Then it burst into flames . . . rescuers, braving the flames, pulled the crew from the plane. But Pete Hill died that afternoon, and Les Tower a little later. Stunned, Boeing and Army investigators sifted through the wreckage. What they discovered demonstrated beyond all else the caution that had to accompany the complexity of new airplanes. The test crew had simply taken off with the elevator controls locked by a device designed to protect the controls from being damaged by wind gusts when the craft was sitting on the ground.

The biplanes of the twenties often had fewer than a dozen controls and instruments demanding the attention of the pilot. By the mid-1930s, this had all changed. Boone Guyton once tallied up a list of forty-eight instruments, switches, and knobs confronting a test pilot preparing for a flight in a single-engine airplane. Largely because of the 299's accident and the danger of similar "oversight" problems with other multiengine airplanes, preflight checklists came into general use. (Reflecting on his own substantial years in the cockpits of large airplanes, Ernest Gann has written: "The mind of man was not designed to remember everything in a modern cockpit. It was remarkable, and sometimes tragic, how many things *two* minds could forget. . . .")[12] The loss of the 299, which nearly ended the career of the fabled Flying Fortress amid the torn earth of Wright Field, came as a brutal reminder that the penalty for carelessness in flying, especially test flying, can be death.

Boeing lost the competition, but by great good fortune the Army also placed an order for thirteen advanced test models of the 299, to be designated Y1B-17, and a fourteenth for static testing. Boeing changed power plants from the Pratt & Whitney Hornet to the more powerful Wright Cyclone, and the first of the new planes flew on December 2, 1936, the direct ancestor of the more than 12,700 Flying Fortresses that Boeing would build. Then, at the behest of Oliver Echols, Boeing modified the "nonflying," fourteenth preproduction Y1B-17 to flight-ready condition, fitting it with General Electric turbosuperchargers, the descendants of the first rudimentary turbochargers that Sanford Moss had tested on Shorty Schroeder's Le Père nearly two decades before. The modified Fortress, designated the Y1B-17A, eventually hit 311 mph at 25,000 feet during flight testing by Johnny Corkille and P. H. Robey in March 1939, presaging later wartime Fortress performance. The United States soon would have an operational unpressurized but turbocharged high-altitude strategic bomber in service, starting with the B-17B, which first flew in June 1939 and showed its stuff by flying coast to coast at an altitude of 26,000 feet and a speed of 265 mph, piloted by cigar-chomping Stan Umstead and L. F. Harmon. The next step, already germinating in the minds of Air Corps and Boeing advanced planners, was for a true high-altitude pressurized "very long range" bomber benefiting from the latest power-plant technology, high-speed NACA airfoil research, and the XC-35 test program—a super Flying Fortress. That would come to pass with the XB-29, the predecessor of the silver giants that devastated Japan and ushered in the horror of the atomic age.

Meanwhile, Boeing sought to apply the technological lessons learned from the XB-17 and B-17 programs to civil aviation, a trend that continued after the Second World War, as evidenced by the technology transfer from the B-47 and B-52 programs to the prototype Boeing 707. Boeing applied the gigantic wing of the XB-15 to the Model 314 flying boats (but used more powerful engines), and built the first of these huge craft outdoors, because the company lacked a hangar large enough to accommodate the plane, with its 152-foot wing, 27-foot height, and 106-foot fuselage-hull. Boeing set the first flight date for June 7, 1938, and thousands of onlookers gathered on the shores of Puget Sound to watch the trials. (Among the onlookers was a teenager named Scott Crossfield, destined to make his own mark on flight testing in a few

years.) Early taxi runs had not gone smoothly; Eddie Allen and Pan
Am's Andre Priester had noted an alarming tendency for the plane to dig
its wing tips into the water. After further tests and ballasting, all was
ready for the first flight, on June 7. That day, in the late afternoon,
Eddie Allen flew the craft off the Sound and up to Lake Washington,
where Boeing planned to do the remaining flight test work. Disappointingly, the Model 314 had revealed a serious directional control
problem, which eventually forced Boeing to change the vertical-fin
configuration from a single fin to triple fins, like the later Lockheed Constellation. Though the discovery disappointed engineers and waiting airline managers, it resulted in the craft being a better and safer airplane.
On March 3, 1939, Eleanor Roosevelt, the wife of the President, christened one of the big Boeings the *Yankee Clipper*. Like the clipper ships
of yore, it soon embarked on the first of its oceanic voyages. But, like the
zeppelin before it, the large flying-boat airliner was rapidly running out
of time, and when the Second World War ringed the tidal shores of the
Atlantic and Pacific with concrete airfields that modern landplanes—such
as the revolutionary four-engine Douglas DC-4—could utilize, the flying
boat followed the zeppelin and the dinosaur into extinction. It disappeared because its peculiar configuration—high wing, floats, boat hull—
limited its utility and raised its operating costs. And it lacked the flexibility of the landplane, requiring smooth debris-and-ice-free waters, not
as easy to find as one might think. But Boeing also had a landplane in the
works, using the wings and tail surfaces of the reliable Model 299 joined
to a new, pressurized fuselage—the Model 307, the Stratoliner, developed
for TWA. Like the Model 299, the 307 was a "taildragger," and on December 31, 1938, Eddie Allen and a picked test crew completed an
uneventful first flight in the portly transport. Tests of the big plane went
smoothly, but then, in the following March, tragedy once again visited
the Boeing test department. During a stability investigation near Mount
Rainier, the Stratoliner broke up in flight. Investigators later pieced the
story together.

A Dutch test crew from KLM (one of the airlines contemplating buying the 307) had joined a Boeing test crew for the flight. The KLM representatives were especially interested in what would happen to the airplane in the event of two engines dying on one side, combined with
maximum yaw into the direction of the dead engines, followed immediately by a stall! Obviously a worst-case situation that most pilots wish
they never see, and a questionable test to perform. Apparently, just
above stalling speed, the Stratoliner prototype had entered a spin. Boeing
test pilot Julius Barr and the KLM copilot had recovered into a dive, but
when pulling out of the dive, the plane broke up from excessive loads,

killing the crew of ten. Eventually the 307 did enter airline service with modifications, including a much larger vertical fin, similar to that on all B-17 models from the B-17E onward. The 307 might have gone on to a great airline career, but with the outbreak of war, Boeing needed all its production capacity for the B-17 and later the B-29, and anyway, the Douglas DC-4 soon eclipsed the 307 in performance and utility. Boeing would not recapture their leadership in air transportation until after the war, with the 707 jetliner.

Every decade in the history of aviation has produced its own distinctive configurations, such as the sweptwing of the 1940s and the lifting body of the 1960s. The 1930s, too, produced its share, culminating most generally in the sleek, low-wing, single-engine pursuit and the equally aesthetically pleasing monoplane transports of the period. But there were other shapes that researchers investigated that required careful flight testing so that their advantages and disadvantages could be impartially and candidly assessed.

Sometimes the flight testing methods researchers resorted to were novel ones. Aerodynamicists had long recognized that a research airplane essentially uses the sky itself as a laboratory, taking the place of the wind-tunnel model tested on the ground. One of the major problems in developing new aircraft has always been the correlation of ground-test results and flight test results, for the limitations of the tunnel and other ground-testing methods (such as towing tanks for seaplane hull experiments) invariably bias trials. There is, simply speaking, no substitute for free-flight testing. Companies naturally were reluctant to proceed with the development of large aircraft if there was much chance that the aircraft might not prove a success.

One novel testing method employed by some manufacturers around the world was to construct a subscale piloted flying model of the larger aircraft, testing it to determine the general suitability of the configuration, before proceeding with the construction of a full-size prototype. Britain did this, for example, with the development of the Short Stirling heavy bomber. In the United States, Martin followed suit when planning the Model 162 flying boat, a large twin-engine experimental design. Martin built a quarter-scale model of the full-size Model 162, designated the little plane the Model 162-A, and flew it in early 1937. Navy test pilot John Jacob put the little single-seat testbed through its paces at Middle River, and it demonstrated that the larger Model 162, with its deep hull and graceful "gull" wing planform, would perform satisfactorily. As a result of these subscale tests, the Navy approved development of the full-size prototype, which became the XPBM-1, first flown in early 1939. Some stability problems with the larger plane forced Martin to modify the tail design of the XPBM-1, but the tests of the small Model 162-A had already proved that its basic design was sound. The XPBM-1 evolved into the versatile Martin PBM Mariner patrol bomber.

ALOFT ON ROTARY WINGS: THE STORY OF THE HELICOPTER

One of the major accomplishments in the history of aviation has been the development of practical vertical-takeoff-and-landing aircraft, best exemplified by the helicopter of the 1930s and early 1940s, and the vectored-thrust jet airplane of the 1960s. Here indeed a major challenge confronted flight researchers. While not perhaps as glamorous as the experimental craft that streaked to new speeds and altitudes, the early vertical-flight testbeds were nevertheless revolutionary in their own unique way, for their potential lay at the other end of the performance spectrum, in vertical ascents and descents, low-speed controllability, and hover. The path to the modern VTOL vehicle is littered with the false hopes and faded promise of many machines. But the result of this work has led to a class of flight craft that have expanded the horizons of air transportation and military aeronautics, and that have, according to one estimate, saved the lives of nearly a half million people through the years. The oil rigger in the Gulf going on leave, the yachtsman waiting for rescue in storm-tossed seas, the infantryman calling in gunships to fend off enemy armor, all can thank the flight researchers of the 1930s and 1940s who made the modern VTOL aircraft, especially the helicopter, possible.

The story of the helicopter begins far before even the First World War. The first rotary-wing devices appeared as children's toys in about the early-fourteenth century. In the 1780s, Launoy and Bienvenu developed a small, draw-string-powered contrarotating helicopter model. George Cayley improved upon this design over a decade later. In the 1840s, W. H. Phillips test-flew a successful helicopter model powered by steam jets in the rotor tips, and Ponton d'Amécourt followed this up with equally successful tests of small clockwork-driven helicopters. Building a full-size, man-carrying machine was quite something else, however. Various inventors had experimented with manned helicopters without success. Then, in the early 1920s, a Spanish aircraft designer, Juan de la Cierva, had taken the first important step, with the development of the Autogiro, an aircraft having a large, free-wheeling rotor mounted above the fuselage and a conventional piston engine and propeller to drive it through the air. Because the rotor and the engine were not directly connected, the Autogiro was incapable of a true vertical takeoff or a hover. After much experimentation, Cierva, a mathematician of exceptional ability, hinged the rotor blades at their roots to compensate for the differences in lift generated by an "advancing" and a "retreating" blade. His research gave the rotary wing automatic stability, a problem that had plagued helicopter developers for years. Alejandro Spencer, a Spanish test pilot, completed the first flight of the Cierva Autogiro at Getafe Aerodrome, outside Madrid, in 1923, and British test pilot Frank Courtney demonstrated it to Air Ministry officials in Great Britain in 1925. Nevertheless, the Autogiro was not a panacea. It still had a number of problems and could pick up enough vertical velocity in a descent to damage or even destroy the machine. Metal fatigue and vibration problems posed threats to the rotor. All these served to limit the immediate utility of the Autogiro, which really remained a semiexperimental craft. It did provide flight researchers with a useful tool to investigate some of the problems of rotary-wing craft and thus pave the way to the true helicopter (which, in fact, followed on the heels of the Autogiro).

In 1931, the NACA purchased an American-built Pitcairn PCA-2 autogiro to provide information for comparing rotary-wing aerodynamic theory with actual data taken in flight. For its day, and even in comparison with later autogiros and helicopters, the PCA-2 had good performance, including an overall lift-to-drag ratio of 6.7 and a maximum speed of 140 mph, still quite respectable today. NACA pilots Bill McAvoy and Melvin Gough undertook a number of flights in the Pitcairn over the next five years, and the NACA reports issuing from this research constituted, in the words of NASA helicopter researcher Frederic Gustafson, the "first authoritative information on autogiro performance and rotor behavior."

The PCA-2 was just the first of a number of autogiros the NACA evaluated at its Langley laboratory. NACA later acquired a more advanced Pitcairn YG-2, first developed for the Army, but NACA testing indicated that its control forces were so high and so variable as to render the craft unsuitable for service. This latter craft gave NACA pilot McAvoy and flight test engineer John Wheatley a particularly bad few seconds during a test flight at Langley on March 30, 1936. McAvoy and Wheatley had taken off and were flying along at about 3,000 feet when suddenly they heard a noise like a steam locomotive: One of the fabric-covered blades had burst open because of the high air-loads generated by centrifugal force on the air *inside* the blade. Immediately, the out-of-balance rotor began to shake the autogiro violently. The heavy control column, equipped with a stick-force recorder, was snatched out of McAvoy's hands and proceeded to rotate furiously around the cockpit as the damaged rotor's malevolent forces whipped it about. With little choice, McAvoy and Wheatley abandoned the autogiro, taking to their parachutes and descending into the shallow waters of the Back River, outside Langley, as the YG-2 crashed and burned.

When Army test pilots H. F. Gregory, Erickson Nichols, and Bud Snyder evaluated the YG-1 for Army service, they had a number of incidents resulting in damage to the craft from resonance effects, and wind gusts forcing its rotors into the ground during hover. On one flight, finally, a hub forging failed and the rotor shed a blade, which went sailing off. The now-out-of-balance rotor ripped the mounting pylon from the autogiro, and the craft, left without any means of lift, fell like a bomb earthward. Nichols and his passenger managed to parachute from the plummeting craft, though the passenger suffered a broken arm when he struck the rear of the autogiro as he exited from it.

Tests of a modified version, the YG-1A, in NACA's full-size wind tunnel (the famed Langley "30 by 60"), at Hampton, were equally dismal. As the wind raced through the open test section, the autogiro's rotor began to twirl. For a while all went smoothly. Then oscillation set in, disturbing the path of the whirling blades. The rotor ripped away from the craft, scattering wreckage in a hail of debris throughout the test section. Eventually, as a result of corrective work, the Army felt confident enough to purchase a batch of much modified and thoroughly tested YG-1B autogiros, setting up an Autogiro School at Patterson Field, Fairfield, Ohio, in April 1938. Yet all recognized that the autogiro should be considered merely a transitory step on the road to the helicopter, a true vertical-flight machine. Cierva himself, at the time of his death, in 1936, in the crash of an airliner, was actively working toward this goal. But the victor's crown in the helicopter field went not to Cierva but to another of aviation's luminaries, the remarkable Igor Sikorsky.

Igor Sikorsky had built his first helicopter before the First World War, in his native Kiev. It whirred, vibrated, and created a lot of excitement, but failed to leave the ground. And Sikorsky, sensing that the problem was more involved than at first apparent, abandoned the concept until he had made his mark as a manufacturer of conventional planes. But he never forgot the dream of flying a machine that could take off and land vertically. And so, when Eugene Wilson, the senior vice-president of United Aircraft, announced in 1938 that United would close down the Sikorsky division, bringing its years of manufacturing large airplanes to a close, but that United would support Sikorsky on any reasonable research project, Sikorsky quickly outlined a proposal to develop an experimental helicopter, estimating that it would cost no more than about thirty thousand dollars to do so. United gave its go-ahead, and Sikorsky set to work.

He had a large order to fill, for many experimental "helicopters" had been built, but few had shown any promise whatsoever. One of the more promising, tested in the early 1920s, had been a large, ungainly craft having four huge six-bladed "paddles" for rotors, the De Bothezat Helicopter, developed and tested at McCook Field by Russian émigré inventor and mathematician George de Bothezat. The enthusiastic Thurman Bane, McCook's commandant, had volunteered to pilot the craft on its first flight. On December 18, 1922, Bane strapped into the strange vehicle and, at 9 A.M., started its engine, which drove the four huge rotors via extension shafts. An eyewitness later reported:

> The movement was graceful and there was no noise of friction in any part of the mechanism. The craft began to move, slowly, ever slowly. Then inch by inch it lifted itself, strained and shook and lifted higher. It was free. Up off the ground, one foot, two feet, three feet and then double that, the height of a man and for one minute and forty-two seconds it remained there. The Army's helicopter had flown. The machine was surprisingly graceful and remarkably steady. Only the slightest oscillations were observed. Hovering at the height of about five feet the ship drifted along with the wind for three hundred feet or more.
> The craft got dangerously near a fence and Major Bane was forced to terminate the flight. He brought it down under absolute control. . . .[13]

Further flight tests of this contraption, the Army's first helicopter, went fairly well, but the craft never climbed above a few feet, and exhibited structural weakness and lack of stability. And so, following a few more trials, the Army abandoned it after having invested over two hundred thousand dollars.

Henry Berliner and Harold Harris experimented at College Park Airport from 1920 to 1924 with a primitive convertiplane having twin rotors mounted on the ends of the wings, but it failed to climb higher than about fifteen feet. Stability and the as yet not fully understood interaction of the rotor upon the controllability of the craft caused all these early machines to remain basically "hoppers." Then, in 1935, French designers Louis Bréguet and René Dorand successfully flew an experimental craft, the Gyroplane Laboratoire, which had two coaxially mounted contrarotating rotors, to a world's airspeed record for helicopters of 67 mph. The next year, Germany developed the Focke-Achgelis Fw 61, a successful double-rotor design.

Sikorsky, in 1938, approached his task with the characteristic thoroughness that was so much a part of this remarkable pioneer. He assembled a small technical staff, and following technical discussions, the team decided to adopt basically the configuration for a helicopter that Sikorsky had patented in 1935: a single-rotor machine having a small tail rotor facing to the side to counteract torque. A single engine would drive both the main rotor and, via extension shafting, the small tail rotor. Design of this experimental craft, designated the VS-300 (for Vought-Sikorsky), began immediately and was complete by the summer of 1939. The Sikorsky technical staff set to work constructing the machine, and it rolled out for its first flight tests—attached to the ground by tethers—in September 1939. On September 14, Sikorsky himself sat in the open framework of the experimental craft and ran up its 75-hp engine to full power. The VS-300 lifted clear off the ground. Sikorsky reduced power and let the craft settle gently back on its four-wheel landing gear. He conferred briefly with the design team, then made a series of short hovers, totaling no more than ten seconds of flight time in all. The VS-300 had proved that it could lift off the ground, but it experienced heavy vibration and uncertain control; the long and arduous flight-research program had just begun.

On December 9, Sikorsky engineer and test pilot Serge Gluhareff crashed the VS-300 when an errant wind gust rolled it, and the rotor broke up when it hit the ground. Sikorsky rebuilt the craft but added two horizontal tail rotors, giving the craft its second configuration and a distinctive (if awkward) appearance. In this form, it completed its first free, untethered flight, on May 13, 1940. Sikorsky followed this with a public demonstration a week later, flying the VS-300 backward and sideways, turning around, and climbing up and down. Most spectators failed to notice that the dapper émigré had not flown the craft *forward*, but not the eagle-eyed Eugene Wilson, who asked Sikorsky why he had not. "That," the confident pioneer murmured in his thick Russian accent, "is one of the minor engineering problems we have not yet solved!"[14]

But solve it he quickly did. The test flights demonstrated the powerful interaction of the main rotor and the tail rotors, resulting in a bobbing flight path, and vibration problems resulted in some structural failures. Sikorsky himself crashed one day from a height of 20 feet when a tail-rotor support failed under load, causing the rotor to slow down and generate less lift, thus heeling the craft over on its side. Sikorsky, who always flew in natty business attire, wearing a gray fedora hat, next installed floats on the VS-300 and flew it from the Housatonic River. After over a year and a half of testing, Sikorsky believed the helicopter ready for an attempt on the world's helicopter endurance record, held by the German Fw 61. On May 6, 1941, Sikorsky piloted the craft on an extended hover lasting 1 hour, 32 minutes, 26.1 seconds, a new record.

Now Sikorsky decided to return gradually to the craft's original and highly desirable single-main-rotor-and-single-tail-rotor configuration. First, he removed the two horizontal tail rotors, leaving the vertical, anti-torque tail rotors. Then he modified the main rotor so that instead of just furnishing lift, it could also provide lateral (roll) control. He added a small horizontal tail rotor mounted on a short tower above the tail to provide pitch-attitude control. This represented the third configuration of the VS-300, and Sikorsky test pilot Les Morris first flew the craft in this form in June 1941.

With the promise of high forward speeds, Sikorsky engineers covered over the structure of the VS-300, giving it a semistreamlined appearance. During testing, Morris quickly reached forward flight speeds of 70 mph. By this time, the Army had contracted with Sikorsky for their second helicopter (the first had been the ill-fated De Bothezat monstrosity), the XR-4, a two-place, fully enclosed machine with a single main rotor and a single tail rotor. To support this effort, Sikorsky modified the VS-300 to its fourth, and final, form, adding the pitch-control function to the main rotor as well and thus obviating the need for the small horizontal rotor at the tail. The VS-300 now had the appearance that has since become standard for most helicopter designs: a single main rotor combining pure lift and pitch and roll control, and a small, side-facing tail rotor to counteract torque and provide directional control. On December 8, 1941, the VS-300 made its first flight in its final configuration. Following some modifications as a result of flight testing, the VS-300, by the end of 1941, was flying in perfect control forward, backward, and sideways. It remained on developmental flight testing duties until mid-1943, enabling a number of pilots to gain their first helicopter experience, including Charles Lindbergh, then a technical consultant for United Aircraft. Finally, on October 7, 1943, Igor Sikorsky piloted the VS-300 on its last flight, delivering it to Henry Ford's Dearborn museum. By that time, the first of the advanced Sikorsky R-4's were entering Army service.

The story of Igor Sikorsky and the helicopter is a classic story of how flight testing can refine a good idea into a workable system. Above all, it is a tale of not losing hope, of being almost excruciatingly patient. Had Sikorsky not been so patient, he might well have abandoned the craft after its first shaky flights, in 1939. Rather, he saw in them the challenge of solving the numerous problems then plaguing the craft. He looked not to its faults but to its promise. He experimented with the configuration, acquired reliable data from test flights, made modifications, and finally, after just about two and a half years, he was rewarded with a fully successful, fully reliable craft whose lessons he could incorporate in a production vehicle, the R-4. Sikorsky died in 1972, the doyen of helicopter developers. Although he had been successful in aeronautics before the VS-300, his reputation had soared upward on rotary wings after it flew. Like the Wright brothers, Sikorsky's success is a tribute to the power of an idea, the tenacity of the individual, and above all, to his meticulous flight research.

THE BIRTH OF THE JET

Had American enthusiasts of gas-turbine propulsion for aircraft had a little of the same tenacity that Sikorsky possessed, the United States might have been the first country to fly a jet airplane. After all, with the work of Sanford Moss of General Electric and the development of the practical turbosupercharger for aircraft, the United States was almost there. What was needed, in simplest form, was to hook the turbine to some form of compressor, such as a centrifugal compressor (usually having a single compressor wheel) or an axial compressor (usually having a series of coaxially mounted compressor wheels), with a combustion section in between. Then a pilot could start the engine, and air coming through an inlet and into the compressor section would be compressed, mixed with fuel, and ignited, and the resulting hot gases would rotate the turbine before exiting through the exhaust, causing the turbine, in turn, to rotate the compressor. It was not a particularly complex scheme, nor a particularly new one. Unfortunately, no one pressed strongly for American gas-turbine development, and for once, even the great NACA missed an opportunity, preferring to stick with the tried and true, especially the reliable piston engine enclosed in a NACA cowling. As late as January 1941, a Navy report stated that gas-turbine propulsion was completely out of the question for aircraft. One wonders how the authors of that report would have reacted had they known that Germany had completed the world's first turbojet flight nearly a year and a half previously, or that Great Britain even then was readying its own experimental jet airplane for its maiden flight.

The development of the gas-turbine engine was one of the major technical accomplishments of the 1930s, and together with the derivation of high-speed aerodynamic theory, it has led aviation to its present state of perfection. Within ten years of the first jet flight, aircraft were flying faster than sound, and within three decades of the first jet flight, the first jet-propelled supersonic transports were entering flight testing. The jet took aeronautics from the confines of subsonic flight and opened up a whole new regime to researchers, a realm where such old terms as propeller and cowling gave way to terms such as inlet shock and afterburner, and "miles per hour" became far less meaningful than "Mach number." Yet even though Frank Whittle and Hans von Ohain, the two principal developers of the jet engine, foresaw the potential of the gas turbine for high-speed flight, they could not have imagined how quickly aviation would jump from 200 mph to 2,000 mph, or how that engine would enable designers to build new jet transports that would eventually drive passenger ships from the seas and alter forever the character and pattern of international transportation.

Frank Whittle, a graduate of the Royal Air Force College, was a promising young engineering officer and pilot. He conceptualized the gas-turbine engine while serving as a flight instructor at the RAF's Central Flying School. Later assigned to often-hazardous duty as a floatplane test pilot at Felixstowe, he continued his research on what fellow pilots joked about as "Whittle's flaming touchhole." Undaunted in spite of occasional self-doubts, Whittle pressed on, earning assignment to Cambridge, where he eventually took an honors degree in science. Eventually, with the help of a small group of enthusiastic supporters, he formed a small company called Power Jets Ltd. and developed a small test engine, the WU, which completed a shaky series of test runs in 1937. Encouraged by Sir Henry Tizard, the former Great War test pilot now serving as Britain's Chairman of the Aeronautical Research Council, Whittle struggled with the numerous problems inevitable in such a program. Against the predictions of many self-appointed critics, and widespread official reluctance, Whittle managed to develop a basically reliable engine by the summer of 1939. At the end of June in that year, the Air Ministry finally agreed to support development of a secret experimental airplane powered by the Whittle engine. Eventually, this led to Great Britain's first jet airplane, the Gloster E.28/39, which first flew in 1941. Like Sikorsky, Whittle had simply never given up, and as a result, success rewarded his efforts.

Hans von Ohain had a smoother time in Germany. A young physicist, Von Ohain had received his doctorate from Göttingen in 1935. While a student, he had, like Whittle, conceived of a centrifugal-flow gas-turbine engine. After graduation, however, he wisely joined forces with maverick aircraft developer Ernst Heinkel, rather than waste precious time trying to win over the many skeptics in the German aero-engine industry. In early 1937, he tested a primitive jet engine fueled by gaseous hydrogen (selected only for test purposes). The bench engine performed satisfactorily, greatly encouraging the young engine developer and Heinkel's technical staff. By mid-1938, he had "frozen" the design of a petroleum-fueled jet engine, and the Heinkel firm already had the design of an experimental airplane, the He 178, underway. Heinkel completed the craft and its experimental engine in the summer of 1939. The plane resembled none previously built. It had a slender monocoque fuselage with a simple nose inlet and a blunt exhaust, with a shoulder-mounted wing and a conventional, tail-wheel-type landing gear. The main wheels retracted into the sides of the fuselage, below the wings. Following ground tests and adjustments to its revolutionary power plant, Heinkel flight researchers deemed the craft ready for its initial flight trials.

On August 27, 1939, company test pilot Erich Warsitz climbed into the cockpit of the little He 178 and, after a final handclasp and "Happy landing!" from Ernst Heinkel, closed the canopy and lit off the engine. A new sound in aviation split the air: the rising wail of a gas turbine building up to full thrust. Engine whistling, the He 178 rolled sluggishly down the runway, then faster and faster, finally racing into the air and climbing to 2,000 feet before the eyes of its creators. Heinkel recollected later that

> something was wrong with the undercarriage. Warsitz did everything he could to retract it; then he gave up and flew with it at 1,500 feet in a wide circle around the field. With or without undercarriage, he was flying. He was flying! A new era had begun. The hideous wail of the engine was music to our ears. He circled again, smoothly and gracefully. The riggers began to wave like madmen. Warsitz had now been three minutes in the air, but it seemed like an eternity. Calmly he flew around once more, and when six minutes were up he started to land. He cut out the jet unit, then misjudged his approach and had to sideslip. Sideslip with a new, dangerous and tricky plane!
>
> We held our breath, but the He 178 landed perfectly, taxied and came to a stop right in front of the Warnow—a magnificent landing. Within seconds we had all rushed over to Warsitz and the plane. The riggers hoisted both of us onto their shoulders and carried us round, roaring with enthusiasm. The jet plane had flown.[15]

Five days after Erich Warsitz secretly ushered in the age of the jet airplane, a different noise disturbed the air: the first cracklings of combat as Nazi Germany plunged Europe into the violence of the Second World War.

CHAPTER 6

COMBAT ON THE
TECHNOLOGY FRONT

During the Second World War, the United States earned for itself the title "Arsenal of Democracy." An arsenal, however, is only as good as the quality of its weapons. Ensuring the quality of those weapons was a task both exacting and demanding, requiring the utmost effort of those charged with this responsibility, especially America's flight testers. Unlike in the First World War, America in the Second World War fielded numerous aircraft designs that eventually fought on all war fronts. Bell's P-39 Airacobra, for example, fought from the South Pacific to the Middle East and on the Russian front. Douglas C-47's, the military brothers of the civil DC-3, carried men and supplies over the Hump into China, shuttled across the North Atlantic, and ferried paratroopers and gliders into action at Normandy and Arnheim. The Consolidated-Vultee B-24 bombed Ploesti's oil fields, in Romania; flew antisubmarine patrols out of Cornwall; and raided Japanese shipping. At war's end, the United States possessed the most powerful land and naval air forces in the world, but such was the pace of technology that most of these aircraft, in the face of the turbojet revolution, were already obsolescent.

Unlike Europe, America was given two years of grace from the time that Hitler's *Wehrmacht* stormed across the Polish frontier. Only when Japanese bombs rained down upon an anchored fleet at Pearl Harbor did the United States at last find itself locked in total war, stilling the protests of America's isolationists. When the United States did enter the war, its combat squadrons still retained some of the first generation of America's monoplane "modern" military aircraft. Basically, however, it was a force in transition. The generation of aircraft with which America would win the war—the Hellcat, Mustang, Corsair, Thunderbolt, and Superfortress, to name just a few—were already in test or just around the corner. They still required, however, thorough proving before the military services could feel confident to depend upon them to serve their crews well and provide the necessary battlefield punch to destroy the hopes of the Axis powers.

NEW FLIGHT RESEARCH CENTERS AND THE BEGINNING OF TEST PILOT SCHOOLS

During the Second World War, the scope of aeronautical research and development expanded rapidly, including the number of sites devoted to test flying and flight research. The older centers—Anacostia, Wright, and Langley—simply could not keep up or support the demands placed upon them by military services and contractors. Additionally, some of the centers were basically unsuited to the testing required by new, advanced combat aircraft. The Navy, for example, had long been bothered by the close proximity of Anacostia to downtown Washington. The possibility of a research aircraft or an experimental prototype going out of control while pointed in the direction of the nation's capital was not pleasant to contemplate. Similarly Wright Field was situated too close to an urban area. High-performance aircraft testing required remote testing sites, convenient to developed areas but not restricted by them. There were also security questions. Both Wright and Anacostia were too populous to generate any confidence that research was safe from prying eyes. The gentle hills east of Anacostia afforded an unsurpassed view of the base, and with enough time, any Dayton local could ride over to "the Field" and see the Army's latest aircraft going through their paces, just by watching from beyond the airfield's boundary.

Eventually, in 1943, the Navy transferred its flight testing activities from Anacostia to a new naval air station at beautiful Cedar Point, Maryland, on the western shore of Chesapeake Bay, at the mouth of the Patuxent River. The new air station opened on April 1, 1943, the home of the Naval Air Test Center. "NATC Pax River" has since become known worldwide, and is still the Naval Air Systems Command's single site for the developmental testing and evaluation of all naval aircraft and their systems. The Army, meantime, did not give up on Wright Field, but perferred to concentrate its more exotic research—such as that on turbojet aircraft—at Muroc, California, now the site of the U. S. Air Force Flight Test Center, Edwards Air Force Base. The NACA, which before the war had already recognized the necessity of having another, Langley-like aeronautical laboratory in close proximity to the West Coast aircraft industry, secured congressional approval for construction of the gigantic Ames Aeronautical Laboratory (now the NASA Ames Research Center), at Sunnyvale, south of San Francisco, which undertook its first research in 1941. The NACA later opened its Flight Propulsion Laboratory, at Cleveland, the basis of the present-day NASA Lewis Research Center. All NACA centers stepped up their pace of flight research to meet the critical demands of wartime. Other centers undertook flight testing as well. The Navy, for example, undertook some testing at Philadelphia, while the Army also developed a series of service testing installations at what eventually emerged as the Eglin complex, in Florida. Each contractor would, of course, maintain a relatively small flight department, with a staff of experimental test pilots and flight test engineers, so that the company could test its prototypes for basic airworthiness before passing them along to the users for more extensive evaluation. Additionally, companies also maintained a staff of production test pilots, who would check aircraft off the production line to see if they were ready for delivery to their operators.

One of the major difficulties the war quickly brought out, however, was how to recognize an acceptable test pilot. Obviously, one had to be interested in the job, had to have good piloting skills, had to have a great measure of common sense, should have a thorough grounding in technical principles, and should have that sense of adventure (as distinct from recklessness) that is so critical to the professional test pilot. How, though, could one take an ordinary pilot and transform this willing and basically qualified individual into a test pilot, skilled in discriminating the good airplane from the bad or the merely mediocre? Already during the 1930s, aeronautical engineers had recognized pilot opinion of new aircraft as a vital consideration in evaluating new aircraft designs. The greatest problem, however, is that not all pilots speak the same language: the pilot of a heavy transport who flies a nimble fighter might feel the controls to be too skittish, too sensitive. On the other hand, a fighter pilot flying that same aircraft might want even greater control response. Some method had to be found whereby a common set of guidelines could be drawn up so that test pilots, engineers, and designers all spoke a common language, especially concerning the vital field of aircraft stability and control.

Fortunately, during the 1930s, the NACA had spearheaded this effort,

drawing upon the earlier work of Edward Warner, who had first proposed tentative requirements for aircraft evaluation. Then, late in the
decade, Hartley Soulé and Robert Gilruth, two flight-research engineers
at the Langley laboratory, had begun their own study on standardizing
evaluation criteria, eventually resulting in a landmark NACA technical
report issued in 1943: *Requirements for Satisfactory Flying Qualities of
Airplanes*. The document influenced the specifications later used by the
military services for evaluating new aircraft designs.

Air Commodore Allen Wheeler, one of Great Britain's most distinguished test pilots and the wartime officer in charge of Boscombe Down,
where British military aircraft underwent their testing, has related an appropriate story that indicates how widespread was the problem of evaluating aircraft properly and accounting for pilot interpretations, even as
late as the dark days of the early 1940s. An experimental naval aircraft
arrived for trials at Boscombe. The highly skilled and experienced flight
test personnel at the field quickly discovered to their dismay that it
needed major—indeed, drastic—development before it could be qualified
as an operational type. But it had already gone through extensive contractor testing. What had gone wrong? An investigation quickly revealed
the cause of trouble. The contractor had needed a test pilot and had
hired an apparently capable returning combat veteran. Lacking a formal
background in flight testing, he had neither the experience nor the understanding to properly appreciate his role. Instead of *criticizing* the
craft's performance, and thus forcing needed redesign, he had simply
taught himself to *cope* with it. As a result, only he could fly it safely, and
much precious time had been lost in the development process.

No incident more clearly indicates that a test pilot is a pilot apart from
his brethren who fly for other reasons. In peacetime, one could take service pilots, post them to an experimental center, and as with the guilds of
old, gradually train them in the art of experimental flying. But as the
need for expanding flight testing appeared, such methods quickly proved
wanting.

Britain responded to this by creating the Empire Test Pilots' School, in
1943, "to provide suitably trained pilots for test flying duties in Aeronautical Research and Development Establishments within the Service and
the Industry," in the words of its charter. Its motto, appropriately
enough, is "Learn to Test—Test to Learn." In 1945, the U. S. Navy followed suit by setting up a formal test pilot school at Patuxent River; so
did the Army Air Forces at Wright Field. These formed the basis of the
present Naval Test Pilot School and the USAF Test Pilot School at Edwards AFB. Other nations have since followed suit. (The search for
standard rating criteria by which pilots could judge experimental aircraft
has continued since the Second World War. In the mid-1950s, George

Cooper, NACA's chief test pilot at the Ames laboratory, derived a ten-point pilot opinion scale, 1 being best and 10 being worst, with 1–3 "satisfactory," 4–6 "unsatisfactory," 7–9 "unacceptable," and 10 "unprintable.") The institutionalization of formal test pilot schools and the establishment of a firm academic tradition for the training of test pilots must be accounted as one of the major developments in experimental flying during the 1940s.

AMERICAN TEST PILOTS GO TO WAR

The wartime work of America's test pilots did not begin with the attack on Pearl Harbor, however. Before the war, both before the actual attack on Poland and then in the hazy period of neutrality afterward, American test pilots had demonstrated and delivered new aircraft fresh from the factories on the East and West coasts to the French and the British. Sometimes, in this period of confused debate over the merits of American isolation from or intervention in European affairs, their actions resulted in unwanted publicity and even political clamor. In January 1939, for example, Douglas test pilot Johnny Cable had perished in the crash of the prototype DB-7B bomber, the forerunner of the wartime A-20 Havoc. Cable had been demonstrating the craft to a team of French air purchasing commission members secretly visiting America, apparently without realizing that one of the commission's members had been inspecting the rear gunner's position on the plane before takeoff and had been inadvertently carried along for the ride. There was no means of communication in the test aircraft, and the luckless stowaway could not inform the test pilot that he was aboard. Cable had feathered the left engine, and as Douglas and French officials watched with increasing alarm, the pilot tramped on the rudder pedals, yawing the plane from side to side to demonstrate its controllability with one engine out. Suddenly, the DB-7B snapped into a spin, from an altitude of only 500 feet. Cable jumped but could not open his parachute in time. The gyrating bomber struck the ground and exploded, but, by a miracle, the stowaway, though badly injured, was still alive, and eventually recovered.

The crash sparked an instant debate in the halls of Congress between isolationist and interventionist congressmen: a new American bomber had crashed with a foreign official on board! Eventually, even President Franklin Roosevelt was drawn into the affair. He responded by calling a meeting of the largely isolationist Senate Military Affairs Committee at the White House a week after the crash, lecturing the senators on the necessity of selling American aircraft to potential allies. He defended the actions of his administration in secretly selling the latest American air-craft to France and Britain by stating, in part, that ". . . it is to our in-terest, quite frankly, to do what we can, absolutely as a matter of peace, peace of the world, to help the French and British maintain their inde-pendence. Literally, their independence is threatened today."

It surprised few in the aviation and diplomatic communities then that there were American test pilots abroad when fighting broke out in Europe. Pilots such as Boone Guyton (Vought), Sam Shannon (Martin), and Gerrardus "Jerry" Clark (Curtiss), among many others, check-tested newly delivered planes as fast as they could be assembled, and then passed them along to the French. They flew by day, spent their evenings (in moderation) at the Ritz bar in Paris, and had their share of close calls before leaving for the States. It was not a small effort. Guyton, in France to test Vought dive bombers for the Aéronavale, recalled that in the hec-tic weeks before September 1939,

> Out at Orly we hurriedly assembled and flew airplanes as fast as the crates were unloaded at the crowded depot. At Bourges, Curtiss P-36 fighters were being tested fast and furiously and turned over to eager French pilots. At Nantes, North Americans were rolling onto the field and getting into the air for their tests. At Bordeaux, Douglas bombers were coming along. In London and Sweden too, Lockheeds and Brew-sters were being assembled and tested. . . .[1]

And unfortunately it was all in vain. France collapsed in 1940, leaving a beleaguered Britain to carry on alone. And then, to add insult to injury, the Vichy French forces used some of these very aircraft to oppose the Allied landings in North Africa during Operation Torch—a distasteful story.

After Hitler's *Wehrmacht* had triumphantly crushed France and the Low Countries in the early summer of 1940, creating the specter of quick British defeat, the American military services quietly but firmly stepped up the development of new warplanes and, in some cases, recalled ex-military personnel to active service. (The triumphant conclu-sion of the pivotal Battle of Britain ended any immediate threat of Nazi hegemony but did little to shorten what would eventually prove to be a prolonged and grueling struggle.) Jimmy Doolittle, a Shell executive and president of the Institute of the Aeronautical Sciences, received a tele-gram ordering him to active duty as a major in the Army Air Corps, and soon found himself troubleshooting various programs and planes, includ-ing the rotund Martin B-26 Marauder, a notoriously unforgiving air-plane seemingly incapable of safe single-engine flight. Air service chief Hap Arnold asked Doolittle to check out the crash-prone plane and recommend whether or not it be continued in production. Doolittle, whose flying background included mastering the wickedly unstable and over-powered Gee Bee racer, tackled the job with relish. He liked the B-26, whose crews had unkindly dubbed it the "Widow Maker" and even the "Flying Prostitute" (because its small wings offered no visible means of support). Doolittle, the consummate airman, visited B-26 units and demonstrated that the craft could be safely flown on one engine, even on takeoff and landing, to skeptical flight crews. The real problem was a training one: Marauder crews transferred to the hot bomber from relatively easy-to-fly trainers that tolerated their mistakes and encouraged a belief that one could get away with sloppiness. Greater attention to procedures, lengthened training, and emphasis on precise flying cut the accident rate to acceptable levels, and the Marauder went on to an outstanding wartime career. After Pearl Harbor, Doolittle next turned to studying how an Army B-25 could take off from an aircraft carrier and raid Tokyo. . . .

One civilian test pilot whose contributions to America's wartime efforts were second to none was Charles Lindbergh. Before Pearl Harbor sounded the death knell to American isolationists, Lindbergh had toured the country as an outspoken foe of American intervention in European affairs. Criticized for his activities by President Roosevelt, Lindbergh had resigned his Army reserve commission with regret. After war broke out, however, he volunteered for service, but the Roosevelt administration coldly rebuffed him. He subsequently flew for the Ford Motor Company and the United Aircraft Corporation.

In October 1938, while living abroad, Lindbergh had made an inspection trip to Nazi Germany, where, for several reasons, his hosts allowed him to examine and fly a wide variety of new German aircraft. Lindbergh left Germany with a profound respect for the technical competency of the Nazi aviation industry, and subsequently warned American aviation officials that the United States would have to increase its aeronautical effort to match the latest German state of the art. While in Germany, Lindbergh had numerous opportunities to pilot German airplanes and assess their characteristics, including the large, four-engine Focke-Wulf 200 transport, the Junkers 90, the Messerschmitt 108 liaison plane, and the Messerschmitt 109 fighter, then flying against Soviet-built opponents in Spain. Lindbergh evaluated the 109 at Rechlin, the great German *Erprobungstelle* (test flight center), north of Berlin. He subsequently wrote in his diary:

> After studying the cockpit, I got out and put on a "chute" while a mechanic started the engine. Then, after taxiing slowly down to the starting point, I took off. The plane handled beautifully. I spent quarter of an

hour familiarizing myself with the instruments and controls, then spent fifteen minutes more doing maneuvers of various types (rolls, dives, Immelmanns, etc.). After half an hour I landed, took off again, circled the field, and landed a second time; then taxied back to the line. The 109 takes off and lands as easily as it flies.[2]

Clearly, with such diverse experience of foreign and domestic flying, ranging from nimble fighters to stately multiengine seaplanes, Lindbergh possessed a background almost unique among American airmen at that time.

Like his friend Antoine de Saint Exupéry, Lindbergh consisted of equal parts pilot and poet, philosopher and technologist, agrarian and sophisticate. Even in the midst of war, he always sought to interpret events and situations in terms of a larger meaning. His book *Of Flight and Life* is a portrait of a thoughtful, humanistic man caught up in the hectic and callous pace of modern war. It contains a series of vignettes, one of which concerns a wartime test flight that he made at Willow Run in a Republic P-47B Thunderbolt, a new fighter plagued by engine failures and other problems. He was aloft at over 40,000 feet, testing the plane for "ignition breakdown" at high altitudes. All went well, and he began his descent. Suddenly he grew vaguely restless; he realized something was wrong, and drawing on experience he had gained during tests in the Mayo Clinic's altitude chamber a few months before, he recognized the onset of anoxia. His oxygen system had failed. With about fifteen seconds of consciousness left, he shoved the control stick forward. As he recalled:

The earth slants upward and the dive begins . . . 35,000 feet . . . 34,000 . . . my cockpit roars through the air . . . the earth fades out . . . the instrument dials darken . . . breath's thin; lungs, empty—I'm blacking out —losing sight. . . . I push the nose down farther . . . faster . . . 33,000 . . . 30,000 . . . the dials become meaningless . . . down . . . down . . . I am dimly aware of a great shriek, as though a steam whistle were blowing near my ears . . . Compressibility dive? . . . I'm not thinking about compressibility . . . it's oxygen I need . . . I'm blind . . . I can't see the needles . . . there are no more seconds left—it's a razor edge—a race between decreasing consciousness and increasing density of air . . .

17,000 . . . 16,000 . . . 15,000 . . . a white needle moves over white figures . . . it's the altimeter—I can see—I'm reading its dial again—I'm aware of the cockpit, the plane, the earth and sky—I've already begun to pull out of the dive—the stick is free; the nose, rising; the seat pressing against me.[3]

He descended and landed, but with greater insight than when he had taken off: "I brought life rather than an airplane back to ground." A mechanic announced that the oxygen pressure gauge had read 50 pounds too high. Lindbergh drove along the flightline back to his office, passing the mammoth assembly lines churning out B-24 bombers, "a terrible giant's womb. . . . This was a temple of the god of science at which we moderns worshipped. . . . Here I watched a steel door lift and an airplane roll outside; while, in reality, the walls of a cathedral fell and children died. . . . This altitude flight at Willow Run taught me that in worshipping science man gains power but loses the quality of life."

Lindbergh went on to other projects, helping make the Vought Corsair a combat-worthy fighter and refining long-range fuel-saving cruise techniques, enabling American fighter pilots to extend the combat radius of their aircraft by as much as 200 miles with proper fuel and power management. He worked and traveled at an intense pace: In January 1944, for example, he attended a top-level conference at the AAF's Eglin Field weapons-testing center. During four days at the field, he flew no fewer than eight different aircraft on evaluations, including the experimental Curtiss XP-60E ("an interesting plane with many good characteristics"), a North American P-51B Mustang ("excellent plane—among best in world today"), two different models of the Bell P-63 Kingcobra, a Curtiss P-40N, a De Havilland Mosquito, a P-47K ("Excessive rudder forces in dive. Ailerons became unstable at 450 mph indicated at 8,000 feet"), and finally a Boeing B-29 Superfortress ("Gives impression of well-engineered plane. However, first impressions are dangerous.").[4]

In April 1944 he went to the South Pacific as a civilian adviser, instructing service pilots how best to utilize the capabilities of their aircraft. No behind-the-lines aviator, Lindbergh flew fifty combat missions over Japanese territory and even shot down a Zero. He convinced the Marines that they could carry a 4,000-pound bombload on their Corsairs, and tested this deadly load (the largest bombload carried by a single-engine fighter up to that time) in actual strikes on Japanese targets. At the end of the war, United Aircraft sent him to Europe to investigate German wartime research. There, amid the stench and degradation of Camp Dora, whose slave laborers built the V-2 missile, he confronted the horror of Nazism in all its sordidness, the perversion of technology to destroy life, not better it. And so Lindbergh changed from technology to philosophy, preaching a return to a society based on "simplicity, humility, contemplation, prayer. It requires a dedication beyond science. . . ."[5] Speaking before The Society of Experimental Test Pilots in 1969, Lindbergh affirmed this stand, adding, "Personally, I believe the mind that leads into experimental test flying is well able to extend its leadership to broader fields."[6] With his death, in 1974, passed a great test pilot—and an even greater man.

NEW SHAPES IN THE SKY

Every decade in the history of aviation has witnessed the flights of new configurations for aircraft, configurations that reflect contemporary desires for increased performance. The biplane of the First World War gradually gave way to the internally braced monoplane; the straight wing gradually gave way to the sweptwing for high-speed transports. The 1940s were no exception. During that time, various weird shapes flew through the air: tailless airplanes, canard configurations, flying wings, and odd lift-producing body shapes. Two of the most intriguing were the elegant and attractive Northrop Flying Wing and the freakish Vought "Flying Pancake."

Of the two, Northrop's Flying Wing came closest to practical success. Jack Northrop had always been intrigued with the idea of developing an airplane having minimal drag and maximum aerodynamic efficiency. What if a designer could come up with a craft housing its payload, crew, and fuel, together with its engines, entirely within the wing, obviating the need for a fuselage? And what if the wing were aerodynamically tailored in such a way that there was no need for balancing tail surfaces? Such a craft would offer extraordinary aerodynamic efficiency. The end result of this was the revolutionary Northrop N1M "Jeep," the world's first true flying wing (having neither vertical nor horizontal tail surfaces, nor a fuselage), which Vance Breese first flew from Muroc's dry lake in July 1940. Piloted by Breese and Moye Stephens, the little bright yellow twin-engine pusher droned along over the Antelope Valley, eventually completing more than two hundred flights and—more important—contributing greatly to development of adequate control systems for such a shape. As a result, Northrop felt confident enough to propose a huge flying-wing design for the AAF. This subsequently evolved into the XB-35, and then the YB-49, an all-jet version that flew after the war but lost out for production contracts to the Convair B-36.

To prove out the general aerodynamic configuration of the XB-35, Northrop built four approximately one-third-scale piloted research vehicles, the graceful N9M series. Unfortunately, one crashed after apparently entering a low-altitude spin, killing its test pilot. But the other three completed hundreds of hours of flight research safely, contributing greatly to the final design of the XB-35/YB-49 series, and eventually served as test pilot training vehicles at Muroc. The flying wings were born at a time when a great deal of skepticism and hostility greeted their configuration, when stability-augmentation systems were still a thing of the future, and when their aerodynamic problems—and possibilities—were still largely unknown. The beautiful Northrop flying wings disappeared, but today, in an era more concerned with energy and aerodynamic efficiency than at any previous time, the flying-wing concept is once again receiving serious consideration for future transports and military aircraft, and justifiably so.

In contrast to the flying wings, however, the freakish Vought V-173 "Flying Pancake" stands alone. This strange, flying saucer-like craft was the brainchild of Charles Zimmermann, who believed that an airplane having a semicircular wing planform; being thick enough to house the crew, fuel, payload, and engine system; and equipped with two huge contrarotating propellers, could fly at both very low and very high speeds. It was, in effect, an early attempt at a semi-V/STOL design, and the 16-foot propellers necessitated a long, stalky landing gear. With Navy and NACA interest in a potential shipboard fighter using this design concept, Vought built the V-173 as a testbed for the future fighter.

The yellow-and-silver V-173, with its ungainly landing gear, gigantic propellers, two stubby rudders, and fish-fin-like horizontal tail surfaces protruding from the manta ray-like wing, completed an inauspicious first flight at Stratford, Connecticut, piloted by Boone Guyton, in late November 1942. The craft took off at about 30 mph but had such sluggish controls and high stick forces—Guyton had to use both hands—that the pilot momentarily considered dumping the plane in the water straight ahead off the end of the runway! Gradually, however, he maneuvered it in a long, wide, and slow turn, landing back on the field at 50 mph. Much reworking of the rotor propellers and control system followed, and thereafter, through the end of the war, the V-173 flew quite regularly, piloted chiefly by Guyton and Dick Burroughs. It did have some fascinating properties: with full power and full-aft stick, the V-173 could wallow about in a 45-degree attitude without stalling (the propellers "wetted" virtually the entire wing surface with their flow). In its own way, it did contribute to a base of knowledge that postwar V/STOL designers would build upon during the 1950s and 1960s and thus cannot be adjudged a failure, though, in fact, the proposed fighter (Vought's XF5U-1) never flew. Both the Northrop "Jeep" and the V-173 eventually found their ways into the collections of the Smithsonian Institution, prime examples of aeronautical esoterica.

EDDIE ALLEN AND THE B-29

Naturally, most designers believed they had difficulties enough with conventional aircraft, let alone unknowns such as the Flying Wing and the "Zimmer-Skimmer." One of the major American accomplishments of the Second World War was the development of truly long-range aircraft, such as the DC-4 transport (which influenced the whole course of postwar propeller-driven transport design) and, especially, the Boeing B-29 Superfortress. It is curious that the development of the B-29 has not received the attention that is fully its due, for design and construction of these substratospheric pressurized "Very Long Range" bombers were by no means easily accomplished. Indeed, other nations were singularly unsuccessful in trying to develop equivalent aircraft. Germany, for example (despite the vaunted myth of Nazi technological excellence), never designed a really satisfactory long-range bomber even in the B-17 class. The B-29 devastated Japan in conventional raids that destroyed her industry and left horrific death tolls. But the development of this beautiful if terrifying weapon (the Japanese referred to it in respect and awe as *B-san:* "Mr. B") had not been without its difficulties, requiring insightful flight testing and, regretfully, human sacrifice.

Boeing turned to its chief test pilot, Edmund T. "Eddie" Allen, to test the new bomber, completed over the summer of 1942. Eddie Allen had come a long way from his early days at Martlesham Heath and Langley. Dressed in a conservative suit, with a quiet, unassuming manner and appearance, he looked more the part of the successful small-town businessman than what in actuality he was: the most capable multiengine test pilot in the world, the undisputed monarch of his fellow American test pilots. A plane with Eddie Allen's stamp of approval upon it was a thoroughbred, for, among his fellow pilots and designers, his pronouncements carried the weight of Mosaic law. A list of the companies and organizations he had test-flown for read like a Who's Who of American aviation: Boeing, Northrop, Chance-Vought, Pan American Grace Airways, Eastern Air Lines, Curtiss-Wright, Douglas, North American, Lockheed, Stearman, Sikorsky, Pratt & Whitney, Spartan, Consolidated-Vultee. In 1939, he had rejoined Boeing full time, convincing the company to establish a special department of aerodynamics and flight research. Company chiefs agreed—and appointed Allen to head it. In that position, he supervised the flight testing of the Stratoliner following the loss of the first prototype, over Mount Rainier, and then played a key role in the aerodynamic development of the Boeing B-29. His accomplishments were recognized by the Institute of the Aeronautical Sciences, which awarded him the first Octave Chanute Award, in 1939, and then designated him the Wright Brothers Lecturer for 1942 (he presented a paper on "Flight Testing for Performance and Stability"), exactly thirty-nine years after the Wrights' first flight).

Allen approached testing the new bomber with a great deal of caution and planning. Air Forces' B-29 program director K. B. Wolfe referred to the bomber at one point as a "three-billion-dollar gamble." It challenged the state of the art in many areas. It had highly refined aerodynamics, a broad (high-aspect-ratio) wing, a flap area larger than the wings of most fighters, very large control surfaces, four turbosupercharged Wright engines (of a new and unproven 2,200-hp design), an electronic fire-control and armament system, forward-and-aft cabin pressurization, a range of over 5,500 miles, a 105,000-pound loaded weight, a bombload of up to ten tons, and a service ceiling of over 30,000 feet with a maximum airspeed of over 360 mph. There were many respected authorities within the military and industry who, when told of what Boeing was attempting to accomplish, flatly stated it to be impossible. Allen knew all of this, knew how much responsibility was resting upon his own work and that of his department, and worked hard, both on the ground and in the air, to make the Superfortress live up to its name.

The first prototype, the XB-29, was ready for flight in early September 1942. Allen undertook a cautious series of taxi tests with the olive-and-gray experimental bomber, lifting off the ground to a height of no more than 15 feet and then settling back down. Disconcertingly, it became clear that the engines used on the XB-29 had a long ways to go before being considered reliable. Nevertheless, Allen believed the craft ready for its maiden flight, and on September 21, the great plane roared down the runway at Boeing's plant and lifted off for a perfect 75-minute first flight. Now, with the first flight behind them, Boeing settled down to the long process of proving the airplane out, with checks of its performance, stall behavior, systems operation, handling qualities, and other matters so vital to flight researchers. The engines quickly proved a painful liability. In the first twenty-six flight-test hours, the unreliable engines required replacement no fewer than sixteen times.

The second prototype flew on December 30. During the flight, the number-four engine (that farthest out on the right wing) caught fire; the propeller-feathering mechanism failed, carbon-dioxide fire bottles triggered from the cockpit had little effect, and Eddie Allen completed a successful emergency landing back at the field, the bomber trailing a long banner of smoke laced with burning oil. An alerted fire truck doused the fire as the crew abandoned the damaged airplane, which did not fly again until February 1943. Meanwhile engine problems continued to plague the other prototype, forcing emergency landings and long periods of maintenance. It appeared that the XB-29 was an outstanding airplane wedded to an unsatisfactory engine system, potentially a problem threatening the very B-29 program itself.

On February 18, Eddie Allen, with copilot Bob Dansfield and a crew of nine flight test engineers, took off in the second prototype on a flight to evaluate the plane's powerplant cooling and propeller operation. Five minutes later, passing through 5,000 feet, the XB-29 developed a fire in its number-one engine nacelle (that farthest from the fuselage on the left wing). The crew feathered the engine as a precaution, and dumped a CO_2 bottle, smothering the fire. Allen turned back for the Boeing plant, radioing his approach. Back at the field, Boeing corporate executives were in a weekly meeting when word came that Eddie Allen was bringing the Superfortress back following an engine fire. The meeting broke up as participants raced out to watch the approach. A few minutes later, the stricken bomber was at 1,500 feet over the Lake Washington Bridge; then it passed over Seattle's business district, streaming smoke from the number-two nacelle, for the plane had now experienced a *second* engine failure. Allen radioed the field with a message that brought all work to a stop: "Have fire equipment ready. Am coming in with wing on fire." The XB-29 continued south toward the haven of Runway 13, trailing bits of burning debris and streaming a banner of thick smoke as Allen and Dansfield performed heroically trying to keep the plane in the air. They lost the struggle just north of the field. The fire spread to the plane's fuel tanks and the bomber erupted in flame and plunged into a meat-packing plant, killing its entire crew as well as twenty people on the ground.

The death of the beloved and respected Allen, together with his crew, stunned the aeronautical community and drew forth calls for an investigation of the B-29's engine problems. Eventually, a congressional investigation committee headed by Senator Harry Truman found that the B-29's engine problems stemmed from poor quality control at the engine manufacturer's plant. With tightened procedures, the engines eventually proved reliable enough for the B-29 to be placed in service (though less serious problems, especially engine-cooling, plagued the large bombers throughout their service careers). It is a sad commentary that Allen and his crew had to perish before others took the B-29's engine problems seriously. By their sacrifice, they ensured the safety of those airmen who subsequently flew the Superfortress into combat. Fittingly, Boeing paid homage to Eddie Allen's scientific nature by dedicating a new research facility in his name at their Seattle plant. He posthumously received the 1943 Daniel Guggenheim Medal, one of aviation's most prestigious awards, and its citation succinctly summarized his accomplishments:

For major contributions to aeronautics leading to important advances in airplane design, flight research, and airline operation; particularly for the presentation of new methods for operational control and for the development of scientific and systematic methods in the flight testing of aircraft for basic design and performance data.[7]

Eddie Allen's legacy was a rich one: a legacy of élan, accomplishment, exactness, and courage—in sum, a legacy of professionalism.

TESTING CAPTURED AIRCRAFT

Among the most important aspects of military flight testing during the Second World War was the evaluation of captured enemy aircraft by American test pilots. Researchers then put the information gained from this comparison testing to use in instructing American airmen fighting these aircraft in the skies over Europe, the Mediterranean, the South Pacific, and Asia, and less frequently, in the design of new aircraft. Writing nearly twenty-five hundred years ago, the Chinese military philosopher Sun Zi stated, "If one knows the enemy and knows oneself, one may fight a hundred battles without a defeat," and it was in this spirit that the service pilots of the United States thoroughly evaluated whatever Axis aircraft fell into Allied hands. Sometimes these "turncoat" airplanes were flown in rear areas overseas, but most were shipped to the United States and evaluated at the military testing centers of Wright Field and Patuxent.

Test pilots flew these planes under simulated combat conditions against various opposing aircraft. (For example, on successive test flights, one captured Japanese Mitsubishi Zero flew against a P-39 Airacobra, a P-38 Lightning, an F4F Wildcat, and an F4U Corsair.) Test pilots would evaluate the enemy plane's climbing, diving, maximum speed, and maneuvering performance, as well as such matters as its controllability, handling qualities, usefulness of equipment, and engine performance. These data would then be reduced into circulars issued to combat squadrons, essentially a guide to combat pilots on how best to utilize their aircraft against an enemy airplane whose characteristics were now thoroughly understood. By war's end, it was not uncommon to visit an American test center and see a pilot warming up a Focke-Wulf 190 or a Messerschmitt 109 or a Zero or any of a number of other enemy types. And after the war, American technical intelligence teams acquired examples of many other Axis airplanes for postwar evaluation, including the sleek and then-exotic Messerschmitt 262 jet fighter.

When the war in Europe drew to a close, the Army Air Forces undertook a special air intelligence effort, Operation Lusty, to acquire test and evaluation examples of the Messerschmitt jet. Ten of the 262's captured at Lechfeld, a former German Luftwaffe airfield, were readied for shipment to the United States. A picked group of American pilots, led by Wright Field test pilot Colonel Harold E. Watson, checked out in the aircraft at Lechfeld under the tutelage of former Luftwaffe test pilots, and dubbed themselves "Watson's Whizzers." They ferried the 262's to Melun, France, in June 1945, and thence to Cherbourg, where the sleek jets were loaded aboard ship for their trip to the United States. Subsequently, Watson and other pilots extensively test-flew the craft at Freeman and Wright fields, and also at Patuxent River. Watson nearly lost his life on one flight at Freeman Field; the elevator controls had been accidentally rigged in reverse during maintenance, and he had to exert all his strength on the control column to prevent the howling jet from diving into the ground. Needless to say, he made a cautious circuit around the field before completing a successful emergency landing. American interest in the captured German jets reflected the already intense interest that researchers had for this novel form of aircraft.

AMERICA ENTERS THE JET AGE: THE XP-59A STORY

One of the major wartime thrusts of flight research involved not the development of conventional aircraft or refining the performance of some existing type, but, rather, the testing of a whole new generation of American aircraft: the first American jets. It is, essentially, a story of urgent catching up, for, embarrassingly, the United States lagged far behind other nations in the turbojet sweepstakes.

America entered the jet era on October 1, 1942, courtesy of the Bell Aircraft Corporation and the British Government. In April 1941, during a trip to England, Air Corps Chief Hap Arnold had learned of British jet research. With shocked awareness, he realized that the British were on the verge of flying a turbojet airplane, the little Gloster E.28/39, powered by a Whittle gas-turbine engine; rumors had already reached the United States of German interest in jet and rocket research. Before his European trip, Arnold, always an innovator, had spurred the NACA to create a Special Committee on Jet Propulsion, under the direction of Dr. William F. Durand, a distinguished engineer and pioneer in aeronautics who came out of retirement to direct this new and vital body. Shortly afterward, Hap Arnold had gone to England and seen the E.28/39, with its radical powerplant.

Arnold returned to the United States in May, just before the British jet made its first test flight. He was deeply troubled that the United States would fall behind Europe in jet-engine research; though the nation was not yet at war, few doubted that it would come, and the jet engine could be a war-winning invention. The air chief sent various representatives to meet with the British, and finally, in September 1941, the Army issued a contract to the Bell Aircraft Corporation, of Buffalo, New York, to develop a jet-propelled airplane using Whittle-derivative engines built by General Electric. Bell engineers busily set to work and came up with the Bell Model 27, a twin-engine single-seat airplane later redesignated the XP-59A Airacomet. The company did not complete the XP-59A until the late summer of 1942, nine months after the Japanese struck Pearl Harbor.

In mid-September 1942, Bell trucked the first XP-59A to the dusty and barren dry lake at Muroc, California. There, at a secret Army test site, established just for the experimental program, on the north end of the 65-square-mile lakebed, technicians readied the olive-and-gray plane for its first flight. Always cautious about security, Bell technicians had disguised the true nature of the craft on its transcontinental journey by placing a dummy four-bladed "propeller" on the Airacomet's nose. (In fact, the Army had assigned the XP-59A designation to confuse the project with an earlier, rejected propeller-driven fighter, the XP-59.) In anticipation of its first flight, company president Larry Bell and NACA jet committee chairman William Durand arrived at Muroc, together with representatives of the AAF.

On September 30, Bell test pilot Bob Stanley began feeling the plane out on the ground. He ran up the two G.E. I-A engines and then, with both jets whining, raced across the lakebed in a series of taxi runs at increasingly higher speeds, until he was momentarily lifting off the lakebed, reducing power, and then settling gently back down. Stanley was one of the outstanding engineering test pilots of the period, having flown first for the Navy, holding a degree in aeronautical engineering from the prestigious and pace-setting Guggenheim school at Caltech, and having set a series of altitude and distance records in sailplanes. Satisfied with the Airacomet's behavior, Bob Stanley wanted to make the first flight immediately, but Larry Bell opted for waiting until the next day, October 1.

The next morning, however, technicians discovered that one engine would not start. But Bell decided to fly anyway, using just the other engine. Early in the afternoon, Stanley ran up the good engine, released the brakes, and accelerated across the sun-baked clay of Muroc's Rogers Dry Lake. The XP-59A picked up speed and lifted smoothly off the lakebed before the anxious eyes of Bell, NACA, General Electric, and Air Force officials. Not wishing to endanger America's infant turbojet program, Stanley limited his altitude and kept the tricycle landing gear down and locked throughout the flight. After thirty minutes, he brought the little jet down. Before the end of the day, he made three more flights, each under the same cautious conditions as the first, as observers watched the Airacomet approach silently, without the familiar noise of a clattering propeller, rumble by overhead, and streak away, trailed by a faint aroma of kerosene.

The next day, October 2, Stanley extended the plane's performance a little more, making one flight to 6,000 feet and another to 10,000. Then Army Air Forces Colonel Laurence C. Craigie, chief of the Aircraft Projects Branch, at Wright Field, stepped into the jet's cockpit. Craigie, one of several Army representatives watching the pioneering flights, had participated in a straw-drawing contest to see who would be the first Army test pilot to fly the Airacomet. Now he won by default, for the others were absent from Muroc. Craigie familiarized himself with the cockpit, lit off the engines, taxied out, and took off. He returned highly enthusiastic over the plane, the first of the Army's jet test pilots, and symbolically clipped the propellers off his collar insignia.

Over the next months, Bell test pilots wrung out the little jet to develop as much information as possible. They did not know that, across the Atlantic, German test pilots of the Messerschmitt company were putting the prototypes of an infinitely deadlier jet fighter, the Me 262, through its paces. Messerschmitt's engineers had embarked on developing a high-performance turbojet fighter capable of sweeping the skies of inferior, propeller-driven planes. The XP-59A was nowhere in the Me 262's class. It had about a 390-mph maximum speed, no better than the latest propeller-driven aircraft, while the Me 262 could streak to 540 mph carrying an armament of four 30-mm cannon. But no one seriously proposed using the sluggish P-59 as a fighter, even though a small batch of production P-59 aircraft were produced and delivered to the Army Air Forces. Rather, the P-59 served in much the same capacity as the earlier German He 178 and the British E.28/39. It was simply an airplane to get jet experience, a precursor of more advanced aircraft to come.

One of Bell's best test pilots was the flamboyant Jack Woolams. Woolams had learned to fly with the Army, serving as a P-36 pilot before returning to college. While at the University of Chicago, Jack Woolams financed his education by teaching flying. After getting his degree, in 1941, he joined Bell, becoming the company's chief test pilot. Woolams had the quick wit and ability to make immediate decisions that seems a necessary hallmark of most successful test pilots. During one test flight from Muroc, Woolams edged his P-59 along a flight of curious Army fighter pilots eyeing his propless plane. They glanced over in time to note that the pilot was a gorilla smoking a cigar and wearing a derby hat! His joke a success, Woolams dived away, still wearing his Halloween mask and adding further to the mystery of the strange operation at Muroc.

Bell chose Jack Woolams to make the high-altitude test flights in the Airacomet. After proceeding cautiously, Woolams took the second prototype XP-59A to 45,765 feet on July 14, 1943. Five months later, he flew a preproduction YP-59A up to 47,600 feet. Then the company recalled him to Buffalo to make maximum-speed dive tests in the Airacomet. Nobody expected the P-59 program to proceed without accidents, and in short order, Jack Woolams experienced two. On one high-speed dive, the main landing gear on the jet suddenly extended, and Woolams, coolly keeping control, managed a successful emergency landing on the runway at Niagara Falls Airport. On another flight, the high air loads buffeted and finally ripped off the entire tail assembly. Woolams had reached that moment of truth when a test pilot has no choice but to abandon his airplane, when there is nothing that his skill can do to prevent a crash. So he prepared to open his canopy, only to find, to his consternation, that it had jammed shut. As the stricken P-59 gyrated and tumbled its way earthward from 25,000 feet, he unstrapped and twisted around in the seat so that his back rested on the seat pan and he could kick against the jammed canopy. Finally the stubborn canopy slid open, and Jack Woolams leapt for his life. His parachute blossomed open with a sudden crack that jerked both flying boots from his feet, and the hapless pilot thus landed stocking-footed in six inches of snow. *Then* he had to jog over a mile to a farmhouse, whose inhabitants called the Bell company, which sent out a helicopter to pick up Woolams before he lost his feet to frostbite. As a result, the Army Air Forces could place a "never exceed" speed of Mach 0.7 at all altitudes on the P-59.

In mid-1943, Great Britain and the United States reached an agreement whereby the two nations would send each other examples of their early jets. The United States shipped a P-59 to England, where it was first test-flown from Moreton Valence by Bell test pilot Frank "Bud" Kelley. In return, Gloster shipped a Meteor F.9/40 twin-jet fighter, having about the same performance, to the United States, accompanied by a technical team and Gloster test pilot John Grierson, a noted prewar aviator. The lanky Grierson found much to interest him during his visit to the United States, from the flora and fauna of the Mojave to the wartime atmosphere of Hollywood. But it was the flying that particularly occupied his time, and he did a great deal of that, both in the XP-59A and in his own

Meteor. During its final check flights before being handed over to an American test team, Grierson had one close call when he encountered severe aileron flutter during a high-speed dive. Fortunately, he was able to land the plane safely, and eventually it was delivered to the Army Air Forces. Before returning across the Atlantic, however, Grierson was able to secure permission for a flight in a new experimental jet, one that he subsequently characterized as "the most delightful machine I had flown":[8] the Lockheed XP-80.

P-80: SYLPH FROM THE "SKUNK WORKS"

The XP-80 grew out of an AAF search for a combat-worthy jet fighter able of countering any aircraft the Axis might come up with. In mid-1943 they selected the Lockheed Aircraft Corporation to design the plane, stipulating that the company use a British-designed De Havilland Halford H-1B turbojet of 2,460 pounds thrust. Lockheed entrusted the challenge to their chief research engineer, Clarence Johnson, known more popularly as "Kelly" Johnson. Kelly Johnson had received advanced degrees in aeronautical engineering from the University of Michigan before joining Lockheed in 1933. He had flown as a flight test engineer with many of the prewar aviation greats, including famed aviatrix Amelia Earhart, Wiley Post, and long-distance pioneer Sir Charles Kingsford-Smith. Already Johnson had an enviable reputation, first as recipient of the Lawrence Sperry Award for 1937 for "Important improvements of aeronautical design of high speed commercial aircraft," gained while flight testing the original Lockheed Electra, and secondly for the design and development of the twin-engine and twin-boom Lockheed P-38 Lightning. With characteristic energy, Johnson assembled a design team and set to work in strict secrecy—the origins of what became the legendary "Skunk Works." The development contract stipulated that Lockheed would deliver a prototype of the plane ready for flight testing in 180 days. Working ten hours per day, six days per week, Johnson and his small team completed the prototype XP-80 in only 143 days.

Early in November 1943, Lockheed trucked the first XP-80 to Muroc's dry lake for flight testing. Dubbed *Lulu-Belle* by Lockheed engineers, the first XP-80 was a trim, compact airplane with a low wing and smoothly faired engine intakes for the H-1B engine. By January 1944, the spinach-green plane was ready for flight. On the morning of January 9, 1944, Lockheed president Robert Gross, Kelly Johnson, and a small group of Lockheed engineers gathered at the north end of Rogers Dry

Lake, heavily dressed against the bitter winds that swept across the lakebed from the surrounding hills. During the night, rains had flooded the lakebed to a depth of several inches, but the winds had blown another section of the lake clear, and now, standing on the firm, hard clay of the lake, Kelly Johnson and his design team awaited the moment of truth. After a last-minute discussion, Lockheed's veteran chief test pilot, Milo Burcham, a renowned aerobatic pilot, climbed up into the XP-80, closed the bubble canopy, ran up the Halford engine, and took off. Suddenly the pilot canceled the flight, landed, and taxied back to the tense little group. In the excitement of the moment, mechanics had failed to remove a safety pin that prevented the landing gear from being retracted on the ground, and Burcham had been unable to retract the gear after takeoff.

Hurriedly, technicians removed the offending pin, and Burcham taxied out for another try. The XP-80 lifted off smoothly, Milo Burcham held it low until it built up speed, and then he pulled back on the stick. *Lulu-Belle* shot skyward and disappeared. At 20,000 feet, the pilot applied full throttle, and the XP-80 accelerated swiftly to 500 mph. Then he dived back to Muroc and put on an impromptu air show that left no doubt that the Shooting Star had the performance of a winner. Using the Halford engine, *Lulu-Belle* could climb at 3,000 feet per minute, hit 502 mph at 20,480 feet, and fly and fight up to 41,000 feet.

But events conspired to stop the XP-80 from entering service with the Halford engine. Allis-Chalmers, supposed to produce the engine for the United States, encountered production delays, forcing the Army Air Forces to look for another engine as a substitute. At this critical juncture, had a substitute engine not been available, the XP-80 might have dropped from the pages of aviation history, never to reappear. Instead, Lockheed had already studied an advanced XP-80, using a General Electric engine readily at hand. This was the G.E. I-40, better known subsequently as the reliable J33. The I-40 completed its first trial run on January 13, 1944, shortly after the Halford-powered XP-80. Immediately recognizing its potential, the Army Air Forces dropped plans to produce the XP-80 with the H-1B, and selected instead the more powerful I-40, authorizing Lockheed to build a prototype with the I-40 engine.

Once again, Kelly Johnson and his team set to work. In 132 days, a phenomenal record, they constructed a similar-looking airplane, but bigger and heavier: the XP-80A, known informally as the *Gray Ghost* because of its light gray external finish. It weighed 25 per cent more than the original *Lulu-Belle* and featured a redesigned landing gear, longer fuselage, revised internal equipment arrangement, pressurized cabin, and a bigger wingspread to keep down the wing loading. It could hit over 550 mph at sea level, climb to 5,000 feet in slightly over a minute, and attain

45,000 feet. It carried an armament of six .50-caliber machine guns and could lug two 500- or one 1,000-pound bomb. A true fighting machine, the new Shooting Star was more than a match for any Axis fighter.

To fly the new plane first, Lockheed turned to one of the company's finest test pilots, A. W. "Tony" Le Vier. He checked out in the earlier *Lulu-Belle*, and after Lockheed trucked the *Gray Ghost* up to Muroc after an all-night drive from Burbank, Tony Le Vier began running high-speed taxi tests across the lakebed. Then, on June 11, 1944, Le Vier taxied out to see what the new XP-80A could do in the air, while Kelly Johnson and his crew of Lockheed engineers, together with representatives of the Army Air Forces and General Electric, looked on.

Gray Ghost got off to a rough start. All first flights are made cautiously, for excessive zeal could cause a first flight to degenerate into a last one. So, for this test, Le Vier was to run the jet engine up to 10,500 rpm for takeoff, and reduce it to 10,000 rpm once he was in the air. At the end of the runway, Le Vier ran the engine up, released the brakes, and trundled down the band of concrete. It was a clear, hot day, the kind of weather that makes Southern California perhaps the best all-around flight test area in the world. But the near-Saharan temperatures of the Mojave Desert also rob turbojets of their power, and as the XP-80A moved along, picking up speed, Le Vier thought the airplane "didn't feel like it had too much steam."[9] Four thousand feet down the six thousand-foot runway, the XP-80A finally wallowed into the air.

At once, the pilot discovered that the plane suffered from longitudinal instability: it wanted to pitch up and down. Flying under a bubble canopy in the midst of a Mojave summer can be uncomfortable, but now Le Vier noted a blast of heat pouring into the left side of the cockpit. Following preflight instructions, he reduced his throttle setting, bringing the engine down to 10,000 rpm. Immediately the airspeed dropped to 160 mph, and the XP-80A settled low over the desert, barely airborne. For a few minutes, Le Vier flew low above the Antelope Valley's desert scrub, the I-40 screaming loudly. Then, as fuel burned off, the plane became lighter, and finally began climbing. Le Vier edged it up to 10,000 feet, still unstable, with heat filling the cockpit. Looking at his test card (containing the flight's planned tests), Le Vier began a stall check in "clean" configuration, that is, with landing gear and flaps up. The plane buffeted, then broke off to the right, just like the earlier *Lulu-Belle*. He recovered, then lowered the wing flaps to check their operation.

Immediately, he had a new problem. The left wing flap lowered properly, as did the right. But when he attempted to retract the flaps, the right flap remained full down. Acting just like an aileron, the errant flap threw the *Gray Ghost* into a series of left rolls. Le Vier applied full right control stick, which would tend to generate a right aileron roll. In this case, the full right stick just canceled out the rolling motion generated by the flap. Sizing up the situation, Tony Le Vier decided he had had enough for one day, and headed back for Muroc. On the trip back, he lowered the landing gear and tried to lower the left flap, to equalize flap deployment, but the left flap refused to come down. Now he had to make a landing with one flap jammed down, avoiding any abrupt control movements that might end the precious balance of forces between the ailerons and the disabled flap, precipitating a crash. He kept his airspeed to a minimum of 180 mph, not risking a stall, and descended to the dry lake. The plane touched down smoothly, and he coasted up to the Lockheed hangar. And as he taxied up, he realized that no one had seen him land! Several minutes after his arrival, Kelly Johnson belatedly came out to greet him, and the Lockheed pilot gave the engineer a complete rundown on the disappointing flight. Then they left for a first flight party—a Muroc tradition then and now.

A few days later, Lockheed came up with the reasons for the harrowing succession of problems that had plagued Le Vier and the *Gray Ghost* on their first flight. There is an old saying that at the root of every crash due to mechanical failure lies a nickel-and-dime item. A faulty engine tachometer installed in the XP-80A had falsely registered high, reading 10,500 rpm at takeoff when, in fact, the engine rpm was considerably less. Reduced rpm means reduced thrust; Rogers Dry Lake sits more than 2,000 feet above sea level. At that altitude, on a hot June day, at reduced thrust, Le Vier was lucky to get into the air and stay there. Lockheed reworked the balky flap mechanism to prevent future asymmetric flap operation, a problem sometimes encountered on test flights in new airplanes. Finally, the longitudinal-instability problem necessitated installing heavy lead bars in the nose gun compartment so as to shift the plane's center of gravity forward. Engineers had determined the center-of-gravity location for the XP-80A based on its carrying a full load of ammuniton. When the XP-80A made its first flight, without this weight, the plane's center of gravity shifted aft, creating the pitching tendency. After installing the lead bars, this problem disappeared. Strangely, Lockheed engineers ignored the cockpit-heating problem until one day when Tony Le Vier landed with a badly blistered arm from 180-degree temperatures, threatening to quit. Inspection revealed that the engine heat seeped into the cockpit through a faulty valve. After correction, cockpit temperatures still lingered around 130 degrees, so Lockheed engineers went a step further and combined the cockpit pressurization system with a refrigeration system, for a comfortable pilot is an efficient and safe pilot.

During additional XP-80A flights, Le Vier and Milo Burcham discovered some peculiarities of jet aircraft, notably duct rumble, caused by turbulent boundary-layer airflow entering the air intakes and distorting flow to the engine, as well as directional "snaking" of the plane. Redesigning the intake ducts to incorporate a boundary-layer bypass cured both problems. Engine flameouts constituted another difficulty. At high altitudes and low engine speeds, the flame burners in the engine often extinguished, like a kitchen stove shutting off. When the XP-80A's engine flamed out, the pilot could open the throttle and let the wind-milling engine relight. One day, Le Vier went aloft in the second XP-80A, which Lockheed, because of its natural metal finish, had dubbed the *Silver Ghost*. This plane had a second seat squeezed in behind the pilot for a flight test engineer. It also was the first Shooting Star to have long-range fuel tanks hung from its wing tips. Le Vier was checking the tank operation when his engine flamed out. Connected with the engine was the airplane's electrical system, which ran the hydraulic system. The hydraulic system controlled landing-gear operation, and if Le Vier could not get the engine running again, he would have to lower the landing gear using a special emergency hand pump in the cockpit. As fate would have it, nothing he tried worked; the engine remained dead. The Muroc lakebed rose to greet the plane, and with visions of a belly landing, Le Vier began pumping away. The cruise at high altitude had chilled the hydraulic fluid in the pump, and despite his best efforts, the landing gear remained up. At 2,000 feet, he was physically exhausted. He yelled to the flight test engineer crouched in the rear seat to give him a hand, but the engineer could just barely reach the pump handle to operate it. At several hundred feet above the ground, one main wheel extended, followed shortly by the other main wheel and then the nose landing gear. Seconds later, Le Vier touched down on the dusty lakebed, the valuable *Silver Ghost*—and its even more valuable crew—unscathed.

Lockheed delivered 13 YP-80A Shooting Stars for Army Air Forces service testing beginning in September 1944, and Lockheed and Army test pilots soon proved that the P-80—and any equivalent Nazi jet—could whip any conventional Allied piston-engine fighter or bomber, a source of concern and anxiety to the bomber drivers and a matter of acute embarrassment to the eager young fighter jockeys tooling around in their Mustangs, Lightnings, and Thunderbolts. As always, bugs in the design remained to be worked out. One morning in late 1944, Milo Burcham took off from Burbank in a new YP-80A. An engine overspeed governor apparently failed to work, and less than 50 feet above the ground the turbine rumbled and stopped. There is an adage that the two most useless possessions a test pilot can have is altitude above him and runway behind him. Milo Burcham had both. He turned toward an open field, the heavy jet sinking rapidly. It was perhaps a misbegotten approach anyway, one of those vain attempts made by a superlative pilot when his airplane has betrayed him. Descent defeated distance, and the

Shooting Star mushed into a gravel pit, exploding in a boiling cloud of black smoke and orange flame. Lockheed's flight test office mourned the passing of a great airman.

Like any new class of aircraft, the jets had their share of problems to be worked out, and the P-80 was no exception. An engine failure similar to Milo Burcham's claimed the life of Army production test pilot Dick Bong, the nation's ace of aces, who had only just returned from the war in the Pacific. Most bothersome, however, were a rash of turbine blade failures on early production I-40 engines. One such accident destroyed *Gray Ghost*, nearly killing Tony Le Vier. He had taken off on a duct-rumbling investigation and had climbed away from Rogers Dry Lake to an altitude of 15,000 feet. Then he nosed into a shallow dive, planning to accelerate to 575 mph before leveling out and beginning the test. As the XP-80A passed through 11,000 feet, Le Vier felt the plane shudder slightly. Then it went berserk, nosing down and snapping to the left, tumbling over. High g loads pinned the pilot to his seat, and as the mortally damaged airplane cartwheeled through the skies of the Antelope Valley, Le Vier experienced the awful realization that he probably would be killed. And still the forces kept him pinned in his seat, preventing him from reaching the emergency cockpit canopy release, only inches away from his left hand. Briefly the plane slowed, allowing Le Vier to wrench on the release. The handle pulled out, but nothing happened. In desperation, the pilot seized the cable itself and pulled. A blast of air swept into the cockpit as the canopy jettisoned. Quickly he unsnapped his seat belt, and the tumbling plane catapulted him out into the sky. With remarkable presence of mind, Le Vier decided to delay opening his chute until he was at a lower airspeed. He glanced to his right, and there, about a hundred feet away, was *Gray Ghost*, tumbling down minus its entire tail section. Le Vier opened his chute, and the XP-80A plowed into the Mojave near Rosamond. As he got close to the ground, his parachute began swinging, and he was too low to control it. With a terrible impact, Le Vier smacked into the desert, crushing two vertebrae. In short order, a rescue party and an ambulance arrived from Muroc, and after five weeks in the hospital and six months on the ground, Tony Le Vier returned to the air.

The question remained: why had *Gray Ghost* shed its tail? Investigators quickly found that the turbine wheel had disintegrated and jumped out of the engine, cutting like a circular saw right through the thin alloy fuselage and weakening it so much that the high structural loads during the dive had ripped it off. But why had the turbine let go? The answer didn't come until weeks after Le Vier's accident, when an Army pilot flying an acceptance flight on a P-80 at Van Nuys had an engine failure. After belly-landing in a bean field, he discovered that the turbine wheel had parted company with the rest of the airplane. Now came the time for official action, lest P-80's begin falling from the skies all across the United States. General Electric discovered that the fault lay in the turbine-wheel manufacturing process. When metal workers poured the molten metal for the blades, the sludge and impurities settled to the bottom of the ingot molds. Thus turbine wheels manufactured from the lower portions of these ingots were structurally deficient. G.E. simply stopped using the lower portions of the ingots, pending the development of satisfactory methods of removing the impurities, and the rash of turbine failures came to an end. The P-80 (later redesignated F-80) went on to a successful career as a fighter-bomber. A specially modified version, the P-80R, set a world's airspeed record of 623.738 mph in 1947 at Muroc, flown by test pilot Albert Boyd. Its finest hour came in Korea; within hours of hostilities beginning, F-80's claimed the first aerial victories for American jet aircraft, and a little later that year (though totally outclassed), an F-80 bagged the first of more than eight hundred Soviet-built MiG-15's to fall before the guns of American fighter pilots. The versatile F-80 served as the basis for the later T-33 and T2V trainers, as well as the F-94 interceptor. Today, nearly four decades since *Lulu-Belle*'s first flight, its T-33 descendants continue initiating neophyte airmen into the mysteries of jet flight.

THE JET GOES TO SEA

The U. S. Navy also followed the growing trend toward turbojet aircraft. This resulted in the first U.S. carrier jet aircraft, the mixed-power Ryan FR-1 Fireball and the pure-jet McDonnell FD (later FH-1) Phantom. Largely through the personal interest of Captain Frederick Trapnell, a veteran Navy test pilot who had flown the original XP-59A Airacomet, the Navy decided to award development contracts for jet-powered fighters capable of operating from aircraft carriers. The poor takeoff and landing characteristics of the early jets caused the Navy to favor a mixed-power fighter, one having a turbojet engine for high-speed boost and a conventional piston engine for takeoff, landing, and also for cruise and high speed. This particular requirement led to the mixed-power Ryan Fireball, a graceful little airplane having a G.E. I-16 engine buried in the rear fuselage and fed by intakes in the wing leading edge. Aside from the exhaust port in the tail, the little Fireball looked much like any other piston engine fighter, and allegedly, this eventually led to one of aviation's classic "Can you top this?" stories. Army pilots flying Lockheed's twin-engine P-38 Lightning enjoyed flying alongside their

single-engine Army and Navy compatriots, shutting down one engine
and smugly cruising along on the other. One day, a Fireball pilot gave his
Army opposite a bad psychological shock. The P-38 had pulled alongside, and the Army pilot shut down one engine, peering across the inter-
vening space at the Fireball jockey. The Navy pilot had both the prop
and jet fired up, so he obligingly shut down the piston engine, and the
big three-bladed propeller slowly feathered to stop. While the shocked
P-38 pilot looked on, the Fireball accelerated away from the Lightning,
streaming a thin trail of smoke, its propeller still motionless!

The Navy recognized, however, that the mixed-power concept did not
give all the advantages at high speed that a pure-jet aircraft possessed.
Once aloft, the pure jets could run circles around anything else in the
sky. During evaluations of the Navy's latest piston-engine fighter, the
magnificent Grumman F8F Bearcat, against the early P-80, the jet clearly
had everything its own way. The F8F was unable to take the initiative in
the fight and could not catch the P-80 in its sights long enough to "shoot
it down." That mock dogfight high over Patuxent River spelled the
death of the piston-engine naval fighter. The chief of the Bureau of
Aeronautics down to the lowliest ensign in the most obscure fighter
squadron realized that the Navy had to develop carrier-based jet fighters
in order to stay in the air combat business.

Fortunately, a suitable testbed aircraft already existed: the McDonnell
XFD-1 Phantom, a twin-jet fighter that the Navy had ordered from
McDonnell in mid-1943. The XFD-1 represented, like the XP-59A, a basically conservative design approach, not being too different in configuration from contemporary piston-engine fighters. It did have two Westinghouse 19XB axial-flow turbojets buried in the wing roots. The
company had dubbed the craft the Phantom, the first of many similar
creations from McDonnell's spirit world; the first of three prototypes
flew in January 1945. Such was company confidence in the plane that its
first flight was conducted with but one of the planned two engines installed. Subsequent flight testing confirmed that the craft was pleasant to
fly, without serious vices, and it had a maximum speed of 487 mph at sea
level, decreasing slightly to 483 mph at 20,000 feet, slower than the contemporary P-80 but much faster than the Army's first jet and any Navy
piston-engine airplane. Navy test pilots soon noted with pleasure the
difference between flying jets and the older, piston-engine types. While
taking off, the pilot could hear the rattling of the landing gear, then the
plane would lift off soundlessly and begin to climb, the shriek of its engine inaudible to the pilot in the cockpit. Trapnell later remarked that
the quiet "was an absolute fact—but, amidst such ominous quiet, it
wasn't convincing to an aviator who had gone deaf listening with grati-
tude to all the din and fuss of the old reciprocating engine and propel-

ler."[10] Operations were much simpler: advance the throttle and move out; no propeller pitch, mixture, cooling flaps, or boost to worry about; truly "kick the tire and light the fire."

The differences, in the public eye, between prop and jet promoted a host of new images of steely-eyed supermen screaming into the blue, and one publicist wrote an article entitled "Jet Guys Are Different," which drew the ire of Navy prop pilots, especially some who flew Grumman's hefty Avenger torpedo bomber, known far and wide through the fleet as the "Turkey." They responded with a parody entitled "Turkey Pilots Are Normal." But, in fact, jet pilots and planes *were* different from their propeller-oriented counterparts. With the 500+ mph jet speeds, the time available to pilots to make critical decisions decreased markedly, and flight test personnel accustomed to testing piston-powered aircraft had to institute special procedures for use with jets. Eventually, specialized guides to gas-turbine aircraft testing, such as Benson Hamlin's *Flight Testing Conventional and Jet-Propelled Airplanes* (1946) appeared. The major question concerning naval jet aircraft advocates as the war drew to a close concerned whether or not jet fighters could operate safely from carrier decks. It was a big day when the Navy's XFD-1 first operated from a carrier.

The Navy did not undertake the first carrier trials of American jet aircraft until after V-J Day, but the trials represented the logical extension of wartime work. In December 1945, British naval test pilot Eric "Winkle" Brown had flown a modified Vampire jet fighter down to a successful landing on the aircraft carrier H.M.S. *Ocean*, and now the U. S. Navy set out to emulate the feat with an American jet. In preparation, engineers laid out the shape of a carrier's flight deck on one of the runways at "Pax River." Then the Bureau of Aeronautics held comparative flight trials between the XFD-1 and the P-80, using Phantom-project pilot Jim Davidson and P-80-project pilot Marion Carl, a wartime Marine fighter ace. Both Davidson and Carl had flown the early P-59 and P-80, and Carl had even piloted a captured Me 262 evaluated at "the River." Daily both men practiced taking off and landing from the marked-out strip of concrete. Both jets accelerated slowly, but even so, Carl and Davidson became convinced that either of the two *could* land on a carrier and, if necessary, have enough of a power reserve to execute a "wave-off" and go around again. Finally, in early July 1946, the Navy bestowed its blessing upon the dark blue XFD-1, sending Jim Davidson and the Phantom to Norfolk. There, plane and pilot joined the new carrier U.S.S. *Franklin D. Roosevelt*, readying for a deployment to the Mediterranean. The Bureau of Aeronautics scheduled the initial American trials of a jet fighter from a carrier for July 20.

The *Roosevelt* left port on the morning of July 20, transiting the restricted waters of the Chesapeake for the open sea. McDonnell technicians discovered an electrical malfunction in the plane, and the XFD-1
was down for the day. Davidson and the Phantom spent the night on the
big carrier. By the morning of the next day, the McDonnell team had set
it right again. Finally all was ready. The carrier's captain turned into the
wind, and Jim Davidson clambered into the cockpit of the plane. As
photographers and newsmen watched from the carrier's island, the test
pilot ran up each of the jet's engines, then stabilized them at full power
while carefully watching the engine indicators for any loss in power. He
also had the plane's flaps fully extended to increase lift. Satisfied the plane
was a "good bird," he released the brakes.

Engines howling, the lithe blue airplane accelerated into the 28-knot
wind across the deck, moving ever so slowly, then faster and faster, toward the carrier's bow. Lest the little jet lose power or fail to fly off the
deck, Davidson kept the cockpit hood open in case the craft fell into the
sea. The XFD-1, picking up speed, shot by the carrier's "island" super-
structure. The airspeed indicator edged toward 85 knots, the plane's lift-
off speed. He pulled back ever so slightly on the control column, and the
XFD-1 lifted into the air abeam of the carrier's forward elevator, after a
takeoff roll of 360 feet. Elated observers saw the XFD-1 bank to starboard and then turn for a landing approach astern of the carrier. Davidson dropped behind the carrier, carefully setting up his landing approach. He concentrated on the landing ship officer waving his paddle
indicators, noting that he was "in the groove." He brought the Phantom
to deck with aplomb, then took off again. Three more times, he touched
down and took off, then came around for a simulated wave-off. The
Phantom settled lower and lower, then Davidson applied full power to
the engines and the plane climbed back into the sky. The pilot circled
over the *FDR*, slow-rolled victoriously, and disappeared in the sky, heading back to Patuxent. The Navy now had a seaworthy jet fighter. The
Marines got their chance a few months later. Marion Carl landed a
"hooked" P-80 on the *Roosevelt* soon after the carrier had returned from
the Mediterranean—and undoubtedly the Navy was happy that a Navy-
sponsored airplane had been first.

Like the Army's XP-59A, the McDonnell FD-1 Phantom saw only
limited service. The Navy eventually procured only sixty, using them
primarily for pilot familiarization. The service did deploy the Phantom
to VF-17A, which became the world's first carrier-qualified jet squadron
when it deployed at sea in mid-1948. When more-advanced aircraft became available, the Navy transferred the hardy Phantoms to the Marines,
which set up that service's first jet fighter squadron, VMF-122, under the

command of test pilot Carl. There the Phantom lived out the rest of its career, in the service of the Corps.

Encouraged by its success, McDonnell designed a larger and more powerful successor, the XF2D-1. In time it evolved into the F2H Banshee, the famed "Banjo." When Korea came, the Banshee and its brethren served valorously, gaining a measure of literary recognition in the pages of James Michener's haunting novel *The Bridges at Toko-ri.* Perhaps the greatest recognition of the Phantom's accomplishments, however, came in 1958, when McDonnell flew another Phantom—the epochal XF4H-1 Phantom II, the finest fighter aircraft of the 1960s.

A JET RETROSPECTIVE

By war's end, then, the United States had several jet fighters in flight testing and others on the drawing boards. North American, the manufacturer of the famed Mustang, was already contemplating a jet-propelled fighter for the AAF, which eventually emerged as the F-86 Sabre, master of nearly a thousand combats against MiG's above Korea's Yalu. Republic, builders of the rugged Thunderbolt, had a promising jet fighter on paper, destined to emerge as the ground-loving F-84 Thunderjet. Not all of these various projects—and there were dozens by war's end—reached fruition; indeed, many certainly deserved not to. Perhaps the most interesting American jet fighter to emerge from the war, however, was the little Northrop XP-79B flying wing.

The XP-79 is a classic example of how a weird concept can seize hold of a design team. In this case, designers stipulated that this single-seat flying wing be constructed of magnesium, with an armament of four .50-caliber machine guns, and be powered by a 2,000-pound-thrust Aerojet rocket engine burning a mixture of red fuming nitric acid and aniline, a violently explosive combination totally unsuited for a combat airplane; further, magnesium decomposes when exposed to nitric acid, raising visions of the XP-79 fizzing itself out of existence. By March 1943, cooler heads had succeeded in securing approval to complete one of the planned three prototypes with two Westinghouse turbojets in place of the nasty rocket engine.

Around the same time, engineers built three wooden piloted gliders of the XP-79 configuration to assess its low-speed flying characteristics, and the gliders received the Army designation MX-324. The first one flew in October 1943, towed aloft behind an automobile and piloted by John

Myers, who was an unusual test pilot by anyone's standards: he possessed an LL.B. from the Harvard Law School. The urge to fly had overcome reading legal briefs, and he had joined Lockheed as a test pilot, then left for Northrop. Myers and fellow pilot Harry Crosby thoroughly evaluated the little gliders before Myers was seriously injured in a crash of another Northrop airplane. Meanwhile, Aerojet had developed a small and barely efficient 200-pound-thrust nitric-acid-and-aniline rocket engine for the MX-324, the engine being known as the XCAL-200. In June 1944, technicians installed the engine in one of the gliders and shipped it to Harper's Dry Lake (near Muroc) for flight testing. Early on the morning of July 5, 1944, a Lockheed P-38 towed the rocket-powered MX-324 into the air. At an altitude of 8,000 feet, Harry Crosby cast off the tow, ignited the XCAL-200, and shot ahead, the little flying wing sputtering red flame and streaming a thick black exhaust banner. The engine ran for four minutes, accelerating the glider to about 270 mph before starving itself and shutting down. Crosby glided down to the lakebed, the first pilot in the United States to make a flight in an airplane designed from the outset for rocket propulsion.

The larger XP-79 program soon fell apart; indeed, it would have taken a miracle to prevent its collapse. The projected 2,000-pound-thrust engine fell farther and farther behind schedule, and finally the AAF decided to concentrate only on the jet-propelled version, designated the XP-79B. Northrop completed the XP-79B in mid-1945 and shipped it to Rogers Dry Lake for flight testing. One morning in September, 1945, Harry Crosby fired up the two jet engines in the wings, taxied out, and took off, trailing a sooty stream of exhaust. For fourteen minutes, the small flying wing pirouetted gracefully over the lakebed. Then it suffered an apparent control failure. Witnesses saw it execute a slow roll that degenerated into a spin. At 2,000 feet, Crosby bailed out, but the spinning plane struck the pilot and, unconscious or dead, he fell to the ground without deploying his parachute. The perverse XP-79 program had come to a tragic close.

The gregarious Crosby died just as the United States was beginning to savor the fruits of victory. In no small measure, the victories on the battlefields and in the skies over Europe and the Pacific represented the contributions of America's flight researchers. They had honed the aerial weapons of war to a fine edge, their evaluations causing designers to add more firepower here, a little more stability there, a little more maneuverability and control response here. The result had been such war-winning aircraft as the P-51 Mustang, the Grumman Hellcat, the B-29, the DC-4, the production Sikorsky helicopters. And had the war lasted for another year, such aircraft as the P-80, the Ryan Fireball, and the

McDonnell Phantom would have proved their worth. By war's end, other weapons were in flight testing: weird "flying bombs" such as the Republic JB-2 (a frank copy of the German V-1 buzz bomb) and advanced piston-engine airplanes. The outline of postwar aviation technology, a technology dominated by long-range jet-propelled aircraft, could already be murkily discerned. The United States had already gone a long ways toward catching up for its tardiness in developing jet engines prior to Pearl Harbor.

And yet a disquiet pervaded the councils of America's aeronautical establishments. It would seem that with Hitler's state crushed beyond hopes of a Nazi resurrection and with Japan beaten into submission, American designers could have luxuriated in their accomplishments, in the contemplation of a new golden age of aviation ahead of them. Such was not the case. The jet engine promised truly high airspeeds, perhaps greater than the speed of sound. Yet if the turbojet revolution was to reach this logical fruition, then a supersonic breakthrough beyond the speed of sound would have to take place. In meeting-rooms of industrial, military, and NACA establishments, engineers and test pilots spoke of the urgent challenge before them: to make the attainment of supersonic flight a practical reality. They spoke of "Mach 1," the speed of sound, and while pessimists hinted darkly of a "sound barrier," optimists preferred to contemplate "traversing transonic tangles and traps."

Flying faster than the speed of sound posed the greatest challenge to aeronautics since the time of the Wright brothers themselves. The mysterious phenomena encountered as a plane approached the speed of sound had already killed many excellent pilots flying what were then some of the world's finest aircraft. And for once, ground research methods were of no help, for wind tunnels routinely "choked" as the airflow around test models reached *transonic* velocities, the strange region just below and above the speed of sound. Here, rather, was a challenge requiring solution by flight research using both unmanned and manned research aircraft. The reward could be a new era of high-speed flight. The penalty for failure could be a legacy of wrecked aircraft and dead pilots. Undaunted, American designers and pilots embarked upon the supersonic breakthrough, a task they began in the midst of the Second World War.

The roots of the supersonic breakthrough had been planted in the 1930s, when engineers and designers had contemplated developing planes capable of flying above 500 mph. But plots of horsepower requirements versus speed indicated that the power required to overcome airplane drag rose enormously. One prominent aerodynamicist, W. F. Hilton, concluded gloomily that the speed of sound loomed "like a barrier against future progress."[11] And hence the term "sound barrier" was born. And there was danger as well.

THE "COMPRESSIBILITY" CRISIS: PRELUDE TO SUPERSONIC FLIGHT

One bright morning in 1941, veteran Lockheed test pilot Ralph Virden took off from Burbank in one of the company's latest preproduction YP-38 Lightning interceptors, a gleaming silver plane. The Lightning represented the latest state of the art in aviation technology, with two supercharged Allison engines fairing into twin booms supporting the tail structure; a stub fuselage large enough for the pilot, a nosewheel, and a potent cannon-and-machine-gun armament; and a promised 400+ mph performance. A few months before, Army test pilot Signa Gilkey had flown one of the planes in a high-speed dive. Suddenly the YP-38 had buffeted violently, the nose tending to "tuck under" and the tail surfaces shaking madly. Cautiously, he retarded the throttles and adjusted elevator trim, and the YP-38 gradually recovered into level flight. Gilkey chalked up the incident to flutter, but Lockheed, after a quick investigation, realized that something else was afoot: the extraordinarily clean plane was clearly encountering disturbed flight conditions as it approached higher and higher dive speeds.

Testing continued, and this morning Virden was aloft to evaluate a boosted elevator system to help Lightning pilots overcome the nose-down tendencies of the big fighter-interceptor during high-speed dives. Virden proceeded with a series of dives to a true airspeed of about 535 mph at about 15,000 feet. Then workers at the Lockheed plant—including Virden's fellow test pilots and Lightning designer Kelly Johnson—heard an altogether unfamiliar sound: a high-pitched scream. Ground observers looked up in time to see the tail break away from the Lightning, and the remainder of the plane tumbled inverted and spun into a housing district in Glendale, exploding on impact. It was the second tragic loss for Lockheed's flight test department within a few months, for previously Marshall "Pop" Headle, Lockheed's chief test pilot since 1929, had suffered serious injuries in a decompression-chamber accident, ending his long and productive career (he died in 1945). What had caused Virden's accident?

Obviously, the YP-38 had experienced structural failure, but the answer was far more complex. As air flows over a wing, it accelerates. Consequently, though a plane may be flying at one speed, the airflow velocity over the wing can be considerably higher: this is simple aerodynamic theory and, in fact, is why a wing generates lift, for the change in velocity also induces a reduction in pressure above the wing. Now, suppose a plane is diving at truly high speeds (by 1941 standards), say seven tenths of the speed of sound: Mach 0.7. The accelerated flow over the wing is likely moving much faster, perhaps greater than the speed of sound (Mach 1) itself. The mixed subsonic and supersonic flow conditions cause turbulent flow separation to occur, and the violent, eddying wake streams from the wing and fuselage of the plane and beats upon the tail section. Further, all the precise design calculations of the engineers go out the window, for the "transonic" flow conditions (i.e., mixed subsonic and supersonic flow conditions) change the aerodynamic trim of the aircraft, greatly changing the control response and controllability of the aircraft. Hence the plane might become nose-heavy (or, conversely, tail-heavy), and the control forces might increase to the point where a pilot needs full strength just to keep the control column from moving forward (or perhaps backward) of its own accord. If an abrupt dive recovery is made, the increased loads from the recovery and from the disturbed air flailing the tail can cause it to fail under load, ripping it from the plane. And this is what had happened to the unfortunate Virden.

And he was not the last. As the United States found itself in the midst of a shooting war, Army pilots discovered that the P-38 could be a killer in high-speed dives. That veteran test pilot Ben Kelsey had his own brush with disaster in a P-38 over California's San Fernando Valley. During a vertical dive past 500 mph, Kelsey began pulling back on the control column. Suddenly

> The plane went into a series of violent maneuvers so confusing and so rapid that I had difficulty recalling in detail the sequence of events, never quite sure until sometime later while floating down in the parachute that the airplane had actually broken up in flight.
>
> After considerable difficulty in getting the cockpit canopy open due to the unusual flight conditions of the plane, I released the safety belt and was thrown into space. Actually, I reached and unsnapped the safety belt and suddenly the plane was gone. . . . The jolt of the parachute opening was severe. . . .
>
> Above was a stream of debris extending for several thousand feet out of sight. The biggest piece looked like the tail, but turned out to be a whole wing floating slowly down. . . .
>
> Seconds later I was riding in dead quiet except for the gentle swishing of the air around the parachute. Suddenly there was a dull thud and explosion, the remains of the airplane destroying itself on the ground.[12]

And the accidents to the P-38 were not unique. Tail failures during dives also plagued such fighters as the Bell P-39 Airacobra, the Curtiss P-40 Warhawk, and the Republic P-47 Thunderbolt. By 1943, such failures were common enough for service pilots to be aware of them, and a mix of wild rumors and strange theories grew up around the accidents. Gradually a general truth emerged from the morass of fact and myth: fighter pilots should not impulsively dive at high speeds from high altitudes. Eventually, the NACA, the military services, and private industry had to spend more and more time trying to make high-performance fighters and dive bombers safer.

During this extensive testing process, near disasters abounded. NACA test pilot Larry Clousing once had the tail of a test P-39 fail during high-speed dive, but he managed to limp back to the Ames laboratory safely. Another NACA pilot, Herbert Hoover, had the canopy come adrift during a test flight in one of the Navy's troubled Curtiss SB2C-1 Helldiver dive bombers. The canopy smashed him across the forehead, but the dazed and bleeding Hoover elected not to abandon the airplane and, instead, managed an emergency landing at Langley, returning the airplane and its valuable recording instruments safely to earth. Lockheed's Tony Le Vier undertook a number of hazardous high-speed dives to over 500 mph in a modified P-38 dubbed *Nosey*—including one to Mach 0.7+ followed by a 7½ g pullout at a mere 1,000 feet—while proving out a new dive-flap installation that prevented the P-38 from tearing itself apart at transonic speeds.

Very quickly, designers recognized that the days of fabric-covered control surfaces were a thing of the past. At the increasingly higher speeds attained by fighters in dives, the fabric surfaces could distort in the airstream, "ballooning" between the ribs and totally losing or negating their effectiveness. In one accident caused by fabric ballooning, Army test pilot Perry Ritchie had to abandon a P-47 that lost its tail during dive trials at Wright Field; he parachuted to earth with a broken back. Compressibility-induced problems afflicted foreign aircraft as well. The famed Hawker Typhoon fighter-bomber began its service with a disastrous series of tail failures during dives.

Researchers attempted to use standard ground-based techniques to study the problem of "compressibility": the concept of air bunching ahead of an aircraft as it flew increasingly faster through the sky. At low speeds, air can be treated as an incompressible fluid, but above 400 mph, its compressibility characteristics have to be taken into account. At about 450 mph, the accelerated flow around an airplane may become locally supersonic, and the plane is now in the *transonic* region, a region of turbulent mixed subsonic and supersonic flow conditions. Shock waves form on the aircraft, move back and forth, and violently disrupt the airflow.

Total airframe drag rises sharply, the pressure field around the plane is disturbed, trim changes occur that change control response and control behavior, and the turbulent flow, as has been seen, can induce severe structural stress.

Testing in wind tunnels proved almost useless. At transonic speeds, shock waves formed on tunnel models and distorted the accuracy of tunnel measurements. (This serious problem with tunnel testing was not resolved until the postwar development of the so-called "slotted-throat," or "ventilated," transonic tunnel, another NACA accomplishment.) Wartime urgency dictated that other means be found for research on high-speed aerodynamics. Meanwhile, aerodynamicists studying the problems broke into two camps: those who believed that manned flight beyond Mach 1 "through the sound barrier" was an impossibility, and those who were encouraged by the supersonic flight of bullets and shells into believing that supersonic flight was just another problem to be solved, one that was a bit more difficult than most.

A variety of novel methods were devised for high-speed aerodynamic research. NACA engineer Bob Gilruth developed the "wing flow" method. Cannily recognizing that the airflow over a wing could be supersonic even when the plane was diving at subsonic speeds, Gilruth persuaded NACA flight researchers to install small test models on the surface of a P-51 Mustang's wing, using the wing's gun bay for housing the necessary recording and operating equipment. The Mustang pilot—usually Herb Hoover—would then dive the fighter. At about Mach 0.75, at which the Mustang still had good controllability, the airflow over the wing around the test model would be about Mach 1.2, resulting in the acquisition of generally useful (if limited) data. Another NACA method involved dropping weighted aerodynamic shapes from a B-29 flying at 40,000 feet, then tracking the descent by radar. Still a third consisted of firing off small rocket-propelled models from the ground or from the air. All these methods involved some risk; Hoover once fired a test model rocket from a NACA P-51 diving at about Mach 0.7. The model immediately broke up, showering the Mustang with wreckage and puncturing the engine coolant tank. Quickly, Hoover returned to Langley with the ailing Mustang streaming a thick banner of smoke from its ruined engine.

What rapidly became apparent, however, was that the most reliable data could only come from piloted instrumented test airplanes. At Langley, NACA engineers took one of the original Allison-powered XP-51 prototypes and modified it with special flight test instrumentation to record such quantities as aileron and elevator control position and control forces, airspeed, altitude, "normal" acceleration, tail loads, pressure distribution, pitching tendencies, and actual distortion of the wing profile during flight. High-speed motion-picture cameras photographed the plane's instrument panel and its left wing. Then Army and NACA pilots dived it to increasingly higher speeds. This modified XP-51 was, in fact, the ancestor of all postwar "X-series" research aircraft. Besides acquiring valuable information on flight above Mach 0.7, it also demonstrated that, with a cautious, well-planned test program, the lives of test pilots need not be risked recklessly. It was with the NACA XP-51 that test pilots first saw the streaming of shock waves from the wings as the airflow over the wing exceeded the speed of sound. (This phenomenon is now occasionally witnessed by airline passengers today as they glance out over the wing under certain lighting conditions.) Thereafter, NACA modified a number of aircraft for high-speed dive research.

One of the NACA's most interesting attempts to assess the aerodynamic characteristics of new high-speed planes involved a proposed series of tests using a propeller-less P-51B Mustang towed aloft behind a twin-engine Northrop Black Widow and then released at altitude to glide back to earth at high speed. The purpose behind this testing was to validate measurements taken during wind-tunnel tests of models on the ground, and full-scale aircraft in flight, without the disturbances induced by a rotating propeller. The NACA carefully evaluated a one-third scale model of a P-51B Mustang, then one of the hottest fighters around, and then instrumented an actual P-51B, removing its propeller but leaving the smooth prop spinner on the nose and attaching releases for towlines. One day in September, 1944, Bill McAvoy piloted the Black Widow aloft, trailing the experimental Mustang and its test pilot, Jimmy Nissen, who had already made several of the potentially risky flights. The two aircraft slowly climbed into the sky west of Muroc, reaching an altitude of about 1,500 feet. Then the left towrope broke from the towplane, came back, and hit Nissen's Mustang with a terrific jolt, wrapping around it. At the same time, the right rope disengaged, and Nissen suddenly found himself gliding like a brick over inhospitable terrain. The Mustang sank quickly. As McAvoy watched anxiously, Nissen skillfully put the fighter down amid some sandpits on base. Although his plane was a crumpled heap, Nissen was shaken but otherwise unhurt. And the flight instrumentation had worked during the all-too-brief mission, furnishing the data NACA engineers needed to correlate wind-tunnel test results with those of flight aloft! All in a day's work . . . but wisely NACA decided not to go ahead with any similar glide tests. As engineer-historian Edwin Hartman concluded:

> The hazards to which NACA test pilots were subjected were considered acceptable only if they could not by any reasonable means be avoided. In this case, the whole project had been rushed and a question remained whether, with a little more deliberation, a little more care and

checking, the failure of the cable attachment could have been avoided. The lesson learned was reasonably cheap, but it could have been otherwise.[13]

Dive testing did involve clear hazards, and it was for this reason that the great prewar pattern of making nearly vertical dives with experimental aircraft had been halted. Now, however, military pilots were having to dive their aircraft at high speeds under combat conditions, and pilots were being lost. The accident to Virden's YP-38, the problems of the P-47 and such other aircraft as the Curtiss Helldiver—all took on more than academic interest. The NACA sought to acquire new aerodynamic information so that designers could prevent such problems in the future, freeing aircraft manufacturers to concentrate on overcoming the problems their aircraft were experiencing. Lockheed, for example, worked long and tirelessly to solve the P-38's dive problems. Eventually, engineers decided to install dive-recovery flaps under the P-38's wings, which enabled a pilot to retain control of his bucking aircraft. This, of course, required in-flight validation during actual dive conditions. Lockheed test pilots Milo Burcham and Tony Le Vier went aloft day after day over the Antelope Valley, diving a modified P-38 equipped with recovery flaps at steeper and steeper angles and higher and higher speeds. The two men alternated flights. One day, Burcham seemed to reach the limit: a 55-degree dive from 35,000 feet to over 500 mph. Then, the next day, Le Vier took off from Muroc in the plane, climbed to 35,000 feet south of Muroc, and pushed over into a 60-degree dive. Everything proceeded smoothly as airspeed built well above 500 mph. Then, at 31,000 feet, Le Vier sensed that the plane "wanted to get away from me." It abruptly started to nose over, and the pilot hauled back with all his strength on the control column to keep the nose up and maintain the original dive angle. The dive flaps saved him from meeting Virden's fate, for though the P-38 behaved like "a mad demon," pitching and bucking, it remained under control. At 20,000 feet, Le Vier had the column practically in his lap, but the nose barely lifted. Then, at 13,000 feet, it began to recover very slowly, finally leveling off. "My strain gauge instruments were set for 100 percent of limit load," Le Vier recollected later, "and they were all over 100 and all the red warning lights were on when I finally got out of the dive."[14] Indeed, Le Vier *had* exceeded the limit load of the plane, but it returned safely to base. Those dive trials confirmed that the dive-recovery flap did prevent the sort of accident that had killed the luckless Virden, and the P-38 went on to an excellent combat career. Flight testing had validated a design fix that turned a dangerous airplane into a useful one.

Abroad, other nations launched high-speed research programs using modified fighters diving to transonic speeds. In Germany, the *Deutsche*

Versuchsanstalt für Luftfahrt (DVL) tested a variety of fighters including the Messerschmitt Bf 109 (stable to Mach 0.79), the Focke-Wulf Fw 190 (trim changes at Mach 0.78), the tricky Messerschmitt Me 163 (uncontrollable above Mach 0.82), and the Messerschmitt 262 (good controllability to Mach 0.85). The most interesting foreign trials, however, were those conducted by the test pilots of Britain's Royal Aircraft Establishment, at Farnborough, using various aircraft ranging from Spitfires and Mustangs to Tempests and the Meteor. Two of the RAE's test pilots, Squadron Leaders J. R. Tobin and A. F. "Tony" Martindale, dived a Mustang III (equivalent to an American P-51B) to Mach 0.82, and a modified Supermarine Spitfire XI to Mach 0.9. The Spitfire mark stands as certainly the fastest speed ever attained by a World War II piston-engine fighter. It was a claim advanced most cautiously and only on the basis of the most thorough evidence, including appropriate corrections for compressibility effects upon the airspeed measurement system. During the course of the trials, several near accidents occurred. On one flight, the Spitfire's supercharger shattered, and Martindale had to make a forced landing near the community of Guildford. "He rang up," one engineer recalled, "from a local pub, where we subsequently found him in the bar having safely extracted the all-important instrumentation cameras from the aeroplane."[15] On another dive, the propeller departed the airplane, ripping off most of the engine cowling, and Martindale, one of Britain's finest airmen, skillfully dead-sticked the airplane down to a safe landing at Farnborough. A typical Spitfire dive would start from level flight at about 40,000 feet. The pilot would push over into a gradually steepening dive, eventually holding a dive angle of approximately 50 degrees. Within thirty seconds, the "Spit" would be passing through 32,000 feet at about Mach 0.88. It would reach about Mach 0.9 in the vicinity of 29,000 feet, moving at just about 610 mph. The pilot would begin a gradual pullout, never exceeding more than 2.2 g, finally returning to level flight about seventy seconds after beginning the dive, and at an altitude of around 19,500 feet. The Spitfire was capable of high-speed performance unattainable by other contemporary aircraft (including the Mustang) largely because of its aesthetically pleasing elliptical-wing planform and the thinness of its wing section, both of which endowed it with a higher "critical Mach number" and reduced drag as compared to other piston-engine airplanes and even some of the early jets. Great Britain, then, can safely claim the distinction of having developed the airplane that came closest to the fabled Mach=1 mark during the wartime years. But even so, how could engineers acquire the detailed data necessary to develop practical transonic and supersonic airplanes? Indeed, was it possible to do so?

CHAPTER 7

THE SUPERSONIC BREAKTHROUGH AND THE ERA OF THE JET

One balmy spring morning in 1940, NACA engineers John Becker and John Stack left the Langley laboratory and drove to a remote beach on the Virginia peninsula. There they stopped, and scanned the skies with binoculars. The throaty rasp of an experimental Navy Brewster XF2A-2 Buffalo fighter plane disturbed the morning's tranquillity, and they focused on the small plane, which was preparing to make a high-velocity dive to 575 mph, followed by a dive pullout at the plane's design load limit. NACA and Navy researchers were interested in studying the pressure distribution over the plane's wing during such a harsh test. At last the Navy test pilot nosed over into the dive, and with an increasing whine, the stubby fighter dived earthward. Becker later recalled:

We were most apprehensive as we watched the dive through binoculars. This was before the possible consequences of compressibility effects on the buffeting and control of diving airplanes had been highlighted by the P-38 tragedy of 1941; nevertheless, our knowledge of shock-stalled flows in the wind tunnel left little doubt about the dangers of this dive. Happily, the flight was completed successfully without any undue difficulties

for the Navy pilot, but we were both left with the strong feeling that a
diving airplane operating close to its structural limits was not an acceptable way to acquire high-speed research information.[1]

The hazardous experiences of test pilots around the world during
high-speed dive research convinced designers and research planners that
there must be better methods of acquiring transonic aerodynamic data
than by risking the lives of pilots in dives. Recoveries had to be made at
lower altitudes, in dense air, where structural loads were high. The dives
themselves lasted only a few seconds, hardly enough time to acquire the
amount of data scientists and engineers were interested in obtaining.
They recognized that a specially designed jet or rocket-propelled airplane could cruise in the relative safety of level flight at high altitudes
and at high speeds for such research purposes. Such a notion caused
Great Britain, in 1943, to launch the E.24/43 program, which led
to the Miles M52, a bold attempt to develop a supersonic jet-propelled
research airplane that, regretfully, never came to fruition. In the United
States, a number of outstanding engineers within the government and
industry pressed for development of specialized aerodynamic research
airplanes, including the NACA's John Stack and Eastman Jacobs, the
Navy's Walter Diehl and Emerson Conlon, and the Army's Ezra
Kotcher. Eventually this resulted in the two aircraft that first exceeded
Mach 1 and Mach 2, the Bell XS-1 (designed by a team led by Robert J.
Woods), and the Douglas D-558-1 and -2 (whose design team was led
by Ed Heinemann).

Design work on both the Bell XS-1 (for Experimental Sonic-1) and
the Douglas D-558 began late in 1944. Of the two, the XS-1 represented
the more ambitious design, for it was intended for flight well above the
speed of sound, using rocket propulsion. The D-558, a turbojet airplane,
was better suited for sustained cruising at about Mach .85 +. In fact, during a trip around the country to various aeronautical laboratories and facilities, two members of the XS-1 design team discovered that no one really could offer any concrete advice on how the plane should be
designed! Bell was on its own. This firm, however, which had earlier
produced such revolutionary designs as the XFM-1, the P-39, and then
the XP-59A, was equal to the challenge. After months of effort at a nonstop pace, the company had completed design of a suitable research aircraft, to be air-launched from a modified Boeing B-29 Superfortress. It
featured a wing of exceptional thinness for the time, and utilized a four-
chamber 6,000-pound-thrust Reaction Motors Inc. rocket engine burning
a mixture of liquid oxygen and diluted alcohol. It also featured a retractable landing gear, for Bell at first had hoped to operate the plane by
itself from the ground, but the risks involved in firing up a rocket engine

circa 1945 and depending upon it for takeoff, together with the wasted fuel consumed during a climb to launch altitude, convinced the AAF, the NACA, and Bell to air-launch it from a B-29. The D-558, a much less radical airplane, could be flown from the ground without the need for air launching. Eventually, the D-558 program split: a "D-558-1," having a straight wing and jet propulsion, and a "D-558-2," having a swept wing and both jet and rocket propulsion. And subsequently, Douglas modified the D-558-2 for air launching and removed the turbojet from one of them, making it all-rocket-propelled and capable of twice the speed of sound (but just).

FIRST FLIGHT TRIALS

Bell completed the first of three XS-1's (later designated by the Air Force as simply X-1, the first of the many postwar "X-series" research airplanes) shortly after Christmas, 1945. The company ferried it under a B-29 from the Buffalo plant to Orlando, Florida, for gliding trials, and there, in mid-January 1946, the little orange airplane, still lacking its rocket engine but ballasted to match the characteristics of the ultimate airplane, completed its maiden flights and dropped from the Super-fortress into the humid southern sky as Bell test pilot Jack Woolams evaluated its handling qualities. It flew nicely but had a minor stability problem just before touchdown that caused some difficulty (this remained a hallmark of the X-1's right until their retirement from flying, in 1958).

Bell next prepared for the first powered flights, but, sadly, Jack Woolams was not around to make them. He died while piloting a racing airplane during preparations for the 1946 Thompson Trophy air race. The company replaced him with Chalmers "Slick" Goodlin, a young former RAF Spitfire pilot who had also flown for the U. S. Navy before joining Bell. Despite his youth (he was only twenty-three), he had had a number of close calls. One time, a P-39 had caught fire and Goodlin had just managed to abandon the smoke-and-flame-filled cockpit in time to open his parachute. On another flight, while testing the experimental Bell XP-83 (a hefty, twin-engine follow-on to the P-59), the jet caught fire and Goodlin stayed with the plane until his test observer could jump, before abandoning it himself.

In October 1946, Bell sent the second XS-1, now equipped with its rocket engine, to Muroc for initial powered flight trials. Following these trials, the first two XS-1's would be readied for a joint assault upon Mach 1. Meanwhile, however, an event had occurred that badly shook the confidence of those who believed the sonic "wall" could be breached safely.

In the summer of 1946, Great Britain had abandoned all efforts to develop piloted supersonic research aircraft, citing the country's postwar financial condition but also intimating that pilot safety had entered into the decision. The director-general of Britain's Scientific Air Research, Sir Ben Lockspeiser, remarked in a press interview, "We have not the heart to ask pilots to fly the high-speed models, so we shall make them radio-controlled." Thus passed the M52 program, begun ambitiously in 1943. Sadly, within weeks of this decision, a tragedy claimed the life of one of Britain's outstanding test pilots, young Geoffrey de Havilland, son of the pioneer who had flown so many years before with Edward Busk.

The De Havilland company had developed a new experimental jet, the radical D.H. 108, based on wartime German research on the so-called tailless configuration. The D.H. 108, known popularly as the Swallow, had shapely swept wings and a swept vertical fin joined to the fuselage of a conventional Vampire jet fighter. Hopes were high that the Swallow could set a new world's airspeed record of well over 615 mph, and Geoffrey de Havilland began practicing for the record attempt in the second of two Swallow prototypes. In the late afternoon of September 27, he took off from Hatfield, the blue-gray D.H. 108 disappearing like its namesake into the sky. Then, thirty minutes later, the first intimation of disaster reached the company. Ground observers had seen a small jet break up and crash into Egypt Bay . . . young "D.H." was missing . . . ten days later his body washed ashore at Whitstable. And he had been the second of De Havilland's sons to die while test flying company aircraft. . . . As Charles Burnet, a noted British authority on flight testing, has written,

> One can well imagine the scene at Hatfield on this occasion. A group of people to whom the team spirit meant everything gradually realizing that a king-pin of their team would never return. The first job then was, briefly, to mourn—the second to determine what had happened—the third to continue with research. Such was, and is, the pattern of test flying.[2]

Analysis of the Swallow's wreckage indicated that the small jet had broken up in the midst of a violent longitudinal pitching oscillation at about Mach 0.875. In the dense lower atmosphere (De Havilland was flying at only 7,500 feet), the high g loads imposed on the structure had destroyed the plane. De Havilland went ahead with plans for a third, refined version of the D.H. 108 for further high-speed trials. The accident demonstrated that even new jets, with advanced aerodynamic developments such as swept wings, were not necessarily immune from the dangers of trim changes and increased loads at transonic speeds. But this did not discourage American researchers readying the XS-1's, though it did convince them to move cautiously. Most recognized that the longitudinal pitching that had afflicted the Swallow could have been damped out had the plane had a conventional horizontal tail. With the XS-1 having a horizontal tail (placed high over the wing wake, and also thinner than the wing, so as to retain its effectiveness even if the wing was experiencing compressibility effects), investigators believed that the XS-1, boosted by its rocket engine, could successfully fly at speeds faster than the Swallow, accelerating through Mach 1. Nevertheless, researchers gave thanks that the XS-1's were heavily instrumented, so that, as NACA flight research engineer Walter Williams recollected, "If we lost the airplane, we could at least find out a little about what had happened."[3]

The story now shifts entirely to Muroc, that almost biblical wasteland in the midst of the Mojave Desert, for there the concept of the "sound barrier" crumpled into myth. In mid-October 1946, carried aloft by a B-29, the XS-1 completed its first glide flights in final operational configuration. Then, in December, Bell initiated the first powered flights. The first attempt, on December 2, was a near disaster, for a valve froze, preventing the XS-1 from either jettisoning its propellants or being launched and firing its engine. As Larry Bell watched anxiously, the Bell test team landed the B-29 and its explosive cargo safely. A week later, however, everything functioned smoothly, and an Air Force test observer quaintly reported:

> The Rocket was dropped at 1154 from an altitude of 27,000 feet. When the first unit was turned on, a streak of flame came from the tail of the Rocket and continued to glow until the unit was shut off. The second unit was fired with results coincidental with those of the first. A FP-80 was following the Rocket to observe its reactions and also to take photographs. When the pilot of the XS-1, Chalmers Goodlin, fired the four units simultaneously, the FP-80 could not maintain a speed consistent with that of the Supersonic.[4]

Subsequent testing confirmed the pleasant flying characteristics of Bell's saffron-colored speedster. As part of its contractor requirements, the company had to demonstrate that the XS-1 possessed satisfactory stability and control characteristics at Mach 0.8—anything above this was in the realm of experimental research. At Mach 0.8, Slick Goodlin reported that the plane possessed "perfect control," with only "very slight shuddering." NACA's comprehensive instrument package indicated that this "compressibility buffet" was negligible. Goodlin and fellow pilot Alvin "Tex" Johnston finished up the XS-1 contractor program on both the first and second planes (the third, ill-fated, was incomplete at Bell) at the end of May, 1947. That June, the AAF and the NACA decided to launch a two-pronged assault on Mach 1. The AAF, using the first XS-1 (which had a thinner wing section than the second), would try to attain Mach 1.1 as quickly as was consistent with safety. The NACA, flying the thicker-wing, second XS-1, would proceed more slowly and in greater detail. NACA assigned Herb Hoover and Howard Lilly as project test pilots. Colonel Albert Boyd, then chief of flight testing at Wright Field and himself an outstanding service test pilot (and then holder of the world's airspeed record, at 623.738 mph, which he had set at Muroc in a modified P-80), had the task of picking the AAF pilot who, it was hoped, would become the first man to fly faster than sound. He selected a twenty-four-year-old fighter pilot from Hamlin, West Virginia, Captain Charles E. "Chuck" Yeager.

CHUCK YEAGER AND GLAMOROUS GLENNIS BREAK THE "SOUND BARRIER"

Of Chuck Yeager much has been written, for he eventually assumed a reputation as legendary as that of Doolittle or even Lindbergh. Chuck Yeager became to the test-flying fraternity after the Second World War what Doolittle or Allen had been before the war: the leader, recognized as first among equals, the role model for his fellows—what Tom Wolfe has insightfully perceived as the quality of possessing "the right stuff." Chuck Yeager had established an impressive reputation in the war-torn skies of Europe, including escaping from occupied France to Spain after being shot down, returning to combat, and successfully matching his P-51 against the best German fighter of all, the jet-propelled Me 262. An aggressive, combative pilot, Yeager fitted the image of the successful air fighter perfectly. Less obvious, however, were his technical skills, for although he had not gone on to a college or university before enlisting in the AAF, he was, in fact, an intuitive engineer. This played a key role in his selection for the XS-1 program. Yeager, in 1946, had completed the flight test pilot training program then being taught at Wright Field. He was perfectly matched for the task of taking the XS-1 through Mach 1 and beyond.

Yeager and two other pilots chosen to support the program, Jack Ridley and Bob Hoover, went to Buffalo for a brief course on the XS-1, then flew back to Muroc in late July 1947, arriving at the desert test center one day after President Harry Truman had signed the Armed Forces

Unification Act, creating a U. S. Air Force separate from and coequal with the Army and the Navy. Yeager flew his first glide familiarization flights in the rocket plane in August, leaving a distinctive impression on those who observed him. Herb Hoover, the NACA project pilot, penned a note to fellow test pilot Mel Gough, at Langley, that "This guy Yeager is pretty much of a wild one, but believe he'll be good on the Army ship. . . . On first drop, he did a couple of rolls right after leaving the B-29! On third flight, he did a two-turn spin!"[5]

Late in the month, on August 29, he reached Mach 0.85 on his first rocket-powered flight, this bringing a cautioning note from Al Boyd that the service considered neither the pilot nor the airplane expendable, "so please approach higher speeds progressively and safely to the limit of your best judgment." Thereafter, Chuck Yeager, in consultation with NACA engineers who had transferred from Langley to Muroc to assist in the XS-1 program, would fly at increasingly higher Mach numbers, edging closer to the speed of sound by two or three hundredths Mach (usually 15 to 20 mph) over the previous flight's speed mark. At Mach 0.88, the XS-1 exhibited its first buffeting, and thereafter, after reaching higher Mach values, Yeager would perform a 2 g or 3 g maneuver to get some idea of how severe the buffet would be at higher numbers.

In early October, he reached Mach 0.94 at about 40,000 feet, rolled over, and pulled back on the control column—and nothing happened: no response whatsoever. Wisely, he decelerated by shutting off the four-chamber rocket engine, and glided back down to a landing on Muroc's baked clay. "I was a little bit worried about the outcome of the whole program," Yeager recollected over three decades later, "because it had been predicted that the X-1 would either pitch up or pitch down when I got in the region of the speed of sound. Now I had run out of ability to control the X-1. We got NACA and all of the engineers together and had a talk about what was happening with the X-1."[6]

The engineers determined that a shock wave moved back on the surface of the horizontal stabilizer, so that at Mach 0.94, it was "standing" right along the hinge line of the elevator, negating its effectiveness. Fortunately, Bell had designed the XS-1 with a manually adjustable horizontal stabilizer (the ancestor of the "all-moving tails" used on many high-performance supersonic jets), and the XS-1 test team decided that Yeager should control the plane with the conventional elevator up to the point where elevator effectiveness was lost, and then use his stabilizer trim switch to move the entire surface for longitudinal (pitch) control. The XS-1 returned to the air.

Yeager had painted *Glamorous Glennis* on the nose of his wartime fighters, and now he again honored his wife by painting the name on the nose of the XS-1. On Friday, October 10, B-29 pilot Bob Cardenas dropped *Glamorous Glennis* over the tawny Mojave on its eighth powered flight. Chuck Yeager lit off the four rocket chambers and nosed the XS-1 upward in the climb, trailing a broad white contrail, accelerating rapidly, and finally reaching Mach 0.94 indicated airspeed. He arced over at 45,000 feet, and on the descent earthward, frost formed on the inside of the canopy. Despite Yeager's best efforts to scrape it off, it persisted, and the two chase pilots, Bob Hoover and Dick Frost, had to fly alongside the XS-1 in their P-80's and talk its pilot down to a "blind" landing on the lakebed.

The big surprise, however, came that night, for NACA data reduction indicated that the XS-1 had, in fact, reached a Mach number of 0.997, infinitesimally close to the speed of sound, and possibly supersonic. But there had not been a "boom," as had been heard when German V-2 missiles had gone supersonic after launch. Nevertheless, Chuck Yeager had touched the sonic wall, and with the confidence generated by his return and the fact that the all-moving stabilizer had given the plane adequate control characteristics, the engineers now planned to fly to a higher indicated Mach number to ensure a clear-cut case of supersonic flight.

The NACA-Air Force XS-1 team's gung-ho spirit might have dampened a bit if they had realized that their test pilot had two broken ribs, courtesy of a horse. On Friday night, before engineers had reduced the data from the rocket plane's flight, Yeager and his wife had gone to aviatrix Pancho Barnes's gathering spot and watering hole for dinner. The Barnes ranch was a favorite off-hours hangout for Muroc's test pilots, and after dinner, Chuck Yeager and Glennis had gone riding in the desert. On their return, Yeager failed to see a gate locked across a corral; at full gallop, he stormed the gate. The horse bolted and threw him off. Sharp pain soon indicated that this was no mere accident, and on Saturday, a visit to a civilian doctor in Rosamond (the pilot was taking no chances on going to a military one) confirmed what Yeager feared: two broken ribs. Stoically, Yeager had them taped and returned to the test base, keeping quiet about the accident except to his good friend and colleague Jack Ridley, whom he informed early on Tuesday, October 14, the morning of the first supersonic flight.

That day, Muroc comes alive at 6 A.M. The XS-1 lies bare, its plumbing and innards exposed, as technicians swarm over the aircraft and prepare it for flight. The B-29 launch crew is aware of Yeager's weekend accident but not the injuries, and present him with glasses, a rope, and a carrot. After coffee at the Muroc service club, he gives *Glamorous Glennis* a preflight check, and then confers with Walt Williams and other NACA engineers. The message: Yeager should not exceed Mach 0.96 unless absolutely certain he can do so safely. Technicians fuel the XS-1, pumping in over 290 gallons of alcohol and over 300 gallons of liquid oxygen, the "lox" swathing the plane in vapor, an otherworldly cloud of fog. They scrub the inner windshield with Drene shampoo, an incongruous but ingenious way of guarding against frost again coating the canopy during the long descent to landing. Finally all is ready, and the launch crew enter the B-29.

The B-29 pilot fires up the four big Wright R-3350 piston engines, which cough to life, belching blue-gray smoke as the large four-bladed propellers swing slowly, and then ever faster. Muroc tower gives taxi clearance, and the Superfort surges along as the pilots advance the throttles. The silver bomber with weathered, dull black undersides, moves along, accompanied by ground support vehicles, bobbing gently on its landing gear, with *Glamorous Glennis* snuggled underneath, liquid oxygen frost coating its skin. The tower signals takeoff clearance, the four big piston engines roar forth, and the Superfort trundles down the runway, taking off to the east, passing over the great baked lake, straining for altitude. Muroc tower closes the field to all unauthorized aircraft. Dick Frost and Bob Hoover strap into their P-80's and whistle into the air. NACA technicians monitor their telemetry reception equipment and two tracking radar sets.

The B-29 continues to climb, nosing upward in a wide and easy spiral. At 5,000 feet, Chuck Yeager leaves the relative safety of the B-29's bomb bay and, assisted by Jack Ridley, squirms through the entrance hatch into the tiny cockpit of the XS-1, pain from the broken ribs knifing through him. Then, using a cut-down broom handle fashioned by Ridley, he locks the hatch into place before bending over the instrument panel, readying the rocket airplane for flight. Outside, Hoover and Frost join up with their Shooting Stars, then take their chase positions: Frost behind the Superfort so he can follow Yeager down during the launch, and Hoover ten miles ahead at 48,000 feet to pick up the XS-1 after it has exhausted its propellants.

Five minutes before launch, Chuck Yeager pressurizes the fuel system, and at the one-minute mark, "NACA Radar" clears the Superfort for launch. Aboard the B-29, Jack Ridley raises Yeager on the intercom and asks, "You all set?" Hunched in the cockpit, ribs aching, but tense and ready for flight, the test pilot replies, "Hell, yes, let's get it over with." The Superfort is now in a shallow descent for speed. The climax of three years of intensive research is just seconds away. And so the B-29 crew intone the countdown, and at 10:26 A.M., *Glamorous Glennis* and its young pilot drop out of the B-29's dark bomb bay, out into the bright light of the California High Desert.

The best account of the flight is, of course, in the words of Chuck Yeager's own pilot report filed after the flight:

SECRET

DATE: 14 October 1947
PILOT: Capt. Charles E. Yeager
TIME: 14 Minutes
            9th Powered Flight

1. After normal pilot entry and the subsequent climb, the XS-1 was dropped from the B-29 at 20,000′ and at 250 MPH IAS. This was slower than desired.

2. Immediately after drop, all four cylinders were turned on in rapid sequence, their operation stabilizing at the chamber and line pressures reported in the last flight. The ensuing climb was made at .85–.88 Mach₁, and, as usual, it was necessary to change the stabilizer setting to 2 degrees nose down from its pre-drop setting of 1 degree nose down. Two cylinders were turned off between 35,000′ and 40,000′, but speed had increased to .92 Mach₁ as the airplane was leveled off at 42,000′. Incidentally, during the slight push-over at this altitude, the lox line pressure dropped perhaps 40 psi and the resultant rich mixture caused the chamber pressures to decrease slightly. The effect was only momentary, occurring at .6 G's, and all pressures returned to normal at 1 G.

3. In anticipation of the decrease in elevator effectiveness at speeds above .93 Mach₁, longitudinal control by means of the stabilizer was tried during the climb at .83, .88, and .92 Mach₁. The stabilizer was moved in increments of ¼–⅓ degree and proved to be very effective; also, no change in effectiveness was noticed at the different speeds.

4. At 42,000′ in approximately level flight, a third cylinder was turned on. Acceleration was rapid and speed increased to .98 Mach₁. The needle of the machmeter fluctuated at this reading momentarily, then passed off the scale. Assuming that the off-scale reading remained linear, it is estimated that 1.05 Mach₁ was attained at this time. Approximately 30% of fuel and lox remained when this speed was reached and the motor was turned off.

5. While the usual light buffet and instability characteristics were encountered in the .88–.90 Mach₁ range and elevator effectiveness was very greatly decreased at .94 Mach₁, stability about all three axes was good as speed increased and elevator effectiveness was regained above .97 Mach₁. As speed decreased after turning off the motor, the various phenomena occurred in reverse sequence at the usual speeds, and in addition, a slight longitudinal porpoising was noticed from

.98–.96 Mach₁ which was controllable by the elevators alone. Incidentally, the stabilizer setting was not changed from its 2 degrees nose down position after trial at .92 Mach₁.

6. After jettisoning the remaining fuel and lox a 1 G stall was performed at 45,000'. The flight was concluded by the subsequent glide and a normal landing on the lakebed.

CHARLES E. YEAGER

Capt., Air Corps

SECRET[7]

In fact, as NACA tracking data and the XS-1's own oscillograph instrumentation later revealed, *Glamorous Glennis* had attained Mach 1.06 at approximately 43,000 feet, an airspeed of 700 mph. It remained at supersonic speeds for about 20.5 seconds before decelerating back to subsonic flight. There had been no violent buffeting, no wrenching of the plane. Indeed, the breaching of the sonic wall had been anticlimactic. Perhaps because of the hoopla that had surrounded the idea of supersonic flight, Chuck Yeager had been expecting some dramatic indication that a milestone had been passed. It wasn't forthcoming—just a few curving traces on a strip of oscillograph film were all, evidence that, to an engineer, signified that the plans and events of the previous three years had been well worthwhile, had been fulfilled. Aviation science had crossed an invisible threshold to flight faster than sound. "I was kind of disappointed," Yeager later recalled, "that it wasn't more of a big charge than it was."[8] But, in fact, observers on the ground had plainly heard the double crack of a sonic boom, the first of thousands laid down over the Mojave by experimental aircraft in the years since.

In 1950, when the Air Force delivered *Glamorous Glennis* to the Smithsonian Institution, Air Force Chief of Staff Hoyt Vandenberg succinctly summarized its importance, stating that the flight "marked the end of the first great period of the air age and the beginning of the second. In a few moments the subsonic period became history and the supersonic period was born."[9] And NACA research chief Hugh Dryden paid notice to a more subtle lesson. "The achievement of Captain Charles E. Yeager as the first man to attain sustained horizontal supersonic flight in a piloted aircraft brings to public attention the power of a new tool, the research airplane, in obtaining the basic aeronautical knowledge essential to the design of military aircraft of outstanding performance. . . ."[10]

Chuck Yeager had driven the final nail in the "sound barrier" coffin when, less than a month after his epochal flight, he reached a speed of Mach 1.35, slightly over 890 mph, flying over twice as fast as most piston-engine fighters that had clashed in the closing years of the Second World War. The next year, Herb Hoover became the first civilian test pilot to "break the Mach" when he flew the NACA's thick-wing XS-1 to Mach 1.065, on March 10, 1948. Then it seemed to become routine, though Mach 1 and beyond remained largely the province of the research airplanes until the 1950s, when the first-generation American and Soviet supersonic fighters entered service.

PROBING THE FRONTIERS OF SONIC FLIGHT

What does strike a curious note is the great variety of aircraft shapes that now appeared for supersonic research: aircraft having sweptwings, delta wings, thin "low-aspect-ratio" wings, tailless configurations. In the United States, a whole "X-series" of transonic and supersonic research airplanes appeared: the Bell X-2 (for Mach 3), the Douglas X-3 (for sustained jet flight at Mach 2), the Northrop X-4 (to evaluate the transonic behavior of tailless airplanes), the Bell X-5 (for variable-wing-sweep research), the Douglas D-558-2 (for supersonic sweptwing research to Mach 2), and the Convair XF-92A (to evaluate the transonic behavior of delta aircraft). Only two of these aircraft proved disappointing: the Bell X-2, which fell behind schedule and did not complete a powered flight until late 1955, and the Douglas X-3. The latter is a sad story, for the X-3 had perhaps the most highly refined supersonic airframe of its day, but the engines originally planned for the aircraft grew too large for installation; substitute engines limited it to transonic performance only, a great waste.

Some of the new breed were great successes, however: the D-558-2, which flew for a number of years, furnished much useful data on sweptwing problems and performance, and became the first piloted aircraft to exceed Mach 2. The XF-92A became the ancestor for all future American delta-wing aircraft (and some foreign ones as well). The X-4 displayed the same disastrous pitching tendency as that which had cost Geoffrey de Havilland his life, but the NACA, by careful testing at high altitude (away from the punishing loads close to the ground) flew it safely for a number of years.

The X-4 is a good example of the problems one encounters in judging an airplane's reputation. It had been designed for transonic research on the sweptwing semitailless configuration, to validate or invalidate this design concept. It flew poorly at transonic speeds, "hunting" about all three axes and porpoising so badly that test pilots Charlie Tucker and

Scotty Crossfield compared its ride to driving fast over a washboard road. But it *did* fulfill its design mission (by disproving the concept), and thus must be judged a success.

Even the X-3 was not a total failure, for during its transonic research, it contributed a great deal of knowledge on the dangerous phenomenon of "inertial coupling," which will be discussed subsequently. There were other weird semi-X-series aircraft as well, such as two modified Bell P-63 Kingcobra piston-engine fighters that Bell modified to have 35-degree sweptwings in an attempt to assess the low-speed performance of sweptwing aircraft. These two testbeds, designated the L-39, furnished much of the low-speed data and airfoil data incorporated on both the North American F-86 Sabre and the Bell X-2.

Still, in this postwar era of jet and rocket, the propeller-driven airplane was not entirely dead, and with the urgency of wartime research a thing of the past, engineers had the leisure to go back and look more closely at propellers. At high speeds, above Mach 0.7, propellers experienced a marked loss in efficiency. When the rotating tip of the propeller neared Mach 1, the propeller—which is, after all, a rotating wing—experienced the very same flow problems afflicting the wings of airplanes. This nagging loss in efficiency caused propeller designers to derive totally new shapes for high-speed flight, as typified by a weird series of three-bladed props developed by Curtiss-Wright Corporation that resembled nothing so much as three Arabic scimitars joined to a single hub. Once again, actual flight testing offered the only real means of evaluating the performance of this strange shape, and so the company installed the prop on a modified Republic P-47D Thunderbolt. The resulting airplane had a very strange appearance indeed.

To fly this beast, Curtiss-Wright turned to their chief test pilot, Herb Fisher. During the war, Fisher had personally flown nearly twenty-five hundred Curtiss P-40's on their production test flights, as well as going to China and, like Lindbergh, flying fifty combat missions over Japanese-held territory to evaluate at first hand the P-40's combat performance. After the war, he had flown a special series of propeller reversal tests on a modified C-54 transport, demonstrating that airline pilots could reverse all four engines of large multiengine propeller-driven transports and thereby rapidly descend for earth at more than two miles per minute. Even with landing gear and flaps extended—with the plane in "dirty" configuration—a transport could normally descend at only about 4,000 feet per minute. Fisher demonstrated in a series of potentially hazardous flights that thrust reversal by changing the pitch angle of the craft's propellers could nearly *triple* this rate of descent. The tests held special significance for the new generation of pressurized transports, such as the DC-6 and the Lockheed Constellation, for if these craft developed leaks at high altitude, a pilot would have to descend to safer, lower altitudes as quickly as possible.

In 1947, Herb Fisher began flying the modified Thunderbolt, and quickly discovered that it had numerous problems of its own. For one thing, the curved propellers fluttered easily, flexing and bending "like a hand-saw" if Fisher applied too much power at takeoff. Their low-speed performance left much to be desired, and the "Jug" required 9,000 feet of runway for takeoff. Fisher would climb for altitude from the Curtiss-Wright plant at Caldwell, New Jersey, flying out over rural Pennsylvania to Reading or Allentown. There, at about 35,000 feet, he would point the Thunderbolt east and dive to over Mach 0.7 and sometimes above Mach 0.8, well above 550 mph, screaming down over New Jersey and New York.

But it was not just a pell-mell, headlong rush. Fisher had to dive to a designated test altitude, depending on the test, and then hold that altitude within ± 50 feet as well as a particular Mach number. Risks abounded, especially the ever-present danger that the thin whirling blades would flutter and disintegrate. One time, the plane's thrust meter—a complex instrument fed by high-pressure oil—ruptured, sending gallons of the viscous liquid into the rotating prop. The airstream instantly coated the airplane in black; Fisher could not see out, and in fact, oil sprayed into the cabin, covering all his instruments, followed by billowing black smoke.

In desperation, he opened the cockpit canopy, and the air blast, rather than helping, atomized the oil, sending some of it into his eyes, irritating them terribly. Fisher, fortunately, was over Caldwell; he radioed his predicament, and groped along above the field. Then the tower radioed that his plane appeared to be on fire. What else could go wrong? Then the air blast blew his radio headphones overboard, ending his communications. Now it was man versus airplane, with no outsiders. Fisher pointed the smoking fighter toward the field, set up a rough landing approach, considered and rejected the idea of a belly landing, lowered the landing gear, and flying blind, touched down perfectly, not wasting time in abandoning the plane when it came to a halt. But it was safe, and would fly again.

The Curtiss-Wright tests proved that the scimitar props had an efficiency of about 90 per cent at 550 mph, compared to standard props, which had an efficiency of only 60 per cent at the same speeds. Their other problems, however, prevented their development and employment on aircraft at that time. In the 1950s, the Air Force and NACA experimented with other proposed "supersonic" propellers, but the concept proved noisy and inefficient—and one curious byproduct was resonance effects from the strange propellers, inducing severe nausea in ground personnel working around the planes when their engines were turning over. Today, however, the scimitar prop is regaining the attention of designers, for they promise greater fuel and energy efficiency than conventional turbojet or fanjet engines at high subsonic speeds. NASA has developed a series of so-called "prop-fans" bearing a remarkable resemblance to the earlier Curtiss-Wright props. Flight tests are already underway on these new shapes, which may appear on the transport aircraft of the late 1980s and the 1990s.

The story of North American's F-86 Sabre jet fighter illustrates how quickly going supersonic became relatively commonplace. North American had designed the Sabre, at first designated the XP-86, using captured German sweptwing data as well as the results of indigenous American research. At first, North American had proposed a straight-wing airplane, and indeed, a version of this proposed craft, the FJ-1 Fury, entered naval service. But with the reports of the advantages that a sweptwing planform could offer an airplane—namely improved performance and lower drag at transonic speeds—North American quickly opted for a fully swept planform for their new jet airplane.

The first of three XP-86 prototypes flew at Muroc on October 1, 1947 (just two weeks before Chuck Yeager's journey past Mach 1), piloted by North American test pilot George "Wheaties" Welch. The new plane, a graceful low-wing craft with distinctly beautiful, sculptured lines (some consider, the author included, that the F-86 was the most attractive airplane ever built), had a performance that matched its looks. During the landing approach, however, the nose landing gear failed to extend fully, and for forty minutes it appeared that the XP-86 would have to ignominiously come to rest on its main gear and the nose itself, but the ever-skillful Welch kept the plane nose-high, bounced it down firmly enough to jounce the nose gear into place, and the plane taxied jauntily back to the flight line.

Flight testing proceeded without further difficulty. As was then the fashion, the craft passed through "Phase I" (contractor) testing, went on to Air Force Phase II evaluations by service pilots, then entered Phase III advanced testing in January 1948—things moved quite rapidly. Then, on April 26, 1948, just over a month and a half since Herb Hoover's first supersonic flight in the rocket-powered XS-1, Wheaties Welch dived the Sabre prototype beyond the speed of sound, an ominous implication for the hundreds of MiG pilots who would clash with the Sabre over Korea's rugged terrain. The first production F-86A Sabres, powered by a more powerful J47 engine, appeared in mid-1948, an unusually rapid development pace even by the standards of the day.

At Muroc, that same month, the XP-86 test team generously let British test pilot Roland Beamont fly the plane, and he promptly raced to an indicated Mach number of 1.005 in a shallow dive, though a great deal of uncertainty surrounded the test conditions, precluding stating with any assurance that his was the first British supersonic flight. (The first British supersonic pilot was the late John Derry, who reached Mach 1.04 in a very dangerous and, in fact, uncontrolled dive in the third De Havilland Swallow, on September 6, 1948. Unfortunately, this fine airman subsequently lost his life together with that of his flight observer in the breakup of an experimental De Havilland jet fighter at the 1952 Farnborough airshow, exactly four years after his courageous flight beyond Mach 1 in the deadly Swallow.)

The NACA had quickly recognized that the Sabre had many of the attributes of an X-series aircraft, and in 1949 the agency acquired an early production Sabre and sent it to the Ames laboratory south of San Francisco, where test pilots George Cooper and Rudolph Van Dyke put it through its paces. In the course of its testing at Ames, Cooper and Van Dyke flew it in a number of shallow dives beyond Mach 1. Simultaneously, newspapers reported a series of mysterious explosions, explosions so loud that a sheriff's posse actually investigated the cause. The cause, of course, were the two pilots laying down sonic booms while flying the Ames F-86.

Just slightly over a year following Chuck Yeager's flight, then, Sabre pilots could routinely nose over into shallow dives and exceed the speed of sound, which, only a few short months before, had seemed so mysterious. Still, many questions concerning sweptwing behavior at supersonic speeds remained, and there is where another flight research airplane made its mark: the Douglas D-558-2 Skyrocket.

The Skyrocket had grown out of the earlier D-558-1 Skystreak program. The Skystreak series of three aircraft had complemented the XS-1 series, for, whereas the rocket-powered XS-1's had limited endurance, the D-558-1's were jet-propelled and could cruise for extended time at Mach 0.8 to 0.9+, freeing the XS-1's to use their limited and valuable time for purely supersonic research. Resplendent in bright scarlet, the first Skystreak had flown at Muroc in mid-April 1947, piloted by company test pilot Gene May, who also flew the second aircraft when it arrived for testing, in August. Navy and Marine test pilots Turner Caldwell and Marion Carl then flew both aircraft in a series of successful flights to boost the official world airspeed record, Carl achieving above 650 mph in a sizzling series of flights over a measured course on Muroc lake, at altitudes below 250 feet. Douglas retained the first airplane for company testing, and later claimed to have reached Mach 1 in a steep dive while testing the plane in September 1948.

The NACA began an extensive transonic research program with the second airplane, but, sadly, this craft took NACA test pilot Howard "Tick" Lilly to his death on May 3, 1948, when its J35 engine disintegrated on takeoff, severing vital fuel and control lines. Lilly became the first NACA test pilot to die in the line of duty, and the street to the NASA Dryden Flight Research Center at Edwards is named in his honor. The third Skystreak, modified to prevent any repetition of the Lilly accident, flew into the early 1950s on a variety of NACA research missions.

During the development of the D-558-1, however, Douglas engineers had decided to try their hand at a sweptwing version of the craft. This eventually emerged as a totally new airplane fabricated from magnesium and aluminum, with a sweptwing protruding from a cigarlike fuselage, powered both by a rocket engine similar to that utilized by the XS-1, and with a jet engine as well. Douglas built three of these aircraft, the three D-558-2 Skyrockets, which NACA research pilot Scotty Crossfield recalled fondly as "the real workhorses of the era. We owe all our transonic and supersonic flight research data on sweptwings to those three planes."[11]

The first Skyrocket, a gleaming white airplane, arrived at Muroc for testing in late 1947 sans its rocket engine. Douglas test pilot Johnny Martin completed its first flight on jet power alone on February 4, 1948, but the plane had a decidedly sluggish performance without its rocket engine, hardly an indication of the Skyrocket successes to come. Martin had been named project pilot on the Skyrocket in one of the more famous tales of corporate flight testing. The Douglas test pilots viewed the new plane with suspicion: after all, the "sound barrier" still loomed as an unknown at the time the Douglas decided to select a project pilot for the D-558-2. The test pilots all agreed to submit exceptionally high fee bids for the test program, bids certain not to be accepted. The only pilot not in on the plot was Martin, over in Europe delivering an airplane. He sent in a reasonable bid, and the plane was his!

As with the Skystreak, Douglas kept the first plane for its own research, and the second went to the NACA, still lacking its rocket engine. The NACA, flying from Muroc, used it for investigations of sweptwing stability and control. In the midst of this program, NACA project pilots Bob Champine and John Griffith discovered the severe problem of sweptwing pitch-up during high-g maneuvers and at low speeds. Eventually, aerodynamicists recognized that the tail location on sweptwing aircraft was critical; at high angles of attack, a tail mounted on the vertical fin could become ineffective in maintaining the craft's longitudinal trim. As a result, most first-generation supersonic military aircraft, such as the F-100 and the Navy's F8U, featured low-mounted horizontal tails to alleviate this problem.

When Douglas finally added the specified rocket engine to the Skyrocket, it quickly flew faster than sound. However, operating the plane from the ground proved unsatisfactory for several reasons, including fuel economy (which limited the performance of the airplane at altitude) and safety. Accordingly, NACA and Douglas, together with the Navy (which had sponsored the entire D-558 series, in the same fashion that the Air Force had supported the XS-1 effort), agreed to modify the second and third Skyrockets for air launching from a modified Super-fortress. The second Skyrocket would have all-rocket propulsion; the space occupied by its jet engine and jet fuel supply would be converted to fuel storage for the rocket, and its inlets would be faired over, together with the jet exhaust. The third would retain both its jet and rocket engines. Douglas began air-launch tests of the Skyrocket in the fall of 1950.

Early air-launch testing proceeded at a slow pace. In January 1951, a near disaster occurred because of a communications foul-up between the launch airplane and the Skyrocket. Bill Bridgeman, the Douglas project pilot on the air-launch tests, noticed the craft's fuel pressure dropping slowly and decided to abort the flight less than a minute before launch, radioing, "No drop, this is an abort," and shutting down the craft's vital systems. And then, to his horror, he heard fellow test pilot George Jansen, the pilot of the launch plane, intoning the countdown. He shouted, "Don't drop me, George!" a call plainly audible to personnel on the ground and mission chase pilots, but Jansen had his thumb on the microphone transmission key and could not hear Bridgeman's protestations.

Frantically, Bridgeman worked to ready the craft for flight, deciding to take a chance and attempt to fire up the rocket engine, should he jettison and have only one tank empty because of the falling pressure, fatally throwing the airplane out of trim. Jansen released the Skyrocket, and it dropped like a bomb before Bridgeman managed to get an engine light and climb shakily for altitude. "Goddam it, George," he growled, "I told you not to drop me!"[12] creating another Edwards legend. The rest was anticlimax: the Skyrocket completed a good flight, and Douglas quickly modified their communication procedures to prevent a repetition.

After this eventful flight, Douglas began slowly expanding the performance "envelope" of the plane, mapping out its performance capabilities. Bridgeman flew well beyond Mach 1, and in May 1951, reached Mach 1.72—1,130 mph at 62,000 feet—pushing this to Mach 1.79 a month later.

These tests had revealed the existence of a potentially serious dynamic instability that caused the plane to roll wildly, and the Douglas test team believed that the Skyrocket could safely fly at higher speeds, possibly Mach 2, if Bridgeman nosed over from his climb at a very low load factor; they suggested about .25 g. Yet when Bridgeman did just that, on his next flight, the Skyrocket rolled violently, dipping its wings as much as

75 degrees. He cut power, but the motions, if anything, became even more severe. Finally he hauled back on the control column, for the Skyrocket was in a steep dive and getting farther and farther from the lakebed. The plane abruptly nosed up and regained its smooth flying characteristics, and he brought it back to Muroc.

Douglas had learned a valuable lesson from the flight, and never again attempted such a low pushover load factor; on subsequent flights, Bridgeman held a higher load factor and eventually reached Mach 1.88 and an altitude of 79,494 feet, making the Skyrocket the world's fastest and highest airplane, but only for a time. Bill Bridgeman went on to receive a well-earned 1953 Octave Chanute Award from the Institute of the Aeronautical Sciences, then left the Skyrocket program for the alluring and disappointing X-3. The Skyrockets, all three of them, wound up in NACA's hands.

There had been a lot of changes at the lakebed by the time the NACA received the three Skyrockets for a comprehensive transonic and supersonic research program. For one thing, Muroc had become a name from the past. The sprawling Air Force-NACA complex had overrun the original town, and then, in January 1950, the Air Force had renamed the base in honor of one of its own, test pilot Glen Edwards. On June 5, 1948, Glen Edwards had taken off with a crew of four in an experimental Northrop Flying Wing jet bomber. Inside the cavernous wing, the crew had set to work for a series of stability tests just north of Muroc. Everything seemed to proceed smoothly, and Edwards radioed that he was returning, descending to 15,000 feet, when something happened—perhaps it stalled and broke up during recovery. In any case, at about 8 A.M., it tumbled down in three huge sections, exploding in the desert north of the town of Mojave. Glen Edwards and his crew had joined the ranks of those who have taken off on research missions and not returned. . . . It was both worthy and fitting, then, for the new center of the supersonic age of flight to be renamed in his honor, for he symbolized, like Otto Lilienthal a half century before, the price sometimes demanded of those who test new aircraft.

THROUGH MACH 2–AND ON TO MACH 3

Additionally, by 1951, a new series of rocket research airplanes, based on the older XS-1 design, had begun to grace the Edwards flight line, the so-called "advanced" X-1's, the first of which were the X-1D and the X-1-3 (the latter the original third XS-1). These had totally new low-pressure fuel-feed systems, giving them greater internal fuel capacity and, hence, potential Mach 2 performance. So, as 1951 progressed, it appeared that the Air Force would shortly achieve Mach 2, barely two and one half years since Chuck Yeager's flight of October 14, 1947. Such, however, was not to be, for in August of that year, the X-1D blew up while being readied for test pilot Frank "Pete" Everest, who leaped from its cockpit for the safety of the launch plane's bomb bay just before the test crew dropped it into oblivion. Two and a half months later, the X-1-3 blew apart while sitting on the ground after a check flight, severely injuring pilot Joe Cannon (who recovered to fly again) and destroying its launch plane in the process. Mach 2 would elude researchers for two more years and when it fell, it fell to that maid of all work, the Skyrocket.

The plodding and diligent worker who stays out of the limelight and toils at his own pace is often the one who makes the greater contribution. And so it was with the Skyrocket. When NACA acquired the D-558-2, it did so to simply continue its sweptwing research on such problems as transonic pitch-up and investigating its supersonic stability and control. Gradually, as time went by, the incremental progression of test flights edged closer and closer to the magic of Mach 2—twice the speed of sound. On October 14, 1953, six years to the day since the XS-1 had first whiplashed the Mojave with its sonic boom, NACA research pilot Scotty Crossfield reached Mach 1.96, again setting a new record for the Sky-rocket and placing the plane within striking distance of Mach 2.

The racetrack atmosphere at Edwards sharpened, for onlookers sensed that the old horse might best its newer rival, the advanced X-1A, just undergoing trials on base. After extensive preparations, including installing special lightweight jettison tubes that would melt off in the exhaust of the Skyrocket's engine, and covering the entire aircraft with sealing tape and a heavy coat of wax, the NACA was ready to go after Mach 2. On November 20, 1953, Superfortress pilot Stan Butchart launched Crossfield and the all-rocket D-558-2 at 32,000 feet. The eager test pilot lit off his engine, and following a carefully planned mission profile, climbed into the stratosphere, streaming a broad white contrail. At 72,000 feet, exactly as planned, Crossfield pushed over into a shallow dive, reaching just over Mach 2 at 62,000 feet, then gliding down powerless to a landing on the Edwards lakebed.

For his "important contributions in aeronautical flight research," Crossfield received a well-deserved Lawrence B. Sperry Award for 1954, and the all-rocket Skyrocket eventually retired to its own well-deserved preservation in the Smithsonian Institution, where it is suspended now, within feet of its companion from Muroc, the *Glamorous Glennis*. The Skyrockets contributed much of the early flight test data acquired on sweptwings, especially in the vital field of stability and control. It is pleasant to record that they accomplished this without injuring any of their crews or support personnel. When they finally retired, in 1957, their research longevity was exceeded only by the original supersonic testbed itself, the X-1 series.

In December 1953, less than a month after Scotty Crossfield piloted the Skyrocket to Mach 2, Chuck Yeager offered the Air Force response by flying the advanced X-1A to Mach 2.44, a speed of 1,612 mph at 74,200 feet. The flight demonstrated that the supersonic arena still held many mysteries. Engineers had predicted that the advanced X-1's might be unstable above Mach 2, and on this flight their hunches were proved with devastating accuracy. After launch from its B-29, the X-1A shot upward, easily surpassing the Skyrocket's mark. Then, ten seconds after leveling out on its high-speed run, it began a slow roll to the left; Chuck Yeager corrected for this, and the X-1A suddenly rolled violently to the right, then tumbled completely out of control, as ground trackers listened nervously on the radio. In the plane, Yeager was fighting for his life. At one point, his helmet cracked the canopy itself. The X-1A fell from over 70,000 feet to 34,000 feet, winding up in an inverted spin at that altitude. Yeager recovered into an upright spin at 29,000 feet, groggy, battered, semiconscious though he was, and then recovered into level flight over Tehachapi, gliding back to Edwards and remarking, as the X-1A touched down in a cloud of dust, "You know, if I had a seat, you wouldn't still see me in this thing."[13] And yes, as incredible as it sounds, the X-1A had been built without an ejection seat, a flaw quickly remedied after Chuck Yeager's wild ride. The flight pointed to the danger of "coupled" motions.

Decreasing directional stability and roll damping at twice the speed of sound caused such aircraft as the X-1 series, the Skyrockets, and the later X-2 to all exhibit deteriorating stability at those speeds. After the Yeager flight, the Air Force decreed that the X-1 series undertake no further all-out flights, though test pilot Arthur "Kit" Murray later flew the plane on a series of research flights to altitudes in excess of 90,000 feet, where the air was so thin and dynamic pressure was so low that the craft's control surfaces were rendered ineffective.

The Air Force later turned over the X-1A to the NACA for aerodynamic heating research, but the old problem of fuel-system dangers cropped up, and the X-1A experienced a minor explosion while aloft under its B-29 mother ship preparing for a flight. For a while, the B-29 test crew and the X-1A pilot, Joe Walker, tried as hard as they could to save the little rocket plane, a courageous decision, for the X-1A might have exploded and taken all of them to their deaths (as had the second X-2 just over two years before, killing its pilot and one member of the mother-ship launch crew). Eventually, however, they recognized that the mother ship could not land back at Edwards with the wounded rocket plane, and so, reluctantly, they dropped it on the Edwards bombing range. A subsequent analysis of the wreckage pointed to chemical breakdown of a critical gasket material that deteriorated and then exploded when pressurized—a nickel-and-dime item that had, over the previous four years, destroyed four research airplanes and one launch airplane, killed two crewmen, and injured another severely.

Two X-1's remained, the X-1B (another advanced model) and the X-1E, a NACA rebuild of one of the original XS-1's. They flew until 1958, piling up more and more data points, and retired only on the eve of a new epoch in flight research: the advent of the hypersonic X-15. So passed the X-1 series, milestone aircraft in the exploration of supersonic flight.

The most spectacular of all these early supersonic research aircraft, however, was another sweptwing design, the Bell X-2. It represented an ambitious attempt, as early as 1946, to develop a Mach 3 airplane, and as a result, had an unconventional structure of stainless steel and a copper-nickel alloy to withstand the expected high temperatures of flight at those speeds. It incorporated a large, two-chamber rocket engine producing a total of 15,000 pounds of thrust. A series of problems with the engine and general difficulties with the craft's fabrication and control-system design prevented it from completing its first powered flight until late 1955, though it had earlier flown a series of gliding trials that had revealed a severe landing problem requiring extensive redesign of the craft's landing gear, which consisted of a series of skids. The same gasket problem that claimed the X-1D and X-1-3 also destroyed the second X-2 during a captive flight near Buffalo in May 1953; unfortunately, the research airplane exploded violently while still attached to the B-50 launch airplane, killing test pilot Skip Ziegler and a Bell launch crewman, Frank Wolko. In a magnificent display of airmanship, Bell test pilots William Leyshon and D. W. Howe had managed to fly the B-50 launch plane back to a safe landing despite its having been slammed upward 100 feet by the blast and riddled with shrapnel from the exploding rocket plane. Needless to relate, after landing, the B-50 never flew again.

In late 1955, powered-flight trials with the X-2 got underway. The next year, Air Force test pilot Pete Everest took the craft to over Mach 2.5 and then, in July, reached Mach 2.87, very close to the fabled Mach 3, before leaving for a staff-college assignment. The program had gone smoothly, but the X-2 was clearly treading in an aerodynamic thicket where caution had to rule. Computer simulation and wind-tunnel studies, plus extrapolated data from earlier flights all indicated that the craft would have very poor stability characteristics near Mach 3; even Everest, at the lower speeds, had experienced marginal control effectiveness. The Air Force, with Everest gone, turned to test pilot Iven C. Kincheloe, a graduate of Britain's Empire Test Pilots' School, to make a series of altitude flights in the plane before it was turned over to the NACA for aerodynamic-heating research studies.

Iven "Kinch" Kincheloe, a Korean jet ace, fitted the popular physical image of the test pilot, with ruggedly handsome good looks and a friendly, personable nature. Articulate and brimming with confidence, he was an Air Force public-relations dream come true—and it *was* all true, for the blond pilot was a superlative airman, a fine engineer, and held in the highest esteem by his peers. Kincheloe completed several check flights in the X-2 and then, on September 7, 1956, reached 126,200 feet (the first human flight beyond 100,000 feet), on a journey that won for him the popular press accolade "First of the Spacemen." In truth, at that altitude, he flew for all practical purposes in space. His view was that of the later cosmonauts and astronauts: a blue-black sky and the visible curvature of the earth. The flight highlighted problems of control in near-space, for at that altitude, his aerodynamic surfaces—the elevators, rudder, and ailerons were ineffective. Above 100,000 feet, the plane had, in fact, started a left bank as it moved through the air on a ballistic arc, and Kincheloe dared not attempt to correct it for fear of tumbling the plane.

The NACA viewed all these record flights with quiet concern, for it desired to acquire the remaining X-2 and put it to serious scientific use. But the Air Force delayed turning over the craft for a little longer, in hopes of yet attaining Mach 3 in the plane. The service requested and received a two-month extension to qualify another Air Force test pilot, Milburn Apt, in the airplane and attempt to exceed the speeds reached earlier by Pete Everest. Apt had no previous rocket-plane experience, but he was familiar with the stability difficulties of supersonic aircraft, having flown the Air Force "inertial coupling" program on the service's troubled F-100 fighter. Further, he was a pilot of extraordinary courage. Once, he had been flying chase for another test airplane that had deployed a spin-recovery parachute. The chute failed to disengage as planned, and the test airplane crashed in the midst of the Edwards lakebed, bursting into flames. Without hesitation, Apt had landed his own aircraft alongside the burning, exploding plane and, at great personal risk, rescued the severely injured pilot.

After several ground briefings on a simulator, Apt made his flight attempt in the X-2 on September 27, launching from the belly of a modified Boeing B-50 bomber into the bright blue of the Mojave sky. His flight plan called, vaguely, for him to follow "the optimum maximum energy flight path." Extrapolated data indicated the likelihood of the plane "diverging" (going out of control) during rolling maneuvers in the vicinity of Mach 3.2, and flight planners had instructed Mel Apt to decelerate rapidly if he encountered any stability problems, and not to make any rapid control movements above Mach 2.7.

Apt raced away from the B-50 and, under the full power of the rocket engine, zipped past the F-100 chase planes. He climbed to altitude following a predetermined schedule matching the plane's g loading versus altitude, based on code numbers radioed from the ground. At high altitude, he nosed over, accelerating rapidly, and the X-2 reached Mach 3.2, 2,094 mph at 65,500 feet. So far, the flight had been flawless; the engine had even burned ten seconds longer than normal. Mel Apt had been the first to break Mach 3, a measure of his unquestionable pilot skills. But what happened next is well known, though why it happened is not, and may never be. Still above Mach 3, he began an abrupt turn back for Edwards. Perhaps the X-2's lagging instrumentation misled him; perhaps he assumed the Machmeter (pegged above Mach 3, as cockpit camera films show, for over ten seconds) had stuck. Perhaps he feared getting too far from the lake. In any case, the move was a fatal one, for the X-2 immediately began a series of diverging rolls, and suddenly it tumbled totally out of control, knocking Mel Apt unconscious and finally winding up in an inverted spin. Apt slowly came to and began fighting for control of the plane. Then he decided to abandon it, and jettisoned the entire nose, which formed an escape capsule for the pilot. Instead, the capsule pitched downward violently, streaming its drogue chute. Mel Apt was just again regaining consciousness and preparing for conventional bailout using his own parachute when the capsule smashed into the desert, killing him instantly. Five miles away, the rest of the X-2 spun into the earth as victory changed to ashes.

Apt's flight illustrated the acute need for reliable cockpit instrumentation. But, more important, it pointed to the need for careful planning of missions, careful training of personnel. A valuable and potentially most useful research airplane had been lost. Worse, so had a skilled, dedicated, and courageous airman. Mel Apt eventually received a posthumous Distinguished Flying Cross for the bleak flight that September morning. If the flight publicly appeared as a major accomplishment, within the Air Force and NACA research and development establishment there existed little doubt that it was otherwise: the official Air Force program history on the X-2 states:

> Only one conclusion can be reached and that is that the Air Force in its determination to attain a record speed and altitude with the X-2 which it did achieve assumed a calculated risk of losing the pilot and the aircraft in the process. . . . Fatigue, miscalculations, and poor judgment entered into the program at a time when unhurried flights were in order and good judgment should have directed and supervised the program.[14]

SWINGWINGS, STILETTOS, AND SUPERSONIC ESCAPE

As flight testing of all the early sweptwing research airplanes revealed, these craft had generally acceptable high-speed performance, but their low-speed performance, especially during takeoff and landing, left much to be desired. As a result, designers tried any number of schemes, the most notable being the development of so-called "variable geometry," or "swingwing," airplanes capable of varying the wing sweep angle in flight. Such aircraft could take off and cruise with their wings extended ("straight") for optimal low-speed behavior, and then sweep their wings fully aft for high speed. The first variable-sweep testbed to exploit in-flight variable wing sweeping for low and high speeds was Bell's exotic X-5 research airplane, two of which the contractor manufactured, and which had been based loosely on an abandoned Messerschmitt fighter project from the Second World War. The X-5 resembled a flying tadpole, powered by a single turbojet engine in the belly of the plane. Its wings moved ("translated," in the terse jargon of the engineers) on a complex track mechanism inside the fuselage that also required shifting the entire wing roots as well. The first of two X-5's arrived at Edwards in 1951, and Bell project pilot Jean "Skip" Ziegler first flew it in June of that year, making the world's first in-flight wing sweeping (from 20 to 30 degrees) the following month, on July 16. A few days later, he swept the wings a full 60 degrees. Generally speaking, the X-5 flew satisfactorily, though it had absolutely vicious stalling characteristics. Following a stall, it would invariably enter a spin, proving most reluctant to recover. This quirk gave NACA's Joe Walker and Scotty Crossfield a few bad moments, and, sad to record, a stall-spin accident in the second X-5 claimed the life of Air Force test pilot Ray Popson. Overall, however, the X-5 did demonstrate that the variable-sweep concept was feasible. "It was like having a whole stable of sweptwing airplanes in one," Scotty Crossfield subsequently recalled. Eventually, in 1955, the X-5 retired, its last NACA flight having been completed by a new pilot by the name of Neil A. Armstrong, and it is now at the Air Force Museum.

Sometimes these specialized research aircraft uncovered problems serendipitously, furnishing unexpected information in areas that had been of little concern to designers when they planned building the planes. The rakish X-3, for example, an airplane that received the popular and altogether appropriate appellation "Flying Stiletto," never attained its design speed of Mach 2 or anywhere near it. Nevertheless, it furnished desperately needed data on the phenomenon of "inertial coupling" or "roll divergence," simply from being in the right spot at the right time. Since the late 1940s, aerodynamicists had predicted that the new aircraft shapes emerging, with their short wingspans and long fuselages, would have significantly different dynamic stability characteristics from those of their predecessors, because the mass of the aircraft was spread out over the length of the fuselage and not, as with traditional airplanes, from wing tip to wing tip. In the event of rolling, it was predicted, these aircraft might "diverge," yawing and pitching *while* rolling, and finally tumbling completely out of control.

While flying the X-3 for the NACA, test pilot Joe Walker entered an abrupt roll just below the speed of sound. The X-3 achieved the desired position, and Walker applied corrective aileron control to halt the roll. Instead, however, the X-3 continued to roll at nearly three hundred degrees per second, while beginning to pitch and yaw violently. The plucky Walker, one of the finest research pilots who ever flew, managed to hang on to the airplane and restore it to normal flight—and, intrigued, decided to repeat the maneuver, but this time just above the speed of sound. And so, a few minutes later, at Mach 1.05, he abruptly rolled the long needle-nosed plane to the left. And the X-3 protested mightily. It yawed more than 20 degrees from the flight path, while, at the same time, rolling violently. The plane experienced a multitude of forces: 2 g side loads, a negative load (during an abrupt pitching downward) of —7 g, and an equally strong pitch-up to a 7 g, positive, load. The loads just avoided breaking up the airplane, and Walker, shaken, managed to regain control and then land. Since the X-3 was a research airplane, its comprehensive instrumentation had recorded every little nuance of the phenomenon, thus providing a unique record of what had happened.

As luck would have it, the X-3's inertial coupling encounter held more than just academic interest. Less than two weeks before, the redoubtable "Wheaties" Welch had perished when his experimental F-100A Super Sabre abruptly sideslipped during a rolling pullout (the most strenuous of maneuvers) from a Mach 1.5 dive, yawing about 15 degrees and then disintegrating. Armed with the X-3's data, North American, NACA, and Air Force test pilots began a program of research on the F-100 that finally led to a complete redesign of its vertical tail surfaces, as well as a thorough understanding of the inertial coupling phenomenon. The F-100 went on to a successful and lengthy service career.

One of the major problems in the first supersonic military aircraft, the first aircraft benefiting from the data base gained by such aircraft as the X-1 and the D-558-2, involved escaping from these planes at high speeds. After the end of the Second World War, the ejection seat had come into general use. Some designs incorporated jettisonable nose escape capsules, but pilots believed them to be death traps, and rightly so. Eventually, the combination of well-designed pilot protection suits, together with aerodynamically stable seats, proved most acceptable, though some individual and two-man capsules did appear on production airplanes. The story of another North American test pilot, George Smith, illustrates just how grim a supersonic ejection could be—but, happily, it is a story with a pleasant ending.

On February 26, 1955, the young North American pilot had dropped by his office at the plant to finish some reports, then decided to go aloft on a production test flight in a new F-100A Super Sabre. Shortly afterward, cruising over beautiful Palos Verdes, Smith noticed the jet begin to nose down—and down. The Super Sabre had experienced a total control-system failure, and Smith could not even move the stick. A chase pilot radioed "George, bail out!" for the big fighter had entered a steep dive and was accelerating rapidly toward the speed of sound. Smith retarded the engine throttle and opened the Sabre's big speed brake, but to no avail. By now, Smith realized he could not save the airplane, and had to save himself. He jettisoned the canopy, and with the F-100A in a vertical dive at an altitude of 6,000 feet and a speed of Mach 1.05 (about five seconds from impact), he ejected from the plane. The shock of supersonic ejection hit him with a force of nearly 1,300 pounds per square foot of body area and a g load of an incredible 64 g smashed him for over a tenth of a second. For a total of three tenths of a second, the forces on his body were over 20 g, ripping off helmet and mask and instantly rendering him unconscious. Smith's chute, whether functioning properly or perhaps ripped from its pack, deployed, though it shed many of its panels. By a miracle, the unconscious pilot dropped into the sea near a fishing boat, and rescuers soon had him in a hospital. Five days later, he awoke, his last memory of the flight being the Machmeter reading 1.05. Despite many severe internal injuries, hemorrhages, sprains, ruptures, and dislocations, Smith recovered fully—and went back to testing for North American.

TESTING THE MILITARY CRAFT OF THE 1950s

The complexity of the postwar generation of combat aircraft resulted in lengthened flight test programs and a much greater time between "first flight" and "initial operational capability" than with previous periods in aviation. Whereas a World War I pursuit could go from testing to the front in a matter of weeks, and a Second World War design with a year or so, the fighters, transports, and bombers of the fifties took much longer. The North American F-86D Sabre, a complex interceptor, required nearly 85,000 engineering man-hours during its flight test program; today, a new fighter prototype, for example, cannot be expected to enter service until about a half decade after first flight, causing critical problems for defense planners, who have to forecast the needs of their services well in advance of the planned operational dates of new equipment. All the advanced aircraft of the 1950s, especially the so-called "Century Series" of Air Force fighters (the F-100, F-101, F-102, F-104, F-105, and F-106) underwent prolonged teething troubles before entering service. So did comparable naval aircraft such as the F3H Demon and the F4D Skyray. These airplanes all represented initial attempts to take the lessons learned from the supersonic breakthrough and apply them to operational aircraft capable of conducting military missions. It was natural that, in some cases, the aircraft proved disappointing or even totally unsatisfactory.

All of the early Century series experienced greater or lesser aerodynamic problems that demanded exhaustive flight testing to overcome. The F-101 and F-104, for example, experienced severe pitch-up problems. Douglas worked long and hard refining the design of the XF4D-1 Skyray's after end to eliminate drag and airflow distortion problems, eventually evaluating twelve separate configurations before selecting the one deemed most satisfactory. The wing and fuselage design of the Convair F-102 required extensive study. The lesson to be learned from all this, however, is that, with flight research, the problems *were* overcome, and these aircraft went on to fruitful service.

Flight testing such airplanes was not without anxious moments. Grumman tried its hand at a variable-geometry wing-sweeping design, the XF10F-1 Jaguar, a story best summed up in the reflective words of its former project test pilot, Corwin "Corky" Meyer: "I had never attended a test pilots' school, but, for me, the F10F provided the complete curriculum." On one flight, the canopy blew off the airplane, ripping loose the ejection-seat face curtain and threatening to activate the plane's ejection seat at the slightest jolt. So Meyer, thinking "What a Grade B movie this is!" grabbed the face curtain's rubber handle and clenched it between his teeth. Afraid that a special switch might trigger the ejection seat after he had slowed down during the landing, catapulting him out of the plane, Meyer unbuckled, and as the plane shot over the Edwards lakebed, actually "scrambled out of the cockpit and straddled the front fuselage ahead of the windshield, facing aft. I had managed to get back on the ground and I had no taste for taking off again in an unattached ejection seat!"[15] The Jaguar came to a rest after wildly swinging across the lake, the seat "live" but still in the plane.

On another flight, the Jaguar pitched up during landing-approach tests. Meyer regained control and added full power, but the engine took a while to produce maximum thrust, and the descent rate reached about twenty feet per second. The XF10F-1 thumped down with an awful crunch, and knowledgeable onlookers expected it to break up. Fortunately, it rolled to a quick stop. To one onlooker, the Secretary of the Navy (blissfully unaware of the close call), the Jaguar had just demonstrated a phenomenal short landing and rollout, and he recommended subsequently that the service purchase an additional thirty airplanes! Fortunately, common sense prevailed, and Grumman consigned the craft to oblivion in favor of more conservative and reliable designs.

Even reliable and otherwise excellent designs could give their share of bad moments. Douglas had developed a prototype supersonic interceptor for the Navy, the XF4D-1, appropriately named the Skyray because of its graceful rounded-delta planform. The first prototype flew in 1951, piloted by Larry Peyton and later Russ Thaw. Numerous small problems and difficulties had to be overcome. In the fall of 1951, Douglas pilot Bob Rahn took over testing the Skyray, and by mid-1952 he had gone supersonic. It proved a generally pleasant aircraft, but even so, Rahn had two close calls. On one flight, a high-speed level run to Mach 0.98, Rahn slowed the craft, which underwent a trim change that caused it to abruptly pitch up, reaching a 9.1 g load, which blacked out the pilot. "Fortunately," he recollected, "vision reoccurred just in time to prevent a vertical dive into the water."[16] He gingerly flew back to base, the overstressed Skyray's external skin wrinkled like a prune's.

On another flight, Rahn was aloft evaluating the craft's spinning characteristics, which were, to say the least, very strange. Early spin testing had proceeded uneventfully, but later, Douglas tested the plane with a much-more-aft center of gravity, significantly altering its dynamic characteristics. Now Rahn entered a planned two-turn left spin. After one and a half turns, the XF4D-1 abruptly reversed spin direction, entering a slow flat spin to the right. When Rahn attempted to recover, the Skyray, without warning, snapped over on its back and kept spinning, with pronounced pitching motions, as much as 120 degrees, totally confusing the pilot, who could not be certain whether the craft was spinning upright or inverted, or even right or left. And then the negative g loads caused the ejection seat to break loose from its mount! Rahn fell against the top of the canopy but gamely continued to hang on to the controls. He wisely decided to deploy the emergency spin recovery parachute, which, fortunately, functioned as advertised. The Skyray recovered into level flight only 4,000 feet above ground level, after a spinning drop of over 30,000 feet. And as the plane taxied back on the runway, Rahn discovered that he could not open the canopy! Had the recovery chute failed. . . . In time, the Skyray's problems were overcome, and this fine aircraft fulfilled the hopes of its designer, Ed Heinemann, by becoming a much-praised interceptor. Douglas and Navy test pilots had given the fleet a reliable and safe airplane that subsequently served with distinction.

Sometimes it wasn't the airframe per se but, rather, its systems—the engine, the armament systems, the electronics—that gave pilots problems. The Douglas XA2D-1 Skyshark, for example, was a fine design powered by a trouble-prone turboprop engine that eventually killed the project—but not before engine failures had destroyed three airplanes, killing Navy test pilot Hugh Wood and seriously injuring Douglas pilot George Jansen. The early Lockheed F-104 Starfighters suffered protracted teething troubles. Company pilot Herman "Fish" Salmon had to abandon one of the Mach 2+ fighters when it shed a hatch cover during gunnery trials. Tony Le Vier pulled off a fine dead-stick landing in another Starfighter when an ejected shell casing from the plane's 20-mm. cannon tumbled into one of the engine intakes and punctured a fuel tank. Another F-104 crashed when the test pilot jettisoned the plane's two wing-tip fuel tanks, which promptly tumbled into the tail surfaces (a redesigned tank fin cured that problem).

Engine problems claimed many F-104's and their pilots, including Iven Kincheloe, of X-2 fame, who lost his life when his Starfighter suffered an engine failure just after taking off from Edwards. Other aircraft had problems with weapons trials. Navy test pilot Wally Schirra (later one of the first seven astronauts selected for Project Mercury) had a unique encounter with a missile during a test flight at the Navy's China Lake proving grounds. He and his test observer had just fired an experimental Sidewinder heat-seeking missile from a Douglas F3D Skyknight twin-jet interceptor when the missile suddenly went berserk, looping back toward the F3D, which was, even in the best of circumstances, not the most maneuverable of airplanes. Schirra later recalled:

> Here was something trying to kill me, and I wasn't even mad at it. I was trying to help it along. All I could think of at the time was that I could not let this little jerk climb up *my* tail pipe. So I made a fast loop, trying to stay behind it. I simply wanted to keep its front end from ever seeing my back end. Obviously I succeeded, although the test engineer who was with me suffered slightly from the "clanks," which is pilot talk for the shakes.[17]

The strangest accident of all, however, nearly claimed Grumman test pilot Tom Attridge one September day in 1956. Attridge, flying a gunnery test in an experimental Navy fighter, the F11F-1 Tiger, entered a high-speed supersonic dive and loosed off a burst of defective 20-mm. shells from the plane's four cannon. The Tiger had better supersonic performance than the shells, which quickly tumbled. Attridge's plane overtook them seconds later, multiple hits ruining the engine and forcing the pilot to make an emergency landing in an oak grove near the company's airfield. Attridge thus established a new first in the annals of aviation: piloting a plane that shot itself down! (Years later, another Grumman product, an F-14A Tomcat, repeated the feat during weapons trials with an errant Sparrow missile off California; again, the fortunate crew escaped unharmed.)

By and large, however, the majority of flight tests were far more routine. So sure had become the grasp of supersonic technology that, when North American, Republic, and Vought flew the first prototypes of their initial supersonic fighters (the YF-100A, the YF-105A, and the XF8U-1 Crusader), the engineers and test pilots had confidence enough to actually go supersonic on the very first flight. And though some problems such as inertial coupling occasionally did show up, the lessons *had* been so well assimilated into engineering practice that, by the end of the 1950s, the first generation of supersonic military airplanes were already in operational service, and their Mach 2 successors were just around the corner from squadron service.

"PROOF OF CONCEPT": VALIDATING WHITCOMB'S "AREA RULE"

One of the major flight testing functions has always been so-called "proof of concept" testing: verifying or refuting new concepts or ideas in aeronautics. Among the major postwar aerodynamic developments validated through experimental flight research was the then-radical concept of "area ruling," an idea first postulated by a young NACA engineer, Richard Whitcomb. While working at Langley in the winter of 1951–52, Whitcomb arrived at what he termed a "rule of thumb, a sort of basic principle: Transonic drag is a function of the longitudinal development of the cross-sectional areas of the entire plane." Simply stated, if designers increased the length (and hence, the "fineness ratio") of an airplane, pinching it in where the wings attached to the fuselage, resulting in a "wasp waist" or "Coke bottle" fuselage shape, the plane would have a much lower transonic drag rise, and hence, be able to go supersonic much more easily. Previous aircraft, such as the X-1, say, or the D-558-2, had simply relied on brute force to go supersonic. Whitcomb's "rule of thumb," on the other hand, represented a cajoling of the airflow around the plane and would revolutionize future transonic aircraft design.

Whitcomb's idea looked sound enough on paper, and so, during a staff meeting at Langley, he modestly explained his concept, sitting down quietly at the end of his talk. For a moment, there was quiet. Then

Adolf Busemann, the German father of sweptwing technology, stood up. "Some people come up with half-baked ideas and call them theories," he stated. "Whitcomb comes up with a brilliant idea and calls it a rule of thumb."[18] But would it pass the harsh judgment of flight testing itself?

The Convair F-102, the Air Force's so-called "1954 Interceptor," offered the perfect opportunity to find out. The F-102 was a delta-wing design, drawing upon Convair's earlier experience with the little XF-92A Dart testbed. Even before the F-102's first flight, company engineers had known of the advantages that the Whitcomb area rule offered, and had planned to incorporate it on future F-102 production aircraft. Flight testing of the original prototype at Edwards by company pilot Dick Johnson confirmed the mediocre performance predicted for the craft by the NACA. Instead of being capable of going supersonic in level flight, as the Air Force had desired, the original YF-102, a stubby airplane, could exceed Mach 1 only in a steep dive. Convair and Air Force test pilots lived with its disappointing performance until the first area-ruled example, the sleek YF-102A (dubbed the "Hot Rod" by Convair) flew at Edwards in December 1954. On its second flight, Johnson reached Mach 1.22 in level flight at 35,000 feet, and in January 1956, another YF-102A reached Mach 1.535 "on the level." Nothing could have been more convincing that area rule really worked.

The production F-102A went on to become the mainstay of the Air Force Air Defense Command, together with its bigger and more capable offspring, the Mach 2+ F-106. It also inspired the design of the world's first Mach 2+ strategic bomber, the Convair B-58 Hustler. Area ruling, first validated in flight testing on the YF-102A, has since appeared to various degrees on all subsequent supersonic aircraft. Once again, flight research had demonstrated the value of yet another concept that extended the frontiers of manned flight. And as for Richard Whitcomb, area ruling, great though it was, did not represent the pinnacle of his fruitful career. In the 1960s and 1970s, he postulated two additional revolutionary concepts: the supercritical wing (SCW) and the Whitcomb winglet, conceived to further improve the aerodynamic and energy efficiency of aircraft. These also required and received validation in the Mojave's aerial proving grounds.

FLIGHT TESTING'S "GOLDEN AGE"

In many respects, the 1950s represented the Golden Age of American Flight Testing, for the skies over Southern California and elsewhere in the United States were almost constantly filled with research aircraft and test pilots going about their business on one project or another. And while the 1950s were particularly noteworthy because of the intensive efforts in supersonic flight technology, the story of flight testing during these years embraces much more than just the quest to go beyond Mach 1. Researchers undertook significant developments on such projects as "parasite" airplanes, nuclear propulsion, sea-based jet fighters and bombers, high-altitude aircraft, and VTOL testbeds.

The expected fuel-consumption deficiencies of the new jets caused the Air Force to devote considerable attention to "parasite" aircraft systems, whereby specially designed fighters could fly on a bomber mission by riding in the larger plane's bomb bay or hanging off its wing tips, schemes reminiscent of the Navy's "flying aircraft carriers," of the 1930s. As a result, McDonnell built an ugly and vicious-flying prototype fighter, the XF-85 Goblin, designed to ride in the bomb bay of a gigantic Convair B-36. Flight tests proved anything but pleasant, and though the Goblin eventually proved capable of hooking onto a modified B-29 under very special circumstances, the scheme was justly abandoned as impractical. The Air Force later undertook project "Tip Tow," mounting two modified Republic Thunderjets locked wing tip to wing tip with a B-29, but these trials came to a horrible end in April 1953, when the strong wing-tip vortex from the B-29 caused one of the jets to flip over and smash into the B-29, all test crewmen on the three-plane combination being killed. Nevertheless, the Air Force proceeded with a similar scheme for the Convair B-36, planning this time to launch and retrieve special reconnaissance airplanes. Once again, the strong wake vortex from the B-36 endangered the little jets used in the tests, fortunately without injuries or damage. The Air Force canceled Tom-Tom, as the later project had been known and, instead, modified a number of Republic Thunderflash reconnaissance airplanes so that they could be air-launched and retrieved in flight from the bomb bays of B-36 mother ships. This unique system actually was operational with the Strategic Air Command from late 1952 until mid-1956, the period before the development of the Lockheed U-2.

The rapid development of atomic energy had led to undue optimism that this new form of energy could be harnessed and utilized for aircraft propulsion. As a result, the Air Force had launched project NEPA: Nuclear Energy for the Propulsion of Aircraft. NEPA had numerous problems; in retrospect, it is hard to find a logical reason why it went forward, for any such airplane would automatically have been so heavy that it would have had poor performance as well as serious safety shortcomings (one critic, science commentator Daniel Greenberg, has called the nuclear airplane a prime example of "technological megalomania"). In any case, the Air Force eventually modified a giant Convair B-36 to carry a small General Electric reactor. The reactor was simply for radiation and systems tests and did not, in fact, operate any of the plane's systems. The company removed the nose of the plane and replaced it with a special lead-shielded pressurized capsule for a five-man test crew; the cockpit glass varied from nine to eleven inches thick. The new plane, designated the NB-36H, first flew in September 1955, and completed about a hundred flights before project termination. Convair project pilot Fred Petty and his test crew spent long hours droning across the Atomic Energy Commission's southwest test sites, avoiding bad weather and being tailed by a C-119 chase plane carrying a load of paramedics to secure the crash site for radiation hazards, in the event that the test plane cratered itself in the desert. A planned follow-on program, the X-6, whereby a B-36 would have had reactor-driven aircraft systems, did not get beyond the planning stage. And so ended actual flight tests of nuclear aircraft technology. The project itself lasted until 1963, when it finally collapsed, the victim of rising costs, lack of interest, and growing criticism.

THE "ULTIMATE" SEAPLANES

The post-World War II years witnessed the decline of the seaplane in civil and military applications. Long-range "DC-4 generation" transports replaced it on transoceanic service, and shore- and carrier-based aircraft replaced military seaplanes for patrol and antishipping duties. Nevertheless, the Navy retained some interest in seaplanes during the 1950s, actively pursuing development of both a water-borne seaplane fighter, the Convair XF2Y-1 Sea Dart (a twin-jet delta design), and the large Martin XP6M-1 Seamaster patrol flying boat. Both represented promising concepts. Convair test pilot Sam Shannon completed the Sea Dart's maiden flight at San Diego in April 1953. A more powerful version flew the next year and accomplished a unique "first" for sea-borne aircraft by exceeding Mach 1 in a dive in August 1954, piloted by Charles Richbourg. Unfortunately, during a press demonstration, this aircraft broke up from a "diverging" longitudinal pitching at low altitude near the speed of sound, killing Richbourg. The remaining two Sea Darts flew on into 1957 on a variety of tests, but the program died from lack of funding and genuine operational need.

The XP6M-1 Seamaster, a large, four-engine flying boat, was canceled because it threatened to draw funding away from carrier-based aircraft projects and seemed overtaken as a strategic concept by the first of the Polaris-equipped ballistic-missile submarines. In fact, this most impressive aircraft almost certainly should have been proceeded with, for it was, as chief project pilot George Rodney has recalled, ". . . truly a Mach 1 aircraft, with all the other performance characteristics of comparable land-based aircraft."[19] Testing of the XP6M-1 began in July 1955 at Martin's Middle River, Maryland plant and continued at Patuxent River. Unfortunately, one major accident claimed the lives of four crewmen in December 1955, and although the exact cause was never precisely determined, investigators believed a runaway powered control system failure sent the plane into a violent pitchover during testing off St. Mary's River. A second accident traced to engineering design error caused another prototype to go into a violent loop during testing off Delaware. Fortunately, this time pilot Bob Turner and his test crew were able to eject safely as the plane began breaking up. Despite these two accidents, however, the Seamaster proved an excellent aircraft, capable of a variety of operational uses ranging from mine laying to nuclear bombing, and it was a sad day when the Pentagon's defense planners canceled development of this promising design. The remaining six preproduction and ten production Seamasters completed were eventually scrapped.

A CLASSY SPY FROM LOCKHEED

The acute need for reliable intelligence information concerning the capabilities of the Soviet Union led to many reconnaissance aircraft programs. Bell, for example, undertook development of the so-called X-16 "Bald Eagle," but this twin-engine long-span aircraft never got off the drawing board, for an even more ambitious design, Kelly Johnson's famed U-2, had already flown. The U-2 represented essentially the world's most refined powered glider. At first, Johnson had envisioned an F-104 fuselage joined to a broad-span, high-aspect-ratio, sailplane-like wing. The final aircraft, of course, represented a very different design, and Tony Le Vier completed its first flight in August 1955.

The U-2 presented some unique challenges, as Tony Le Vier discovered on its first flight. Attempts to land it like a conventional sailplane proved unsuccessful; the U-2 simply would not quit flying. Johnson, in resigned tones, advised Le Vier finally to climb to altitude and abandon the prototype. At that point, Le Vier summoned up all his years of experience and decided to land the plane, which had a unique bicycle-like landing gear, like any "tail dragger." And it came in smoothly and gracefully. Future U-2 pilots learned to stall the plane just off the ground before touchdown, otherwise it would coast and coast down the runway.

It had other peculiarities: At altitude, its plexiglass canopy became extremely strong in the intense cold, preventing pilots from ejecting through it, as with conventional planes. U-2 pilots learned to jettison the canopy first, in the event that they had to eject. At maximum altitude, the plane's stall speed and critical "never-exceed" speed came close together: only *4 knots* separated the "V_s" (stall speed) from "M_{crit}" (the never-exceed speed). Routinely the plane broke all existing recognized altitude records, flying well above 70,000 feet. Pilots had to wear pressure suits and helmets, for otherwise, should they lose pressurization at high altitudes, they would die.

Sadly, the U-2 program did not proceed without fatalities; crashes during development testing claimed the lives of Robert Sieker and Pat Hunerwadel early in the program.

Nevertheless, testing at Edwards and at a secret Nevada test site known as Watertown Strip and dubbed "The Ranch" confirmed the basic excellence of the design. In time, it appeared stealthily in the skies over the Soviet Union, flying with impunity until a Soviet surface-to-air missile blew Francis Gary Powers's U-2 out of the air and into front-page headlines in 1960. The U-2 proved surprisingly adaptable, and a much larger version (with a 15-knot safety margin at altitude), the U-2R, flew at Edwards in 1967. And today, still-more-advanced versions are planned, even as NASA utilizes two modified U-2's on earth-sciences research missions, flying out of Ames Research Center.

THE QUEST FOR TRULY VERTICAL FLIGHT

One of the most interesting developmental efforts in the 1950s concerned vertical-takeoff-and-landing (VTOL) airplanes. Military planners already recognized the vulnerability of tying a nation's air defense to vulnerable runways and a few large aircraft carriers. Specialized short- and vertical-takeoff aircraft could revolutionize military operations. In an attempt to overcome the limitations of conventional strike aircraft, designers sought to take advantage of the new class of rocket takeoff boosters then being used to "zero-launch" such cruise missiles as the Regulus and the Matador off ramps. A conventional fighter-bomber such as the F-100, it was thought, could be based just behind the front lines, away from an airfield complex. If war came, it could be launched off a ramp with rocket boost. The pilot would jettison the burned-out booster, attack his target, and then land at a conventional airfield. The first test of this system went smoothly: North American test pilot Al Blackburn strapped into a modified F-100D perched on a ramp, ran the jet engine up into afterburner, triggered the rocket booster, and with a thunderous roar and a cloud of orange smoke, took off into the blue, circled, and landed safely. The next test, however, did not go as well; the booster failed to separate from the Super Sabre after launch, and Blackburn ejected just before the plane wallowed into the Edwards lakebed and exploded. Despite continued interest (and even some tests with a Lockheed Starfighter), the ZELL program (for zero-length launch) was quietly and deservedly shelved as impractical. The only true answer to the short-field problem is a genuine STOL or VTOL airplane.

And so, a number of those were flown as well. Eventually, with the development of the British Hawker Siddeley P.1127, first flown by Bill Bedford in 1961, true V/STOL military flight by craft other than helicopters came of age. The P.1127 eventually spawned the Kestrel research airplane and then, finally, the Harrier ground-attack aircraft, in service with several of the world's air arms, including the Royal Air Force and the U. S. Marine Corps. The predecessors of the Harrier, however, were generally unsatisfactory flying machines. Most were properly termed "tail sitters," for they would have rested on their tail sections and literally taken off and landed vertically. (The Harrier, as well as such unconventional machines as the Bell X-14 and other convertiplanes, utilized vectored engine thrust for propulsive lift, changing over to aerodynamic lift as the plane accelerated away from its takeoff site. Conversely, when the plane slowed for landing, it changed back to propulsive lift for landing.) Stability and control of VTOL aircraft are, of course, quite critical, and one can almost think of a vectored thrust VTOL airplane as a four-poster bed, which requires all four posts to remain upright! The problem with the various tail sitters is that, in fact, they could do little else *but* take off and land vertically, for they did not have the flexibility permitting STOL operation.

During the 1950s, flight researchers in the United States flew three basic tail sitters: the Navy-sponsored Convair XFY-1 "Pogo" and the Lockheed XFV-1 Salmon, and the Air Force-sponsored Ryan X-13. All took advantage of the powerful gas-turbine engines then being developed to achieve vertical flight. Of the three, the two Navy aircraft were intended as actual fighters, designed to operate from the decks of merchant ships and escort vessels at sea. The X-13, on the other hand, was purely a research vehicle to study transitions from vertical flight to horizontal flight and back again. (For example, it did not even incorporate flush riveting.) The two Navy aircraft were also turboprop-driven, incorporating large contrarotating propellers. Of these two, only the Convair design, flown by test pilot James "Skeets" Coleman, achieved true vertical flight. Lockheed never did make a vertical lift-off or landing in the XFV-1, preferring to take off horizontally using a special takeoff dolly attached to the belly of the plane.

Lags in the control system, "spool-up" times for the engine, and general handling-quality problems limited the performance of the planes and contributed to growing official disinterest. Above all, the concept of backing down to land seemed risky, especially, say, for an operational pilot trying to come aboard a small ship pitching in open seas. As Lockheed project pilot Fish Salmon subsequently pronounced, "It's awful hard to fly an airplane looking over your shoulder."[20] Nevertheless, following a series of tethered tests, Skeets Coleman completed the first "free" hover (at an altitude of 150 feet), on August 1, 1954. On November 2 of that year, at Moffett Field, he took off vertically, changed to horizontal flight, flew around, changed back to vertical flight, and backed the big delta XFY-1 down to a smooth touchdown.

Ryan meantime concentrated on developing its pure jet, the X-13. Subsequently, the X-13, known as the Vertijet, did duplicate Coleman's feat. The two X-13's Ryan eventually built utilized a British Avon engine, with ducted air venting for low-speed attitude control. At first, engineers and project pilot Pete Girard tested the propulsion system on a special rig. Finally, they left San Diego for initial trials with the actual aircraft at Edwards. At first, in December 1955, Girard made conventional takeoffs and landings using a quickly installed temporary landing gear fixed on the underside of the plane. Following verification of its basic aerodynamic safety, Ryan next undertook a series of vertical hovers just off the ground, in May of 1956.

The X-13 was designed to hook onto a special "trapeze" launch platform, and Girard undertook a number of development flights to verify the craft's ability to maneuver while balanced on the Avon's hot exhaust jet. In November 1956, following a conventional takeoff, he changed to a vertical hover at altitude, then back to conventional flight before landing. Finally, on April 11, 1957, Girard ran up the engine to full power, edged off the wire on the special launch trailer, and lifted into the air. The X-13 nosed down into level flight, scooted away, and circled around; then came word that technicians were having problems readying the trapeze launch platform for the X-13's landing. Ryan engineers decided to use a backup platform wisely placed nearby for just such an eventuality, and Girard completed a smooth transition and backdown to hook onto the trailer. Three months later, Girard and the Ryan test team felt confident enough to demonstrate the X-13 in Washington, at the river entrance of the Pentagon, while a crowd of one hundred thousand watched. Aviation had come a ways since Ryan's *Spirit of St. Louis*.

In spite of all this, however, researchers quickly realized that the tail-sitting approach to VTOL flight left a lot to be desired. The future clearly lay in aircraft that would "sit" in a horizontal attitude, while taking off and landing vertically by using vectored jet thrust and tilt wings (so that props or ducted fans could furnish both vertical lift and horizontal propulsion), or in craft having both rotors and conventional wings. On May 24, 1958, Bell test pilot David Howe passed a milestone in the history of vertical flight by piloting the experimental X-14 on a vertical takeoff followed by conventional flight, transition, and a vertical landing during testing at Niagara Falls Airport.

What made the X-14 different from all its predecessors, however, was that it was not a tail sitter but, rather, used a venetian-blind-like vane system to deflect the exhaust from the craft's two small jet engines for vertical lift. Compressed-air "reaction controls" kept the craft in balance during takeoff, hovering, and landing, when its conventional aerodynamic control surfaces lacked effectiveness. The flight demonstrated the practicality of vectored thrust. Howe took off straight up, hovered like a helicopter, flew away at about 160 mph, climbed to 1,000 feet, circled back, approached at about 95 mph, deflected the engine thrust (which caused the plane to slow to a hover a mere ten feet off the ground), made a 180-degree turn, and then settled down. There was no need for a hazardous, groping backing down, no need for a special trailer rig. It was the dawn of vectored-thrust flight, brought to practicality with the later Harrier and Soviet Yak-36 *Forger*.

As for the X-14, it later flew for NASA at the Ames Research Center, piloted by Fred Drinkwater and his colleagues on a variety of research investigations ranging from evaluating electronic control systems to simulating the characteristics of a lunar lander in support of the Apollo effort. Research on the problems and potential of VTOL aircraft continued through the 1960s and early 1970s, both in the United States and abroad, with such strange craft as the Ling-Temco-Vought XC-142A, the Curtiss-Wright X-19, the Bell X-22, the Lockheed XV-4A and XV-4B, and the Ryan XV-5A. Problems and crashes plagued all these programs, claiming the lives of several crewmen, and indeed only the Harrier program stands as an unqualified success in the still-strange field of vertical flight. (Eight Harrier predecessors, the Hawker XV-6A Kestrels, underwent trials at Edwards and "Pax River" from 1965 through 1967. Two later flew with NASA's Langley Research Center piloted by Lee Person, Jack Reeder, and Bob Champine, contributing to the success of what eventually became an Anglo-American joint venture.)

THE DAWN OF THE 707

The story of flight testing in the postwar years would be incomplete without reference to one of the truly milestone commercial airplanes in aviation history: the Boeing 367-80, better known as simply the "Dash 80," the first of the 707 family. With the dawn of the 707, commercial jet aviation came of age, and the airplane, as the prime mover of people in intercontinental and transoceanic service became an established reality. Ever since the advent of the DC-3, the United States had dominated world transport aviation, and the field itself had in turn been dominated by Douglas products. In December 1947, on the forty-fourth anniversary of Kitty Hawk, Boeing test pilots Bob Robbins and Scott Osler had completed the maiden flight of the radical XB-47 Stratojet—a six-engine jet bomber capable of lugging a "Fat Man" atomic bomb and having a sharply swept, slender wing combined with pods for the engines. Eventually the XB-47 went into production and became one of the mainstays of the Strategic Air Command, remaining in service until 1966. But it had numerous flaws as well as good points, especially poor high-speed performance and aeroelasticity difficulties.

Boeing, at the same time, had a proposed "XB-52" under development, a moderately swept airplane powered by four turboprop engines. Then, one Friday when Boeing engineers were presenting the latest report to Air Force officials at Wright Field on the XB-52, the service chieftains asked Boeing to consider a pure-jet aircraft instead. Working that weekend in a suite of rooms at Dayton's Van Cleve Hotel, Boeing engineers came up with the general configuration of what eventually flew as the XB-52, with eight engines. Test pilots Alvin "Tex" Johnston, formerly of Bell and now with Boeing, and Guy Townsend demonstrated the B-52's fine handling characteristics following the series' first flight (by the second airplane, the YB-52), in April 1952. Though Convair attempted a similar configuration with its XB-60 (basically a sweptwing and jet-powered derivative of its monstrous B-36), Boeing clearly had the inside track. Eventually the B-52 went on to yeoman service, and indeed it is expected today that upgraded models of this combat-proven airplane will continue to form a vital branch of the nation's nuclear defense triad through the year 2000—though this is less a tribute to the plane's excellence than it is to the shoddy record of defense planners, who have been trying, ever since the days of the XB-70, to develop a suitable replacement.

As Boeing's military ventures of the 1930s and 1940s had encouraged the development of such airplanes as the 307 Stratoliner, the 314 flying boat, and the 377 Stratocruiser (based on the B-29 and B-50 series), the technology base from the XB-47 and XB-52 programs now encouraged the company to pursue development of a jet transport that could also be produced as a jet tanker to air-refuel Boeing's Stratojet and Stratofortress bombers. Eschewing some of the more exotic aspects of the two bombers, such as the high wing and the bicycle-style landing gear, com-

pany engineers instead opted for a low-wing design incorporating podded engines, a moderately swept wing, and such items as vortex generators (proved beneficial in improving transonic airflow over a wing by
NACA flight testing). Landing-gear design proved a problem, and indeed, during an early taxi test, one gear leg actually collapsed. But on the
afternoon of July 15, 1954, Tex Johnston and Dix Loesch took the trim
brown-and-yellow Dash 80 aloft from Seattle on its maiden flight, a success.

Boeing had invested almost a quarter of the company's total net worth
in developing the Dash 80, and if ever the future of a company rested
truly in the hands of its test pilots, then so did the future of Boeing in
the capable hands of Johnston and his test crews. Testing proceeded rapidly and without difficulty. The Air Force, originally cool to the idea of
a pure-jet tanker to match its increasingly pure-jet bomber force, decided to take another look. American airline corporations, skeptical about
jet transports following the disastrous in-flight structural failures that had
grounded Great Britain's ill-fated Comet, took another look as well. So
confident, however, was Tex Johnston about the plane's capabilities and
performance, that at the annual Seattle powerboat races he was not content with just a sedate flyby. As Boeing vice-president John Steiner subsequently recalled:

> Our chief test pilot could not pass up the opportunity to show off his air-
> plane in front of 200,000 people or so. With a full test crew aboard, he
> made a couple of barrel rolls at altitude, then came down to about 200
> feet and barrel-rolled over the speedboat course, returning to do the same
> thing in the other direction. A lot of people went home thinking about
> jet transports instead of hydroplanes.[21]

Nor was this the last time that Johnston took the Dash 80 up for
aerobatics. Reputedly, Boeing chairman Bill Allen once took a fishing
trip with his friend Larry Bell, who suffered from a weak heart. They
were out on the lake, lines cast and bait waiting, when the rumble of a
large jet disturbed the tranquil scene. Overhead appeared Johnston and
the brown-and-yellow transport prototype. Slowly it wheeled over into
a majestic roll, then straightened out and flew off. "Larry," said Allen to
his stunned friend, "pass me some of your heart pills."

The Dash 80 was responsible for introducing a design trend fully as
influential as that introduced earlier by the four-engine DC-4. Since the
time of the prototype 707, all jet transports have tended to look alike,
with moderate sweptwings and podded engines. Boeing did not find the
road to commercial success with the Dash 80 free of challenges. Though
the company won numerous orders from the Air Force for a tanker

derivative—the slightly wider KC-135—Douglas rose up to challenge Boeing for dominance in the jetliner marketplace. Boeing eventually won, with the even wider production 707 airliners, with a variety of wing, fuselage, and engine combinations. (The DC-8, Boeing's Douglas rival for the jetliner market, did well in its own right, and can claim a unique distinction: in 1961, as part of a Douglas test program, a crew headed by Bill Magruder took an advanced DC-8 through the speed of sound in a shallow dive over Edwards, reaching Mach 1.012, the first supersonic excursion by a commercial aircraft.) Boeing's 707 prototype continued flying on company projects for a number of years, testing such concepts as aft-mounted engines (for the 727), externally blown flaps, triple-slotted flaps, and noise-reduction schemes, before being honorably retired to the Smithsonian Institution, in 1972.

So, by the end of the fifties, the promise of the airplane had been fulfilled—a meeting of the hopes of the Wrights and all those who had preceded and followed them. The rumble of the jet could be heard daily, and the days of the twelve-hour transcontinental flight ended in the four- or five-hour flights common with the 707-generation jetliners. And when Robert Little and Lew Nelson completed the maiden flights of the Mach 2+ McDonnell XF4H-1 Phantom II and the supersonic Northrop N-156T (the predecessor of both the T-38A trainer and the F-5 multinational fighter), toward the end of the decade, it signaled the end of the first era of supersonic flight and the beginning of the second: the routine ability to fly at speeds considered little short of fantastic only a decade before. Aviation had matured into adulthood.

THE CREATION OF THE SOCIETY OF EXPERIMENTAL TEST PILOTS

And so had the profession of test pilot. The seeds of professionalization planted by the First World War had germinated and, in the mid-1950s, the test pilot was regarded as a vital and valued member of the research-and-development team, an individual whose opinions and judgments were solicited and accepted, a person whose credentials for employment almost always included specialized technical or scientific training and, frequently, education at a test-pilot school as well. Increasingly, test pilots recognized that they *were* a new class of aerospace professionals, as much as, say, members of the various engineering organizations such as the Institute of the Aeronautical Sciences. They had a heritage, a tradition; they had much in common with each other. They shared the same risks, undertook the same kinds of tasks, had the same concerns in safety.

And thus, in the late summer of 1955, one test pilot, Northrop's Ray E. Tenhoff, took it upon himself to serve as the catalyst for such an organization of test pilots. On September 14, 1955, Tenhoff and five civilian test pilots met for lunch at Aleck's Valley Club Cafe, in Lancaster, California, the heart of the Edwards-Palmdale flight testing arena. Tenhoff's five colleagues were Scotty Crossfield (NACA), John Fitzpatrick (Convair), Dick Johnson (Convair), Tom Kilgariff (Douglas), and Joe Ozier (Lockheed). These six concluded that a "Pilot Organization" should have the general objective of being "a group dedicated to assist in the development of superior airplanes." Then they went forth with plans for an organizing conference of pilots in the Edwards area. A group of seventeen met one night at Juanita's Bar and Grill, in Rosamond, near the Edwards gateway, and besides five of the original six, this group numbered such luminaries as Bill Bridgeman, George Jansen, Charles Tucker, Bob Rahn, Bob Drew, John Conrad, Lew Nelson, Pete Girard, W. L. Everitt, Skeets Coleman, Al McDaniel, and Al Blackburn. Out of this meeting, held on September 29, 1955, came an organization known, for lack of a better working title, as the "Testy Test Pilots Society." Another organization meeting, on October 13, back at Aleck's, resulted in a new title: The Society of Experimental Test Pilots (SETP). Within weeks, sixty-five of the nation's leading test pilots had signed on as charter members. Al McDaniel came up with a simple and appropriate insigne: a gold X superimposed upon a blue oval, representative of the sky and experimental flying—an uncomplicated logo, yet one that has gained the worldwide respect of the aeronautical community. By November 1956, over a hundred had joined; today, SETP membership is worldwide, numbering close to fifteen hundred, and including foreign chapters as well. Truly it is impossible to visit a major aerospace company in the non-Communist countries whose flight test staffs do not include at least a few members of SETP.

Within a few months of its organization, SETP members were appearing at professional symposia and colloquia. In 1957, they held the first of their since justly famous annual meetings in Beverly Hills, inducting four highly appropriate honorary fellows: Jimmy Doolittle, Frederick Trapnell, Albert Boyd, and Howard Hughes. Sadly, within months of its founding, the society lost its first member to perish in a flight testing accident: Harry Brackett, who died north of Edwards in the crash of an experimental XF8U-1 Crusader on February 1, 1956. (The SETP Headquarters building in Lancaster is named in his honor.) Founder Joe Ozier died in the crash of an F-104 at Palmdale, and Tom Kilgariff perished when a Douglas A3D Skywarrior betrayed him at the same field. Early in the formation of the society, the officers had decided to present a special award at their annual banquet, an award in memory of all the society's deceased members. At first tentatively called the Test Pilots Achievement Award, it was renamed the Iven C. Kincheloe Award, in honor of the personable young Air Force test pilot—and SETP member —who had died at Edwards in July 1958 in the crash of a Lockheed F-104. This fitting honor has since been awarded to some of the most outstanding of America's research test pilots. Today the SETP acts like many professional technical societies: it issues a journal, holds symposia, participates in national meetings with other, related organizations and societies, and promotes active dialogue and a forum for professional discussion. But there is a difference: there are very few societies in this world whose members consistently face a chance, however remote, of injury or death, and where uncommon courage of the membership seems to be a common characteristic. The success of the SETP has gone far beyond anything that Ray Tenhoff could have hoped for in his most optimistic dreams. And it is a pity that he did not live to see the society flourish as it has, for he, too, died in pursuit of his profession, in the crash of a Convair B-58 at Great Salt Lake, on April 22, 1960.

CHAPTER 8

FROM AIR TO SPACE

The two-decade period from 1960 to 1980 saw the aerospace sciences reach levels of achievement and complexity that would have dwarfed even the most optimistic predictions of forecasters viewing the horizon from the 1950s. By 1980, men had walked on the moon, hundreds of millions of passengers flew each year in craft ranging from light, general-aviation airplanes to SST's, and flights by manned and unmanned orbiting spacecraft were commonplace. A dualistic drive governed aerospace development in this period. At the same time that researchers drew upon the missile programs of the 1950s to generate the manned spacecraft of the '60s and '70s, others concentrated on furthering the capabilities of aircraft for flight within the atmosphere—a two-pronged approach that eventually spawned both the spectacular triumph of Apollo and the advanced commercial and military airplanes of today.

It is a modern truism that advanced aircraft are expensive. In 1945, a standard P-51 Mustang had a "flyaway" price of just about $51,000. Today, the Navy's Grumman F-14A Tomcat costs $22 million per copy, and even a less-sophisticated machine such as the General Dynamics F-16A costs $15 million. With overall program costs running into the billions of dollars, it is clearly necessary that defense planners—and commercial airplane developers as well—be thoroughly convinced that the products they acquire are capable of fulfilling national needs. A modern country simply cannot afford a multibillion-dollar mistake. In the 1960s, the United States underwent a period in which actual competitive flight testing of rival prototypes (such as the 1950s matching of the XF4H-1 Phantom versus the XF8U-3 Crusader III, or the 1970s fly-off between the Northrop A-9 and the Fairchild A-10) was deemphasized in favor of extensive paper analysis. This weakness is equivalent to the oft-expressed view that the test pilot could be replaced by the unmanned, "robot" airplane.

The legacy of such misplaced thinking is that great aeronautical debacle of the 1960s, the F-111 program. The F-111, developed to meet a poorly thought-out government specification for both an Air Force strike aircraft and a Navy interceptor, fell between the two. Eventually, the Navy version collapsed entirely, forcing that service to hurriedly develop the F-14. Serious flight testing deficiencies arose, and one pilot referred to the F-111's performance envelope as a "three-dimensional maze." Eventually, after a great deal of hard work, the Air Force and the manufacturer managed to turn that service's F-111's into reasonable aircraft, but the entire program must be counted a disappointment—and for the Navy, a failure. The 1970s saw a return to the notion of "fly before buy," and heavy costs and lengthy development times of modern aircraft have forced a more stringent blending of ground and flight analysis, and even on an international scale, as witnessed by the multinational Jaguar, Tornado, and F-16 programs.

Once again, the historical record points to the increasing importance of the test pilot and flight test engineer in the development process. When the F-111 program appeared in dire straits, and Grumman, the manufacturer charged with responsibility for the Navy version, was beginning the process of growing disenchantment that would eventually lead them on the path of the superb F-14, a company official journeyed out to Edwards to meet with the F-111's test pilots. He did so, he testified subsequently before a congressional committee, because

> there is something that we say in the aerospace industry, that any aircraft company president who doesn't have a very close communication with his chief test pilot is going to be in grave danger. That is the final place where engineering and operational skill come together to evaluate the performance of the final product.[1]

And this, of course, implies the notion of the two-way street. The test pilots, for their part, have to be discerning individuals operating as free as possible from irrelevant bias. As Mike Collins has written,

> A test pilot, more than any other type of aviator, must be objective. It is all right for a squadron pilot to fall in love with his airplane; it is all he

has to fly, and he might just as well enjoy it because it has already been designed. . . .

The test pilot cannot fall into this trap. . . . He must carefully analyze the possible uses to which a new airplane might be put and judge it accordingly.[2]

And so, in test flying as in so many other aspects of human society, unreasonable prejudice and simplistic beliefs serve only to cloud issues and must ultimately call into question the competence of those who propound them. The professional test pilot realizes this and recognizes that duty dictates a forthright and constructive analysis of an airplane's potential—or lack thereof. When, for example, the Grumman official asked the Edwards pilots whether (in pilot parlance) the F-111 was a "dog" (i.e., unsatisfactory) airplane, one pilot replied, "I would define it as a goat, because that is the only thing that smells worse than a dog. But," he added, "that doesn't mean that a lot of these things can't be fixed and corrected, but at the present moment this is not a satisfactory airplane." And fixed and corrected they were. Today and for the future the F-111 is a valued and trusted weapon in the nation's arsenal, notwithstanding its early history.

There is no better recent example of the willingness of test pilots to risk their lives to prevent possibly inferior airplanes from entering service than the dramatic case of the Lockheed Electra airliner. The Electra, a stubby and powerful four-engine propjet transport, had entered airline service to the general acclaim of flight crews, passengers, and airline operators. Then disaster struck. An Electra broke up and crashed over Buffalo, Texas. Tragically, a few months later, on St. Patrick's Day 1960, another Electra crashed, in a "mirror-image" of the first. An intensive and exhaustive investigation pinned the cause on an obscure aeroelastic and flight-dynamics problem called whirl-mode instability. Under certain and very rare conditions, the dynamic interaction of the racing propeller, the bobbing engine nacelle, and the flexing wings would lead to "frequency coupling," with the result that the wings would fail under load, sending the plane into an inevitable crash.

Lockheed came up with a solution involving complete beefing up of the engine nacelles, the engine installation and mountings, and the wings themselves. Lockheed test crews (with parachutes) strapped into Electras and roared aloft from the company's Burbank plant in special tests designed to impose maximum loads on the engine-nacelle design, including deliberately inducing flutter and loosening the propellers so that they would wobble. In all cases, the reenforced nacelles prevented the onset of destructive whirl mode and frequency coupling. Then the FAA asked

Lockheed for one more series of tests: take a test Electra with deliberately weakened engine mounts into conditions of high speed and turbulence, to see if the reenforced nacelle just by itself could temper the violence of whirl mode. It was a dangerous request, for should the nacelle
fail, a very real accident could occur, and the test crew might not have
time to abandon the gyrating transport before it smashed into the
ground. But the Lockheed flight test crews volunteered to a man, and
eventually the company selected Herman "Fish" Salmon and Roy
Wimmer to run the tests. The crew had full confidence in the plane.

To simulate a worst-possible condition, Lockheed weakened the engine
mounts of all four engines, then disconnected one propeller so that it
would windmill in the onrushing airstream. High over the California
Sierras, Salmon and Wimmer took the weakened Electra beyond its "red
line," never-exceed speed. Slightly at first and then more pronouncedly,
whirl mode set in, rocking the nacelles and wings. But the strengthened
nacelles themselves prevented the fatal frequency coupling. Then Salmon
and Wimmer deliberately dived the Electra to an indicated airspeed of
nearly 400 mph, pulling out in a punishing way that further imposed
heavy loads on the nacelles—and they held. The Electra returned safely.
A further six flight tests confirmed the results of the first, and the FAA
restored the plane to unrestricted service. It has since served without
difficulty, and a military derivative, the P-3 Orion patrol bomber, is in
worldwide naval service—thanks, in no small way, to Lockheed test
crews who were willing to lay their lives on the line to demonstrate a
product that they had faith in, so that others might fly safely.

THROUGH MACH 3 IN THE BLACKBIRDS AND XB-70A

One of the most challenging and secretive of the 1960s flight test programs involved the alluring Lockheed "Blackbirds." At government
behest, Lockheed undertook the design of a Mach 3+ aircraft suitable
for long-range strategic reconnaissance at altitudes in excess of 80,000
feet. The basic technical challenges were not inconsiderable. As with the
U-2 and the P-80 before it, the Blackbird was a product of Lockheed's
Advanced Development Projects Group—Kelly Johnson's Skunk Works.
It represented an innovative and creative application of the latest in
aerodynamic theory and structural and propulsion knowledge. Literally
nothing could be incorporated from existing hardware. The 30,000-
pound-thrust Pratt & Whitney engines had not previously flown. Johnson selected a largely titanium airframe—in itself a major and radical

departure from traditional aircraft design—to better withstand the heat-soaking Mach 3 cruise temperatures the Blackbird would encounter. Special hydraulic fluids and fuels were developed. Indeed, Johnson subsequently wrote, "It is said truly that everything on the aircraft from rivets and fluids, up through materials, and power plants had to be invented from scratch."[3] At Mach 3 speeds, the J58 engines functioned more as ramjets than as turbojets.

But what immediately struck observers privileged enough to see the new plane was its futuristic shape. Johnson's design team had selected a "blended wing-body" shape having a basically delta planform, with two large engine nacelles at mid-span, one on each wing. The fuselage itself had an aerodynamic cross section, with prominent "chines" running along the fuselage from the leading edge of the wing. On the original prototypes, the A-12 (as it was known within the company) and the YF-12A, these chines ran almost up to the tip of the nose, and they did extend to the tip of the nose on the later SR-71A, the definitive strategic reconnaissance airplane. The YF-12A, an experimental interceptor not placed in production (and possibly never intended to be more than just a testbed for the development of advanced radar, fire-control systems, and missiles), had a prominent nose radome that necessitated deleting the chines (they ended abruptly in small infrared sensors), and thus the changed nose contours necessitated Lockheed adding a large ventral fin that could fold to one side for takeoff and landing, and would extend at supersonic speeds for added directional stability, as well as two smaller ventrals on the bottom of the engine nacelles. These ventral fins, together with the large vertical fins mounted above the engine nacelles, gave the A-12/YF-12A a very distinctive appearance, as did the overall black finish (though the initial fights were in bare metal).

The audacity of this design is hard to comprehend. At the time Johnson and his team drew up the plane's tentative shape, the first Mach 2 aircraft were just entering operational service. The only Mach 3 experience had been Mel Apt's unhappy flight. Both the X-15 and the proposed XB-70A bomber were expected to furnish useful data on flight at and above Mach 3, but the A-12 quickly outpaced the development of the XB-70A (which did not fly until late 1964), and the X-15 did not encounter the problems faced by an "air-breathing" Mach 3 airplane soaking its structure for long periods of time with the temperatures incurred at that speed. Lockheed truly found themselves on their own, an unenviable position for any company to be in, but a position that did not particularly bother Johnson and his staff.

The first Lockheed A-12 flew at "The Ranch" on April 26, 1962, far away from prying eyes. Other prototypes (including a mix of single- and two-seat aircraft, perhaps as many as twenty-four in all) soon joined it in the air, and Lockheed proceeded with both aerodynamic testing of the airplane and tests of its various systems, including supersonic firing trials of air-to-air missiles. The Blackbird could not be tested simply in the Nevada-California corridor, for unlike even so exotic an airplane as the X-15, it sustained Mach 3+ speeds for far longer, and hence covered a lot of territory. So some of its test flights covered the whole southern half of the United States, ranging, for example, from California to Miami and back. It proved a pleasant airplane to fly, but the strange interactions of its inlet system with the airflow could, at some times, cause the craft to "diverge" from its flight path, necessitating a complex stability-augmentation system to offset the objectionable motions. Sometimes the shock wave contained within the inlet would pop "outside" the lip of the inlet, inducing a violent engine "unstart," marked by greatly increased drag on one side and an abrupt swerving motion that rocked the crew in the cockpit. ("Helmets," the YF-12A project manager later stated, "have hit the canopy hard at times."[4]) Accidents claimed several Blackbirds, but the losses were cloaked in secrecy.

It is virtually impossible to keep such a program a complete secret, and soon airline pilots caught glimpses of the Blackbirds far above their craft, and FAA traffic controllers watched in amazement at blips that occasionally raced across their screens at fantastic speeds. In February 1964, Lyndon Johnson announced the existence of the A-12. Several things happened nearly simultaneously. With the program now no longer a secret, testing was transferred from the remoteness of "The Ranch" to Edwards; Kelly Johnson received the Presidential Medal of Freedom and later the Collier Trophy for the design of the plane; finally, Lockheed's A-11 test pilots, Louis W. Schalk, William C. Park, Robert J. Gilliland, and James D. Eastham, received the coveted Kincheloe Award of The Society of Experimental Test Pilots for their part in the program.

Subsequent testing went without much difficulty. The first SR-71A flew at the end of December 1964, just before Christmas. By mid-decade, the Strategic Air Command had received the first of these sophisticated intelligence-gatherers, and it was soon involved in the thick of the air war in Southeast Asia. Back at Edwards, advanced testing of both the YF-12A and SR-71A's continued. In May 1965, the Air Force's YF-12 Test Force set seven new speed and altitude records, including a maximum speed over a straight course of 2,070.101 mph. But such figures gave little indication of the plane's maximum performance potential, a potential highly classified to this day. NASA and the Air Force launched a joint test program on the YF-12 in late 1969, using the plane for aerodynamic and propulsion studies as well as measuring its structural characteristics. One caught fire, forcing its crew to safely eject before it blew up, but two others, known as "935" and "937" (the latter being a

YF-12C having some features of the SR-71A), flew for nearly a decade on NASA research flights from the Dryden Flight Research Center at Edwards, crewed by test pilots Fitz Fulton and Don Mallick, and flight test engineers Vic Horton and Ray Young.

NASA's flight test program on the Blackbirds has provided a wealth of data that is certain to be incorporated in the design of future sustained-cruise supersonic aircraft. Some of the research areas explored in the course of hundreds of experimental flights included studying high-altitude turbulence, integrated aerodynamic and propulsion controls, analysis of propulsion-system operation, tests of advanced structural materials, and the problems of holding a particular altitude when cruising at Mach 3—a critical issue for the future development of any commercial supersonic transport. Interesting conditions turned up; for example, at Mach 3, fully 50 per cent of the Blackbird's drag came simply from air vented out of inlet bypass doors. Indeed, in the "gray area" between the disciplines of stability and control on the one hand and flight propulsion on the other, researchers discovered that, under some conditions, motion of the adjustable inlet "spikes" and the inlet bypass doors could actually cause the craft to alter its flight path—hence the interest in integrating the operation of the propulsion inlet system and the operation of the plane's flight controls.

Sometimes things did not go as planned, either. On one flight in the YF-12C, a stuck inlet spike caused the plane to burn fuel at a tremendous rate, forcing Don Mallick and Ray Young to make an emergency landing in Nevada. On another flight, the agency's YF-12A, "935," shed its huge ventral fin in flight; the big fin ruptured a fuel tank, and Mallick and Young brought the ailing plane back to Edwards trailing a long banner of fuel vapor. On another flight, while undertaking a complicated heat-transfer investigation at Mach 3, the YF-12A suddenly encountered a simultaneous "unstart" on both engines. As it descended earthward, the test crew setting up a relight procedure, the chase plane—NASA's YF-12C—also experienced multiple unstarts! Back at Edwards, mission controllers listened anxiously, but both crews managed to fire up their recalcitrant beasts and limp back home.

Today, visitors to the Air Force Museum can see "935" on exhibit; it stands in marked contrast to the rest of the museum's collection. Occasionally, at an air show or under special conditions, one may see an SR-71A from close up, but much more infrequently, for today, more than fifteen years since its initial flight, this airplane is still the world's most advanced reconnaissance aircraft. What will its successors be like? It is a commentary on the state of aeronautical research that the United States has not been able to proceed with another high-Mach aircraft that is anywhere in the league of the SR-71A. But perhaps the choice of a successor to the Blackbird is a question best left up to the Skunk Works itself, one of whose senior engineers is fond of remarking, "We did things ten years ago that you haven't even heard of."[5]

The only other air-breathing Mach 3+ manned aircraft the United States has flown was, of course, the huge North American XB-70A Valkyrie, a contemporary of the Blackbirds. Unfortunately, this beautiful six-engine airplane was, at the time of its development, the wrong design for the wrong mission. Conceived as a high-altitude strategic bomber, even before its first flight it fell victim to the extremely rapid advances made by the Soviet Union in the field of surface-to-air missile technology. Those advances spelled defeat for any airplane attempting such a penetration of Soviet airspace, and the aircraft was incapable of undertaking a feasible low-altitude penetration. Nevertheless, NASA, the FAA, and the Air Force expected that this large supersonic airplane could furnish information directly applicable to the planned American Mach 3+ SST then under consideration (and which would, of course, fall victim to technological inadequacy and the congressional ax in 1971). Accordingly, North American completed two of the monstrous planes, shapely delta aircraft with canard control surfaces and twin vertical fins, as well as wing tips that could be lowered in flight to furnish necessary supersonic stability. Each of its large General Electric XJ93 turbojets could produce 30,000 pounds of thrust. Like the A-11, it posed enormous design challenges, for example, having to survive 630 degrees F., use its own fuel supply as a "heat sink," and have a complicated inlet ramp system to adjust the position of shock waves so that the engines would receive an adequate amount of air under ideal conditions. It had a length of 189 feet, a height of 30 feet, and spanned 105 feet, being the world's largest supersonic airplane, weighed over 250 tons, and featured a structure of mixed titanium and brazed stainless steel "honeycomb."

The first XB-70A, a gleaming white airplane, took to the air from North American's Palmdale plant on September 21, 1964, for a short trip across the Mojave to Edwards. But after takeoff, test pilots Alvin White and Joseph Cotton discovered that the flight would be out of the ordinary. The landing gear would not retract, one engine had to be shut down as a precaution, and when White and Cotton did land the roaring giant on Edwards Runway 04, it blew out most of its tires, coming to a halt with dramatic orange flames boiling from its landing gear. Nevertheless, in early October it returned to the air, and then, on its third flight, went supersonic. On March 24, 1965, it first broke Mach 2. In July 1965, the second XB-70A joined the test program. The second plane had wing dihedral to give it better supersonic stability, a more refined inlet control system, and much more extensive instrumentation for recording research data. Both Valkyries now proceeded to exceed Mach 3 routinely, starting, appropriately enough, with a flight to Mach 3.02 on October 14, 1965, eighteen years to the day since Chuck Yeager had first whiplashed the Mojave with a sonic boom.

Like the A-11 Blackbirds, the pure-white Valkyries needed a lot of airspace, and their test flights often covered whole tracts of the Far West. Unlike the smaller and lighter Blackbirds, the XB-70A's needed time to build up to Mach 3. On a typical flight, the North American or Air Force (and later NASA) test crew would take off from Edwards, afterburners crackling, climb at Mach 0.95 to about 32,000 feet, again light the burners, and accelerate past the speed of sound, lowering the outer wing panels to full down position by the time the large research plane had reached Mach 1.4. Under the best of all possible conditions, a Valkyrie could go from brake release to Mach 3 in about thirty minutes.

Like the Blackbirds, pilots of the Valkyries found them difficult to hold at a particular altitude, and the large planes would often seesaw through the air at Mach 3, drifting above and below their assigned altitude by as much as 2,000 feet (not surprising, since a 1-degree pitch change could induce a 3,000-foot-per-minute rate of climb or descent). Clear-air turbulence was quite uncomfortable to pilots sitting at the end of the long, snake-like fuselage. Even worse was "unstart" caused by poor inlet-ramp performance. If an "unstart" occurred, the entire plane would buffet badly for about ten seconds while the crew got the ramps and engines sorted out again. One B-70 pilot remarked that unstart might not damage an SST transport, but at its next stop, passengers would almost certainly disembark and take the next available train!

There were other, more serious problems, especially with the first airplane. The lack of dihedral on its wing caused it to exhibit generally poor stability characteristics above Mach 2.5. But its major difficulty involved in-flight shedding of its bonded-steel honeycomb skin! Poor bonding techniques led to the XB-70A actually peeling substantial portions of its skin on Mach 3 flights. The second airplane did not exhibit this problem, but NASA eventually decided to limit the first airplane to Mach 2.7 when they received charge of the Valkyrie. In support of the nation's SST effort, the Air Force and NASA announced a joint program to study the operational aspects of SST-like aircraft (including sonic-boom strength and propagation), to begin in mid-June 1966. NASA designated Joseph A. Walker as the agency's project pilot.

Joe Walker was, at the time, NASA's chief pilot at the agency's Flight Research Center at Edwards, and a test pilot much respected within the flight testing community. A physicist, Walker had contributed substantially to such early programs as the X-1, the advanced X-1E (nicknamed "Little Joe," in his honor), the occasionally frightening X-3 and X-5, a B-47 aeroelasticity study, and the X-15. Flying the third of the X-15's, he had flown to a height of 67 miles, then executed a precision reentry and landing from that height. A gregarious, pleasant airman with a "country-boy" manner that belied a fine technical mind, Joe Walker could lay claim to being the nation's finest research pilot during the 1960s. But fate was to deal him a cruel blow.

On June 8, 1966, the second XB-70A thundered aloft from Edwards on a checkout flight for a new Air Force project test pilot, Carl Cross, and to calibrate its airspeed system as well as take some sonic-boom data over a special test range. And the flight plan also included a "fluff" item: a rendezvous with four airplanes also powered by General Electric jet engines for some in-flight public-relations photography. After completing all the requisite duties called for in the flight plan, Valkyrie pilot Al White and copilot Carl Cross headed for Lake Isabella, the rendezvous point, followed by a T-38 trainer piloted by Pete Hoag and Joe Cotton. There a Navy Phantom from Point Mugu, a Northrop YF-5A from Edwards, the T-38, and the XB-70A all joined up—together with a Lockheed F-104N from NASA's Flight Research Center, piloted by Joe Walker. Clouds forced the gaggle to divert to the vicinity of Three Sisters Dry Lakes, where they set up a tight racetrack pattern, with the T-38 and the Phantom off the Valkyrie's left wing, and the F-104N and the YF-5A off its right wing. A passing F-104 on a test mission saw the formation and noticed that the F-104N and the YF-5A were flying an extremely tight formation off the XB-70A's right wing.

Forty-three minutes after forming up, as an escorting Learjet took photos, Joe Walker's Starfighter closed with the gigantic Valkyrie, his horizontal stabilizer touching the downturned outer wing panel of the XB-70A. The F-104N, caught in the powerful turbulent vortex rolling off the leading edge of the huge delta wing, hooked its wing against that of the XB-70A, spinning around violently, smashing across both of the Valkyrie's vertical fins, and then breaking up as it hit the bomber's left wing, exploding in flames. Joe Walker was dead. And in the huge bomber, time was running out for Carl Cross.

White and Cross did not realize that the plane had been hit—the long structure had damped out the impact, and the initial radio calls of "Midair! Midair!" as the flock of escorts scattered caused White to suspect that two of the escorts might have collided. For sixteen seconds, the mortally wounded Valkyrie sailed serenely along, and then it abruptly yawed and rolled to the right, tumbling over so violently that Al White thought the nose would break off. Hoag and Cotton radioed, "Bail out, bail out, bail out" over and over, and finally one of the XB-70A's escape capsules appeared, under a parachute canopy. White was out—but in seriously injured condition, for the capsule's clamshell doors closed prematurely, injuring his shoulder. Worse was to come. The landing-shock attenuation bag did not deploy, and Al White took a 45 g impact load that left him with severe internal injuries, though he recovered. Carl Cross's ejection system also failed to function properly, but he was unluckier, and perished in the wreckage. . . .

The loss of the second XB-70A drastically altered research plans for the airplane. But airplanes can be replaced—test pilots cannot. The loss of Joe Walker stunned the nation's flight testing community as much as the death of Eddie Allen had, over two decades earlier. It is a measure of his well-deserved popularity that some of his fellow test pilots petitioned NASA to rename the Flight Research Center in his honor. Though the effort was unsuccessful, Joe Walker has a suitable monument at Edwards: the little X-1E, plinth-mounted in front of the Dryden Flight Research Center.

The Air Force quickly lost interest in the XB-70A program following the loss of the second Valkyrie and, a year later, turned over program responsibility to NASA. NASA flew the first aircraft for the next two years on SST-related research, piloted by Fitz Fulton, Don Mallick, Van Shepard, Joe Cotton, and Emil "Ted" Sturmthal, before retiring it in 1969. Much of its research had examined the sonic-boom problem. As a result, the exuberant holdover atmosphere of the 1950s that tolerated the occasional sonic boom gave way to a more sober realization that it could be plain annoying, especially on a routine basis, and might, under certain circumstances, even be damaging. The XB-70A, having the size of an SST and an equivalent sonic-boom "footprint," provided quantitative data indicating that overland SST operations would generate intolerable sonic-boom phenomena. By and large, the XB-70A was not as productive a program as, say, the Blackbird effort. Today the surviving XB-70A is at the Air Force Museum. There visitors can still marvel at its futuristic look, blending an angular shape with a cobra-like body. Its immense size symbolizes the immense complexity and grandiose vision that spawned its development. It is huge, like the dinosaurs—and like the dinosaurs, it has passed from the scene.

CONCORDE, A NEW GENERATION OF JET TRANSPORTS—AND NEW PROBLEMS

The whole American SST effort collapsed in 1971, a disaster for the city of Seattle and an unnerving experience for Boeing. The collapse had a variety of causes, including the peculiarities of American domestic politics, a reaction against the "military-industrial complex," unsupported generalizations that it would cause environmental havoc, as well as thoughtful and cogent arguments that pointed to its extravagant fuel consumption and questioned its technical design. What was truly unfortunate was the manner of the cancellation: Congress simply cut off all funding, terminating plans to complete two of the Boeing SST prototypes. It must be noted that Congress could have terminated the program but still funded completion of the two test aircraft. Indeed, it cost more to cancel the program outright than it would have to complete both prototypes *and* then have flown each in a one-hundred-hour flight test program! The economic dislocation on Seattle would have been far less severe, and the gains to our knowledge about SST operating problems and impact upon the environment would have been tremendous. As it was, nothing remained. The Cassandras had made their point, and flight research itself was the poorer for the result.

In contrast, Great Britain and France proceeded with the development of their own supersonic jetliner, the seductively beautiful Concorde. Unlike the United States, which had hoped to build a Mach 3 SST (a decision that greatly increased its cost and complexity), the Anglo-French design team settled on Mach 2, enabling them to use conventional structural materials, though they still faced considerable technical challenges. They met the challenges with a creative research and development program heavily dependent on blending ground research with flight research aloft. Special research airplanes tested the Concorde's engine system and wing shape. Then, starting in 1969, the first prototypes of the Concorde itself flew, each loaded with about twelve tons of specialized recording instrumentation. Test crews headed by André Turcat, Brian Trubshaw, and Jean Franchi undertook a cautious, incremental approach to Mach 2. On March 2, 1969, the first Concorde flew at Toulouse. Seven months later, on October 1, it first exceeded Mach 1, nearly twenty-two years since the flight of the XS-1 at Muroc. Over a year later, on November 4, 1970, it exceeded Mach 2 for the first time. Thereafter, the first two Concordes and five others assigned to the test program thoroughly proved out the configuration and characteristics of the revolutionary airplane. When Concorde finally entered airline service with Air France and British Airways, in 1975, it was the world's most thoroughly tested jetliner, with more than a decade of ground testing and nearly four thousand flight test hours having been accumulated. One can argue that the Concorde's operating economics are undesirable in a fuel-conscious age, but one cannot criticize it on the basis of its technical design, for it has been thoroughly tested and thoroughly proved.

Concorde, of course, does not constitute the only air transport story of the 1960s. During that turbulent decade, the first of the "jumbo" jet-powered transport aircraft appeared: Lockheed's controversial C-5A and Boeing's 747. At the same time, the practical medium-range jetliner also made its debut, in the form of the highly successful Boeing 727 trijet. And for the first time, the business executive could rely on his own personal jet, typified by the graceful and speedy Learjet, which first flew in 1963 and could outclimb a 1950s-vintage F-86 Sabre to 40,000 feet and outturn the older fighter once it got there!

The new jetliners were not entirely trouble-free, and their idiosyncrasies required a great deal of cautious study, leading noted multiengine test pilot David P. Davies to write what subsequently became a jet transport "bible," Handling the Big Jets, which thoroughly explored the qualitative differences between the new generation of airliners and their predecessors. Unexpected problems cropped up, sometimes with unpleasant results. One such was the problem of the "super stall," whereby a transport having a "T-tail" configuration could enter a stall and then simply lack the ability to recover. Sadly, such an accident in a BAC 1-11 claimed the lives of a crack British test crew headed by the legendary Mike Lithgow, one of Europe's finest test pilots.

Another and even graver problem concerned wake vortices. Because of the pressure differential above and below a wing, every airplane streams a vortex from its wing tips, sort of a horizontal tornado. The strength of the vortex is directly related to the size and weight of the aircraft, and the wake vortex streaming behind a "jumbo jet" such as a C-5A or a 747 can have a rotational rate as high as 150 mph and persist as far as twenty miles behind the airplane. These invisible whirlwinds can easily throw other aircraft out of control, including smaller jet transports. Small general-aviation airplanes face a special threat.

Flight researchers quickly recognized that the vortices posed a twofold problem, posing a hazard and also robbing the larger planes of performance due to drag. This eventually led to a series of research flights by NASA and the FAA. In one test, a T-37 deliberately entered a vortex four miles behind a 747 and did two inadvertent snap rolls, developing a roll rate of 200 degrees per second. At low altitude, such an episode could well prove fatal. The studies did demonstrate that extending the spoiler surfaces above the transport's outer wing panels did reduce the magnitude of the vortex, leading FAA test pilot Joseph Tymczyszyn to remark that he would "prefer to fly three miles behind a 747 using spoiler alleviation than six miles behind one in standard configuration."[6] Today's air traveler flies with greater safety as a result of flight research on these and related air transport problems.

X-15: PRELUDE TO SPACE

The past two decades, however, will be remembered primarily as the period in which humanity first journeyed into space. With the steps taken so far, we have learned more about our capacity for technological and scientific accomplishment. And we have also acquired a greater appreciation for the fragility of our planet Earth.

On March 16, 1926, Robert H. Goddard, a physics professor at Clark University, fired the world's first liquid-fuel rocket. The test flight lasted only a few seconds and covered only 184 feet, but it constituted, nevertheless, the "Kitty Hawk" of rocketry, a true milestone that had opened up the pathway to the stars. Unfortunately, Goddard's desire for isolation and his obsession with secrecy stymied the subsequent prewar development of American rocketry, and the next major steps in the development of rocket propulsion were made by Nazi Germany.

As early as 1937, aircraft manufacturer Ernst Heinkel and rocketry expert Wernher von Braun had directed the first experiments with airplanes utilizing liquid-fuel rocket engines. German test pilot Erich Warsitz piloted a piston-engine He 112 fighter with a small booster rocket mounted in the rear of the fuselage. Encouraged, Heinkel next proceeded with development of a pure-rocket testbed (complementing the testbed being simultaneously developed for Von Ohain's jet engine), and this aircraft, the He 176, completed a very shaky first flight on June 20, 1939, flying less than fifty seconds before Warsitz gingerly set it back down on earth. But small developments often lead to big ones, and before the end of the war, Germany had placed a flashy (if mediocre) rocket-propelled interceptor, the Me 163 Komet, into service.

The Nazis had also undertaken the development of a large liquid-fuel rocket-propelled terror weapon, the V-2, which caused thousands of direct Allied civilian casualties, and thousands of others among slave laborers worked to death building it. A major theoretical study by two other leading rocketeers, Eugen Sänger and Irene Bredt, postulated the design and construction of a large rocket-propelled winged spacecraft capable of orbital bombardment missions. Von Braun's own Peenemünde team examined various winged versions and follow-ons to the V-2, flight testing one of these, the so-called A-4b, in early 1945. Fortunately, most of these remained paper studies, and in the major wartime technological and scientific sweepstakes—the development of an atomic bomb—Nazi Germany was not even seriously in the running.

Following the collapse of Hitler's state, all of Nazi Germany's technical work became grist for the ex-Allies' technical mills. Wartime fraternity quickly chilled amid the quest for artifacts, documents, and personnel from the fallen regime. America's major acquisitions were trainloads of V-2's, and most of the Peenemünde staff, together with Von Braun and, later, his supervisor, Walter Dornberger. Shortly thereafter, the first of America's own captured V-2 rockets was racing aloft on research flights from White Sands, New Mexico. As at Peenemünde, many of the missiles met unplanned ends. One hooked south, crashing near a cemetery just outside of Juárez, Mexico. But these trials formed much of the basis for America's major postwar rocket programs, all the way from the first Redstones through the Jupiter and on up to the mighty Saturns, of Apollo fame. And thousands of miles away, at Kapustin Yar, in the midst of the Russian steppes, Soviet technicians under the direction of Sergei Korolev were also launching captured V-2's and learning.

With the powerful rocket engines now available to engineers, many began wondering about the possibility of manned space flight, either by flying out into space in a special winged airplane-like rocket, or by boosting into space in something more closely resembling a V-2. The Sänger-Bredt report gave encouragement to those who thought that hypersonic flight—flight at speeds five times that of sound and above—might be possible, including winged reentry from space at about Mach 25, with all the concomitant problems of heating, guidance, and stability and control. As a result, as the 1940s gave way to the 1950s, a number of scientists and engineers gave thought to America's future in space. Many believed that the best (and most reasonable) course of action would be to develop specialized hypersonic rocket-propelled flight-research vehicles, eventually leading to an orbital craft that could provide the necessary technology base for the later development of orbital space transportation and military weapons systems. This thinking paved the way for the X-15 and the abortive X-20 "Dyna-Soar," as well as forming the initial stimulus for what eventually emerged as the NASA Space Shuttle.

What these adherents to winged flight missed, of course, was the emphasis on ballistic and semiballistic spacecraft that eventually spawned both the Soviet and the American satellite and manned-spacecraft programs, such as Vostok, Mercury, Gemini, Soyuz, and Apollo. And this ballistic wave grew out of the tremendous impact made in the 1940s and 1950s in both the Soviet Union and the United States on the development of intermediate- and intercontinental-range ballistic missiles (IRBM's and ICBM's).

Any such manned-spacecraft effort would, of course, require a very cautious and thorough incremental approach involving development research vehicles of increasing complexity and performance. The early "Round One" rocket research airplanes such as the X-1, X-2, and D-558-2 series provided useful information on such questions as aerodynamic heating, high-altitude physiological protection, use of "reaction control" thrusters, and reusable rocket propulsion systems. Any "Round Two" effort (what became the X-15) would have to confront such questions as use of superalloy construction, hypersonic stability and control, pilot control during atmospheric exit and reentry, and the approach and landing problem. Any "Round Three" (as NACA dubbed what eventually became Dyna-Soar) would have to consider actual orbital problems, including the demanding lifting reentry from space with some form of thermal protection system for the returning spacecraft. First, of course, came Round Two. And by the end of 1954, a joint Air Force-Navy-NACA team had drawn up the specifications for what would eventually become the most ambitious of the rocket airplanes actually flown, the X-15. The specs called for an air-launched airplane capable of flying at 6,600 feet per second (over 4,100 mph), withstanding 1,200 degrees F., and attaining an altitude of 250,000 feet. Following an intense design competition between Bell, Republic, Douglas, and North American, the Air Force informed North American in September 1955 that it had won the competition. North American subsequently received a contract for the fabrication of three of the research airplanes.

Eventually, the hypersonic X-15 program demonstrated just how complex and well organized the flight testing process had become by mid-century. Behind the pilot and his research plane were literally thousands of people working with him nationwide. The X-15 program also required creation of a special test corridor 485 miles long and 50 miles wide, running from Utah to Edwards, just for the use of this rocket-propelled aircraft, with radar tracking, telemetry, real-time physiological monitoring of the pilot, and interstation communications and data-link services. Nothing this extensive had previously existed for flight research, and the X-15's special "High Range" (as it came to be known) foreshadowed the worldwide tracking network later developed and utilized on the subsequent American manned space program. The X-15 pilot required, just for his safety, a complete environmental protection system as well as a full-pressure suit (the descendant of Wiley Post's original efforts) in case the aircraft lost cabin pressurization at high altitudes. Aeromedical experts decided to furnish him with "real-time" (i.e., as it was happening) physiological monitoring in case he got into difficulty, as well as to provide data useful for future manned space-flight operations. An ejection seat capable of operation at Mach 4 and altitudes up to 120,000 feet afforded him a means of abandoning his complex airplane if that became necessary.

The airplane itself, of course, made its own demands upon its developers. At its heart was a large, 57,000-pound-thrust rocket engine burning a mixture of liquid oxygen and anhydrous ammonia, the Thiokol XLR-99. Capable of being throttled from 40 to 100 per cent of its rated thrust, this powerplant presented so many difficulties for its developers that it was not ready for flight when North American completed the first X-15 airplanes, and as a result, the initial flight trials were undertaken with the X-15 powered by two of the earlier XLR-11 engines (used in the X-1) mounted one above the other in the tail cone of the airplane. The plane had three separate control sticks—a conventional stick for landing and touchdown, a "sidestick" mounted off to the side of the cockpit for the pilot to use during launch, acceleration, climb-out, and reentry prior to the landing approach, and a reaction controller to manage small hydrogen-peroxide thruster jets to provide tiny bursts of H_2O_2 steam to keep the craft under control at the extreme altitudes where its conventional aerodynamic control surfaces would be ineffective. It also had a landing gear consisting of a nosewheel unit and two skids under the after fuselage.

For the requisite hypersonic stability, it had a large, wedge-shaped vertical fin above and below the fuselage that resembled a huge cleaver. The lower half of the bottom fin could be jettisoned by the pilot prior to landing so that the skids could reach the lakebed and cushion the touchdown. It utilized a then-radical structure of Inconel X chrome-nickel alloy "heat sink" construction, for in the Mach 6 "thermal thicket" it would encounter temperatures on the surface as high as 1,200 degrees F. At the end, North American engineers under the direction of Harrison "Stormy" Storms and Charles Feltz, with the valuable assistance of Scotty Crossfield (who left the NACA and joined North American to help them with the project), gave the Air Force, the NACA (soon to become NASA), and the Navy what they wanted: a rugged, dependable aeronautical research tool designed to probe the frontiers of space at theretofore unattainable airspeeds and altitudes.

The X-15 most closely resembled a long, heavy dart, with narrow wings, a rakish tail, and a hooded cockpit. It spanned a mere 22 feet, with a length of 50 feet. North American completed the first one in October 1958, and then Vice-President Richard M. Nixon presided over the gala roll-out ceremony, a traditional aerospace-industry event, held at Los Angeles on October 15, 1958. The reason for this attention was, of course, as much political as technical: on October 4, 1957, the Soviet Union had orbited Sputnik I, the first earth satellite, and the X-15 now became a vital segment of America's national prestige. It would be disastrous, all concerned agreed, if anything were to cause the program to fail. And so the responsibility for the first contractor flights rested in the capable hands of none other than A. Scott Crossfield, the man who first broke Mach 2.

THE X-15: RESEARCH ON THE EDGE OF SPACE

North American trucked the first X-15 to Edwards the day after its roll-out ceremony, and the second aircraft joined it at the lakebed in April 1959. The third remained at North American pending completion with the first available XLR-99 "large engine." The first two thus had the interim XLR-11's (each boosted to produce 8,000 pounds of thrust) and were thus capable of flying at only a little above Mach 3, more than satisfactory for the first contractor proving flights. The National Aeronautics and Space Administration, created toward the end of 1958, had selected NASA test pilot Joe Walker as its project pilot. The Air Force had at first selected Iven Kincheloe, but following his death, they chose another experienced veteran, Bob White. The Navy selected test pilot Forrest "Pete" Petersen. These three would fly the X-15 on its initial research flights following Crossfield's contractor demonstration program.

The first captive flights got underway in March 1959, the X-15 being carried to altitude under the right wing of a modified Boeing B-52 Stratofortress. A number of nagging failures of the craft's auxiliary power units (to provide on-board electrical power) plagued the early flights. The X-15's on-board power generators would burn out, sending clouds of smoke into the cockpit. "Smoke in the cockpit" became such a by-word that when, on the final captive flight, Crossfield muttered "Holy smoke!" about an unrelated matter, North American engineer Charles Feltz (monitoring the mission at "Earphone One," the main mission-control center) leaped to his feet with an anguished "Wha'd he say? Wha'd he say?" Eventually the team solved the burnout problem, and next turned to the first real milestone, a free flight.

In preparation for the first flight, Crossfield had flown a number of "low-lift-to-drag" approaches in F-100's and F-104's, simulating the rocklike characteristics of a gliding X-15 by making steep nose-high approaches with idle engine power and the craft in "dirty" (i.e., high-drag) configuration. He could also draw upon his years of research flying with the NACA, when he had handled some of the trickiest of the nation's X-series airplanes. On June 8, 1955, Crossfield dropped away from the B-52 mother ship at 38,000 feet, flying the first of the three X-15's. It handled well during the descent, and as it sank down to a touchdown, Crossfield blew off the ventral fin bottom and set up his landing approach. And then the X-15 turned sour, beginning to pitch wildly, as the oversensitive boosted control system took every pilot control input and magnified it. Crossfield tried to get into phase with the pitching, but to no avail. He recalled later:

> Now the nose was rising and falling like the bow of a skiff in a heavy sea. Although I was putting in maximum control I could not subdue the motions. The X-15 was porpoising wildly, sinking toward the desert at 200 miles an hour. I would have to land at the bottom of an oscillation, timed perfectly; otherwise, I knew, I would break the bird. I lowered the flaps and gear.
>
> My mind was almost completely absorbed in the tremendous task of saving the X-15, of getting it on the ground in one piece. But I could not push back a terrible thought that was forming. *Something was dreadfully wrong. We had pulled a tremendous goof. The X-15 in spite of all our sweat and study, our attempt at perfection, had become completely unstable.*[7]

Fortunately, on one oscillation, just as the nose pitched up, the tailskids pounded into the lakebed and the X-15's nose gear then slammed down on the lake, the rocket plane streaming a long rooster tail of playa dust as it skidded across the lake, Crossfield "engulfed in disappointment" as he sat in the cockpit.

Things were not what they seemed to be, however, and despite the wild first flight, the X-15 did not have any serious design flaws. Rather, a valve in the control system required adjustment to prevent the pilot's control inputs from getting out of phase with the actual operation of the control surfaces. With this simple adjustment, the X-15 demonstrated fine flying characteristics. On September 17, 1959, flying the second X-15, Crossfield completed the first rocket-powered flight, a simple check flight to Mach 2.11—pretty tame stuff by 1959. In early November, however, another check flight nearly ended in disaster. Just after launch, an engine explosion shook the plane. Crossfield was unable to jettison all the craft's propellants and had to make an emergency landing on Rosamond Dry Lake, a few miles from Edwards. During the landing, the heavy propellant load broke the back of the X-15, necessitating long and costly repairs. NASA accepted the first X-15 in early 1960; in March and April, Joe Walker and Bob White undertook its first research flights, beginning the actual X-15 research program.

Obviously, until the X-15 received its large rocket engine, it had only limited utility as a research tool equipped with just the two XLR-11's. A ground explosion while testing the large engine in the third X-15 virtually destroyed the craft's midsection and tail, and could have claimed Crossfield's life, for he was sitting in the cockpit when the plane blew up, because of a stuck pressure regulator. The plane's rugged structure and sealed cockpit saved him. Eventually, in November 1960, Crossfield demonstrated the large XLR-99 engine during a flight in the re-engined second X-15 to Mach 2.97. The flight was, of course, no challenge to the X-15's capabilities, the large engine essentially idling as it propelled the craft at nearly Mach 3. NASA, the Air Force, and the Navy now turned to using the X-15's for what they had been intended: aerodynamic research at Mach 6. The program went relatively quickly and smoothly.

By the end of 1961, the X-15 had attained its Mach 6 design goal and had reached altitudes in excess of 200,000 feet. Generally, the flights demonstrated remarkable correlation between wind-tunnel test results and those acquired from flight testing, with the exception of drag around the after end of the craft. Heating at Mach 6 buckled a portion of the wing leading edge, requiring redesign, and fractured some of the outer panes of the X-15's multilayer cockpit windshield. The "cruciform" tail contributed, oddly enough, to a serious roll problem that prevented the X-15 from being flown at angles of attack greater than 20 degrees during reentry. When engineers removed the lower portion of the ventral fin (the jettisonable portion), the problem disappeared, and the X-15 eventually completed reentry profiles with an angle of attack as great as 26 degrees and a steep descending-flight-path angle of -38 degrees, at speeds up to Mach 6. This presented, in fact, a much trickier and demanding reentry piloting problem than an actual return from earth orbit.

A number of other research pilots soon joined Joe Walker, Pete Petersen, and Bob White on the program. From the Air Force came Bob Rushworth, William "Pete" Knight, Joe Engle, and Mike Adams. NASA contributed Neil Armstrong, Jack McKay, Milt Thompson, and Bill Dana. Their flights demonstrated that pilots could fly a winged rocket-propelled vehicle out of the atmosphere, change from conventional aerodynamic controls to using reaction-control thrusters, and then fly back and glide down to a precision landing using energy-management techniques. Their flights also reaffirmed the wisdom of manned research vehicles: had the X-15's been strictly ground-controlled, they would have crashed on thirteen of the program's first forty-four flights.

The program was not without its share of close calls. One day in 1962, for example, Milt Thompson took off in a NASA F-104 to check on weather conditions "up range" before making an X-15 flight. After lowering flaps for an approach to Edwards, the F-104 rolled crazily—only one flap had deployed. For a while, he was able to barely keep the plane in control by using full power and full opposite aileron. But the plane obviously could not land that way. He tried raising the flaps to takeoff position, but the plane immediately went out of control. On the ground, NASA monitors heard Thompson exclaim, "It's going!" Then silence.

And then, from "Eddy tower" came word that a pall of smoke had blossomed on the Edwards bombing range. . . . "The gloom was so thick," one engineer recalled, "you could cut it with a knife." Then, a half hour later, Thompson drove up to the main entrance of the center, delivered by a pickup truck that had come across him in the desert. The plucky pilot had stayed with the faithless plane through four rolls before finally ejecting from it.

The Air Force also developed a special rocket-boosted version of the F-104 that could exceed 100,000 feet (the NF-104), enabling pilots to execute X-15-like approaches from high altitude. It also featured reaction-control thrusters for high-altitude control. This nasty beast, three of which were built, claimed one pilot's life and almost claimed that of Chuck Yeager, who had returned to Edwards in the 1960s as commandant of the Air Force test pilot school. Yeager ejected from a spinning NF-104 low over the desert after tumbling from over 100,000 feet. He was struck and seriously injured by the ejection seat, suffering burns from its still-dribbling rocket exhaust, but recovered to fly again and resume his career.

Another X-15 simulation flight in an F-104 almost ended disastrously for two Air Force test pilots, Dave Scott (who later flew on the Gemini and Apollo programs) and Mike Adams (who later joined the X-15 program). During a landing approach, a propulsion-system failure caused the heavy Starfighter to mush toward the runway. Both men made the correct decision for their survival. Adams, sitting in back, ejected. Scott stayed with the plane through its crash landing, and a postaccident investigation revealed that if he had ejected, his seat would have worked only partially, probably killing him. On the other hand, the Starfighter's huge engine had broken loose and would certainly have killed the hapless Adams had he not "punched out."

During a flight in the first X-15, Air Force test pilot Pete Knight experienced a total electrical failure while climbing through 107,000 feet at Mach 4.17. Suddenly, in the world's most complex and sophisticated airplane, Knight lost all computed flight information and aircraft guidance. Calmly, he set up a visual approach—no mean feat—and managed, during the descent, to restart one generator unit, giving him some instrument indications. He glided down to a safe emergency landing at Mud Lake, receiving a well-earned Distinguished Flying Cross for the feat.

On other flights in the modified second X-15, thermal stresses caused the nose gear to extend at Mach 4, generating nearly uncontrollable motions and giving pilot Bob Rushworth "an awful bang." Rushworth retained control, and as expected, the damaged tires blew out on landing, the plane coming to rest on the magnesium rims of its wheels. Such episodes stand as a tribute to the skill and courage of the pilots involved in them.

Eventually, the X-15 program changed completely, from just hypersonic aerodynamic research to using the first and third aircraft to carry special "experiment packages" into near space and using the second aircraft for special advanced reentry tests. In November 1962, during an emergency landing at Mud Lake, Nevada, the second X-15 crashed, seriously injuring NASA pilot Jack McKay. Though he survived to fly again, his injuries, sadly, forced his retirement from flight testing and eventually contributed to his death. Despite the severe damage to the airplane, X-15 program officials decided to rebuild it, with huge, jettisonable fuel tanks for increased performance. The virtually new aircraft was redesignated the X-15A-2, and it completed its maiden flight at Edwards in late June 1964. Later, in 1967, a dummy ramjet installation was added in support of a NASA ramjet research project, and a special claylike "ablative" thermal-protection coating was applied to enable the plane to safely attain flight speeds as high as Mach 7.5 without damaging its structure. NASA engineers hoped that tests of the coating would confirm that future reusable winged spacecraft could utilize a simple refurbishable ablator over a conventional structure, thus reducing development time, cost, and complexity.

On October 3, 1967, Pete Knight took the craft aloft for an all-out, maximum-speed attempt. It was a flight in the grand Edwards tradition. High over Nevada, Knight dropped away from the launch B-52, fired off the large engine, and began his climb. When the X-15A-2 exhausted its propellants from the two large external tanks he punched them off and rocketed onward, leveling off at full power just over 100,000 feet. The rocket plane, boosted by over 140 seconds of engine-burn time, shot to Mach 6.72, over 4,520 mph, the fastest winged flight to that date by a manned vehicle.

But all was not well with the airplane. Complex heating conditions seared the craft, and temperatures of over 3,000 degrees F. burned the ramjet model right off of its pylon mounting, punching a hole in the plane that acted like a ram air scoop shoveling superhot air into the craft and weakening the internal structure. A few more seconds would have spelled disaster. As it was, the unexpected flow interactions caused a failure in the craft's propellant jettison system, and Knight was left with the X-15A-2 nearly a ton heavier than planned. The X-15A-2 slowed, dropping down from the skies over Edwards, as the chase planes looked on in amazement at the blackened and charred research airplane, which resembled burnt firewood. Knight completed a successful landing, bringing this potentially dangerous flight to a pleasant close. It was the nearest that any of the X-15-series aircraft ever came to suffering major structural damage from aerodynamic heating, and it pointed to the occasional unexpected problems that can crop up during a flight testing program.

As one NASA engineer later stated, the X-15A-2's condition "was a surprise to all of us. If there had been any question that the airplane was going to come back in that shape, we never would have flown it."[8] To John Becker, NASA's X-15 founding father, the experience of Pete Knight and the X-15A-2 furnishes a valuable lesson for the future. Engineers and designers must "underscore the need for maximum attention to aerothermodynamic detail in design and preflight testing."[9] The X-15A-2, though repaired, never flew again, and today it is on exhibit at the Air Force Museum, the world's fastest airplane.

Following Pete Knight's epic flight, the X-15 program gradually entered its twilight. Sadly, at this point, the project claimed the life of test pilot Mike Adams. The third X-15 had flown primarily as a high-altitude research aircraft and experiments carrier, and featured a very advanced electronic control system. In 1963, on another of the program's milestones, NASA test pilot Joe Walker had attained an altitude of 354,200 feet—still a record for winged aircraft—and then glided down from that height to a precision landing on the Edwards lakebed. On November 15, 1967, during another altitude flight, the X-15 began a slow, gradual heading drift as it climbed upward. At its peak altitude, of 266,000 feet, it had yawed 15 degrees off its heading. While descending through 230,000 feet, it entered a Mach 5 spin. On the ground, mission controllers worked urgently to try to help Adams—possibly disoriented and confused from vertigo—to get down safely; a lack of instrumentation in the control room prevented them from understanding fully what was happening, and they realized they had only seconds left. Eventually Mike Adams recovered into a steep Mach 4+ dive at around 120,000 feet. And then the plane's complex flight-control system betrayed him, beginning a pitching oscillation that quickly built to destructive levels, a technical fault that spelled the end to Adams' heroic efforts to return the stricken X-15 to earth. At 62,000 feet, approaching the old mining town of Johannesburg, California, the wildly pitching X-15 broke up, killing its pilot. As a result of this tragic flight, NASA installed an X-15-type attitude indicator in the mission-control center to furnish controllers with "real-time" pitch, roll, heading, angle-of-attack, and sideslip information simultaneously available to the pilot of the actual airplane. Plans to modify the third X-15 as a slender delta-wing ramjet research aircraft had to be abandoned, and now only the original, first X-15 remained flying.

But not for long. Weather and maintenance problems caused rescheduling and cancellation of a number of flights. The X-15 had outlived its research utility, and NASA did not seek funding to support flight operations after December 1968. For nostalgic rather than scientific reasons, X-15 test personnel hoped to get to the magic 200 flight mark for the series, and on October 24, 1968, the first X-15 completed its 81st flight, the 199th flight of the entire X-15 series. A 200th flight seemed assured. But then maintenance and weather problems crept in. Time went by. Finally, on December 20, test crews had the X-15 and the B-52 "mated" and ready to go—and a snow squall struck Edwards! That afternoon, the sky cleared, but it was too late. Mother Nature had defeated any plans for the 200th flight. Technicians "de-mated" the pair, then left for a wake at Juanita's saloon. The operational X-15 logbook closed with the entry, "This ends an era in flight research history," and indeed it did. In 1969, NASA shipped the original X-15 to the Smithsonian Institution for permanent exhibition.

Without question, the X-15 constituted the most successful research airplane of all time. It contributed at least twenty-seven major advances to aerospace technology, ranging from being the first application of hypersonic theory and wind-tunnel work on an actual flight vehicle to demonstrating that a pilot could function in a weightless environment (this in the days before Project Mercury), and that a pilot could fly a lifting atmospheric reentry from space. It was the first aircraft to have a reusable "superalloy" structure capable of withstanding the stresses and thermal gradients of Mach 6 flight. Additionally, it made no less than sixteen "testbed" investigations, carrying research experiments ranging from ultraviolet stellar photography to micrometeorite collection. It had flown in support of the nation's Apollo program, carrying aloft experimental insulation for the Saturn booster, and advanced celestial-navigation equipment. The X-15 served as a general focal point for hypersonic research. Even before the program concluded, engineers and scientists had generated nearly eight hundred research reports, equivalent to the output of a typical four-thousand-person federal research center working full time for two years. Overall, it materially assisted in the derivation of future hypersonic aircraft design criteria and technology, helping pave the way for the later NASA Space Shuttle.

The decade-long X-15 test program spanned a tumultuous period in American history, from the self-confident and buoyantly optimistic 1950s to the doubt-filled 1960s. At the beginning of the X-15's flight research, Sputnik and successive Soviet space triumphs had shattered the myth of American omnipotence in rocketry. At the end of the X-15 program, America was on the eve of its Apollo triumph, the first manned lunar landing by a team of astronauts led by former X-15 pilot Neil Armstrong. While the X-15 was not a direct part of the American space program, it occupied a place in between purely atmospheric flight and flight in space, and preceded such space ventures as the abortive X-20A

Dyna-Soar effort. There were other half-air, half-space programs like the X-15.

In 1959, Air Force test pilot Joseph Kittinger lifted off in a series of special polyethylene high-altitude balloons in tests of pressure suits and parachutes at the fringes of the atmosphere. Kittinger undertook a number of courageous parachute jumps; the final test, project *Excelsior III*, had him leap from a balloon at an altitude of 102,800 feet. In related tests, the Navy ran a series of its own high-altitude balloon flights for research on upper-atmospheric conditions, physiological studies, and pressure-suit technology. On the final of these flights, Malcolm Ross and Victor Prather reached a record 113,700 feet in the open-gondola *Strato-Lab V* balloon, but the unfortunate Prather drowned during recovery operations at sea—a poignant and tragic end to a fine flight. (Balloon research has since come full circle from the days of the Montgolfiers and J. A. C. Charles, as has recently been reaffirmed by the heroic transatlantic flight of the crew of *Double Eagle II:* Ben Abruzzo, Larry Newman, and Maxie Anderson).

THE ROAD TO TRANQUILLITY BASE

The American manned-space-flight program triggered another stage in the continuing metamorphosis of the test pilot and flight researcher. When, in the late 1950s, space-program planners opted in favor of the "blunt body shape" for the initial Project Mercury man-in-space program, rather than a winged configuration such as a development of the X-15 or a Dyna-Soar-like craft, some of these planners believed that the days of having to have a qualified pilot—and preferably a test pilot—in command of such vehicles had come to an end. After all, the Mercury "capsule" would follow a basically ballistic reentry trajectory, with minimal piloting demands (it was thought). Indeed, the original NASA plan for hiring potential Mercury crewmen stated that the agency required individuals who had demonstrated willingness to accept hazards and tolerate rigorous and severe environmental conditions, and could react adequately in stressful or emergency conditions. Such characteristics could be met by those who had experience in such occupations as

> test pilot, crew member of experimental submarine or arctic or antarctic explorer. Or they may have been demonstrated during wartime combat or military training. Parachute jumping or mountain climbing or deep sea diving (including SCUBA). . . . Or they may have been demonstrated by experience as an observer-under-test. . . .[10]

Fortunately, common sense prevailed, and when President Dwight D. Ei-
senhower received the proposed plan he scratched it at once, and
directed that NASA look to the pool of trained military test pilots already available. As finally established, NASA determined that the first of
the agency's astronauts should be selected from trained test pilots who
were less than forty years old, less than five feet eleven inches in height,
in excellent physical condition, possessors of a bachelor's degree or equivalent, have a minimum of fifteen hundred hours total flying time, be a
rated jet pilot—and be a graduate of a recognized test pilot school. Yet
among the test-flying fraternity there were those who, used to the freedom of actual atmospheric flight, were unwilling to be simply ballistic
"spam in a can." As Edwards-test-pilot-turned-Gemini-and-Apollo-astro-
naut Michael Collins has written,

> Man, they were here to *fly*, not to be locked up in a can and shot around
> the world like ammunition. They flew, in smooth control, in command.
> They flew day after day, in various machines to prove various things, but
> they *flew*. In Project Mercury, on the other hand, one rode; granted
> there had been only one Mercury flight so far, Al Shepard's fifteen-
> minute up-and-downer, but he was a passenger, man, a talking monkey.[11]

Nevertheless, the space program did not lack for test pilot volunteers,
and no one could fault the first seven astronauts (Al Shepard, Gus Grissom, Wally Schirra, John Glenn, Scott Carpenter, Gordon Cooper, and
Donald "Deke" Slayton) on the basis of their test-flying background.
Eventually, others joined the ranks too, such as X-15 veterans Joe Engle
and Neil Armstrong, and many more. As Mercury gave way to Gemini,
and then Apollo, a gradual cry rose within the scientific community to
select not test pilots but scientists, an often not-so-hidden elitism. NASA
chose—and has continued—to select both test pilots *and* scientists, engineers, and medical personnel. But, in the early and dangerous days of the
first steps into space, NASA wisely recognized that the crews of the first
manned missions should be heavily weighted in favor of test pilots having strong backgrounds in the problems and complexities of flight
research. The test pilot-astronauts felt the same way; as one bluntly
stated, "It's a lot easier to train a test pilot to pick up a rock than it is to
train a scientist to land on the moon." And there were certainly instances
enough in the actual Mercury, Gemini, and Apollo program to confirm
the wisdom of NASA's emphasis.

On John Glenn's Mercury orbital flight, for example, mission controllers received a faulty indication that his heat shield had come loose.
Reluctantly they passed the word to the orbiting astronaut, who, taking
it in stride, piloted the craft on a precise and uneventful reentry. On
Gemini VIII, astronauts Neil Armstrong and Dave Scott suddenly were

confronted by an out-of-control thruster rocket that sent their spacecraft (docked with an Agena target vehicle) into a violent left roll. As the official Gemini program history reports,

> After backing away from the Agena, the spacecraft had started to whirl at a dizzying rate of one revolution per second. Armstrong suspected that the maneuvering thrusters were about finished. He and Scott were also having trouble seeing the overhead panel dials; their physiological limits seemed near. They were dizzy, and their vision was blurred. Something had to be done. "All that we've got left is the reentry control system," Armstrong said. "Press on," Scott responded. The two men began to throw switches to cut out the Orbit Attitude and Maneuvering System and cut in the reentry control system. Armstrong tried his hand controller—nothing. Scott tried his—still nothing. They started switching circuitry again—maybe something had been set in the wrong position.
> The hand controllers responded!
> Armstrong steadied the motion and then turned off one ring of the reentry control system to conserve fuel. He then carefully reactivated the maneuver thrusters; now they were able to tell that No. 8 had "failed on" —that is, it had stuck open![12]

With Gemini VIII back under control—albeit emergency—the two astronauts, with assistance from Mission Control at Houston, executed a successful reentry, splashing down off Okinawa, where rescue forces quickly picked them up none the worse for wear.

The professionalism and courage required of the nation's test pilot-astronauts were nowhere more evident than in the Apollo program itself. Poor design of the original Apollo Command Module had led to the deaths of Gus Grissom, Ed White, and Roger Chaffee during a check of the Apollo I spacecraft at Kennedy Space Center on January 27, 1967. The task of proving out the revised CM design fell to astronauts Wally Schirra, Donn Eisele, and Walter Cunningham, who undertook a grueling ten-day, twenty-hour earth orbital mission in Apollo VII that left no doubt that Apollo was ready for the moon.

A trickier question involved landing on the moon itself. Using a typical flight testing approach, engineers at the NASA Flight Research Center had developed a jet-and-rocket-propelled "flying bedstead" called the Lunar Landing Research Vehicle (LLRV). A "production version" built by Bell Aerosystems, the Lunar Landing Training Vehicle (LLTV), went into service at NASA, as did the original LLRV rebuilt to LLTV standards. The LLTV's used a jet engine to lift five sixths of the vehicle's weight (simulating lunar gravity), and the LLTV trainee astronaut could use small rocket engines to regulate his "lunar descent" while other reaction controls kept the craft from tumbling out of control.

Neil Armstrong flew many LLTV missions in preparation for the first lunar landing. On one flight in the rebuilt original LLRV, the strange craft suffered a loss of helium pressure in one of its propellant tanks, and the vital attitude control rockets shut down prematurely. As it started to nose up and roll over, Armstrong immediately ejected, safely descending by parachute as the stricken LLRV plunged into the Texas soil and exploded. A month before the actual Apollo XI mission, Armstrong had remarked that the LLTV flights were giving the astronauts "a very high level of confidence in the overall landing maneuver."[13] And so they were.

On the actual flight itself, as the lunar lander *Eagle* edged down to the dusty Sea of Tranquillity, Armstrong discovered that the planned landing site was strewn with boulders. He coolly maneuvered away, as available fuel dropped lower and lower, searching for a suitable spot. Would he have to abandon the approach and rocket away from the lunar surface so temptingly close? Armstrong spotted a suitable site. Dust kicked up by the descent rocket exhaust raced across his field of vision, obscuring the landing site. Yet he pressed on, as fellow astronaut Buzz Aldrin called out his altitude and fuel supply, and Mike Collins listened from the orbiting Command Module *Columbia*. The lander drifted backward, and Armstrong corrected for the drift backward but could not stop a steady drift to the left. As the Apollo program official history relates,

> He was reluctant to slow the descent rate any further, but the figures Aldrin kept ticking off told him they were almost out of fuel. Armstrong was concentrating so hard on flying the lunar module that he was unable to perceive the first touch on the moon nor did he hear Aldrin call out "contact light," when the probes below the footpads brushed the surface. The lander settled gently down, like a helicopter, and Armstrong cut off the engine.[14]

Hours later came the "one giant leap for mankind" as Neil Armstrong first set foot on the lunar surface. It had been the flight of a lifetime, a fitting triumph of flight research fittingly undertaken by a veteran test pilot team. The Society of Experimental Test Pilots recognized it as such by naming the Apollo XI astronauts—together with Lockheed test pilot Darryl Greenamyer—corecipients of the Kincheloe Award, a most appropriate honor among those they would subsequently receive.

Unlike the Soviet Union's, the American space program proceeded on the assumption that the astronaut crew should be endowed with as much command and control ability over their vehicles as was practicable. By the time of the Apollo program, this meant that the astronauts were fully in command of their craft, and really were, in an actual sense, "piloting" the vehicle on its mission in space. In contrast, the Soviet Union did not adopt such an approach, favoring, instead, treating the cosmonaut as pretty much a passenger in an underinstrumented spacecraft at the mercy of ground control. The attitude of those running the American space program was best summed up in 1964 by Walter C. Williams, a NASA administrator who had participated in every major NACA/NASA flight-research program from the 1940s until Project Mercury. Reflecting on his years spent with test pilots and flight research, Williams stated:

> I never bought the philosophy that this is a dangerous business and we're going to kill people. I always felt that by careful preparation, careful planning in carrying the flight out in a careful manner, you can do some pretty exotic things, like orbiting a man or breaking the sound barrier, without killing people.[15]

And when followed, this philosophy paid off, with the tragic exception of Apollo I, in 1967, pointing the lesson of never relaxing one's vigilance. When, on Apollo XIII, another design flaw, coupled with human error on the ground, caused an explosion that critically damaged the spacecraft and placed the lives of crewmen James Lovell, John Swigert, and Fred Haise in jeopardy, the astronaut crew, reflecting their flight testing backgrounds, made rapid life-or-death decisions without having to rely for their survival completely upon Mission Control back at Houston. They jury-rigged emergency survival equipment, temporarily abandoning the Command Module *Odyssey* in favor of using the Lunar Module *Aquarius* as an "emergency lifeboat," and with the support and advice of the NASA-industry technical community, returned safely to a splashdown in the South Pacific, salvaging a shattered mission and turning it into a shining example of human triumph over mechanical adversity in the hostile depths of space.

THE PATH TO THE SPACE SHUTTLE

The space program's advanced planners had always hoped that NASA would follow the Apollo program with a more utilitarian space venture, and in fact they saw the Mercury-Gemini-Apollo evolution as a logical sequence of steps toward developing some sort of orbiting space station. An orbiting space station had been a fixture of science fiction for years, dating even to the nineteenth century. Whether a large station with hundreds of crewmen, or just a small platform with a crew of five or ten, such a space vehicle could perform a variety of scientific and defense-related tasks. In the optimistic climate of the mid-1960s, NASA's senior staff saw the development of such a station in the 1970s or 1980s as inevitable. Such a station would, of course, require some logistical support. One could launch supply rockets to the station, delivering small payloads. A better scheme, however, seemed to be the development of some sort of hybrid aircraft-spacecraft, drawing upon the work of the X-15 and the abortive X-20A Dyna-Soar effort. Such a craft could take off from the earth, either horizontally like an airplane or vertically like a pure rocket, boost into orbit, supply the station, and then reenter the atmosphere at about Mach 25, gliding down at hypersonic speeds until it reached about 100,000 feet, then slowing down to subsonic speeds and, at about 40,000 feet, deploying some sort of retractable air-breathing engines and cruising down to land at an airfield like a conventional airplane. Such a scheme had one obvious advantage: it was not necessary to send out half the Navy to patrol the ocean where a landing was expected. Further, such a vehicle would be fully or almost fully reusable, with but minimal refurbishment. A fleet of such vehicles could be built, and they would "shuttle" between the earth and the orbiting space station. Thus sprang forth the notion of a "Space Shuttle," which eventually evolved into the present-day NASA Space Shuttle Space Transportation System. And if the promise of this concept is as yet unfulfilled, it is clear that eventually such craft will be built by the United States and other nations, and will bring about the dawn of practical and economic mass space transportation.

Eventually, of course, NASA had to modify its plans. After Neil Armstrong's historic step on July 20, 1969, public interest in space exploration and utilization waned. Many Americans believed the nation should turn inward, to solving the obvious social problems faced here on earth, away from the expansive and expensive scientific and technological vistas lying ahead. NASA had to cancel plans for its proposed space station development, and instead, the Space Shuttle itself became America's manned spacecraft venture, following on the heels of Apollo. Justification shifted from having a logistical support spacecraft to having a reusable transportation system that could effectively replace costly "throwaway" launch vehicles, undertake limited scientific research in space (using the crew on board the vehicle, or in special modular-manned experiment facilities such as the European Spacelab carried in the Shuttle's payload bay), and perhaps undertake space rescue and repair duties. With this change in rationale, NASA proceeded with its plans for the Shuttle, eventually receiving a presidential go-ahead in 1972.

Interest in the Space Shuttle concept dated to Eugen Sänger's ambitious studies of the 1930s and 1940s, and indeed, various European nations examined the concept in great detail. Only the United States and the Soviet Union have found themselves in the position to actively proceed with developmental work leading to actual manned craft. The Shuttle concept posed a number of thorny technical problems, ranging from reentry heating (the most serious difficulty) to hypersonic stability and control. Numerous quandaries forced compromises. For example, an aerodynamic shape for hypersonic flight is often totally unsuitable for supersonic and, especially, subsonic flight. Yet a reentry spacecraft would have to decelerate from Mach 25 down to subsonic speeds, maintaining adequate stability and control the entire way, then execute a precision landing under perfect control. It was, in fact, this problem—the problem of changing from high speeds in weirdly shaped craft down to a landing—that caused NASA and the Air Force to pursue construction and flight testing of a unique class of vehicles called "lifting bodies," and to actually consider, at one point, constructing a piloted scale model of the Shuttle and air-launching it from a modified B-52.

In the early 1950s, NACA scientist H. Julian Allen had postulated the concept of the blunt-body reentry. A blunt body, during reentry, streams a strong "detached" shock wave that carries off much of the heat of reentry. But it gives the reentering spacecraft pretty much a ballistic flight path. Other engineers recognized that if one streamlined a blunt body, elongating it and perhaps giving it an airfoil cross section, it could be made to reenter with a modest lift-to-drag ratio, permitting varying the landing point and perhaps generating enough lift so that it could land like the early rocket-research airplanes. Such thinking eventually spawned three basic concepts: the Ames laboratory M2 shape (a modified half cone), the Langley laboratory HL-10 (a fattened delta), and the Air Force/Martin SV-5 (which resembled a finned potato). All three exhibited generally good hypersonic characteristics; the SV-5D, an 850-pound, small model, had actually been test fired out over the Pacific Missile Range, reentering and maneuvering at over 15,000 mph following launch by a Convair Atlas missile. But could they fly safely at low speeds?

In 1962, following tests with small radio-controlled models, engineers at the NASA Flight Research Center decided to build a plywood glider of the M2 shape. The end result was a twenty-foot-long vehicle having a steel tube frame and a mahogany plywood hull built by the Sailplane Corporation of America. It weighed a mere 1,140 pounds, and following wind-tunnel tests with this craft mounted in the Ames Research Center's huge 40 × 80-foot tunnel, it returned to Edwards for its first flight trials, towed behind an automobile—but not just any automobile: a stripped-down, much-modified Pontiac convertible specially primed for high

speed by "funny car" expert Mickey Thompson. Following the first
ground tows, NASA approved air tows behind a modified C-47, and on
August 16, 1963, NASA research pilot Milt Thompson piloted the little
glider, designated the M2-F1, from takeoff up to 10,000 feet, where the
C-47 cut it loose for the glide to earth. All lifting bodies had X-15-like
approach characteristics, and the M2-F1 would sink rapidly, touching
down about two minutes after release, landing at about 90 mph. Chuck
Yeager, then chief of the Air Force's test pilot school at Edwards, flew
the craft and pronounced his blessing upon it. Eventually, it completed
approximately one hundred flights by NASA and Air Force pilots. The
M2-F1 demonstrated that such an aircraft could fly, though it had some
dangerous quirks, including poor lateral stability. Encouraged, NASA
decided to proceed with two "heavyweight" lifting bodies capable of
supersonic flights with rocket propulsion, the M2-F2 (a similar half-cone
shape), and the HL-10, both built under contract by Northrop. Both utilized advanced versions of the famed XLR-11 engine, which had first
powered the pioneering Bell XS-1. The M2-F2 completed its first flights
in July 1966 and quickly exhibited generally poor lateral (rolling) and
directional (yawing) stability. During a test flight on May 10, 1967, the
craft crashed, seriously injuring NASA pilot Bruce Peterson, who nevertheless recovered to fly again. NASA rebuilt the vehicle as the M2-F3,
equipped with a different vertical fin arrangement and a reaction-control
"thruster" system. It subsequently completed a further twenty-seven
flights, reaching Mach 1.613 and an altitude of 71,500 feet, its peak performance marks, before NASA retired it to the Smithsonian.

The heavyweight HL-10 was a much pleasanter-flying craft than the
occasionally vicious M2 series. On its first flight, in December 1966, the
plane experienced marginal control because of unanticipated aerodynamic flow problems, and only Bruce Peterson's skillful handling saved
the craft from a perhaps disastrous crash—once more proof that there is
no substitute for the well-trained test pilot in the cockpit of today's
aerospace machines. Following modifications to its fin design, it returned
to the air. On May 9, 1969, the HL-10 completed the first flight of a lifting body to supersonic speeds, demonstrating that it could traverse the
transonic region without difficulty—a major lifting-body program milestone. In 1970, Air Force test pilot Peter Hoag reached Mach 1.86 (1,288
mph), a record for the lifting-body program, and later NASA pilot Bill
Dana reached 90,303 feet before piloting a precision entry and touchdown on the lakebed at Edwards. NASA then equipped it with small
rockets so that it could land with power, rather than glide in, but the
powered tests revealed that the piloting tasks were harder than if pilots
executed unpowered landings. As NASA research pilot Milt Thompson

subsequently stated, "The Shuttle, whether it has landing engines or not, must be maneuvered, unpowered, to a point near the destination, because the engines cannot be started until the vehicle is subsonic and only limited fuel will be available. To us, it seems ridiculous to maneuver to a position where power must be relied upon to reach the runway." NASA Headquarters agreed, and today's Shuttle lands powerless, like the earlier X-series airplanes.

The Air Force SV-5 program underwent the most interesting metamorphosis. After testing the unmanned hypersonic SV-5D models, the service and Martin built a piloted low-speed testbed like the heavyweight M2-F2 and HL-10, designated the SV-5P and known as the X-24A. After ten flights as a glider, piloted by Air Force test pilot Jerauld Gentry and NASA's John Manke, the X-24A completed its first powered flight in March 1970. Disconcertingly, the craft exhibited a pronounced nosing-up tendency when the engine was firing, a warning to NASA to beware of similar problems on the far more complex Space Shuttle. In the summer of 1971, the downright-ugly X-24A concluded its flight test program, because NASA and the Air Force had decided to transform it into a swan. Eventually, it flew again as the X-24B, but this time with a new hypersonic body shape that changed it into the most attractive of the lifting bodies. John Manke and Air Force test pilot Mike Love began flying the craft in mid-1973, and from then until late November 1975, it completed a total of thirty-six flights.

The highlight of the program came in August 1975, when Manke and Love piloted the craft on its first precision landings on a concrete runway. The X-24B had exhibited superlative handling characteristics, characteristics, in fact, better than its F-104 chase planes. This, combined with the craft's steerable nosewheel, encouraged the two pilots that the X-24B could land on the Edwards 15,000-foot concrete runway, a convincing verification that the Shuttle itself could be expected to complete precision landings at Kennedy Space Center and Vandenberg on runways, without the necessity of always landing on the vast dry lake at Edwards. Mission planners gave their go-ahead, and Manke and Love practiced for three weeks by flying simulated X-24B approaches to the runway using T-38 and F-104 airplanes in "dirty," high-drag low-lift configuration. On August 5, 1975, Manke launched from the B-52, fired up the craft's rocket engine, and climbed to 60,000 feet. Then he began his swift descent to the Edwards runway, landing precisely at the selected landing spot, seven minutes after launch. He subsequently reported to The Society of Experimental Test Pilots that, due to careful flight research, "We now know that concrete runway landings are operationally feasible and that touchdown accuracies of ±500 feet can be expected." Two weeks later, Mike Love duplicated the feat. Following a series of checkout flights for other NASA and Air Force pilots, the X-24B was retired to the Air Force Museum.

THE SHUTTLE: A LONG WAY FROM KITTY HAWK

The lifting-body flight-research programs of the 1960s and 1970s gave great encouragement to advocates of the actual Space Shuttle, which was, by the end of the X-24B program, on the verge of its initial flight tests. In 1972, the NASA Shuttle program had received an official go-ahead from President Richard M. Nixon. In contrast to the sometimes exotic craft that various conceptualizers had drawn up for the Shuttle mission, the final shape was a relatively modest-appearing craft, whose conventional lines hid what was, in reality, a most complex and demanding vehicle. As a cost measure, NASA had abandoned the fully-reusable approach, developing, instead, a delta-wing orbiter nestling on top of a large external fuel tank that would supply the orbiter's three large engines with fuel. Two solid-fuel "strap-on" boosters flanked the jettisonable fuel tank, and each of the boosters could generate 2.9 million pounds of thrust (each of the Shuttle's three liquid-fuel engines produces 375,000 pounds of thrust). Roughly the size of a Douglas DC-9 transport, the Shuttle orbiter itself spanned just over 78 feet, with a length of 122 feet, and its cargo bay alone measured 60 feet in length and 15 feet in diameter. Rather than incorporate some exotic form of metal superalloy construction for the craft's thermal protection system, NASA instead opted for a Lockheed-developed tile system that would cover the skin of the craft. The entire Space Shuttle would take off vertically from Kennedy Space Center or Vandenberg, rocketing upward under the full power of its solid-fuel and liquid-fuel engines. Then the strap-ons would jettison away from the craft, to be recovered at sea and refurbished for reuse. The Shuttle would continue onward into space, jettisoning the external fuel tank (which would tumble down to destruction) and going into orbit. It would perform its orbital mission and then reenter the atmosphere, portions of it glowing from the intense heating. After decelerating to subsonic speeds, the Shuttle crew would prepare for landing, setting up an approach and gliding down to earth. Because of the necessary compromises to develop such a vehicle, the Shuttle would fly a landing approach similar to the X-15's, sinking down rapidly then "flaring" for the landing just before touchdown. Initial orbital test flights would land at the lakebed at Edwards; operational missions would land on special runways constructed back at Kennedy or at Vandenberg. In late July 1972, NASA gave Rockwell International approval to proceed with the final design, construction, and development of the Space Shuttle, following extensive review of proposals from Rockwell, Grumman, Lockheed, and McDonnell-Douglas. Rockwell began construction of the first Shuttle, Orbiter OV-101, in June 1974, and completed it in September 1976.

NASA had long recognized that the first actual high-speed test of the Shuttle in flight would be made on the all-important first orbital flight itself. But at least some questions could be answered earlier, namely, how the Shuttle behaved at low speeds, during its subsonic glide down to landing. Actual full-scale testing of the Shuttle itself at low speeds could verify the wind-tunnel predictions made for its performance. Accordingly, NASA planned a series of approach-and-landing tests for the Shuttle at Edwards.

The Shuttle's approach-and-landing tests drew upon the full panoply of flight research. They involved blending intensive wind-tunnel work on the ground with flight research aloft, using a variety of airborne simulators, rigorous analysis of data, the efforts of thousands of individuals nationwide, and of course, careful planning and execution. Obviously, the Shuttle required some means of being carried up to launch altitude, and NASA solved this difficulty by procuring a 747 jetliner formerly flown by American Airlines and modifying it to carry the Shuttle on its back. The agency selected veteran test pilot-astronaut Donald K. "Deke" Slayton to direct the overall test program. In January 1977, the first orbiter, by now named the *Enterprise*, arrived at Edwards following an overland journey from the Rockwell plant at Palmdale. Technicians set to work readying it for flight.

The 747-*Enterprise* combination completed its maiden flight on February 18, 1977, crewed by NASA pilots Fitz Fulton and Tom McMurtry and flight engineers Vic Horton and Louis "Skip" Guidry. The flight went smoothly, the test crew reaching a maximum airspeed of 288 mph at 16,200 feet, and finally, after over two hours, the two craft linked and as one returned to earth. But what struck most observers was the outlandish joining of the strange-looking Shuttle to the gigantic 747. Further, to smooth the airflow around the 747's vertical fin, the Shuttle had a huge tail cone covering its after end. With the first flight behind, engineers and test personnel cleared the craft to "expand the envelope," and the next flight, four days later, was at a higher weight, of 313 tons, a higher altitude, a higher speed (330 mph), and a longer duration. After three more flights, NASA was so satisfied that it abandoned plans for a sixth captive "inert" (i.e., without a Shuttle crew in the spacecraft), and readied the orbiter for its next series of tests: captive flights with the Shuttle occupied by two teams of astronauts: a team consisting of Fred

Haise and Charles Fullerton, and Joe Engle and Dick Truly as the second.

On June 18, 1977, the 747-*Enterprise* took to the air on the first "captive active" flight. Astronauts Haise and Fullerton sat in the Shuttle as Fulton et al. piloted the awkward-looking combination from the cockpit of the 747. Once again, NASA was so satisfied with the test results that a planned four-flight series was cut to three. On the last flight, the 747 flew a launch separation maneuver, Fulton and McMurtry pushing the combination into a shallow dive simulating the maneuver that would be flown before Haise and Fullerton launched away from the 747 on the first free flight. Now all attention turned to the actual free flights themselves.

In preparing for the actual approach and landing of the Shuttle, NASA had contracted with Grumman to develop a special in-flight simulator. Grumman had taken two conventional Gulfstream II bizjets and drastically modified them so that they could simulate the Shuttle's approach characteristics from about 35,000 feet down to landing. This represented a creative approach to flight testing that has gained increasing favor since the Second World War—modifying actual airplanes to simulate the characteristics of other aircraft or flight vehicles under development. An instructor pilot would sit in the right seat (normally the copilot's position), while an astronaut sat in the left. An on-board digital computer could vary the performance characteristics and control behavior of the Gulfstream II to mimic those of a returning Shuttle flying at subsonic speeds and gliding down to landing. Instead of the Gulfstream's normal 10:1 gliding ratio (i.e., ten feet forward for every foot of altitude lost), the modified craft could match the Shuttle's anticipated 3:1 ratio, and had a 15,000-foot-per-minute sink rate. Specialized flight controls provided "direct lift control" and "side force control" (the latter furnished by two stub vertical fins installed under the wing of the jet), so that the astronaut would have the same control response and feel as if he were flying the actual Shuttle. The complex control system enabled the astronaut to let the computer "fly" the "Shuttle" down to the landing flare maneuver, or he could fly it himself, relying on the control system and instrumentation for cues. In the weeks prior to the first free flight, the Shuttle astronauts flew simulations of the Shuttle in the Gulfstream II training aircraft on a regular basis.

The actual first flight occurred on August 12, 1977. That day, at 8 A.M., Fitz Fulton and Tom McMurtry added full power to the 747-*Enterprise* duo, and the combination accelerated slowly down Edwards' runway, taking off with the magnificent Tehachapi Mountains forming a perfect backdrop for the unique aircraft. A flock of T-38 chase planes followed, piloted by other NASA research pilots and astronauts. For just over forty-five minutes, the 747-*Enterprise* cruised over the Antelope

Valley, scene of so many flight testing accomplishments. Then, at 8:48, due east of Rogers Dry Lake, Fulton and McMurtry nosed into a shallow dive from an altitude of just over 28,000 feet. Seconds later, Fred Haise radioed, "The *Enterprise* is set; thanks for the lift," and punched a separation button firing a sequence of explosive bolts. The *Enterprise* was on its own. As the Shuttle went swiftly upward, Fulton rolled into a diving left turn, for some feared the Shuttle might possibly collide with the 747's tall vertical fin. Haise, for his part, rolled to the right, then, as planned, began a banking turn to the west, beginning the descent to the lakebed. As thousands of onlookers at the lakebed watched, the white speck of the Shuttle grew rapidly. In the cockpit, Haise checked the control of the big delta; it handled well. The Shuttle dropped down over Leuhman Ridge, across Highway 58 north of the base, then turned toward the lakebed. Haise set up his landing approach, and sinking like a rock, the *Enterprise* touched down on the lakebed a mere five and a half minutes after launch, its maiden flight an unqualified success.

Late-summer rains flooded the lakebed, preventing Joe Engle and Dick Truly from emulating Haise and Fullerton's flight until the following September 13. Ten days later, Haise and Fullerton completed the third so-called "tail-cone-on" flight, and NASA, highly pleased with the program, authorized the first "tail-cone-off" flight for the very next mission. Without the airflow-smoothing tail cone, the disturbed air behind the Shuttle's blunt after end might cause a dangerous buffeting problem for the 747's vertical fin. But, without the tail cone, the Shuttle would have the very same flying configuration as a Shuttle returning from space would possess, and thus be better able to furnish useful data than if all the flights were flown with the drag-reducing tail cone. "Real-time" analysis of telemetered data from the 747 would furnish a warning in case the buffeting was severe enough to cause structural damage; if so, and the 747 was still on the runway, the takeoff would be aborted. If the 747 had just become airborne, Fitz Fulton would chop power and land straight ahead on the lakebed. But, in fact, the actual "tail-cone-off" flight on October 12, 1977, came off without a hitch. The 747 rumbled down the runway and into the air with no visible problems, the Shuttle resting on its supports, and three dummy "main engine" nozzles protruding from its after end in the space previously covered over by the tail cone. Buffeting did occur but was well within planned tolerances. The flight proceeded toward drop, and finally, Fulton entered into the now-familiar shallow dive, and along the way Engle triggered separation. The changed drag characteristics of the Shuttle were immediately apparent, and this time the Shuttle landed not in five and a half minutes but in just over two and a half minutes, flying like a big X-15.

NASA now turned to the final verification flight: a landing on Edwards Runway 04/22, the main 15,000-foot concrete runway. On October 26, 1977, Haise and Fullerton launched from the 747 on a straight-in approach to 04/22. Just as the *Enterprise* touched down, however, it rolled to the left; Haise corrected for this and the Shuttle bounced back into the air. The crewmen relaxed on the controls to prevent the onset of a persistent oscillatory motion, and the Shuttle bounced once more before finally touching down and rolling to a stop. This final flight had pointed to a potentially serious landing problem and resulted in some changes to the craft's control system. All in all, however, NASA concluded that the Shuttle could safely fly at subsonic speeds down to landing. Flight research and analysis had verified that. The Shuttle faced other challenges before it would be ready for its first orbital missions, but flight research had enabled it to clear one of the major hurdles to such flights. Appropriately, the four Shuttle crewmen subsequently received the SETP's Kincheloe Award.

THE FLIGHT OF THE SPACE SHUTTLE COLUMBIA

In March 1979, NASA delivered the second Space Shuttle, orbiter OV-102 *Columbia*, to the Kennedy Space Center at Cape Canaveral. *Columbia*, named both after the historic Apollo XI spacecraft and one of the Navy's first frigates to circumnavigate the globe, did not get its chance to rocket into space for over two years. A series of frustrating problems with its engines and the thermal protection system (essentially a series of 30,759 silica-base tiles having the consistency of styrofoam, plus other materials including a carbon composite structure for the Shuttle's nose cap and wing leading edges) delayed hopes of an earlier launch. As time went by, pessimism grew, until NASA's Shuttle team found themselves not only faced with the challenges of the upcoming launch but buffeted by a rising chorus of criticism ranging from sniping at its cost overrun to predictions of disaster in space. But by early 1981, the $9 billion program was, at last, "go" for launch, and the actual participants exuded confidence. The selected crew, astronauts John Young and Robert Crippen, were ready; Young remarked, "We're 130% trained and ready to go. We have more time in the mission simulators than 20 astronauts in the entire Gemini program and we haven't even launched yet."[16] Young, NASA's chief astronaut at age 50, was known for his ready humor and personable manner. He had flown four previous times on Gemini and Apollo, was a graduate of the Naval Test Pilot School, and had set a series of climb records in the Navy's McDonnell F4H-1 Phantom II back in 1962. "Crip" Crippen, another naval aviator, had graduated from the Air Force's test pilot school at Edwards, served there as an instructor, and then had been selected for the abortive Manned Orbiting Laboratory program in 1966. When MOL collapsed, he transferred to NASA's astronaut corps. *Columbia's* first flight would culminate a fifteen-year wait for a journey into the black void of space by the 43-year-old astronaut.

Still, there were always the unknown concerns. Veteran astronaut Donald K. "Deke" Slayton, manager of the Shuttle orbital flight test program, cautioned: "In my opinion, about 90% of your risk in a total program comes with a first flight. There is no nice in-between milestone. You have to bite it all in one chunk."[17] And John Yardley, NASA's associate administrator for space transportation systems, stated, "I'm not worried over any of the problems we *have* worried about. They're in good shape. The things that you have to be careful about are the unknowns, things that have never happened before, things that people have never thought of simply because we have a configuration that's considerably different from the thirty years of the history of launch vehicles. This is entirely different. A new engineering gremlin could crawl out of the woodwork, one nobody could have predicted."[18] NASA, in any case, was not taking any chances. Alternate emergency landing sites had been prepared around the world. Finally, the crew sat in two SR-71-type ejection seats capable of hurling them away from the Shuttle should anything go wrong with the Shuttle during launch or reentry. For such ejection to be made in safety, the speed of the Shuttle would have to be Mach 3 or less, at 120,000 feet or less. At speeds and altitudes above these figures, the crew would have to trust their lives to the Shuttle until, with luck, the opportunity to eject from the stricken craft would present itself.

The space agency had set a tentative launch date of April 10, at 6:50 A.M. eastern time. That morning found nearly a million people lined along the Banana River and swarming in the Cape area, all attention riveted on the Shuttle. But, that Friday, Shuttle would not fly. A critical computer failed to interact properly with its electronic colleagues and, frustrated, mission controllers scrubbed the launch after a prolonged delay. Over the next day, computer technicians worked to resolve the problem and, finally, all was set for launch the next morning, Palm Sunday, April 12.

April 12, 1981, was the twentieth anniversary of Yuri Gagarin's first orbital flight, but this day belonged to the United States. In the early hours before launch, preparations and the countdown moved inexorably toward ignition. A Soviet trawler snooping in the expected impact area where the two solid-fuel boosters would land had to be shooed away by a Coast Guard cutter. Security remained tight, and

NASA had even taken special precautions to prevent the Shuttle's air-to-ground communications links from being interfered with by Soviet or terrorist organizations. Security forces maintained a close watch at the Cape. President Ronald Reagan, recuperating from a would-be assassin's bullet, watched from the White House. Weather conditions at the Cape and at the emergency landing sites were perfect: warm, almost like summer.

The moment of truth came at 7:00 A.M. Cape time. The countdown reached T−3.8 seconds, and the *Columbia*'s onboard computer system sent a command to the Shuttle's three main liquid-fuel engines. Hydrogen met oxygen in an explosive mix, was ignited in a controlled explosion, and by T+0.24 second, all engines were firing at 90 per cent thrust, and a timer, set for 2.64 seconds, began to run down to trigger the two solid-fuel boosters on either side of the Shuttle's huge external fuel tank. Once the solids fired, Shuttle would be committed to launch. The first rumble of ignition had not even reached the ears of observers before the solids erupted at about T+3 seconds. An igniter shot a twenty-foot sheet of flame down the core of each solid rocket, instantly triggering ignition. Under a full 7.5 million pounds of thrust, the Shuttle lifted quickly away from Pad 39A, rising above a cloud of steam from the pad's water exhaust quenching system, away from the palmetto scrub and toward space in a spectacle that staggered the imagination. It was a fantastic vision: the three liquid-fuel engine exhausts glaring with that peculiarly clear flame coming from hydrogen-oxygen combustion, bright shock-diamonds streaming in each exhaust trail; the two solids, burning with a characteristic dazzling white-yellow flame, generating a broad banner of grayish exhaust smoke; as one observer noted, *Columbia* looked for all the world like some gigantic Fourth-of-July firework thundering into the sky. Above all was the rumbling, crackling roar—greater, even, than the Saturn's—and the ground itself trembled.

As planned, when the Shuttle reached an altitude of four hundred feet, eight seconds after launch, it began an automatic roll and pitch maneuver that placed it in a climbing arc on its back as it rocketed over the Atlantic Ocean. Inside the spacecraft, the unflappable Young's heart rate idled along at 85 beats per minute while Crip Crippen's enthusiastically touched 135. Shortly after two minutes into the flight, the spent solid boosters, their job done, separated from the *Columbia* at an altitude of 27 nautical miles, descending to earth under bright orange and white parachutes. Four minutes into the flight, as *Columbia* raced along faster than the X-15, Crip Crippen proclaimed, "Man, what a view, what a view!"[19] At T+6:30, the *Columbia* was at Mach 15, pressing on to orbit. At T+8:32, the Shuttle entered a low earth orbit at an altitude of 63 nautical miles; the crew jettisoned the spent external fuel tank twenty seconds later. The tank broke up and tumbled, as planned, into the Indian Ocean. Racing around the globe at Mach 25, in excess of 17,400 mph, Young and Crippen utilized the Shuttle's two orbital maneuvering system rocket engines to loft the craft into a circular 130 nautical mile orbit, then set down to the routine of *Columbia's* planned 36 orbit, 54.5 hour mission.

During the launch, as expected, the blast from the Shuttle's engines had caused some damage to the launch pad, hurling handrails around and melting, scorching, and searing some other parts of the structure. Unexpectedly, however, the launch had also damaged some of the Shuttle's tile thermal protection system. After Young and Crippen opened the Shuttle's cargo bay doors, exposing radiators to carry away the accumulated heat of the craft's electronic equipment and testing the door operation, a TV camera panning the open payload bay and the back of the Shuttle revealed that a small number of tiles had separated during launch. Experts knew that these tiles, situated on the fairings for the Shuttle's orbital maneuvering and reaction control systems, were not critical for the reentry. Nevertheless, the nagging question remained: Had any of the tiles from the critical underside of the craft been lost? NASA arranged for special long-range photography of the Shuttle using Air Force space surveillance cameras situated around the globe. The agency remained confident, however, that no tiles had, in fact, been shed from the *Columbia's* underside. Intensive preflight "pull" tests at the Cape and tests with the tiles mounted on experimental aircraft at Edwards had convinced mission planners that the critical tiles would remain on the craft, no matter what. For two days, Young and Crippen checked out the orbiter and its systems, and aside from very minor problems, nothing remotely serious showed up. Then, on the morning of Tuesday, April 14, the two astronauts prepared for the return to earth, *Columbia's* second moment of truth.

NASA had planned the Shuttle to land at 10:30 A.M. local time at Edwards, one hour after beginning the reentry engine "burn" to drop out of orbit. Two and a half hours before the reentry burn, Young and Crippen closed the Shuttle's payload bay doors, which shut snugly. The Shuttle was now orbiting tail forward, on its back, with the astronauts in a heads-down position. At 9:22 A.M. Edwards time, the orbital maneuvering engines fired, slowing Shuttle fractionally, enough to drop it out of orbit, while it passed over the Indian Ocean. Shuttle was soon within range of the Yarragadee tracking station in Australia, and the crew called Mission Control in Houston, informing them that the "deorbit" burn had been a success. About the same time, four

Northrop T-38 Talon chase planes took off from Edwards, to escort Shuttle down to the lakebed about forty-five minutes later.

In 1907, Alexander Graham Bell had written, "There are two critical points in every aerial flight—its beginning and its end."[20] And so it was with the Shuttle. *Columbia* had already successfully passed launch. But now came the most critical—indeed, most perilous—portion of the flight: reentry. In preparation, Young rotated the Shuttle in an "inverted pitch" nose-down position with the belly facing the earth and the craft's nose pointing about eighteen degrees below the horizon. As Shuttle raced onward, it gradually changed its orientation until, at the moment it entered the upper atmosphere, it had assumed a nose-high attitude, flying with the nose forty degrees above the horizon. *Columbia* passed within range of the Guam tracking station, and ground monitors verified that the craft was right on the planned reentry profile. At 400,000 feet and about Mach 24, *Columbia* entered the tenuous upper atmosphere. Now was when all the predictions of engineers and scientists would be verified—or refuted. Any returning spacecraft creates an ionized sheath of gases that prevent radio transmission during the period of intense reentry heating. Just before *Columbia* entered radio blackout, Mission Control in Houston radioed, "Easy does it, John, we're all riding with you," to which the confident Young briskly answered, "Bye bye."[21] And then all was silence, for minutes.

The Shuttle had begun its entry at 9:50 A.M. Edwards time, passing into the upper atmosphere over the central Pacific while the ocean and islands below remained in deep predawn darkness. Four minutes later, as heating built up to temperatures nearing 3,000 degrees F., the *Columbia* passed into radio blackout. Inside, Young and Crippen saw the sky outside glow redly; Young later recalled that the reentry gave him the feeling of "flying in a pink world."[22] But there was work to be done, and the two men could not simply sit back and enjoy the spectacular view. Already the dynamic pressure around the craft was high enough to permit maneuvering the *Columbia* with its conventional aerodynamic control surfaces; the craft began a series of carefully planned S turns to dissipate speed and altitude. During the first of these "reentry roll reversals," the *Columbia* wandered a bit before settling down to its proper eighty-degree bank angle. Later in the reentry, with Shuttle having slowed to Mach 18 and down to an altitude of about 220,000 feet, Young monitored a second automatic banking maneuver. So far so good. By 10:05 A.M., Shuttle was down to Mach 18 and 213,000 feet, one thousand miles from Edwards, and flying in its "equilibrium glide phase," in which the craft's guidance system automatically maintained a constant lift and "g" force.

Speed and altitude continued to drop as *Columbia* approached the California coast near Big Sur.

Meanwhile, on the ground, flight controllers waited anxiously. Shuttle was on its way back, but in what shape? And then came one of the most exciting calls in aviation history. Young and Crippen came out of radio blackout to announce, "Hello Houston, *Columbia* here, we're doing Mach 10.3 at 188. Our L over D is nominal."[23] *Columbia* had withstood reentry and was now pounding along toward the California coast at over ten times the speed of sound, at 188,000 feet (but sinking fast), and with its lift-to-drag characteristics right where the engineers had planned. Astronaut Joe Allen, NASA's spacecraft communicator back at Houston, verified that *Columbia* was right where it should be, with "perfect energy, perfect ground track."[24] The Shuttle flew another roll reversal to bleed off a little more energy and altitude at Mach 9, then crossed the coastline at Mach 6.6 at an altitude of 139,000 feet. As it headed southeast down the coastal range south of Bakersfield, Young took control of the Shuttle, wheeling it around in another series of S turns to reduce its speed. More than a half million people had journeyed out to the great lake in the Mojave, braving desert dryness and even the nasty tempers of mating rattlesnakes to see the Shuttle land. And they were not to be disappointed.

Columbia returned to Edwards at 54,000 feet and Mach 1.3, jolting the desert with a double whiplash of a sonic boom, a fitting enough reminder to old timers that Edwards *née* Muroc had spawned the whole supersonic and hypersonic revolution. Not for Shuttle the untidy semi-ballistic drop into the sea—it would land with grace and style, as a decent aircraft should. As Crip Crippen whooped, "What a way to come home to California!"[25] *Columbia* sank earthward in a descending left turn, angling around to line up on lakebed runway 23. And suddenly it was all old hat, once again back to the days of *Enterprise* in the Shuttle summer of 1977. Four of the ubiquitous T-38 chase planes sidled up to the orbiter, and one passed by underneath, surveying it for any signs of damage that might preclude safe operation of its landing gear. Then all was clear, and Shuttle dropped down like a huge X-15, Young executing a smooth landing flare, lowering the landing gear and then waiting as Shuttle coasted along, using up excess energy before the mainwheels gently met the baked clay of Rogers Dry Lake. As with all delta craft, the nose slowly dropped until its gear, too, had touched the earth. Then Shuttle was down and rolling, speed brakes fully open, braking to a halt as the T-38's whistled by and a convoy of support vehicles raced across the lake to meet the craft. The first flight of the shuttle had ended, an unqualified success.

Though Shuttle housed a fatal flaw that would eventually kill seven astronauts before the horrified gaze of the world, the presence of that flaw did not signify an inherent weakness in either the concept or basic value and desirability of a Shuttle system, despite the more hysteric comments of anti-Shuttle partisans in the wake of the *Challenger* tragedy. What it *did* signify, unfortunately, was the change in style and management of an agency between the time of Apollo and that fateful January day when Dick Scobee and his crew launched to their deaths: "Not the NASA I recall," was how one Apollo astronaut veteran put it. The "technological maestros" (as technology commentator Professor Arthur M. Squires has termed them) that shepherded Mercury, Gemini, and Apollo had been replaced over the decade of the seventies by less responsive and more detached decision-makers who too willingly accepted the compromise notion of "good enough."[26] *Challenger*'s loss needs to be put into perspective, however. The loss of the *Titanic* did not end the era of the big ocean liner; rather, it resulted in changed procedures and policies. The loss of the de Havilland Comets did not, fortunately, retard the subsequent development of improved Comets and other jet airliners. So it must be with the Shuttle. When *Columbia* landed in 1981, a new era dawned in space transportation, and the subsequent loss of the *Challenger*—or any other spacecraft—could not change that fact, nor turn back the clock to pre-Shuttle days. As if in recognition of this, one has only to consider the various international Shuttle-like programs now gestating: in the Soviet Union, with Germany's *Sänger II*, France's *Hermes*, Great Britain's HOTOL, and even within the United States, where government-industry teams are busily studying the potential for NASP—the National Aero-Space Plane. The Soviet Shuttle can be expected to fly in the near future; whether other of these programs reach the hardware stage remains to be seen. But no matter: any will follow in the wake of the *Columbia*'s historic 1981 excursion into space. There was a casualness in the flight testing community after that flight that underscored an important point: flight researchers are, as a group, not inclined to waste time on speculation or unproductive introspection. As before, there were—and always would be—challenges enough to keep them plenty busy in the years ahead.

CHAPTER 9

TODAY—AND TOMORROW

It was fashionable, not too many years ago, to predict the imminent demise of the test pilot. Automation, some boldly stated, would soon take over his job; the test pilot would go the way of the weaver or the buggy maker, passing into the mists of folklore. Such thinking came at a time when many of these selfsame prophets predicted that missiles would replace the manned military airplane and that the day of the highly maneuverable fighter had passed. Even genuine experts were not immune from the seemingly persuasive logic of such claims: When, shortly before his death in 1959, pioneer test pilot Sir Henry Tizard was asked whether the test pilot had a future, he cautiously replied, "If I had a son who was a test pilot, I would advise him to stick to it; but perhaps I wouldn't advise it for *his* son."[1]

Yet, today, the profession of test pilot and flight researcher is secure, and appears so for as far as the future-focused eye can see. Flight testing and flight research are deeply ingrained in the aerospace research-and-development consciousness. Every day, over Edwards, Patuxent, Boscombe Down, Istres, Manching, Wichita, Shenyang, Caselle, at any of the dozens of flight research centers worldwide, the skies echo to the sounds of aircraft undergoing test. The Marine test pilot evaluating the F-18's carrier landing performance, the NASA pilot preparing for a flight in the AD-1 oblique-wing testbed, the Israeli aloft in an experimental Kfir, are the heirs and guardians of a tradition dating to the time of Eilmer, just as they themselves will be the ancestors to the flight researchers of future centuries. And in the fast-paced world of experimental flight, time literally flies: there are test pilots today who as children built models of the F-104 and X-15.

Modern flight testing and research encompasses many aspects. Some, such as careful planning and safety, are unchanged from the past. Others, such as the increasing emphasis on aerodynamically- and energy-efficient flight, reflect newer concerns. A casual and by no means extensive listing includes the following:

> *Aerodynamically- and Energy-Efficient Flight*
> *Use of Automated Telemetry Systems*
> *Remotely Piloted Research Vehicles*
> *Ground and In-Flight Simulation*
> *Control of Cost Escalation*
> *Changing Sociological Patterns*

To be sure, each of these requires explanations: some cover a multitude of activities; others are narrower in focus. All, however, are important for the continuing evolution of the flight research profession, and to our understanding of it.

AERODYNAMICALLY- AND ENERGY-EFFICIENT FLIGHT

In a sense, the history of aviation is a history of the quest for aerodynamically- and energy-efficient flight. But only in the very recent years—principally the past two decades—has this quest been emphasized. In part, the search for greater aerodynamic and energy efficiency has led to such notions as the supercritical wing (SCW), the Whitcomb winglet, the oblique wing, the "circulation control wing," fly-by-wire (FBW) control systems, "control configured vehicles" (CCV), advanced VTOL rotorcraft, and the imaginative aircraft of Burt Rutan and Paul MacCready.

As is apparent, much of this attention has centered on the wing itself. Just as the Guggenheim Fund sponsored a STOL competition that generally demonstrated the value of the wing slat and flap, recent flight research work has aimed at demonstrating the value of certain developments by testing them on special experimental airplanes. One early-1960s attempt that met with indifferent success was the notion of laminar flow control. Northrop developed a duo of X-21A test aircraft, modifying two Douglas B-66 bombers to incorporate special wings having a series of spanwise slots only a few thousandths of an inch in width. Gas-turbine air pumps would suck away the turbulent boundary layer through the slots, thus generating smooth (laminar) airflow and eliminating up to 80 per cent of the friction drag, enabling an airplane with such a wing to fly much farther and with a greater payload than if it possessed a conventional wing. Unfortunately, the two X-21A's proved especially vulnerable to dust plugging the tiny slots and rendering the whole scheme impractical. The hulks of both now lie forlornly in the midst of Edwards' photographic test range. Today, however, other researchers are again examining "suction-stabilized" airflow, for it promises a minimum fuel savings of 20 per cent over conventional transport aircraft.

A much more immediately successful concept has been Richard Whitcomb's supercritical wing, which is appearing on current aircraft. The supercritical wing (SCW) has a flattened top combined with a pronounced downward turn at the trailing edge. Since it has less drag than a conventional airfoil, it can enable a jetliner to cruise at higher speeds by as much as 100 mph, and the aircraft also burns less fuel. NASA tested the concept on a modified Vought F-8A Crusader equipped with the new and beautiful wing shape, and also on a modified F-111A, and the extremely promising results culminated in Whitcomb's receiving yet more honors and awards, including the 1974 Wright Brothers Trophy. Whitcomb also postulated the notion of the "winglet," a stubby vertical finlike appendage added on to the wing tips of an airplane to reduce the drag penalty of the wing-tip vortex. This concept also underwent validation by flight testing, and is now appearing on production aircraft such as the Learjet Longhorn.

A more radical idea is that postulated by Robert T. Jones, the American father of the sweptwing, and one of NASA's senior scientists. Jones conceived of the oblique wing, a wing having a central pivot point about which it could rotate on the fuselage. Such a wing would, in effect, function like a scissors, with one tip swinging forward while the other swings aft, avoiding the mechanical complexities, weight penalties, and aerodynamic-trim problems associated with conventional variable-sweep wings. As doubtful as this sounds to the casual observer, the concept is theoretically valid. NASA tested the wing shape on a small radio-controlled model, and then went ahead with the development of a small piloted research airplane, the Ames/Dryden AD-1. It is currently undergoing testing at Edwards, and may well point to the future shape of at least some transport airplanes.

A team of Navy researchers led by Robert Englar, of the Naval Ship

Research and Development Center, developed a "Circulation Controlled Wing" concept, blowing a high-velocity sheet of air over a rounded trailing edge (termed a "Coanda surface") and thus causing the sheet of air to "adhere" to the surface, following the curve and inducing a strong circulation around the airfoil that effectively increases the lift of the wing. After rigorous wind-tunnel research, the Navy contracted with Grumman to apply the concept to the wing of a modified A-6 Intruder attack bomber. The modified Intruder could land in 1,080 feet, as compared to a normal 2,050, could touch down at about 90 mph, compared to a normal 140 mph, and could maintain flight speeds as low as 77 mph. Further work remains before this promising system appears on production aircraft, but flight research has clearly validated the concept.

Researchers have done and are continuing to do exciting work in the field of electronic flight controls and so-called "control configured vehicles" (CCV). Essentially, using the advantages of advanced electronics technology, engineers can develop airplanes having much more rapid control response than was possible previously, with older, direct-force or hydromechanical systems. Aircraft with "fly-by-wire" (FBW) electronic-control signaling and operation can also avoid some of the safety pitfalls inherent in complex older systems involving pumps, valves, and fluids. Damaged hydraulic systems were a major cause of aircraft losses in Vietnam; otherwise-perfectly good aircraft became uncontrollable, forcing their pilots to abandon them, all too often for the dismal rigors of captivity.

In December 1970, a multiple hydraulic failure caused the loss of Grumman's first F-14 Tomcat prototype. Though test pilots Bob Smyth and Bill Miller did their best to save it, they had no choice but to abandon the expensive prototype when it went totally out of control during final approach to Grumman's Calverton test facility. With an electronic primary-flight-control system and with multiple electronic backups, such problems can now be overcome. Indeed, the advantages of electronic sensors coupled with "active" (i.e., constantly functioning) flight controls can lead to true CCV aircraft that can, for example, fly straight and level even while in yawed flight or with the nose angled down to the ground. Such aircraft can be designed as basically unstable (to enhance maneuverability), with the stability generated artificially by a sensor system constantly deflecting control surfaces to compensate for any tendency of the airplane to go out of control. This, together with advances in propulsion and flight structure, is likely to generate strange-looking aircraft of the future that will have swept-forward wings, direct lift control, integrated aerodynamic and propulsion controls, canard control surfaces, and other nontraditional items. Designers are now free to design what is best for performance, not what is demanded by the constraints of stability. FBW technology was first convincingly demonstrated by NASA in tests of a modified Vought F-8C Crusader at Edwards, using surplus Apollo computer equipment. Today, there are fly-by-wire testbeds flying around the world, and the first production airplane to incorporate a full-time FBW system without any sort of mechanical backup, the General Dynamics F-16, is in service.

The traditional helicopter has also undergone many changes, thanks in part to the efforts of flight researchers. The complex and troublesome rotor arrangements of the 1940s and 1950s are giving way to advanced new concepts, and the performance envelope of the helicopter has already opened up to include flight speeds above 200 mph. Flight testing has validated such concepts as the rigid rotor (first tested on the Lockheed XH-51 series), and today such ideas as contrarotating rigid rotors and also the tilting prop-rotor are being tested on such experimental craft as Sikorsky's ABC (Advancing Blade Concept) research helicopter and the Bell XV-15 tilt-rotor testbed. Both may push rotorcraft technology toward the 350 mph mark.

Special mention must be made concerning the efforts of two particular individuals, Burt Rutan and Paul MacCready, to develop efficient new aircraft. Rutan has shown an uncommon gift for combining the latest advances in structural technology with high aerodynamic "cleanliness" to achieve outstandingly performing general-aviation "homebuilt" airplanes. Such designs as the VariEze and the Defiant have set new standards for light-aircraft performance. The Defiant, for example, offers cruise performance efficiency 65 per cent greater than comparable conventional airplanes. Much of his success has been due to methodical and careful flight testing and verification of his designs; appropriately, his development organization (a total of three people, including brother Dick Rutan, the test pilot) is based at Mojave Airport, not far from Edwards, in the midst of the Antelope Valley.

Paul MacCready and his team achieved one of humanity's fondest dreams: the ability to fly using human muscle power for propulsion. Project test pilot Bryan Allen completed the world's first human-powered, sustained, and controlled flight on August 23, 1977, piloting a frail craft named the *Gossamer Condor* over a special course at Shafter Airport, California, and thus winning the long-unclaimed Kremer Prize. Subsequently, he piloted a derivative, the *Gossamer Albatross*, across the English Channel on June 13, 1979, emulating the flight of Blériot not quite seventy years before, and securing another Kremer award. In both cases, the propulsion system consisted of a bicyclelike pedal rig connected to a pusher propeller. But the apparent simplicity of these two record-breaking airplanes—they had an externally braced framework with clear plastic covering over the flight surfaces and "cabin"—should not be allowed to obscure the very original and highly analytical research that went into their design. MacCready and project aerodynamicist Peter Lissaman undertook detailed analysis of stability and control requirements, the effects of loads upon the structure, and the appropriate choice of airfoil cross section for the wings, the horizontal control surface, and the propeller. They opted, unlike other human-flight enthusiasts, for very low flight speeds, about 10 to 15 mph. This alone placed them in what Lissaman subsequently termed "a relatively unexplored domain of flight."[2] They chose also to incorporate a construction scheme that would permit rapid repair and, if necessary, redesign. They selected thin-wall aluminum tubing for the *Condor*'s wing spar, but opted for advanced carbon-epoxy composites for that of the *Albatross*. The external skin consisted of DuPont Mylar only .0005 inch thick. MacCready and his team followed a flight test program as demanding as that of the Wright brothers. Approaches were taken, then rejected. Time after time, the frail airplanes crashed and were rebuilt. But the team learned, and in the end, success crowned their efforts. Today and for the future, a trip on gossamer wings is more than just a dream. It is a reality born of the desire for more efficient flight and the hard work of a unique group of flight researchers.

USE OF AUTOMATED TELEMETRY SYSTEMS

Today, automated "real-time" telemetry analysis of test flights while they are in progress has wrought a revolution in flight testing procedures. In days gone by, a test pilot like Shorty Schroeder would take off, perform some stipulated tests, land, and then write up his impressions of the plane. Even as late as 1944, for example, the Army Air Forces Flight Test Section at Wright Field utilized a sixteen-page "Pilot's Observation" form to record the data taken during the test flight. A little later, however, and the X-series aircraft were going aloft with comprehensive instrumentation packages. But still, after the plane landed, technicians would have to unload the on-board records of the flight (usually recorded on a strip of oscillograph film), as well as any data that might have been telemetered to the ground, and begin a lengthy process of "data reduction" and interpretation to try to find out what conditions the airplane had experienced. Sometimes, on other experimental production airplanes, data analysis fell behind the progress of the flights, with the result that, occasionally, test airplanes operated ahead of the latest data, data that might warn of undesirable and unsafe conditions. Tragically, every now and then a plane would crash because the latest information had failed to get to the test team in time before a scheduled flight. Such accidents were quite rare, but they did, nevertheless, occur. And there were other concerns as well. Increasingly, with the expensive, high-performance aircraft of the 1960s, it was simply too costly to fly an airplane on a test flight having but a few limited objectives. It greatly prolonged the length of the flight test process, at a time when the increasing complexity of new airplanes was already adding considerable amounts of time to aircraft development cycles.

With the enormous potential of the computer, some flight researchers believed the time had come when this powerful tool, in conjunction with data acquisition systems, could aid flight test personnel not only *after* the flight but *during* the flight. Grumman data-acquisition specialists combined experience gleaned in developing the Apollo program's Lunar Module with advanced communications and display equipment, backed by a CDC 6400 computer. The result was a real-time automated telemetry system (ATS) which, keyed to cathode-tube displays and voice communication, enabled a flight test conductor based on the ground to have instantaneous reports of conditions on board test aircraft in flight. The ATS system was first put to use in the testing of the F-14 Tomcat shipboard fighter. During test flights, the ATS presented analysts with readouts of aircraft behavior and performance. If all looked well, they could clear the test crew to proceed to the next test point. But if something looked suspicious, or if an undesirable trend appeared (say, for example, the data indicated that at some future point the plane would experience a marked decrease in directional stability), the ground personnel could notify the crew to bring the plane back home until the data could be fully worked up and analyzed. For once, test crews and ground test personnel operated with as much knowledge as they liked to have, greatly increasing confidence and safety. With modern automated telemetry systems, engineers on the ground can monitor the progress of a flight test as it is taking place, advising the crew of upcoming conditions and what they might expect at the next test point. For example, as a modern jet fighter maneuvers through a structural test, engineers on the ground may see an immediate readout of lift coefficient versus angle of attack, drag coefficient versus Mach number, vertical fin root bending moment versus vertical fin root torsion, together with Mach number, the airplane's airspeed, gross weight, and altitude, on their cathode ray monitors, enabling them to advise whether or not a test should continue. With the ATS in operation, Grumman generated a time saving in the F-14 test program of 67 per cent, as compared to previous company programs, in which earlier forms of data analysis had been utilized. The test F-14's made 46 per cent fewer flights, as well, a considerable cost and energy saving. These lessons were not lost on the flight testing community. Derivatives of the Grumman ATS are now in operation at both Patuxent River and Edwards, as well as at Manching, West Germany, where a Grumman system is utilized for the multinational European Tornado fighter-testing program. It is one more valuable tool for researchers, one that blends increased flight safety with highly desirable cost and time savings as well. In the future, such systems will undoubtedly proliferate.

REMOTELY PILOTED RESEARCH VEHICLES

One June morning at Edwards, a small red experimental airplane dropped away from a Boeing B-52 mother ship, fired up its engine, and flew off on a research mission to investigate use of advanced flight controls to prevent wing flutter. For ten minutes all went well. Then, suddenly, something went wrong. The experimental wing broke up, and the research airplane plummeted to the ground, crashing north of the base. Fortunately, the test pilot survived—he was, in fact, sitting safely on the ground in a special console at NASA's Dryden Flight Research Center. The airplane had been unmanned, a new kind of research tool, a "Remotely Piloted Research Vehicle" (RPRV).

There are no panaceas for the difficulties that flight testers sometimes encounter. There is no substitute for Wilbur Wright's advice that if you wish to fly, "you must mount a machine and become acquainted with its tricks by actual trial." Nevertheless, it is foolish to take unnecessary risks or incur unnecessary costs, and to the ends both of safety and economy, the RPRV is eminently suited.

In its simplest form, the RPRV can be thought of as a small radio-controlled model airplane. Unlike conventional "RC," or "drone," airplanes, however, the RPRV system features comprehensive instrumentation in a ground cockpit that is data-linked to the airplane. A fully qualified test pilot flies the RPRV remotely from the ground. NASA undertook the first RPRV tests in 1969 at Edwards, with pilot Milt Thompson flying an advanced lifting-body shape, the Hyper III, down to a landing. Interestingly, researchers discovered that the RPRV pilots experienced similar stress levels to those of pilots actually aloft on test missions. The NASA Flight Research Center then embarked on tests of a remotely controlled full-size airplane, the Piper PA-30 Twin Comanche, and eventually, in 1971, test pilot Einar Enevoldson flew the PA-30 from takeoff through landing, including precision maneuvers and stalls, all while sitting in the shirt-sleeve environment of the test center. The first major research use of the RPRV concept came during the Air Force F-15 program. At

NASA behest, McDonnell-Douglas constructed two ⅜-scale models of the F-15 shape, installing instrumentation enabling them to be piloted down to a landing following air launching from a modified B-52. The agency wished to study the spin-recovery characteristics of the novel-looking fighter before the onset of manned spinning trials.

Spin trials have always been among the more dangerous of flight tests. An experimental airplane is usually equipped with a special spin-recovery parachute, so that if the pilot finds that he cannot maneuver out of the spin, he can deploy the parachute, which will assist the plane in recovering, then jettison the chute. Nevertheless, there have been situations in which even the spin-recovery chute has not sufficed. In one case, a plane recovered from a spin when the pilot streamed the chute, but then reentered a spin in the opposite direction when the pilot jettisoned it. In another case, a test crew at Edwards were aloft on spinning trials with a modified F-4 Phantom II. The Phantom entered a flat spin, and when it was obvious that the plane would not recover on its own, the crew deployed the chute—which, due to an equipment problem, promptly separated from the airplane. The crew ejected safely, and the offending Phantom, in otherwise perfect condition, dug a hole in the desert. With an RPRV, flight test personnel could get a feel for the spin behavior of an airplane without actually risking the lives of a test crew and an expensive prototype. The F-15 RPRV first flew in 1973; it contributed information to researchers that lent confidence and encouragement to Air Force and McDonnell test personnel before they embarked on manned spinning trials in the full-size F-15.

Today the RPRV is an accepted part of flight testing, and a new RPRV, the Rockwell-NASA-USAF HiMAT (for Highly Maneuverable Aircraft Technology) is now flying, furnishing information for the advanced fighter designs of the 1990s. But a word of caution has to be inserted. The RPRV is by no means a substitute for the test pilot and piloted flight research. Rather, like the wind tunnel on the ground, it complements piloted flight research. Certainly the RPRV represents a testing method that will continue to find application.

GROUND AND IN-FLIGHT SIMULATION

With the increasing complexity of modern aerospace vehicles, it is often necessary to undertake development of appropriate simulation methods, both for research and for training purposes. This is especially true in the field of flight testing. Ground-based simulators possess varying degrees of complexity, from simple cardboard mock-ups to full-size multimillion-dollar motion simulators duplicating the entire cockpit area of some vehicle, together with appropriate visual, aural, and tactile cues. For example, in the early and mid-1960s, the Martin Company, under NASA contract, conducted seven-day simulations of the Apollo lunar landing mission. Team leader Milton Grodsky directed an effort at simulation that included a full-scale mock-up of the Apollo Command Module and the proposed lunar landing vehicle. The lander was supported on a three-axis gimbal system, and the test subjects—three-man teams of test pilots—could "see" the earth, stars, and moon outside the craft. Researchers piped in "radio communications" with "Mission Control," and a loudspeaker system duplicated the actual noise of the craft in operation. This effort typifies the creative role that simulation can play in developing criteria—in this case on crew performance during the mission—for use in an actual flight situation. During the X-15 program, the craft's test pilots trained on a cockpit simulator, "flying" it as much as ten to twenty hours before making each actual ten-to-twelve-minute flight. NASA's Ames Research Center pioneered using ground-based simulators for prediction of the critical problems encountered by an SST-type aircraft during flight. Today, the current state of simulator technology is represented by the massive Space Shuttle crew-procedures trainer at NASA's Johnson Space Center. This simulator includes a huge representation of the approach area to Edwards, and this is scanned by a camera to give the crew a realistic portrayal of what they will see during their approach to landing. Additionally, the astronaut crew can "fly" an entire Shuttle-type mission from lift-off through reentry and landing.

But even the best ground-based simulation methods are limited, and a much more satisfying method is simulation aloft. Once again, in-flight simulators can be used both for research and for training. In-flight simulation can be as routine as a pilot using an F-104 to mimic the approach and landing characteristics of a lifting body. Or it can be as complex as a multimillion-dollar aircraft having a sophisticated electronics package integrated with its control system so that the crew can duplicate the handling characteristics of another vehicle—such as NASA's Gulfstream Shuttle training airplanes. A particularly useful class of aircraft have been so-called "variable-stability" research vehicles, both fixed-wing and helicopter.

Variable-stability aircraft have a control system enabling the pilot or test crew to vary its characteristics, so that the plane can simulate a wide range of other aircraft or even hypothetical vehicles. The fidelity and realism of the variable-stability simulator can be checked by comparing its *simulation* of an actual airplane with the *known* characteristics of that actual airplane. In most cases today, variable-stability airplanes are multiplace vehicles, with a test cockpit having the variable-stability control system, and a "safety" or instructor cockpit, where the safety pilot or instructor monitors the performance of the airplane, ready to abort the flight should the plane enter a dangerous flight condition. While a variable-stability airplane cannot, in most cases, imitate the actual speed and altitude profile of another plane it is simulating, it must be remembered that this is not the intent. The intent is to simulate the other craft's actual or expected *handling* qualities, including the aerodynamic forces to be experienced by the plane and the control response expected. By adding such items as direct-lift flaps and "side force" control surfaces, the plane's lift-to-drag ratio, accelerations, and attitude can be totally changed; a variable-stability testbed such as the Calspan Corporation's NC-131H can, therefore, simulate the characteristics of even so different an aircraft as the Rockwell B-1 bomber.

During the 1950s, the NACA undertook development of a variety of variable-stability aircraft and helicopter testbeds. One of these, a modified Grumman F6F-5 Hellcat flown out of the Ames laboratory, furnished information for the design of the F-104; its control system was modified in such a way that the plane flew as if its wing were set at a variety of dihedral angles, depending on what the pilot selected in the cockpit. Later, a modified North American F-100 simulated the characteristics of the X-15. In the 1960s, the Martin Company modified two Convair F-106B Delta Darts to incorporate a variable-stability system and "side-stick" flight controllers so that they could act as trainers for the Air Force test pilot school, simulating the approach and landing characteristics of an SV-5P lifting body returning from space. NASA modified the Bell X-14B VTOL jet as a variable-stability aircraft for hover research. Princeton University modified and operated two Ryan Navion general-aviation airplanes as variable-stability testbeds.

The one organization whose name is inextricably linked to the development of variable-stability airplanes is, however, a private firm, the Calspan Corporation (formerly the Cornell Aeronautical Laboratory). Calspan began research on variable-stability aircraft, under the direction of Waldemar Breuhaus, as early as 1948, using a modified Vought F4U-5 Corsair developed for the Navy. In the early 1950s, a Calspan-modified Lockheed F-94 Starfire interceptor provided Convair with information on the expected longitudinal (pitch) handling qualities of the then-unflown B-58 Hustler bomber. Arguably the most successful variable-stability research aircraft ever built, however, is a modified Lockheed T-33A Shooting Star developed by Calspan in conjunction with the Air Force and now known as the Calspan NT-33A. It is still flying today. At one point, the craft featured retractable "drag petals" installed on its wing-tip fuel tanks so that it could vary its lift-to-drag ratio from the craft's standard 14:1 to about 2:1, enabling it to simulate an X-15 reentry and approach. During its career it has simulated a number of planned aircraft, ranging from Great Britain's abortive TSR-2 to the present-day McDonnell Douglas F-18 Hornet. Calspan also flies two Douglas B-26 attack bombers originally modified by the Air Force as variable-stability aircraft capable of simulating bomber-type handling qualities. The two B-26's and the NT-33A also help train student test pilots at the Navy and Air Force test pilot schools, acquainting them with the handling characteristics of a wide range of aircraft. (Soon Calspan will introduce a modified Gates Model 24 Learjet as a more suitable trainer in this era of high-performance jets.)

In recent years, Calspan has built on its earlier work with two other variable-stability testbeds, the modified Convair NC-131H TIFS (Total In-Flight Simulator), and a modified Bell X-22A V/STOL aircraft. The TIFS aircraft, operated on behalf of the Air Force's Wright Aeronautical Laboratory, is one of the most elaborate and versatile variable-stability aircraft developed to date, equipped with a variety of specialized control surfaces, sophisticated computer systems, and a complete second cockpit mounted on the nose of the craft for a test crew. It has successfully simulated the handling qualities and characteristics of such craft as the Rockwell B-1, the Anglo-French Concorde supersonic transport, and the NASA Space Shuttle Orbiter.

The X-22A is a specialized V/STOL variable-stability simulator, and in fact was the first aircraft designed and built from the outset as a variable-stability vehicle. This unique (if bizarre-looking) research airplane has simulated the qualities of a wide range of helicopters, and such V/STOL craft as the McDonnell Douglas AV-8B advanced Harrier, while flying a number of research programs for the Naval Air Systems Command. As long as flight researchers remember the prophetic words of the Wrights and Lilienthal, and regard the Sirenlike appeal of the ground simulator with skepticism, it can be expected that variable-stability aircraft will continue to play a major role in advancing the state of the art in flight research.

CONTROL OF COST ESCALATION

Costs have always been a key factor in limiting the growth of technology. Today, in an era of complex "high technology," economic questions become critical; presently, aircraft costs increase fourfold every ten years. At this rate, by the mid-twenty-first century, the federal government will be able to afford buying and flying only *one* military airplane! The initial XS-1's cost in the vicinity of $500,000 apiece; the X-2, a great step into the unknown, ran $2 million. And the X-15 cost $50 million. Today, NASA's estimates for a new hypersonic airplane having the X-15's general performance, range anywhere from $300 million to $600 million. The *entire* postwar transonic, supersonic, and hypersonic research-airplane program cost less than $500 million, in fact less than just one Apollo moon shot.

What is to be done? The answer is to search for alternative solutions that do not require developing unique research aircraft from scratch. There are several alternatives. A growing trend is the use of testbeds modified from existing designs. Recent examples have included NASA's YF-12 Blackbirds, the modified F-8's flown at Dryden, an Air Force F-4 Phantom modified with an FBW control system and a "short-coupled canard," and future plans to modify a present-day fighter as an advanced technology demonstrator. Another approach is to limit one's goals and not try to accomplish many research objectives using a single airplane. The present-day Ames/Dryden AD-1 oblique wing testbed aircraft is an example of the latter philosophy. It is a low-speed, unsophisticated aircraft powered by two small jet engines and intended strictly to validate the principle of oblique-wing operation.

Another approach is greater reliance on RPRV technology. This is, of course, not entirely satisfactory. However, an RPRV aircraft system can validate many of the general concepts and theories that a designer might need rough answers for. The present-day HiMAT program is a good example of the constructive use of the RPRV concept, furnishing data without requiring the Air Force or NASA to proceed with the costly and time-consuming development of an actual manned airplane. Two unmanned HiMAT's have been built for $17 million. A single larger manned HiMAT would have cost taxpayers $60 million.

Finally—though this is an alternative that is not popular with many flight researchers, for both traditional and practical reasons—one can make greater use of ground simulation facilities to derive data useful for the development of future flight technology. There is, of course, the serious problem of ensuring adequate correlation between the test data acquired on the ground and the likely data one would expect to acquire aloft. This problem is serious enough to warrant very careful structuring of any ground simulation and ground testing research program.

The best answer, of course, is for researchers to "try everything and reject nothing." The blending of all these approaches, together with creative management techniques emphasizing rigorous adherence to cost and time estimates, represents the best course of action for future flight researchers coping with the increasing costs associated with advancing aerospace technology.

CHANGING SOCIOLOGICAL PATTERNS

Through the years, changes in technology have forced changes in the flight testing and flight-research processes. There have been equal and significant changes in the sociological aspect of flight research, in the makeup of the flight researchers themselves. And one can safely forecast that continued sociological changes, in some cases reflecting patterns in society as a whole, will take place.

One such area concerns women in flight testing. Women have always been involved in flight testing but have never been fully represented among professionals in the field, especially among the ranks of test pilots themselves. Katharine Wright staunchly supported the work of her more famous brothers. As early as 1912, Bernetta Miller, a graduate of the Moisant training school, at Hempstead, Long Island, flew a Moisant monoplane on official demonstration trials before representatives of the government at the Army's College Park flight test center. In the 1930s, Amelia Earhart evaluated new aircraft designs for the federal government, even setting altitude records in an experimental autogiro. In the 1930s, aviatrix Jacqueline Cochran undertook high-altitude aeromedical research with Dr. W. Randolph Lovelace, and also tested new aero engines. (Later, she became the first woman pilot to exceed Mach 1 and Mach 2.) In Germany, before and during the Second World War, Flugkapitän Hanna Reitsch flew many experimental aircraft (including the Me 163). So did her fellow countrywoman Flugkapitän Melitta Gräfin von Stauffenberg, who courageously perished in the "kith and kin" murders following the failure of the bomb plot against Hitler instigated by her brother-in-law, Colonel Claus von Stauffenberg. A wartime WASP pilot, Ann Baumgartner, became the first American woman to fly a jet aircraft, when she evaluated an experimental Bell YP-59A Airacomet at Wright Field in 1943. Barbara Jayne, Elizabeth Hooker, and Cecile "Teddy" Kenyon, three production test pilots Grumman employed during the war, logged thousands of flight hours piloting newly produced Avengers, Wildcats, and Hellcats on their initial flights. British test pilot Joan Hughes test-flew in England and is perhaps best known for her work on the pioneer Demoiselle monoplane flown in the cinematographic epic *Those Magnificent Men in Their Flying Machines.* (She was selected because she was both a skilled pilot—and the only pilot light enough to fly it!) Jacqueline Auriol distinguished herself as a French test pilot, flying such aircraft as the Dassault Mystère IV and the later Mirage. She graduated from the French test pilot school in 1960, the first woman ever to complete a formal test pilot training program. The Society of Experimental Test Pilots recognized the accomplishments of Jacqueline Auriol, Jacqueline Cochran, and Hanna Reitsch by awarding each of them Honorary Fellowships in SETP in the early 1970s.

Nevertheless, the ranks of female test pilots worldwide are thin. Recently, since the military services have started training female pilots, some women aviators have joined naval test and evaluation squadrons at such centers as China Lake. It is to be expected that as the number of available female pilots increases, some, possessing the requisite technical and flying background, will be selected to attend the Air Force or Navy test pilot schools. (The ranks of nonpilot flight test engineers have already been increased by women entering that profession.) And a major step, of course, has been the selection of female astronaut-mission specialists for the upcoming Space Shuttle program. Eventually, it can be presumed that NASA will select the first female astronauts for piloting duties as well, probably from the ranks of female military-service pilots.

One area, of course, where women have always participated is in engineering and data support on the ground. In fact, from the 1930s onward, the old NACA and other governmental scientific bodies placed special emphasis upon utilizing women for mathematical computational tasks. By the 1950s, the first women engineers were entering the flight testing process, and today, the national research and development centers are, in this respect, generally free from traditional bias. Interestingly, for such a staunchly "macho" field, there seems to be little of the prejudice that hinders women in, say, the business world at large. Perhaps this is because flight testing is a remarkably pragmatic endeavor, and it little matters if a male or a female has come up with some answer, only that the answer be right.

Recent decades have witnessed a growing concern for the rights of America's older citizens. Especially pernicious is the notion that after some certain age, a person should be "put out to pasture," and if necessary, forcibly retired. But what of the test pilot? Does the older test pilot represent a special case? Some industrial lawyers and work specialists think not, and believe that as long as a pilot is demonstrably fit and mentally alert, he is capable of fulfilling his duties as a test pilot. Others disagree, arguing that it is well and good to have a senior airline captain who flies under basically "tame" conditions, but a test pilot, who often flies tense, stress-inducing and physically demanding missions is, they argue, quite another matter. Such questions, one would think, must be decided on the individual merits of each case. Certainly this issue will be raised in the future, as it already has been in the past. At least nowadays, nobody seriously believes, as William Faulkner did, that today's test pilot "begins to train in his teens and is through in his thirties." Today there are a growing number of test-flying grandfathers who quite capably and confidently zip through the air at Mach 2—and long may they do so.

The modern test pilot also has a substantially different educational background than his predecessors. In the late teens and twenties, it was not uncommon for the test pilot to have some technical-school training and perhaps a degree in mechanical engineering. Then, after the Second World War, there was a subtle shift toward such specialities as mathematics, electronics, physics, and sometimes geology and chemistry. Today, many test pilots are multiple degree holders with, for example, a bachelor's degree in an engineering area, and a postgraduate degree in the same field or in an area such as administration or business management. In the test pilot field as in many other professions, there is a growing trend toward acquiring a master's degree in business administration or general administration, or even a law degree. This trend will probably become firmly established as some test pilots opt for leaving the cockpit for the corporate boardroom. One characteristic, however, remains unchanged from the days of Lilienthal, Busk, and Eddie Allen: the test pilot must be knowledgeable in aerospace science and technology. As British test pilot John Derry remarked before the Royal Aeronautical Society in 1951, "He and the scientist must speak the same language, but not the same dialect."

One important facet of modern society is its increasing dependence upon information and communications—in short, the exchange of knowledge. It is encouraging to note the importance that the Western world's flight testing community places upon technical exchanges. The various American, British, French, and Italian flight test pilot schools are in close touch with one another, and for example, it is standard procedure for the graduates of the two American schools to take a "graduation tour" of foreign flight test establishments to better acquaint them with their colleagues' work in progress. Professional aerospace organizations, notably the SETP, the Society of Flight Test Engineers (SFTE), and the Test Pilots' Group of the Royal Aeronautical Society (founded in 1963) also do much to promote the international exchange of information on flight testing and flight research. This too is a trend certain to continue, as is the practice of foreign governments routinely admitting selected students from other countries, and instructors as well, to their test pilot schools. The Australian trainee pilot, for example, who is attending Britain's Empire Test Pilots' School, may well have an American Navy instructor for one of his classes. The American student pilot at Patuxent River may likewise find himself studying under an instructor whose accent is more at home at Boscombe or Bedford than on the shores of the Chesapeake Bay.

There is also an emerging corporate presence in flight testing and flight research. Increasingly, specialist firms have evolved for the purpose of undertaking contractor flight testing programs. This trend first began in the 1940s, with the establishment of the old Curtiss-Wright Research Laboratory, at Buffalo, New York. In 1945, Curtiss-Wright, "in the interest of aviation and the welfare of the nation," presented the laboratory to Cornell University, thus spawning the Cornell Aeronautical Laboratory (CAL), which functioned largely independently of the university. Over the subsequent years, CAL's research was contract-oriented and broad-based. As mentioned previously, the laboratory made its greatest contribution in the field of variable-stability aircraft. But CAL also tested captured Russian-built Yak and Ilyushin aircraft during the Korean War, undertook investigations of a poststall gyration problem plaguing the semitailless Vought F7U-3 Cutlass, tested experimental low-level high-speed terrain-following systems on board a modified Martin B-57B bomber, and evaluated other major American military and civilian aircraft. In 1972, the organization changed its name to Calspan Corporation, reflecting the range and scope of its activities. Other private organizations concerned with operational test and evaluation work have emerged, such as the BDM Corporation (founded in 1959), which is currently involved in a wide range of American military aviation projects, and Flight Systems, Inc., of Mojave, California, which maintains a small fleet of research aircraft (including ex-military jet fighters) for specialized testing. For a firm that may not have its own "in-house" flight testing department, the presence of a growing number of "for hire" flight testing firms offers one answer to meeting the testing need. And there are a number of supplier companies that are involved in furnishing governmental and private flight research organizations with specialized testing equipment ranging from small cockpit instruments to entire test and evaluation air ranges over which an airplane can fly.

Finally, there are ethical concerns as well. The decades since the Second World War have not been easy ones. While we must recognize the truth of the old Latin proverb that he who desires peace must be prepared for war, we must equally recognize that our control over science and technology is far greater than our control over ourselves, and consequently, for the first time in history, humanity possesses the ability to destroy itself and all the trappings of civilization. Should the dark time come when the world is plunged into a nuclear holocaust through the work of madmen, blunderers, or, ironically, perhaps by technological error itself, it will represent, as Lindbergh recognized, the folly of worshiping science and technology at the expense of human values. And the price may be all that we have achieved as humans, centuries wiped away by the flicker of nuclear fires. Any impartial witness to the past eight decades would recognize that aerospace technology has played a very special role in bringing humanity to this point; indeed, the nuclear balance of terror, with peace maintained only through the ethically questionable doctrine of "mutually assured destruction," is ensured only by reliance on aerospace technology. The same technology that can build new and better airliners can produce the bombers that bring down the world around us; the technology that safely returns astronauts and cosmonauts to earth can return multimegaton bombs through the fiery hell of reentry to ensure fiery hells on earth. One could easily look at the history of aviation, especially the role flight research and flight testing have played in developing such capabilities, and become totally discouraged. But there is hope, for increasing numbers of aerospace technologists are recognizing that one cannot legitimately separate technology from social and ethical values. To do so is to succumb, in Hannah Arendt's damning phrase, to the banality of evil.

Thus, today and for the foreseeable future, flight researchers and test pilots have a special responsibility to ensure that their activities accrue to the general benefit of humanity and not to the support of any misguided escalation of destructive technology. As Charles Lindbergh stated to his fellow pilots after receiving an Honorary Fellowship in The Society of Experimental Test Pilots in 1969,

> We are proud to have helped expand the scale of time on the charts of space. But I believe our pride should be tempered by the realization that man and his awareness, in fact all the basic qualities of life, developed under conditions of low power and slow movement.
>
> To what degree can life adjust to the commercial and military impacts that eventuate through our profession? This, I think, is the greatest test we, and everyone who works in professions of space and air, must face.
>
> I do not know the answer; but surely the first step in searching for it is recognition of the problem. . . .[3]

If each of these areas poses its own set of challenges and responsibilities, it is comforting to realize that at least one constant exists in the flight research / flight testing equation: the continued demand for highly motivated and highly trained test pilots and flight test engineers. In the final analysis, the research-and-development problem eventually does reduce itself to the test crew sitting in the airplane at the end of the runway. As British test pilot A. W. "Bill" Bedford remarked while giving the inaugural lecture of the Royal Aeronautical Society's Test Pilots' Group in 1964, "In simple terms, the test pilot is the designer's hand on the final product, and he must convey back to the designer how the project behaves in a manner as convincing as though the designer were himself a test pilot."[4]

After the lecture, Sir Sidney Camm, Hawker's legendary designer, commented that the test pilot is "certainly the designer's best guide, philosopher, and friend."[5] Another commentator, summarizing a lecture by Sir George Edwards, the great Vickers designer, noted:

> Sir George paid tribute to the work of test pilots, who were, he said, the only men in the whole design and production chain who really risked their lives to prove the products. It was the test pilot who could make a poor start into something worthwhile; and it was fatal either to employ bad test pilots or to take no notice of what the good ones said.[6]

No better example of the coolness and decisive actions required of a test pilot exists than an incident involving General Dynamics test pilot Phil Oestricher and the YF-16 experimental fighter. Oestricher was making a series of high-speed taxi runs along the Edwards runway when the little plane's control system proved too sensitive. Suddenly the brightly painted airplane began rolling and bobbing violently, scraping one wing tip on the runway and veering toward the scrub desert beyond. Oestricher realized that he would have a far better chance of saving the airplane if he actually took off, so he added full power and roared into the air as startled witnesses and test personnel looked on. After cautiously evaluating the airplane, he returned it safely to earth, where it underwent extensive control-system modifications before its "official" first flight. With skill and verve a test pilot had saved a valuable prototype to fly another day by knowing when to abandon the illusory safety of the ground for the actual safety of the sky.

In 1967, James E. Webb, the perceptive administrator of the National Aeronautics and Space Administration, testified before Congress that

> Flight testing of new concepts, designs and systems is fundamental to aeronautics. Laboratory data alone, and theories based on these data, cannot give all the important answers. . . . Each time a new aircraft flies, a "moment of truth" arrives for the designer as he discovers whether a group of individually satisfactory elements add together to make a satisfactory whole or whether their unexpected interactions result in a major deficiency. Flight research plays the essential role in assuring that all the elements of an aircraft can be integrated into a satisfactory system.[7]

As long as humanity flies in or beyond earth's atmosphere, the test pilot and flight researcher will continue to lead the way.

THE SAGA OF THE VOYAGER

On December 14, 1986, an aircraft unlike any the world had ever seen took off from Edwards Air Force Base, heading west. Nine days later it appeared in the skies above the great dry lake and landed, having completed the first round-the-world flight made without using aerial refueling, or landing to refuel enroute. Thus did Dick Rutan, Jeana Yeager, and the *Voyager* enter into aviation history books, having (in Dick Rutan's words) picked "the last plum": the last great epic atmospheric flight remaining to be plucked.

The story of *Voyager* is a fascinating one, all the more so because it was not the product of a major aerospace conglomerate or the government, supported by laboratories and special facilities scattered around the country and drawing on the experience and skill of thousands of individuals expending millions of man-hours. Rather, it was the product of Dick and Burt Rutan, Jeana Yeager (no relation to Chuck), and a small team of individuals at Mojave airport, aided by private donations from enthusiastic individuals around the country; it was more in the spirit of Lindbergh and his small team of backers than the era of high tech—but there was high tech enough for those familiar with the program.

Voyager could not have succeeded without two major advances since the Second World War: the refinement of aerodynamics including the application of numerical solution techniques to determine "optimized" aerodynamic shapes, and (more importantly) the development of the so-called composite structure from a materials revolution that began in the mid-1960s, but which had roots going as far back as the Second World War. Grumman's radical forward-swept X-29 technology demonstrator typified the application of these advances (coupled with electronic fly-by-wire flight control technology) to high-speed transonic and supersonic aircraft design. *Voyager* encompassed the application of these to a much different flight regime. Both programs demanded creative solutions to unique engineering problems—but, again, whereas one was the product of the military services, NASA, the Defense Advanced Projects Research Agency, and a major aerospace contractor, the other was the product of but a single small team working out of a single hangar at Mojave.

As discussed previously, Burt Rutan had made his name with a family of radical "homebuilt" canard aircraft designed for construction by individuals for their own use. Eventually, Rutan's interest led him to form a small company, Scaled Composites, which built subscale flying demonstrators of proposed designs being developed by major aerospace manufacturers, notably the Fairchild T-46 (which the government eventually abandoned), and the Beech Starship, the latter a truly elegant canard business and corporate airplane. But such success was not enough, and Burt Rutan set his sights on a far more difficult accomplishment: designing an airplane to fly all the way around the world, without refueling. To both Burt and Dick Rutan, it seemed the last major challenge remaining in atmospheric flight. Very early, the two brothers decided on two important goals: fly a full 25,000 miles, and fly over the oceans to have the freedom to avoid the problems associated with overflight clearances as well as to have the freedom to fly around weather. One day in 1981, Burt Rutan, Dick Rutan, and Jeana Yeager sat down in the dining room of a now defunct restaurant in Mojave and discussed the project. Burt doodled a sketch of a large flying wing having a sweep-back angle of 15 degrees, his initial concept for the world-girdling craft. Over the next few weeks Burt Rutan recognized that the wing alone could not hold enough fuel; the craft would need long fuel tanks projecting ahead of and behind the wing. When he added the tanks, he recognized the need for a canard connecting the nose of the fuselage to the tanks to eliminate torsional problems with the structure. The next addition was vertical fins to the back of the booms. The fuselage would have both a pusher and tractor engine, the latter to be utilized only at the beginning and end of the flight as an additional propulsion unit (during the record flight, the front engine would fly with its prop feathered—i.e., in minimal drag position—to reduce drag). Thus was born the generalized *Voyager* configuration.

Many enthusiasts draw up visions of dream airplanes. But transforming those dreams into a hardware reality is something else again. The Rutans recognized that *Voyager* would be quite impossible if built with conventional aluminum or Fiberglas construction. The key was lightness: but with sufficient strength to ensure that the plane could hold out for the long and arduous voyage. That meant using graphite composites. Eventually *Voyager* used a solid Magnamite graphite spar for its 111-ft wing, and used graphite composite sheeting bonded to Hexcel honeycomb cores for the skin. This huge two-place airplane—larger than a Boeing 727 in span—weighed only 1,858 pounds (and six pounds *less* than originally estimated); in contrast, when fueled for its round-the-world flight, it weighed 9,760 pounds. Graceful drag-reducing winglets sprouted from its wingtips. To build the airplane, the Rutans needed money—and they got it, as stated previously, from private donations. In the years prior to the flight, Dick Rutan and Jeana Yeager, the crewmen, were familiar sights on the aviation lecture circuit, particularly in Southern California. No donation was too small, no group too insignificant for them to make the effort to raise funds. They refused some donations from groups they did not believe in; for example, they turned down an offer of lucrative sponsorship by a major tobacco company.

It would have been easy to dismiss the whole project as a crank effort were it not for the proven track record of the Rutans, and the reputation of Dick Rutan and Jeana Yeager as pilots. Rutan had retired from the Air Force as a Lieutenant Colonel, having been a career fighter pilot. He served in the Vietnam war as a so-called "Misty FAC," a high-speed Forward Air Controller working over the southern half of North Vietnam in aging F-100's. Even among Vietnam aircrews, the "Hun"-flying Misty FAC's were legendary for their courage and aggressiveness, and among the Misty's, Rutan was a standout who had himself survived being shot down and parachuting into the Gulf of Tonkin. After retirement he had joined his brother Burt as the family test pilot on Burt's radical designs; quiet and reserved, Rutan quickly established a reputation for himself even in the high-rolling flight testing arena of the Mojave. So too had Yeager, whom Dick had met in 1980. Petite and serious in manner, she had led an adventurous life, including, for a time, serving as the planned "project pilot" for rocket-pioneer Robert Truax's effort to develop a private-enterprise rocket capable of boosting ordinary citizens into the upper atmosphere. An accomplished draftsman and pilot, Jeana Yeager had set numerous records flying Rutan canards. Together, these two, then, planned to take Burt Rutan's airplane around the world, nonstop.

Voyager rolled out of Hangar 77 at Mojave at 2:00 P.M. on June 2, 1984. It looked—different. In overall shape, it vaguely resembled a gigantic remotely piloted vehicle, such as the Compass Cope surveillance aircraft of the 1970s. Like Lindbergh's *Spirit of St. Louis* it lacked a "traditional" cockpit. Indeed, one of the most challenging aspects of the entire flight was how two people could stay in the tiny airplane for nearly two weeks. Only one could sit—the pilot. The "off-duty" pilot would rest on a fuel bladder bed. The "on–duty" pilot could see forward through a small bubble canopy protruding above the fuselage lines, but the entire flight would be very demanding and downright uncomfortable. With *Voyager* built, all attention focused on its first flight. The first flight subsequently came off without incident, though, as Rutan afterward recalled, "As you look down the runway it gets very lonely; you always wonder what the next five minutes of your life will be like." Very quickly, and as expected, the Rutans and Yeager discovered that the *Voyager* flew nowhere nearly as good as it looked. It had barely marginal lateral and directional handling qualities, but they were adequate for the shallow climbs and turns the craft could be expected to make on its round-the-world flight. It had pronounced adverse yaw tendencies, requiring judicious use of rudder and aileron to overcome. Though initial flight testing revealed no serious flutter tendency, subsequent testing indicated that at mission weight, the *Voyager* could experience a short-period "divergent" oscillatory motion that would lead to break-up in three to five cycles—approximately fifteen seconds— unless the pilot took immediate corrective action. It was so sensitive in pitch that the application of a mere quarter-pound of force in pitch control would add an additional g to the airplane, giving it a Cooper-Harper rating of 7 or 8—bordering on unacceptable. Conversely, lateral control forces were so heavy that aileron deflection required both hands. In short, it was a downright dangerous airplane, and would be a killer in the hands of the unwary. After its round-the world flight, the Rutans had no intention of ever flying it again.

Test flying proceeded relatively smoothly. In July 1986, *Voyager* set a closed-course record for distance while flying a racetrack-pattern between Point Reyes (north of San Francisco) and Santa Barbara; for twenty laps, Rutan and Yeager droned around off the California coast. After the second day, they found that they had acclimatized to the environment, but the high noise level in the cabin—about 110 decibels, equivalent to front-seats at a rock concert—demanded ear protection. Thirst and hunger did not prove to be problems, but dehydration did, and shortly after landing back at Mojave, while attending a press conference, Yeager fainted. Accordingly, more work went into the human factors questions.

Following its record flight in July, *Voyager* seemed on schedule for making its record attempt during the middle of its optimum weather window—the period in which it could be expected to encounter the most favorable weather conditions for the flight. But then disaster struck. On a test flight, the front engine shed one propeller blade, narrowly missing a chase plane, and setting up such a serious vibration that, for a brief time, Dick Rutan was uncertain which engine had failed. Fortunately, the front engine mounts failed "gracefully," allowing the engine to remain in the plane without wrenching it out of its mounts and sending *Voyager* and its crew to their doom. The ailing plane limped back to an emergency landing, and the team, who had thought themselves on the verge of the actual record attempt, now had to face serious questions: could the craft be repaired? And could it be repaired in time for a flight in the weather window? Fortunately, the answer to the first was an emphatic *yes*, but the second was a certain *no*, in part because all of *Voyager*'s electronic equipment had to be replaced, and the Rutans decided to abandon the planned wooden prop design that had failed, going, instead, with an all-metal prop from the Hartzell Company that required its own series of modifications. At this point, things began to look up again. Testing demonstrated that the new Hartzell prop gave 8–12 percent better fuel consumption characteristics than the wooden prop it replaced, this factor alone making up for the additional weight of the metal propeller. (Subsequently, the flight indicated that had the wooden propeller been utilized, *Voyager* would never have returned to its takeoff site).

At last, two months after the accident, *Voyager* was ready for flight. *Voyager* had lingered beyond its desirable weather window, but the Rutans and Yeager decided that they would press on in any case. The late date necessitated revising the flight plan to minimize undesirable weather, and included what Dick Rutan had feared most: an unavoidable track across central Africa, possibly crossing several unstable countries. During the flight, the *Voyager* crew planned to rely upon a project mission control center set up at Mojave. Originally, the mission control center was to be located on the first floor of the National Air and Space Museum in Washington, but this plan fell through and, instead, the *Voyager* team set up special trailer facilities at Mojave. It was not quite as primitive as it might seem; the team could rely upon the services of a project flight surgeon and project meteorologist; the meteorologist would contribute information from orbiting weather satellites to provide the crew with six-hour updates including recommendations on what course to fly to take advantage of favorable weather and avoid bad weather. Even so, as events turned out, *Voyager* had more than its share of problems with weather. On December 13, the crew and other team members determined that they were ready. Jepperson navigational charts were put on microfiche for use with a small microfiche reader. On the afternoon of December 13, the crew ferried *Voyager* to Edwards, whose runway and lakebed offered maximum safety; fueling operations took place that night, as with the early rocket research aircraft of the 1950s and 1960s. Dawn found the *Voyager* poised for flight on the west end of Edwards' 15,000-foot runway. The chill Mojave night had deposited a coating of ice over the plane, and members of the team and even the center's vice commander, Colonel Bob Ettinger, cleaned the ice from its surfaces. There had been no desire to take off at maximum gross weight except for the world flight itself, and thus *Voyager* was sitting at the end of the runway at a heavier gross weight than ever before, its drooping wing tips about 8 inches off the runway.

Unknown to the team, three small occurrences now conspired to make the *Voyager*'s takeoff even more exciting than anticipated. First, to improve safety and controllability during the first moments of flight, the *Voyager* team had shortened the nose landing gear strut, thus lowering the angle of incidence of the wing. Secondly, concerned that the drooping tips might scrape the runway as the plane accelerated on takeoff, the team pumped up the main landing gear to give a little more tip clearance; this had the effect of further lowering the angle of incidence. Thirdly, the heavy boom tanks imparted a slight twist to the wing that reduced the angle of incidence even more. The result of all this, when taken together, meant that as *Voyager* accelerated down the runway, its wing would be driven by aerodynamic forces toward the ground—in effect, pounding the wing tips, with their fragile composite structure, into the ground.

At 8:00 A.M., *Voyager* began its takeoff roll, its 130-horsepower supplemental engine in the nose and the 110-horsepower tail-mounted cruise engine both rasping loudly. Built by Teledyne, the two engines differed in their cooling; the front engine, as expected, used air-cooling from the ram air stream. The aft engine relied upon liquid cooling; it was the latter engine that would be most heavily taxed during the flight, as the front engine would only be used at the beginning and end of the flight. As *Voyager* began trundling down the runway, observers and the onboard crew began noting its acceleration as measured against checkpoints along the runway. At its first checkpoint, it was close to its planned speed. But at the second it was 2 knots low, and at the third, 4 knots low. At about the same time, observers noted the wingtips dragging the ground. Aloft, Burt Rutan, in a chaseplane, watched as Dick Rutan pounded along; neither Dick nor Jeana Yeager was aware of the wingtip drama occurring just out of view of the cockpit. *Voyager* had a narrow margin of safety for a "go no-go" decision, and Dick Rutan was determined to stop only in the face of certain catastrophe. When he rotated the plane, the tips cleared the runway, the wing began operating at a positive angle of attack, and *Voyager* gracefully—if ponderously—lifted into the air. At 100 knots it climbed out into the east over the lake bed, then turned and began its western journey, its damaged winglets fluttering in the breeze. On the advice of Burt Rutan, Dick Rutan and Jeana Yeager decided to dispense with the damaged wingtip winglets, and Dick skidded the aircraft to cause the tips to fail under the added air loads. This posed a potential problem, for the *Voyager* had to skid in such a fasion that the up-wind tip would fail. As it failed, it naturally would tear a portion of the composite covering from the upper surface of the wing near the tips. The Rutans feared that the tearing might possibly extend over the fuel tank itself, generating a possibly fatal leak and imbalance that would spell disaster. But both tips separated relatively cleanly, and the tanks remained undamaged and intact. Another danger might have been if one tip had separated as planned and the other had not—the trim forces to keep the plane in trim would have prevented *Voyager* from completing its flight due to high drag and resulting additional fuel usage. Losing the tips cost *Voyager* in range and fuel consumption, fortunately not critically. Even more important, the exposed composite core did not erode as much as might have been expected, and thus *Voyager* preserved its desired airfoil cross-sections despite the extensive surface damage near the tips.

It would be pleasant to report that *Voyager* flew onward, the real excitement behind it, and just piled up the hours and miles until it returned to Edwards. Such, of course, was not the case. The mission called for the plane to fly at an average airspeed of 115 mph, though in reality the plane would considerably exceed this at first in its loaded condition and with both engines operating, and would fly considerably less than this toward the end of its journey as it neared Edwards. Because of its anticipated divergent oscillatory motions at loaded conditions, *Voyager* depended upon a King Radio autopilot, which the team fine-tuned. Likewise, King furnished a comprehensive navigational system consisting of a Very Low Frequency (VLF) Omega navigation system, weather radar (installed at Rutan's request over the objections of brother Burt), and a global positioning receiver so that *Voyager* could always determine its position relative to orbiting navigation satellites. *Voyager* benefited from its extensive weather planning and the project meteorologist; throughout the flight, the plane averaged a ten knot tailwind, which helped offset the loss of the wingtip winglets, the longer than planned running of the front engine, and course deviations demanded by the weather. Over a day after takeoff, nearing the Marshall Islands, *Voyager* encountered its first bad weather as it passed near Typhoon Marge. Dick Rutan was still flying the airplane—he flew it for the first fifty-five hours, in fact—and the turbulence jolts buffeted the plane greatly. Yeager became airsick, but when Rutan finally relinquished the controls, she took over despite her sickness, and pressed on. December 17, the anniversary of the Wright brothers first flight at Kitty Hawk, found Rutan near disquietingly familiar territory: the South China Sea off Vietnam. Well aware of how the North Vietnamese had feared and loathed the Misty FAC's who had flown so determinedly to end the North's aggression against the ill-fated South, Rutan wondered if, as a payback, the Vietnamese might attempt to intercept the round-the-world flight. Fortunately not; and *Voyager* continued onward. By this time, the crew were aware of a serious fuel discrepancy; backflow into the tanks was generating misleading fuel consumption statistics. Rutan and Yeager reasoned that the fuel consumption was acceptable, but determined to check on it later. Eventually the opportunity came while flying over Africa. A Beech Baron from Nairobi joined up on *Voyager*, and on the basis of a series of single and twin engine climb tests, Dick and Jeana confirmed that *Voyager* was healthy after all. It was at this point that the *Voyager* mission experienced some of the worst weather—if not its worst moment, which would come later, off Mexico— of the entire flight.

When the Rutans and Yeager had first planned their round-the-world flight, they had intended to follow a flight path that would take them over the world's oceans, since overflying land raised complications due to the necessity of getting overflight permits; additionally, the constraints of geography and weather would be greater with land crossings. But by the time *Voyager* launched on its trip, the conditions at the time forced a more northerly route that, of necessity, required crossing Africa. Several African nations—notably Uganda, Sudan, Chad, and Ethiopia—had denied *Voyager* overflight permission. Now, confronted with violent thunderstorms over Lake Victoria, Rutan and Yeager had to accept the danger of weather in order to avoid possibly being shot down. (Nevertheless, they overflew Uganda's Entebbe airfield, where Israeli antiterrorists had taught dictator Idi Amin some of the finer points of international law a decade previously). Not wishing to risk overflying war-torn Ethiopia, Chad, and Sudan, however, the *Voyager* crew opted instead to press through the weather, but avoid most of it by going to high altitude. They climbed as high as they could, and went on oxygen. Despite this, the flight over central Africa was physiologically grueling. As with Lindbergh during his own Atlantic crossing in 1927, Dick Rutan experienced hallucinations as he piloted the craft, at one point imagining the *Voyager* exploding. Hypoxia and airsickness added to their misery. In time they passed over the front, and then *Voyager* was out over the South Atlantic.

Two significant crises marred the last major ocean crossing of the flight. Midway across the Atlantic, an oil warning light for the aft engine startled the crew into quickly adding more oil from a reserve tank. The engine temperature returned to normal and *Voyager* droned on. Then, just off the coast of Brazil, an emergency warning from *Voyager* mission control at Mojave warned Rutan and Yeager of a severe but small storm directly in their flight path. Unable to aovid it, the crew continued onward, into the most violent turbulence of the entire flight. Repeatedly, turbulence buffeted the craft and threw it into extreme banks, which, given *Voyager*'s marginal controllability, posed a grave danger to its survival. As Rutan recalled, at one point, the storm "spat us out at 90 degrees of bank . . . we unloaded to a quarter of a g, added in full rudder, added aileron, and slowly recovered." This, too, passed, and *Voyager*, now nearing its eighth day, pressed onward. Unlike the original plan, which called for a return through the Caribbean and a crossing of the United States from Texas onward, the *Voyager*'s hardy crew crossed over Costa Rica, and turned northward over the Pacific coast of Central America. At this point, headwinds slowed *Voyager*'s ground speed to as little as 65 knots; the flight was now a contest of human endurance, engine reliability, and a dynamic equation of remaining fuel vs. distance vs. weather conditions.

A chain of events now began that nearly spelled disaster for *Voyager* hours later. One of the plane's two electric fuel pumps failed. The rear engine's mechanical fuel pump now fed directly from a canard fuel tank, bypassing the pump that failed. Unfortunately, the engine needed to draw fuel in a nearly level attitude. Concerned about headwinds causing high fuel consumption, Rutan initiated a descent off Baja in a bid to find slower winds at low altitude. As *Voyager* nosed downward, gravity played a cruel joke and the rear engine abruptly quit; *Voyager* was now a glider, only 700 miles from home. At mission control, and even in the cockpit of the plane, pandemonium erupted. Instinct took over, and Rutan set to work isolating and identifying the problem. Just 5½ minutes later, Rutan fired up the front engine—a desperation move to save the aircraft, for running the front engine for any amount of time would doom the mission to failure from fuel exhaustion. On the ground, one mission controller reported he had "teeth marks on his heart." For *Voyager*, time had run out. Then, as the plane leveled out, the crew were able to restart the aft engine. Thanks to its broad wing and high lift to drag ratio (on the order of 30 or 33 to 1), the plane had lost only 2,500 feet. Now the crew rearranged the tubing for the fuel feed system so that the rear engine could draw fuel from the right side to improve its weight and balance distribution. On its rear engine alone, *Voyager* headed home. At sunrise on December 23, about seventy miles off Long Beach, Burt Rutan and team member Mike Melvill rendezvoused with *Voyager* in a Beech Duchess chase plane. Overcome with emotion, Burt Rutan cried for forty-five minutes. And so it was that *Voyager* returned to Edwards as the project team went delirious with joy. In contrast to the approximately 100 people that had seen the takeoff, this time, 50,000 awaited its return. Accompanied by the Duchess and two other chase planes, *Voyager* appeared below the thinning cloud deck over Edwards at 7:35 A.M., still droning along at 67 mph. Anxiously Rutan asked if any test flights were in progress, for morning is a busy time at "Eddie Air Patch"; the tower replied that all the pilots were watching *Voyager:* center commander Major General Ted Twinting had shut Edwards down until *Voyager* returned. And now *Voyager* and its crew received the attention that was their due. Diek Rutan cruised above the lakebed along the rows of people, showing off *Voyager* in clean configuration. Then, as Jeana Yeager pumped arduously in the cockpit, the three landing gears came down one by one. They flew around for a few more minutes to make it an even nine days; Nancy Reagan informed them later that the president had said "Land the damn plane!" as it kept circling. Finally, all was set, the gear was down, and *Voyager*—a difficult airplane to fly under any condition—made its landing approach, both engines ticking over, as Melvill in the chase aircraft read off altitudes to Dick Rutan while *Voyager* sank earthward. Nine days, 3 minutes, and 40 seconds after liftoff, *Voyager*'s wheels brushed the lakebed, and Edwards could record another successful first.

It had been a remarkable flight. Just over eighty-three years previously the Wright brothers had remained aloft for twelve seconds and had covered scant feet. The accomplishment of *Voyager* required no less daring and imagination, and the family nature of the feat seemed to bring it full circle to the experience of the Ohio brothers. It had been a near thing, given the number of close calls aloft. When *Voyager* landed, it had only 18½ gallons of fuel left—just 1½ per cent of its fuel load, sufficient for another 600 to 700 nautical miles. It seemed a lot, but slightly less tail winds, slightly stronger headwinds coming up the Pacific coast, slightly less efficient propellers, a slightly larger fuselage, all would have made a difference between victory and defeat. Some cited the closeness and called *Voyager* a triumph of luck—but that was both misleading and unfair. Professionals—especially those in the flight testing arena—make their own luck by planning and hard work. The team at Mojave, the crew of the *Voyager*, possessed luck—but it was the luck of Lindbergh—the luck that they had earned. Ahead lay international recognition; President Ronald Reagan awarded the Rutans and Jeana Yeager Presidential Citizens Medals. *Voyager* had captured the attention of the nation, demonstrating yet again that aviation is dynamic and the stuff of epic adventure. It fittingly symbolized the mastery of winged flight within the atmosphere. Beyond the atmosphere, of course, lay the ever-present challenge of space.

The *Voyager* discussion is based on a lecture by Dick Rutan and Jeana Yeager at the University of Dayton, Ohio 24 March 1987; from conversations with Dick Rutan and Jeana Yeager in 1983–84; and from numerous press accounts, particularly Sandra Blakeslee, "Voyager Succeeds in Historic Flight," *New York Times*, 24 Dec. 1986; Michael Specter, "Voyager Completes Record-Breaking Flight," *Washington Post*, 24 Dec. 1986; and Michael Specter, "Reagan Hails Flight That 'Inspired a Nation' ", *Washington Post*, 30 Dec. 1986. I have also benefited from discussions with Col. Bob Ettinger, USAF, Lt. Col. Bill Flanagan, and Pete Merlin, who were present at Edwards during the launch and recovery of *Voyager*.

APPENDIX

THE COOPER-HARPER HANDLING QUALITIES RATING SCALE

DEFINITIONS GOVERNING THE INTERPRETATION OF THE COOPER-HARPER SCALE

Required Operation: The designation of flight phase and/or subphases with accompanying conditions.

Compensation: The measure of additional pilot effort and attention required to maintain a given level of performance in the face of deficient vehicle characteristics.

Handling Qualities: Those qualities or characteristics of an aircraft that govern the ease and precision with which a pilot is able to perform the tasks required in support of an aircraft role.

Mission: The composite of pilot-vehicle functions that must be performed to fulfill operational requirements. May be specified for a role, complete flight, flight phase, or flight subphase.

Performance: The precision of control with respect to aircraft movement that a pilot is able to achieve in performing a task. (Pilot-vehicle performance is a measure of handling performance. Pilot performance is a measure of the manner of efficiency with which a pilot moves the principal controls in performing a task.)

Role: The function or purpose that defines the primary use of an aircraft.

Task: The actual work assigned a pilot to be performed in completion of or as representative of a designated flight segment.

Workload: The integrated physical and mental effort required to perform a specified piloting task.

Source: Rating scale and definitions from TND-5153, National Aeronautics and Space Administration.

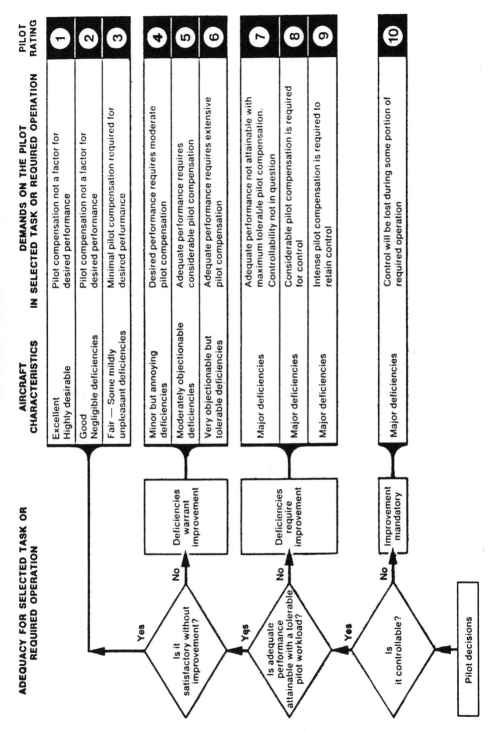

SOURCES

PREFACE

1. Otto Lilienthal, "Practical Experiments for the Development of Human Flight," in James Means, ed., *Epitome of the Aeronautical Annual* (Boston: W. B. Clarke Co., 1910), p. 8.
2. Wilbur Wright, address to the Western Society of Engineers, September 1901, reprinted in Charles H. Gibbs-Smith, *Aviation: An Historical Survey from Its Origins to the End of World War II* (London: HMSO, 1970), pp. 222–23.
3. Cyril F. Uwins, "Experimental Test Flying," paper presented to the Bristol branch, The Royal Aeronautical Society, March 21, 1929.
4. Antoine de Saint-Exupéry, *Wartime Writings, 1939–1944* (New York: Harcourt Brace Jovanovich, 1986) p. 9.

CHAPTER I

1. Account by William of Malmesbury, quoted in Lynn White, Jr., "Eilmer of Malmesbury: An Eleventh Century Aviator: A Case Study of Technological Innovation, Its Context and Tradition," *Technology and Culture* (Spring 1961). Abbot's alleged prohibition on further flights is from Bernulf Hodge, *A History of Malmesbury* (Minety, England: Taylor & Sons, 1976), p. 8.

2. From the *Journal de Paris*, Nov. 22, 1783, reprinted in Edita Lausanne, *The Romance of Ballooning: The Story of the Early Aeronauts* (New York: The Viking Press, 1971), p. 20.

3. Marquis d'Arlandes, "The First Aerial Voyage," in Neville Duke and Edward Lanchbery, *The Saga of Flight: From Leonardo da Vinci to the Guided Missile* (New York: The John Day Company, 1961), p. 42.

4. Charles H. Gibbs-Smith, *The Invention of the Aeroplane, 1799–1909* (London: Faber & Faber, 1965), pp. 7–8.

5. Constance Babington-Smith, *Testing Time: The Story of British Test Pilots and Their Aircraft* (New York: Harper & Brothers, 1961), p. 43.

6. Otto Lilienthal, "Practical Experiments," in James Means, ed., *Epitome of the Aeronautical Annual*, p. 8. (This quotation has previously been cited, in truncated form, in the Preface.)

7. Otto Lilienthal, "At Rhinow," from *Zeitschrift für Luftschiffahrt* (March 1895), reprinted in James Means, ed., *Epitome of the Aeronautical Annual*, pp. 32–33.

8. C. H. Gibbs-Smith, *The Aeroplane: An Historical Survey of Its Origins and Development* (London: HMSO, 1960), p. 35.

CHAPTER 2

1. Washington *Post*, Oct. 8, 1903.

2. Roger Bilstein, "The Airplane, the Wrights, and the American Public," in Richard P. Hallion, ed., *The Wright Brothers: Heirs of Prometheus* (Washington, DC: Smithsonian Institution, 1978), p. 41.

3. Letter, Orville Wright to Katharine Wright, Nov. 1, 1903, reprinted in C. D. B. Bryan, *The National Air and Space Museum* (New York: Harry N. Abrams, Inc., Publishers, 1979), p. 47.

4. Orville Wright, "How We Made the First Flight," *Flying and The Aero Club of America Bulletin*, Dec. 1913.

5. Tom D. Crouch, *A Dream of Wings: Americans and the Airplane, 1875–1905* (New York: W. W. Norton & Co., 1981), p. 305.

6. Marvin W. McFarland, ed., *The Papers of Wilbur and Orville Wright*, Vol. I, *1899–1905* (New York: McGraw-Hill Book Co., 1953), p. 397.

7. C. H. Gibbs-Smith, *The Rebirth of European Aviation, 1902–1908: A Study of the Wright Brothers' Influence* (London: HMSO, 1974), p. 287.

8. Harry Combs with Martin Caidin, *Kill Devil Hill: Discovering the*

Secret of the Wright Brothers (Boston: Houghton Mifflin Co., 1979), p. 309.

9. Roger Bilstein, "The Airplane, the Wrights, and the American Public," in Richard P. Hallion, ed., *The Wright Brothers: Heirs of Prometheus*, p. 47.

10. George van Deurs, *Wings for the Fleet: A Narrative of Naval Aviation's Early Development, 1910–1916* (Annapolis, MD: U. S. Naval Institute, 1966), p. 15.

11. Flint O. DuPre, *Hap Arnold: Architect of American Air Power* (New York: Macmillan, 1972), p. 20.

12. George van Deurs, *Wings for the Fleet*, p. 70.

CHAPTER 3

1. Constance Babington-Smith, *Testing Time*, p. 91.

2. From Martin biographical file, National Air and Space Museum.

3. Grover Loening, *Takeoff into Greatness: How American Aviation Grew So Big So Fast* (New York: G. P. Putnam's Sons, 1968), p. 95.

4. Conversation with the author, Jan. 23, 1980.

5. George B. Patterson, *Notes on Practical Airplane Performance Testing* (Dayton, OH: Air Service Engineering Division, June 1919), pp. 29, 35–36.

6. Copy transmitted to author by Walter J. Boyne.

7. U. S. Army, Division of Military Aeronautics, *Test Report on Performance of Le Pere Two-Seater Fighter* (Dayton, OH: DMA Technical Section, Aug. 22, 1918), p. 1.

8. Ibid., pp. 17–18.

9. U. S. Army Air Service, Division of Military Aeronautics, *Air Service Medical* (Washington, DC: War Department, 1919), p. 432.

10. Dean C. Smith, *By the Seat of My Pants* (Boston: Little, Brown, 1961), pp. 102–3.

11. From Rohlfs biographical file, National Air and Space Museum.

12. Quoted in *The Nartopix* (monthly newsletter of the Naval Air Facility, Washington, DC), Oct. 1979.

CHAPTER 4

1. Quoted in J. C. Hunsaker, "Forty Years of Aeronautical Research," in *Smithsonian Report for 1955* (Washington, DC: Smithsonian Institution, 1956), p. 246.

2. Edward P. Warner and F. H. Norton, *Preliminary Report on Free Flight Tests*, NACA Report No. 70 (1919), p. 575.

3. Ibid., p. 581.

4. John A. Macready, "Exploring the Earth's Atmosphere," *The National Geographic Magazine*, Dec. 1926.

5. Harold R. Harris, "Sixty Years of Aviation History: One Man's Remembrance," address given at the annual meeting of the Northeast Aero Historians, Windsor Locks, CT, Oct. 12, 1964.

6. Extracts cited in U. S. Army Air Corps, *Wright Field* (Dayton, OH: AAC Materiel Division, 1938), p. 32.

7. Sally Macready Liston, "Perils and Pitfalls of Early Test Pilots," *Journal of the American Aviation Historical Society*, Spring 1969.

8. Douglas J. Ingells, *They Tamed the Sky: The Triumph of American Aviation* (New York: D. Appleton Century Company, 1946), p. 179.

9. H. R. Harris, "Sixty Years of Aviation History."

10. Memo from I. F. Peak, M.D., to Richard V. Rhode, June 8, 1928, quoted in Richard V. Rhode, *The Pressure Distribution over the Horizontal and Vertical Tail Surfaces of the F6C-4 Pursuit Airplane in Violent Maneuvers*, NACA Report No. 307 (1928), p. 552.

11. Le Corbusier, *Towards a New Architecture* (New York: Praeger Publishers, 1970), p. 101.

12. Thomas G. Foxworth, *The Speed Seekers* (Garden City, NY: Doubleday & Co., 1975), p. 278.

13. U. S. Army Air Service, *A Little Journey to the Home of the Engineering Division* (Dayton, OH: AAS Engineering Division, n.d.), pp. 25, 27.

14. Lowell Thomas and Edward Jablonski, *Doolittle: A Biography* (Garden City, NY: Doubleday & Co., 1976), p. 128.

15. Charles A. Lindbergh, *Autobiography of Values* (New York: Harcourt Brace Jovanovich, 1977), p. 303.

16. Charles A. Lindbergh, *The Spirit of St. Louis* (New York: Charles Scribner's Sons, 1953), pp. 121–22.

17. John Grierson, "Charles A. Lindbergh," in Tom D. Crouch, ed., *Charles A. Lindbergh: An American Life* (Washington, DC: Smithsonian Institution, 1977), pp. 3–4.

18. C. A. Lindbergh, *The Spirit of St. Louis*, p. 325.

19. Jerome C. Hunsaker, *A Survey of Air Transport and its Communication Problems* (Bell Telephone Laboratories, July 1, 1927), pp. 6–7. Copy in Hunsaker papers, National Air and Space Museum.

20. James H. Doolittle, "Early Blind Flying: An Historical Review of Early Experiments in Instrument Flying," Third Lester Gardner Lecture, presented at the Massachusetts Institute of Technology, Cambridge, Apr. 28, 1961.

21. Ibid.
22. D. J. Ingells, *They Tamed the Sky*, p. 23.
23. Ibid., p. 27.
24. Ibid., p. 30.
25. R. H. Mayo, *History of The Daniel Guggenheim Fund* (unpublished manuscript in The Papers of The Daniel Guggenheim Fund for the Promotion of Aeronautics, Manuscript Division, Library of Congress), p. 196.
26. The Daniel Guggenheim Fund for the Promotion of Aeronautics, *The Daniel Guggenheim International Safe Aircraft Competition: Final Report* (New York: Daniel Guggenheim Fund, 1930), p. 9.
27. U. S. Army Air Service Engineering School, *Flight Testing of Aircraft* (Dayton, OH: AAS Engineering School, May 1926), p. 2.
28. Cyril F. Uwins, "Experimental Test Flying," paper presented to the Bristol branch, The Royal Aeronautical Society, Mar. 21, 1929.

CHAPTER 5

1. Albert W. Stevens, "Man's Farthest Aloft," *The National Geographic Magazine*, Jan. 1936.
2. Oklahoma City *Times*, July 24, 1933.
3. Theon Wright, "They Take the High Road," in John F. Loosbrock and Richard M. Skinner, eds., *The Wild Blue: The Story of American Airpower* (New York: G. P. Putnam's Sons, 1961), p. 176.
4. Francis Vivian Drake, "Test Pilot," in Max J. Herzberg, Merrill P. Paine, and Austin M. Works, eds., *Happy Landings* (Boston: Houghton Mifflin, 1942), pp. 44–57.
5. Edmund T. Allen, "Here Goes Nothing: Flight Testing From Daredeviltry to Scientific Research," *Aviation*, Dec. 1937.
6. Quoted in The Society of Experimental Test Pilots, *The Society of Experimental Test Pilots: History of the First Twenty-Five Years* (Covina, CA: Taylor, 1978), p. 78.
7. Edward H. Heinemann and Rosario Rausa, *Ed Heinemann: Combat Aircraft Designer* (Annapolis: U. S. Naval Institute Press, 1980), p. 35.
8. Jimmy Collins, *Test Pilot* (Garden City, NY: Doubleday, Doran & Co., 1935), p. 174.
9. William Faulkner, "Folklore of the Air," *The American Mercury*, Nov. 1935.
10. Ibid.

11. H. Lloyd Child, "Faster than a Bullet," *The Saturday Evening Post,* Sept. 16, 1939.

12. Ernest K. Gann, *Fate Is the Hunter* (New York: Simon & Schuster, 1961), p. 388.

13. H. F. Gregory, *Anything a Horse Can Do: The Story of the Helicopter* (New York: Reynal & Hitchcock, 1944), p. 22.

14. Frank J. Delear, *Igor Sikorsky: His Three Careers in Aviation* (New York: Dodd, Mead & Co., 1976), p. 190.

15. Ernst Heinkel, *Stormy Life: Memoirs of a Pioneer of the Air Age* (New York: E. P. Dutton & Co., 1956), p. 224.

CHAPTER 6

1. Boone T. Guyton, *This Exciting Air: The Experiences of a Test Pilot* (New York: McGraw-Hill Book Co., 1943), pp. 79–80.

2. Charles A. Lindbergh, *The Wartime Journals of Charles A. Lindbergh* (New York: Harcourt Brace Jovanovich, 1970), p. 108.

3. Charles A. Lindbergh, *Of Flight and Life* (New York: Charles Scribner's Sons, 1948), pp. 8–10.

4. Lindbergh, *Wartime Journals,* pp. 759–60.

5. Lindbergh, *Of Flight and Life,* p. 55.

6. SETP, *The Society of Experimental Test Pilots: History of the First Twenty-Five Years,* p. 240.

7. G. Edward Pendray, ed., *The Guggenheim Medalists: Architects of the Age of Flight* (New York: Board of Award, 1964), p. 84.

8. John Grierson, *Jet Flight* (London: Sampson Low, Marston & Co., 1945), p. 159.

9. Tony Le Vier with John Guenther, *Pilot* (New York: Harper & Brothers, 1954), p. 175.

10. Frederick Trapnell, "A Test Pilot Looks at the Jets," *Aeronautical Engineering Review,* May 1950.

11. Walter T. Bonney, "High-Speed Research Airplanes," *Scientific American,* Oct. 1953.

12. Douglas J. Ingells, *They Tamed the Sky,* p. 170.

13. Edwin P. Hartman, *Adventures in Research: A History of Ames Research Center, 1940–65* (Washington, DC: NASA, 1970), p. 83.

14. Tony Le Vier and John Guenther, *Pilot,* pp. 146–47.

15. Charles Burnet, *Three Centuries to Concorde* (London: Mechanical Engineering Publications Limited, 1979), p. 38.

CHAPTER 7

1. John V. Becker, *The High-Speed Frontier: Case Histories of Four NACA Programs, 1920–1950* (Washington, DC: NASA, 1980), p. 88.
2. Charles Burnet, *Three Centuries to Concorde*, p. 104.
3. Statement of W. C. Williams at the American Institute of Aeronautics and Astronautics' history session, San Francisco, CA, July 28, 1965, in the NASA History Office.
4. Muroc Army Air Field Historical Report, Oct. 1 to Dec. 31, 1946, p. 11, in the Air Force archives, Maxwell AFB.
5. Letter, Herbert H. Hoover to Melvin Gough, Aug. 22, 1947, in the files of NASA Langley Research Center.
6. Charles E. Yeager, "Flying Jet Aircraft and the Bell XS-1," in Walter J. Boyne and Donald S. Lopez, eds., *The Jet Age: Forty Years of Jet Aviation* (Washington, DC: Smithsonian Institution, 1979), p. 107.
7. Report from the files of the Historical Office, Air Force Flight Test Center, Edwards AFB.
8. Charles H. Gibbs-Smith, *Flight Through the Ages* (New York: Thomas Y. Crowell, 1974), p. 158.
9. Remarks by General Hoyt S. Vandenberg, USAF, Aug. 26, 1950, from the files of the National Air and Space Museum.
10. Statement by Dr. Hugh L. Dryden, June 15, 1948, from the files of the National Air and Space Museum.
11. Conversation with the author.
12. William Bridgeman with Jacqueline Hazard, *The Lonely Sky* (New York: Henry Holt & Co., 1955), p. 259.
13. From transcription of flight communications, in the files of the Historical Office, Air Force Flight Test Center, Edwards AFB.
14. Ronald Stiffler, *The Bell X-2 Rocket Research Aircraft: The Flight Test Program* (Edwards, CA: AFFTC, Aug. 12, 1957), copy 2 of 7, p. 30, in the Air Force archives, Maxwell AFB.
15. Quotes from Corwin H. Meyer, "Wild, Wild Cat: The XF-10," XXth Symposium, SETP, Beverly Hills, CA, Sept. 25, 1976.
16. Robert O. Rahn, "XF4D Skyray Development: Now It Can Be Told," XXIInd Symposium, SETP, Beverly Hills, CA, Sept. 30, 1978.
17. M. Scott Carpenter, et al., *We Seven* (New York: Simon & Schuster, 1962), p. 61.
18. Brian Welch, "Whitcomb: Aeronautical Research and the Better Shape," *Langley Researcher*, Mar. 21, 1980.
19. Richard C. Knott, *The American Flying Boat: An Illustrated History* (Annapolis: U. S. Naval Institute Press, 1979), pp. 238–39.

20. Herman R. Salmon, "XFV-1," XXth Symposium, SETP, Beverly Hills, CA, Sept. 25, 1976.
21. John E. Steiner, "Jet Aviation Development: A Company Perspective," in W. J. Boyne and D. S. Lopez, eds., *The Jet Age: Forty Years of Jet Aviation*, p. 154.

CHAPTER 8

1. U. S. Congress, Committee on Government Operations, Senate, *TFX Contract Investigation (Second Series), Part 3* (Washington, DC: GPO, 1970), p. 537.
2. Michael Collins, *Carrying the Fire: An Astronaut's Journeys* (New York: Farrar, Straus & Giroux, 1974), p. 21.
3. Clarence L. Johnson, "Some Development Aspects of the YF-12A Interceptor Aircraft," *Journal of Aircraft*, July–Aug. 1970.
4. Richmond L. Miller, "Flight Testing the F-12 Series Aircraft," *Journal of Aircraft*, Sept. 1975.
5. Ben Rich, quoted in Michael E. Long, "They're Redesigning the Airplane," *The National Geographic Magazine*, Jan. 1981.
6. Philip J. Klass, "Wake Vortex Sensing Efforts Advance," *Aviation Week & Space Technology*, Apr. 25, 1977.
7. A. Scott Crossfield with Clay Blair, Jr., *Always Another Dawn: The Story of a Rocket Test Pilot* (Cleveland: World Publishing Co., 1960), p. 343.
8. Conversation with Jack Kolf, Dryden Flight Research Center.
9. John V. Becker, "The X-15 Program in Retrospect," *Raumfahrtforschung*, Mar.–Apr. 1961.
10. Cited in Loyd S. Swenson, James M. Grimwood, and Charles C. Alexander, *This New Ocean: A History of Project Mercury* (Washington, DC: NASA, 1966), p. 130.
11. Michael Collins, *Carrying the Fire*, p. 25.
12. Barton C. Hacker and James M. Grimwood, *On the Shoulders of Titans: A History of Project Gemini* (Washington, DC: NASA, 1977), pp. 314–15.
13. Zack Strickland, "Series of Lunar Landings Simulated," *Aviation Week & Space Technology*, June 30, 1969.
14. Courtney G. Brooks, James M. Grimwood, and Loyd S. Swenson, *Chariots for Apollo: A History of Manned Lunar Spacecraft* (Washington, DC: NASA, 1979), p. 344.
15. Interview of Walter C. Williams by Eugene M. Emme, Mar. 25, 1964, on file with the NASA History Office.

16. Dave Dooling, "Launch the Shuttle," *Astronautics & Aeronautics*, March 1981.
17. Ibid.
18. Ibid.
19. "Columbia Exceeds Flight Goals," *Aviation Week & Space Technology*, Apr. 20, 1981.
20. Alexander Graham Bell, "Aerial Locomotion," *The National Geographic Magazine*, Jan. 1907.
21. John J. Fialka, "Space Saga Lifts Hopes for Future," Washington *Star*, Apr. 15, 1981.
22. "Young and Crippen Comment on Flight," *Aviation Week & Space Technology*, Apr. 27, 1981.
23. "Crew Flies Precise Reentry," *Aviation Week & Space Technology*, Apr. 20, 1981.
24. Ibid.
25. J. J. Fialka, "Space Saga Lifts Hopes for Future," Washington *Star*, Apr. 15, 1981.
26. The best analysis of the *Challenger*'s loss (despite the many newspaper accounts and several books that have appeared) remains the *Report of the Presidential Commission on the Space Shuttle Accident* (Washington, D.C.: Government Printing Office, 1986). The Apollo astronaut comment is from an interviewee who must remain anonymous. Squires' "maestro" notion is more completely discussed in his collection of case studies on technological bureaucracy, *The Tender Ship* (Boston: Birkhäuser, 1986). See also Hal Bowser, "Maestros of Technology: An Interview with Arthur M. Squires," *American Heritage of Invention & Technology* Vol. 3, No. 1 (Summer 1987), pp. 24–30. For an excellent accounting of the preparations and training involved in a Space Shuttle flight see Henry S. F. Cooper, Jr., *Before Lift-Off: The Making of a Space Shuttle Crew* (Baltimore: The Johns Hopkins University Press, 1987).

CHAPTER 9

1. Constance Babington-Smith, *Testing Time*, p. 206.
2. P. B. S. Lissaman, "Wings for Human-Powered Flight," in American Institute of Aeronautics and Astronautics, *Evolution of Aircraft Wing Design* (Dayton, OH: AIAA, 1980), p. 49.
3. Reprinted in The Society of Experimental Test Pilots, *SETP: History of the First Twenty-Five Years*, p. 240.
4. A. W. Bedford, "The Role of the Test Pilot," *Journal of the Royal Aeronautical Society*, June 1964.
5. Ibid.
6. Neil R. Anderson and Philip F. Oestricher, "F-16 Progress Report," XIXth Symposium, SETP, Beverly Hills, CA, Sept. 24, 1975.
7. U. S. Congress Committee on Aeronautical and Space Sciences, Senate, *Aeronautical Research and Development Policy* (Washington, DC: GPO, 1967), p. 7.

ACKNOWLEDGMENTS

This book is the outgrowth of research first begun when I was an undergraduate in the Department of History at the University of Maryland in 1969. Since that time, I have had the pleasure of working and consulting with a number of individuals and organizations who have been especially helpful. I would like to acknowledge my debt to the following institutions and individuals for their assistance through the years:

At the National Air and Space Museum, Smithsonian Institution: Michael Collins, Melvin Zisfein, Jack Whitelaw, Paul Garber, Frederick C. Durant III, Dr. Howard Wolko, Donald Lopez, Walter Boyne, Robert Meyer, Dr. Tom Crouch, Dr. Paul Hanle, Ed Chalkley, Walter Flint, Louis Casey, Claudia Oakes, Frank Winter, Dr. Joseph Corn, Jay Spenser, Lynne Murphy, Louise Hull, Catherine Scott, Pete Sutherd, Mimi Scharf, Phil Edwards, Bob van der Linden, Richard Crawford, Bob Mikesh, Tim Wooldridge, Walt Dillon, Dominick Pisano, Tony Bâby, and Jan Steenblik.

At the National Museum of American History (formerly the National Museum of History and Technology), Smithsonian Institution: Dr. Otto Mayr.

At the University of Maryland: Dean Milton Grodsky and Professors Walter Rundell, Wayne Cole, J. Kirkpatrick Flack, Keith Olson,

Gordon Prange,* John Anderson, Jewel Barlow, Bruce Donaldson, Alfred Gessow, Fred Suppe, and Colonel Dale Eppinger, USAF.

At NASA Headquarters: Dr. Walter C. Williams, Dr. Eugene M. Emme, Dr. Monte Wright, Dr. Frank Anderson, Dr. Alex Roland, Lee Saegesser, Carrie Karegeannes, Les Gaver, and Jim McCulla.

At the NASA Ames Research Center: Dr. Robert T. Jones and Larry King.

At the NASA Dryden Flight Research Center: Ralph Jackson, Trudy Tiedemann, Milt Thompson, Karen Puffer, the engineering and technical staff (especially Wen Painter), and the research pilots and flight test engineers, including Bill Dana, Einar Enevoldson, Fitz Fulton, Vic Horton, Steve Ishmael, Gary Krier, Tom McMurtry, Don Mallick, John Manke, Mike Swann, and Ray Young.

At the NASA Goddard Space Flight Center: Bob Burns, and Paul Ondrus.

At the NASA Johnson Space Center: Fran Gentry, Jim Grimwood, Sally Gates,* Dick Laidley, and Joe Engle.

At the NASA Langley Research Center: John Becker, Ralph Bielat, Dr. Robert Helton, Bob Champine, Macon Ellis, Axel Mattson, Neva Brooks, Thomas Toll, Harold Turner, Bud Mulac, Dr. Richard Whitcomb, Jack Reeder, and Richard Layman.

At the Office of Air Force History: Major General John W. Huston, Carl Berger, Lawrence Paszek, and Jack Neufeld.

At the Air Force Museum: Royal Frey and Charles Worman.

At Air Force Systems Command: Dr. Donald McVeigh.*

At the Air Force Flight Test Center: Brigadier General Philip J. Conley, J. Ted Bear, and Johnny Armstrong.

At the Air Force Still Photo Depository: Dana Bell.

At the Air Force Albert F. Simpson Historical Research Center: Lloyd Cornett, Jr.

At Air Force Military Airlift Command: R. Cargill Hall.

At Naval Air Systems Command: Hal Andrews, Dr. Lee M. Pearson, and Dr. William Armstrong.

* Deceased

At the Naval Air Test Center: Captain Carl M. "Tex" Birdwell, Captain Alex Kirby, Bill Frierson, and Valerie von Allmen.

At the Library of Congress: Len Bruno, Marvin McFarland, Arthur Renstrom, and Dr. Ronald Wilkinson.

At the Naval Ship Research and Development Center: Bob Englar and Jim Nichols.

At the U. S. National Archives and regional record centers: Jo Ann Williamson, John Taylor, Thomas Thalken, Elaine Everly, James Paulauskas, and Nancy Malan.

At the University of Houston at Clear Lake City: Dr. Roger E. Bilstein.

At Kansas State University: Professor Robin Higham.

At Texas A & M University: Professor Richard E. Thomas.

At the University of Georgia: Professor William Leary.

At Duke University: Professor I. B. Holley.

At Yale University: Judith Schiff.

At the Ministry of Defence, London: Air Vice Marshal H. A. Merriman, RAF.

At the Royal Aircraft Establishment, Farnborough: Rhys P. Probert,* and B. C. Kervell.

At Malmesbury, Wiltshire: Stan Hudson and the staff of the Athelstan Museum.

At The Aerospace Corporation: Everett Welmers.

At Bell Aerospace, Textron: William Gisel, Armand "Swede" Manson, and Charles Kreiner.

At Boeing-Vertol: Stan Smith.

At British Aerospace: John Fozard, John E. Scott, A. P. S. Jones, Charles Burnet, A. W. "Bill" Bedford, Darryl Cott, Philip Birtles, Mike Newell, Graham Weller, Rex Griffiths, and Norman Cox.

At Calspan Corporation: Arno Schelhorn, Nello Infanti, and Robert Wolf.

At Fairchild Industries: John Stack.*

* Deceased

At General Dynamics: George Vila, Frank Davis, Richard Johnson, Sam Shannon, Fred Petty, and Phil Oestricher.

At General Electric: Dick Passman and Bob Harris.

At the Grumman Corporation: Joseph Blazosky and Frank McQuade.

At Lockheed Aircraft Corporation: Bob Ferguson.

At McDonnell Douglas: John Fredericks, Harry Gann, and A. M. O. Smith.

At The National Geographic Society: Mike Long.

At Rockwell International: Robert A. Hoover and Ralph Oakley.*

At the Northrop Corporation: Charles Eyres.

At United Technologies: Sergei Sikorsky, Frank Delear, and Harvey Lippincott.

At the Institute for Defense Analyses: Waldemar "Walt" Breuhaus.

At The Society of Experimental Test Pilots: Billye McMains.*

At the Science Museum, South Kensington: Charles H. Gibbs-Smith, John Bagley, and Peter Mann.

At the offices of Aeroplane Monthly and *Flight International:* Richard Riding, Philip Jarrett, Stephen Piercey, and Mike Hirst.

At Air International: Bill Green and Gordon Swanborough.

And: Milton Ames, Bill Armour, Neil Armstrong, Paul Bikle, Dick Blaylock, Adolph Burstein, Clinton Brown, Jacqueline Cochran,* Don Cole, A. Scott Crossfield, Derek Dempster, Leo Devlin, Captain Walter S. Diehl, USN (ret.),* Bob Dodd, General James H. Doolittle, USAF (ret.), Jeff Ethell, Dr. Edward Ezell, Frank Fleming, René Francillon, Richard Frost, Colonel Jerauld Gentry, USAF, Dr. Robert Gilruth, John Glendinning, Dr. David W. H. Godfrey, Chalmers "Slick" Goodlin, Benson Hamlin, Brigadier General Harold R. Harris, USAAF (ret.), Edward Heinemann, Gail Hickman, Harold Hoekstra, Malcolm Holcomb, Dr. Abraham Hyatt, Admiral John Jacob, USN (ret.), Steve Johnson, Margaret Kane, Brigadier General Benjamin S. Kelsey, USAF (ret.),* Doug Kitchener, Professor Otto Koppen, Ezra Kotcher, Jerome Lederer, Brigadier General Charles A. Lindbergh, USAF (ret.),* Gertrude Lippisch, Professor W. A. Mair, John Mayer, Ferdinand and Ulrike Mikel, Jay Miller, Dee Mosteller, Brian Nicklas, Robert Parke, Dana

* Deceased

Phelps, Flugkapitän Hanna Reitsch,* Richard Rhode, G. Edward Rice, Lieutenant Benny Rich, USAF, Donna Richards, Douglas Robinson, M.D., Jean Roché, Dr. L. Eugene Root, Larry Ruberl, Ralph Schick, Colonel David Scott, USAF (ret.), Vice Admiral Thomas G. W. Settle, USN (ret.),* Dr. Richard K. Smith, Robert M. Stanley,* Harrison Storms, Floyd Thompson,* Gerald Truszynski, Joseph Vensel,* Major General Leigh Wade, USAF (ret.), Eric Walgren, John and Jane Ward, Air Commodore Allen Wheeler, RAF (ret.), Brigadier General Charles E. "Chuck" Yeager, USAF (ret.).

To these and all others that I have called upon on occasion, I extend my very grateful appreciation.

* Deceased

BIBLIOGRAPHICAL NOTE

The study of any subject as broad as flight research and flight testing requires that a historian examine and draw upon an equally broad range of both published and unpublished primary and secondary sources. Naturally, the assistance of the participants themselves in the various activities traced in this book was of vital importance. With unfailing courtesy, they furnished the author with much valuable information and the benefit of their insights and recollections. The following record collections contain much useful material on the history of flight research and flight testing:

At the U. S. National Archives: RG 18 (Records of the USAAS/AAC/AAF); RG 72 (Records of the USN Bureau of Aeronautics); RG 40 (Records of the Department of Commerce); and RG 255 (Records of the NACA and NASA).

At the Manuscript Division, Library of Congress: the papers of Henry H. Arnold, Washington I. Chambers, Octave Chanute, Benjamin D. Foulois, Grover Loening, Igor I. Sikorsky, the Wright brothers, The Daniel Guggenheim Fund for the Promotion of Aeronautics, and the Institute of the Aeronautical Sciences (the AIAA collection).

The following federal government offices contain useful documentary and photographic materials: The NASA History Office, Washington, D.C.; the Office of Air Force History, Washington, D.C.; the Historical Office of the Naval Air Systems Command, Crystal City, Virginia;

the Historical Office of Air Force Systems Command, Andrews AFB, Maryland; Office of the Historian, Air Force Flight Test Center, Edwards AFB, California; Public Affairs Office, Naval Air Test Center, Patuxent River, Maryland; Office of External Affairs, NASA Ames Research Center, Moffett Field, California; Office of External Affairs, NASA Dryden Flight Research Center, Edwards, California; the Historical Office, Air Force Logistics Command, Wright-Patterson AFB, Ohio.

The National Air and Space Museum of the Smithsonian Institution has a comprehensive file collection of materials (primarily photographic) on specific aircraft and individuals, in addition to the Jerome Hunsaker papers and the McCook-Wright Field papers collection. The Air Force Museum (Wright-Patterson AFB) has a useful collection of documentary materials on USAAS/AAC/AAF/AF research aircraft, personalities, and projects. The Albert F. Simpson Historical Research Center at Maxwell AFB, Alabama, is the Air Force central repository for service records. As such, it contains a number of useful items, including individually organized project histories and, especially, the semiannual historical reports generated by such research centers as Edwards and Wright-Patterson. The latter reports are quite useful in tracing the chronology of events and also in determining what was considered important to individuals at the time.

The historical archives of the NASA Langley Research Center, Hampton, Virginia, contains an especially valuable collection of flight research documents, including flight logs, photographs, personal papers, and reports, assembled by Richard Layman.

The Columbia University Oral History Collection includes records of many interviews and recollections of American flight researchers and test pilots, most of which are available for reference by researchers.

The following is a selected bibliography of works that were of use in the preparation of this book.

SELECTED BIBLIOGRAPHY

Allen, Edmund T. "Here Goes Nothing: Flight Testing From Daredev-iltry to Scientific Research," *Aviation*, Dec. 1937.

Allen, Richard S. *Revolution in the Sky*. Brattleboro, VT: Stephen Green Press, 1964.

American Institute of Aeronautics and Astronautics. *Evolution of Air-craft Wing Design*. Dayton, OH: AIAA, 1980.

Anderson, John D. *Introduction to Flight*. New York: McGraw-Hill, 1978.

Anderton, David A. *Progress in Aircraft Design Since 1903*. Washington, DC: NASA, 1974.

——. "Lockheed's Lone Ranger: Reconnoitring at Mach 3," *Air International*, Oct. 1974.

Andrews, Hal. "Douglas F4D Skyray," *Aeroplane Monthly*, May 1977.

Anon. "The Miles Supersonic," *The Aeroplane*, Sept. 13, 1946.

Anon. "MX-324: Step to Manned Rocket Flight," *Astronautics & Aeronautics*, Oct. 1964.

Anon. "Columbia Exceeds Flight Goals," *Aviation Week & Space Technology*, Apr. 20, 1981.

Anon. "Crew Flies Precise Reentry," *Aviation Week & Space Technology*, Apr. 20, 1981.

Anon. "Young and Crippen Comment on Flight," *Aviation Week & Space Technology*, Apr. 27, 1981.

Archer, H. B. "Operational Experiences with Flying Test Bed Airplanes," National Aeronautic Meeting, Society of Automotive Engineers, Los Angeles, CA, Oct. 1–4, 1952.

Armstrong, Johnny G. *Flight Planning and Conduct of the X-24B Research Aircraft Flight Test Program.* Edwards, CA: AFFTC, 1977.

Armstrong, Neil A.; and Reynolds, Peter T. "The Learjet Longhorn Series: The First Jets with Winglets," XXIInd Symposium, SETP, Beverly Hills, CA, Sept. 29, 1978.

Arnold, Henry H. *Global Mission.* New York: Harper & Row, 1949.

Askins, William. "The Ultimate Fighter Pilot," *Air Progress*, Sept. 1970.

Babington-Smith, Constance. *Testing Time: The Story of British Test Pilots and Their Aircraft.* New York: Harper & Brothers, 1961.

Ball, John. *Edwards: Flight Test Center of the USAF.* New York: Duell, Sloan & Pearce, 1962.

Barksdale, E. H. *Flight Testing of Aircraft.* Dayton, OH: Air Service Engineering School, May 1926.

Beaghen, A. *Malmesbury Abbey.* Minety, England: Taylor & Sons, 1974.

Beamont, Roland. *Testing Years.* Shepperton, England: Ian Allan, 1980.

Becker, John V. *The High-Speed Frontier: Case Histories of Four NACA Programs, 1920–1950.* Washington, DC: NASA, 1980.

——. "The X-15 Program in Retrospect," *Raumfahrtforschung*, Mar.–Apr. 1969.

Bedford, A. W. "The Role of the Test Pilot," *Journal of the Royal Aeronautical Society*, June 1964.

Bell, Alexander Graham. "Aërial Locomotion," *The National Geographic Magazine*, Jan. 1907.

Benford, Robert J. *The Heritage of Aviation Medicine.* Washington, DC: Aerospace Medical Association, 1979.

Berger, Carl. *B-29: the Superfortress.* New York: Ballantine, 1970.

Bikle, Paul F. *Performance Flight Testing Methods in Use by the Flight Section.* Dayton, OH: AAF Materiel Command, Jan. 15, 1944.

Bilstein, Roger E. *Prelude to the Air Age.* Ann Arbor, MI: University Microfilms, 1973.

Bonney, Walter T. "The Research Airplane," *Pegasus*, June 1952.

——. "High-Speed Research Airplanes," *Scientific American*, Oct. 1953.

——. *The Heritage of Kitty Hawk*. New York: Norton, 1962.

Bonté, Louis. *L'Histoire des Essais en Vol* (Vol. III of *Collection Docavia*). Paris: Éditions Larivière, 1974.

Bowers, Peter M. *Forgotten Fighters and Experimental Aircraft, 1918–1941*, 2 vols. New York: Arco, 1971.

Boyne, Walter J. *Messerschmitt 262: Arrow to the Future*. Washington, DC: Smithsonian Institution, 1980.

——. "The Treasure Trove of McCook Field," *Airpower*, July 1975.

——. "The Treasures of McCook Field," *Wings*, Aug. 1975.

——, and Lopez, Donald S. *The Jet Age: Forty Years of Jet Aviation*. Washington, DC: Smithsonian Institution, 1979.

Briddon, Arnold E.; Champie, Ellmore A.; and Marraine, Peter A. *FAA Historical Fact Book*. Washington, DC: FAA, 1974.

Bridgeman, William. "Supersonic Flight from the Pilot's Seat," Meeting of the National Capitol Section, Institute of the Aeronautical Sciences, Washington, DC, Oct. 2, 1951.

——, with Hazard, Jacqueline. *The Lonely Sky*. New York: Henry Holt & Co., 1955.

Bright, Charles D. *The Jet Makers: The Aerospace Industry from 1945 to 1972*. Lawrence, KS: The Regents Press of Kansas, 1978.

Brooks, Courtney G.; Grimwood, James M.; and Swenson, Loyd S. *Chariots for Apollo: A History of Manned Lunar Spacecraft*. Washington, DC: NASA, 1979.

Brooks, Peter W. *The Modern Airliner: Its Origins and Development*. London: Putnam, 1961.

Brown, Eric. *Wings on My Sleeve*. Shrewsbury, England: Airlife Publications, 1978.

——. "An Ill-fated Swallow—but a Harbinger of Summer," *Air Enthusiast Ten*, July–Sept. 1979.

Bryan, C. D. B. *The National Air and Space Museum*. New York: Harry N. Abrams, Inc., 1979.

Burke, James D. "Human-Powered Flight," *AIAA Student Journal*, Spring 1980.

Burnet, Charles. *Three Centuries to Concorde*. London: Mechanical Engineering Publications Limited, 1979.

Busk, Mary. *E. T. Busk: A Pioneer in Flight, with a Short Memoir of H. A. Busk, Flight Commander, RNAS.* London: John Murray, 1925.

Caidin, Martin. *Test Pilot.* New York: E. P. Dutton, 1961.

Carpenter, M. Scott, et al. *We Seven.* New York: Simon & Schuster, 1962.

Casey, Louis S. *The First Nonstop Coast-to-Coast Flight and the Historic T-2 Airplane.* Washington, DC: Smithsonian Institution, 1964.

Chanute, Octave. *Progress in Flying Machines.* New York: Forney, 1894.

Child, H. Lloyd. "Faster than a Bullet," *The Saturday Evening Post,* Sept. 16, 1939.

Cierva, Juan de la, and Rose, Don. *Wings of Tomorrow: The Story of the Autogiro.* New York: Brewer, Warren & Putnam, 1931.

Clark, Ronald W. *Tizard.* Cambridge, MA: MIT Press, 1965.

Clayton, Donald C. *Handley Page: An Aircraft Album.* London: Ian Allan, 1970.

Clousing, Lawrence A. "Three Rules to Guide Test Pilots," *Aviation Week,* May 10, 1948.

Cochran, Jacqueline. *The Stars at Noon.* Boston: Little, Brown, 1954.

Cochrane, Rexmond C. *Measures for Progress: A History of the National Bureau of Standards.* Washington, DC: NBS, 1966.

Collins, Jimmy. *Test Pilot.* Garden City, NY: Doubleday, Doran & Co., 1935.

Collins, Michael. *Carrying the Fire: An Astronaut's Journeys.* New York: Farrar, Straus & Giroux, 1974.

Collison, Thomas. *The Superfortress Is Born: The Story of the Boeing B-29.* New York: Duell, Sloan & Pearce, 1945.

Combs, Harry, with Caidin, Martin. *Kill Devil Hill: Discovering the Secret of the Wright Brothers.* Boston: Houghton Mifflin, 1979.

Constant, Edward W. *The Origins of the Turbojet Revolution.* Baltimore: The Johns Hopkins University Press, 1980.

Cooper, George E. "Understanding and Interpreting Pilot Opinion," *Aeronautical Engineering Review,* Mar. 1957.

Cooper, Henry S. F. *13: The Flight that Failed.* New York: Dial Press, 1973.

Courtney, Frank T. *The Eighth Sea.* Garden City, NY: Doubleday, 1972.

Courtney, W. B. "Under His Wing," *Collier's,* Nov. 13, 1937.

Craven, Wesley Frank; and Cate, James Lea. *Men and Planes.* Vol. VII of *The Army Air Forces in World War II.* Chicago: University of Chicago Press, 1955.

Crossfield, A. Scott; with Blair, Clay. *Always Another Dawn: The Story of a Rocket Test Pilot.* Cleveland: World Publishing Co., 1960.

Crossfield, A. Scott; and Williams, Walter C. "When Flight Test Was the Only Way," XXIInd Symposium, SETP, Beverly Hills, CA: Sept. 30, 1978.

Crouch, Tom D. "December: Diamond Anniversary of Man's Propulsion Skyward," *Smithsonian,* Dec. 1978.

——. *A Dream of Wings: Americans and the Airplane, 1875–1905.* New York: W. W. Norton & Co., 1981.

——, ed. *Charles A. Lindbergh: An American Life.* Washington, DC: Smithsonian Institution, 1977.

Daniel Guggenheim Fund for the Promotion of Aeronautics. *The Daniel Guggenheim International Safe Aircraft Competition: Final Report.* New York: Daniel Guggenheim Fund, 1930.

——. *Solving the Problem of Fog Flying: A Record of the Fund's Full-Flight Laboratory to Date.* New York: Daniel Guggenheim Fund, 1929.

Daniel Guggenheim Medal Board of Award. *Pioneering in Aeronautics: Recipients of the Daniel Guggenheim Medal, 1929–52.* New York: Board of Award, 1952.

Davenport, William Wyatt. *Gyro! The Life and Times of Lawrence Sperry.* New York: Scribner's, 1978.

Davies, David P. *Handling the Big Jets.* Redhill, England: Brabazon House, 1971.

Davis, Frank W. "Problems of Gas Turbine - Propeller Combinations," *Aeronautical Engineering Review,* Apr. 1948.

Delear, Frank J. *Igor Sikorsky: His Three Careers in Aviation.* New York: Dodd, Mead & Co., 1976.

Dempster, Derek. *The Tale of the Comet.* New York: David McKay, 1959.

Donovan, Frank. *The Early Eagles.* New York: Dodd, Mead, 1962.

Dooling, Dave. "Launch the Shuttle," *Astronautics & Aeronautics,* Mar. 1981.

Doolittle, James H. "Early Blind Flying," *Aerospace Engineering,* Oct. 1961.

Dorman, Geoffrey. *British Test Pilots*. London: Forbes Robertson, 1950.

Dryden, Hugh L. "A Half Century of Aeronautical Research," *Proceedings of the American Philosophical Society*, Apr. 1954.

——. "Supersonic Travel Within the Last 200 Years," *The Scientific Monthly*, May 1954.

Duke, Neville; and Lanchbery, Edward. *Sound Barrier*. London: Cassell, 1953.

——, eds. *The Saga of Flight: From Leonardo da Vinci to the Guided Missile*. New York: The John Day Company, 1961.

Duke, Neville, with Mitchell, Alan W. *Test Pilot*. London: Allan Wingate, 1953.

DuPre, Flint O. *Hap Arnold: Architect of American Air Power*. New York: Macmillan, 1972.

Ege, Lennart. *Balloons and Airships*. New York: Macmillan, 1974.

Emme, Eugene M. *Aeronautics and Astronautics: An American Chronology of Science and Technology in the Exploration of Space, 1915–1960*. Washington, DC: NASA, 1961.

——. *The Impact of Air Power: National Security and World Politics*. New York: Van Nostrand, 1959.

——, ed. *The History of Rocket Technology: Essays on Research, Development, and Utility*. Detroit: Wayne State University Press, 1964.

——. *Two Hundred Years of Flight in America: A Bicentennial Survey*. San Diego: American Astronautical Society, 1977.

Englar, R. J., et al. "Design of the Circulation Control Wing STOL Demonstrator Aircraft," AIAA Aircraft Systems and Technology Meeting, New York, August 20–22, 1979.

Eppley, Charles V. *The Rocket Research Aircraft Program, 1946–1962*. Edwards, CA: AFFTC, Feb. 1963.

Ethell, Jeffrey L. *Komet: The Messerschmitt Me 163*. New York: Sky Books, 1978.

Ettinger, Robert C.; and Thigpen, Dave. "Flight Testing the Fighter CCV," XXth Symposium, SETP, Beverly Hills, CA, Sept. 24, 1976.

Everest, Frank K., with Guenther, John. *The Fastest Man Alive*. New York: E. P. Dutton, 1958.

Fahey, James C. *U. S. Army Aircraft (Heavier-than-air) 1908–46*. Falls Church, VA: Ships and Planes, 1946.

Farren, W. S. "Research for Aeronautics: Its Planning and Application," *Journal of the Aeronautical Sciences*, Apr. 1944.

Faulkner, William. "Folklore of the Air," *The American Mercury*, Nov. 1935.

Feeny, William D. *In Their Honor*. New York: Duell, Sloan & Pearce, 1963.

Fialka, John J. "Space Saga Lifts Hopes for Future," Washington *Star*, Apr. 15, 1981.

Fisher, Herbert O. "Investigation of Reversing Propeller Pitch on a Multi-Engine Aircraft in Flight," National Aeronautic Meeting, Society of Automotive Engineers, New York, Apr. 17–20, 1950.

Foxworth, Thomas G. "North American XB-70 Valkyrie," *Historical Aviation Albums*, Nos. 6 and 7, 1969–70.

———. *The Speed Seekers*. Garden City, NY: Doubleday & Co., 1975.

Francillon, René J. *McDonnell Douglas Aircraft Since 1920*. London: Putnam, 1979.

Gast, Robert de. "Pax River: The Naval Air Test Center," *United States Naval Institute Proceedings*, Dec. 1969.

Gentzlinger, William H. "Modified Gulfstream II Will Teach Space Shuttle Pilots How to Drop In from Outer Space—Deadstick," *Grumman Aerospace Horizons*, 1976.

Gerhardt, W. F.; and Kerber, L. V. *A Manual of Flight-Test Procedure*. Ann Arbor, MI: University of Michigan Department of Engineering Research, 1927.

Gibbs-Smith, Charles H. *The Aeroplane: An Historical Survey of Its Origins and Development*. London: HMSO, 1960.

———. *Aviation: An Historical Survey from Its Origins to the End of World War II*. London: HMSO, 1970.

———. *The Invention of the Aeroplane, 1799–1909*. London: Faber & Faber, 1965.

———. *The Rebirth of European Aviation, 1902–1980: A Study of the Wright Brothers' Influence*. London: HMSO, 1974.

Glines, Carroll V. *Jimmy Doolittle*. New York: Macmillan, 1972.

———; and Moseley, Wendell F. *The DC-3: The Story of a Fabulous Airplane*. Philadelphia: Lippincott, 1966.

Goldberg, Alfred, ed. *A History of the U. S. Air Force, 1907–1957*. Princeton, NJ: Van Nostrand, 1959.

Gray, George W. *Frontiers of Flight: The Story of NACA Research.* New York: Knopf, 1948.

Great Britain, Aeronautical Research Council. *Research on High-Speed Aerodynamics at the Royal Aircraft Establishment from 1942–1945.* London: HMSO, 1950.

Great Britain, Empire Test Pilots' School. *The Empire Test Pilots' School: Twenty-five Years.* Boscombe Down: ETPS, 1968.

——. *Thirty Years On: Empire Test Pilots' School, 1973.* Boscombe Down: ETPS, 1973.

Green, William. *Rocket Fighter.* New York: Ballantine, 1971.

——. *The War Planes of the Third Reich.* Garden City, NY: Doubleday & Co., 1970.

——; and Swanborough, Gordon. "Airacomet: A Jet Pioneer from Bell," *Air International,* Mar. 1980.

——. "The Untossed Pancake: The Story of the Ill-fated XF5U-1," *Air Enthusiast,* June 1973.

——. *U. S. Navy and Marine Corps Fighters.* New York: Arco, 1977.

Gregory, H. F. *Anything a Horse Can Do: The Story of the Helicopter.* New York: Reynal & Hitchcock, 1944.

Grierson, John. *Jet Flight.* London: Sampson Low, Marston & Co., 1945.

Grosser, Morton. *Gossamer Odyssey: The Triumph of Human-Powered Flight.* Boston-Houghton Mifflin Company, 1981.

Gruenhagen, Robert W. *Mustang: The Story of the P-51 Fighter.* New York: Arco, 1969.

Gunston, Bill. *Attack Aircraft of the West.* London: Ian Allan, 1974.

——. *Bombers of the West.* London: Ian Allan, 1973.

——. "Burbank's Blackbirds," *Aeroplane Monthly,* Mar. 1974.

——. *Early Supersonic Fighters of the West.* New York: Scribner's, 1975.

Gurney, Gene, ed. *Test Pilots.* New York: Franklin Watts, 1962.

Gustafson, Frederic B. "History of NACA/NASA Rotating-Wing Aircraft Research, 1915–1970," *Vertiflite Magazine,* Apr. 1971.

——. "A History of NACA Research on Rotating-Wing Aircraft," *Journal of the American Helicopter Society,* Jan. 1956.

Guyton, Boone T. *This Exciting Air: the Experiences of a Test Pilot.* New York: McGraw-Hill Book Co., 1943.

Hacker, Barton C.; and Grimwood, James M. *On the Shoulders of Titans: A History of Project Gemini.* Washington, DC: NASA, 1977.

Haggerty, James J. *First of the Spacemen: Iven C. Kincheloe, Jr.* New York: Duell, Sloan & Pearce, 1960.

Hall, G. Warren. "Research and Development History of USAF Stability T-33," *Journal of the American Aviation Historical Society,* Winter 1974.

Hallion, Richard P. *Supersonic Flight: Breaking the Sound Barrier and Beyond.* New York: Macmillan, 1972.

——. "American Rocket Aircraft: Precursors to Manned Flight Beyond the Atmosphere," XXVth Congress, International Astronautical Federation, Amsterdam, the Netherlands, Oct. 4, 1974.

——. *Legacy of Flight: The Guggenheim Contribution to American Aviation.* Seattle: University of Washington Press, 1977.

——. "American Flight Research and Flight Testing: An Overview from the Wright Brothers to the Space Shuttle," *Cockpit,* Jan.–Feb. 1977.

——. "X-15: Highest and Fastest of Them All," *Flight International,* Dec. 23, 1978.

——. "Convair's Delta Alpha: The XF-92A," *Air Enthusiast Two,* Nov. 1976–Feb. 1977.

——. "X-4: The Bantam Explorer," *Air Enthusiast Three,* Mar.–June 1977.

——. "Serendipity from Santa Monica: The Story of the Douglas X-3," *Air Enthusiast Four,* July–Oct. 1977.

——. "Saga of the Rocket Ships: The X-1, D-558-2, and the X-2," *Air Enthusiast Five,* Nov. 1977–Feb. 1978.

——. "Saga of the Rocket Ships: The X-15," *Air Enthusiast Six,* Mar.–June 1978.

——. "Saga of the Rocket Ships: The Lifting Bodies," *Air Enthusiast Eight,* Oct. 1978–Jan. 1979.

——. "Lockheed P-80: The Story of a Star," *Air Enthusiast Eleven,* Nov. 1979–Feb. 1980.

——. "T-33 and F-94: More Stars in the Lockheed Galaxy," *Air Enthusiast Twelve,* Apr.–June 1980.

——. "Lifting Bodies," *Air & Space,* Mar.–Apr. 1980.

——. "Antecedents of the Space Shuttle," *AIAA Student Journal,* Spring 1980.

——, ed. *The Wright Brothers: Heirs of Prometheus.* Washington, DC: Smithsonian Institution, 1978.

——; and Crouch, Tom D. *Apollo: Ten Years Since Tranquillity Base.* Washington, DC: Smithsonian Institution, 1979.

Hamlin, Benson. *Flight Testing Conventional and Jet-Propelled Airplanes.* New York: Macmillan, 1946.

Hart, Clive. *The Dream of Flight: Aeronautics from Classical Times to the Renaissance.* New York: Winchester Press, 1972.

Hartman, Edwin P. *Adventures in Research: A History of Ames Research Center, 1940–65.* Washington, DC: NASA, 1970.

Heiman, Grover. *Jet Pioneers.* New York: Duell, Sloan & Pearce, 1963.

Heinemann, Edward H.; and Rausa, Rosario. *Ed Heinemann: Combat Aircraft Designer.* Annapolis: U. S. Naval Institute Press, 1980.

Heinkel, Ernst. *Stormy Life: Memoirs of a Pioneer of the Air Age.* New York: E. P. Dutton & Co., 1956.

Hello, Bastian. *Final Report of Development, Procurement, Performance and Acceptance—XP-80 Airplane.* Dayton, OH: AAF Air Technical Service Command, June 28, 1945.

Henshaw, Alex. *Sigh for a Merlin: Testing the Spitfire.* London: John Murray, 1979.

Herzberg, Max J.; Paine, Merrill P.; and Works, Austin M., eds. *Happy Landings.* Boston: Houghton Mifflin, 1942.

Hewlett, Richard G.; and Duncan, Francis. *Atomic Shield: 1947–1952.* Vol. II of *A History of the United States Atomic Energy Commission.* Washington, DC: AEC, 1972.

Hodge, Bernulf. *A History of Malmesbury.* Minety, England: Taylor & Sons, 1976.

Holland, Maurice; and Smith, Thomas M. *Architects of Aviation.* New York: Duell, Sloan & Pearce, 1951.

Hughes, Thomas Parke. *Elmer Sperry: Inventor and Engineer.* Baltimore: Johns Hopkins, 1971.

Hunsaker, Jerome C. *Aeronautics at the Mid-Century.* New Haven, CT: Yale University Press, 1952.

Hurley, Alfred F.; and Ehrhart, Robert F., eds. *Air Power and Warfare.* Washington, DC: USAF, 1979.

Ingells, Douglas J. *The Plane that Changed the World: A Biography of the DC-3.* Fallbrook, CA: Aero Publishers, 1966.

———. *They Tamed the Sky: The Triumph of American Aviation*. New York: D. Appleton Century Company, 1946.

Johnson, Clarence L. *Development of the Lockheed P-80 Jet Fighter Airplane*. Burbank, CA: Lockheed, 1946.

———. "Some Development Aspects of the YF-12A Interceptor Aircraft," *Journal of Aircraft*, July–Aug. 1970.

Johnson, Edward C.; and Cosmas, Graham A. *Marine Corps Aviation: The Early Years, 1912–1940*. Washington, DC: USMC, 1977.

Keats, John. *Howard Hughes: A Biography*. New York: Random House, 1972.

Keil, Sally Van Wagenen. *Those Wonderful Women in Their Flying Machines*. New York: Rawson, Wade Publishers, Inc., 1979.

Kelly, Fred. *The Wright Brothers*. New York: Harcourt, Brace, 1943.

Kinsey, Gordon. *Martlesham Heath: The Story of the Royal Air Force Station, 1917–1973*. Lavenham, England: Terence Dalton, 1975.

Knaack, Marcelle Size. *Post World War II Fighters, 1945–1973*. Vol. I of *Encyclopedia of U. S. Air Force Aircraft and Missile Systems*. Washington, DC: USAF, 1978.

Knott, Richard C. *The American Flying Boat: An Illustrated History*. Annapolis: U. S. Naval Institute Press, 1979.

Lambermont, Paul; and Pirie, Anthony. *Helicopters and Autogyros of the World*. London: Cassell, 1958.

Lanchbery, Edward. *Against the Sun: The Story of Wing Commander Roland Beamont*. London: Cassell, 1955.

Lausanne, Edita. *The Romance of Ballooning: The Story of the Early Aeronauts*. New York: The Viking Press, 1971.

Lehman, Milton. *This High Man: The Life of Robert H. Goddard*. New York: Farrar, Straus, 1963.

Lerche, Hans-Werner. *Luftwaffe Test Pilot*. London: Jane's Publishing, Inc., 1980.

Le Vier, Tony. "P-80 Development," XXth Symposium, SETP, Beverly Hills, CA, Sept. 25, 1976.

———, with Guenther, John. *Pilot*. New York: Harper & Row, 1954.

Lindbergh, Charles A. *Autobiography of Values*. New York: Harcourt Brace Jovanovich, 1978.

———. *Of Flight and Life*. New York: Charles Scribner's Sons, 1948.

———. *The Spirit of St. Louis*. New York: Charles Scribner's Sons, 1953.

———. *The Wartime Journals of Charles A. Lindbergh*. New York: Harcourt Brace Jovanovich, 1970.

———. *We*. New York: Putnam, 1927.

Liston, Sally Macready. "Perils and Pitfalls of Early Test Pilots," *Journal of the American Aviation Historical Society*, Spring 1969.

Lithgow, Mike. *Mach One*. London: Allan Wingate, 1954.

Loening, Grover. *Takeoff into Greatness: How American Aviation Grew So Big So Fast*. New York: G. P. Putnam's Sons, 1968.

Long, B. J. "Seadart, USN XF2Y-1 and YF2Y-1," XXth Symposium, SETP, Beverly Hills, CA, Sept. 25, 1976.

Long, Michael E. "They're Redesigning the Airplane," *The National Geographic Magazine*, Jan. 1981.

Loosbrock, John F.; and Skinner, Richard M. *The Wild Blue: The Story of American Airpower*. New York: G. P. Putnam's Sons, 1961.

Lundgren, William R. *Across the High Frontier: The Story of a Test Pilot—Major Charles E. Yeager, USAF*. New York: Morrow, 1955.

McCollum, Kenneth G., ed. *Dahlgren*. Dahlgren, VA: Naval Surface Weapons Center, 1977.

McFarland, Marvin W., ed. *The Papers of Wilbur and Orville Wright*, 2 vols. New York: McGraw-Hill Book Co., 1953.

Mackersey, Ian. *Into the Silk: True Stories of the Caterpillar Club*. London: Robert Hale, 1956.

Macready, John A. "Exploring the Earth's Atmosphere," *The National Geographic Magazine*, Dec. 1926.

Manke, John A.; and Love, Michael V. "X-24B Flight Test Program," XIXth Symposium, SETP, Beverly Hills, CA, Sept. 26, 1975.

Mansfield, Harold. *Billion Dollar Battle: The Story Behind the "Impossible" 727 Project*. New York: David McKay, 1965.

———. *Vision: A Saga of the Sky*. New York: Duell, Sloan & Pearce, 1956. (Rev. ed., *Vision: the Story of Boeing*. New York: Duell, Sloan & Pearce, 1966.)

Markgraf, Gerry. "Skyshark: Son of SPAD," *Journal of the American Aviation Historical Society*, Fall 1977.

Marschak, Thomas A. *The Role of Project Histories in the Study of R & D*. Santa Monica, CA: The Rand Corp., 1965.

Martin, James A. "The Record-Setting Research Airplanes," *Aerospace Engineering*, Dec. 1962.

May, Gene; and Halferty, Guy. "My Biggest Thrill," *Flying*, June 1953.

Means, James, ed. *Epitome of the Aeronautical Annual.* Boston: W. B. Clarke Co., 1910.

Meyer, Corwin H. "Wild, Wild Cat: The XF-10," XXth Symposium, SETP, Beverly Hills, CA, Sept. 25, 1976.

Miles, John, with Prescott, John. *Testing Time.* Victoria, Australia: Neptune Press, 1979.

Miller, Jay. "The X-Series: X-1/X-14," *Aerophile*, Jan.–Feb. 1977.

———. "The X-Series X-15/X-28," *Aerophile*, Mar.–Apr. 1977.

———. "Tip-Tow and Tom-Tom," *Air Enthusiast Nine*, Feb.–May 1979.

Miller, Richmond L. "Flight Testing the F-12 Series Aircraft," *Journal of Aircraft*, Sept. 1975.

Miller, Ronald; and Sawers, David. *The Technical Development of Modern Aviation.* New York: Praeger, 1970.

Mohler, Stanley R.; and Johnson, Bobby H. *Wiley Post, His Winnie Mae, and the World's First Pressure Suit.* Washington, DC: Smithsonian Institution, 1971.

Moolman, Valerie. *The Road to Kitty Hawk.* Alexandria, VA: Time-Life Books, 1980.

Moore, John M. "Wheels Up Landing Development Program," XIXth Symposium, SETP, Beverly Hills, CA, Sept. 27, 1975.

Moss, Sanford A. *Superchargers for Aviation.* New York: National Aeronautics Council, 1942.

Myers, Larry J. "Pioneers of the Sky," *Soldiers*, Sept. 1975.

Neal, Ronald D. "The Bell XP-59A Airacomet: The United States' First Jet Aircraft," *Journal of the American Aviation Historical Society*, Fall 1966.

Oakes, Claudia M. *United States Women in Aviation Through World War I.* Washington, DC: Smithsonian Institution, 1978.

Oestricher, Philip F.; and Ettinger, Robert C. "F-16 High Angle of Attack Testing," XXIInd Symposium, SETP, Beverly Hills, CA, Sept. 28, 1978.

Olmsted, Merle. "The Era of the Martin Bomber," *Journal of the American Aviation Historical Society*, Fall 1962.

Palmer, A. D. *Buffalo Airport, 1926–1976.* Buffalo, NY: Niagara Frontier Transportation Authority, 1976.

Parsons, Henry McIlvaine. *Man-Machine System Experiments.* Baltimore: Johns Hopkins, 1972.

Patterson, George B. *Notes on Practical Airplane Performance Testing.* Dayton, OH: Air Service Engineering Division, June 1919.

Paul, Franklin K. "Flight Test," *Pegasus,* Oct. 1949.

Pendray, G. Edward, ed. *The Guggenheim Medalists: Architects of the Age of Flight.* New York: Board of Award, 1964.

Penrose, Harald. *British Aviation: The Adventuring Years, 1920–29.* London: Putnam, 1929.

——. *No Echo in the Sky.* New York: Arno, 1972.

Perkins, Courtland D.; and Dommasch, Daniel O. *AGARD Flight Test Manual,* 3 vols. Princeton, NJ: Advisory Group for Aeronautical Research and Development of the NATO and the Aeronautical Engineering Department, Princeton University, n.d.

Perry, Robert. "The Antecedents of the X-1," Second Annual Meeting of the American Institute of Aeronautics and Astronautics, San Francisco, CA, July 26–29, 1965.

Pinson, Jay D. *Diamond Jubilee of Powered Flight: The Evolution of Aircraft Design.* Dayton, OH: AIAA, 1978.

Powell, H. P. "Sandy," *Test Flight.* London: Allan Wingate, 1956.

Powers, Richard D. "Monstro and the Goblin," *Journal of the American Aviation Historical Society,* July–Sept. 1973.

Pratt, Edward L. *Flight Test Manual.* Dayton, OH: Air Corps Materiel Division, Mar. 8, 1928.

Price, Wesley. "Jet Buggies Are Tough to Test," *The Saturday Evening Post,* Nov. 13, 1948.

——. "They Fly Our X-Ships," *The Saturday Evening Post,* July 1, 1950.

Rae, John B. *Climb to Greatness: The American Aircraft Industry, 1920–60.* Cambridge, MA: MIT, 1968.

Rahn, Robert O. "XF4D Skyray Development: Now It Can Be Told," XXIInd Symposium, SETP, Beverly Hills, CA, Sept. 30, 1978.

Reed, R. Dale. "RPRV's: The First and Future Flights," *Astronautics & Aeronautics,* Apr. 1974.

Reitsch, Hanna. "Flying the V-1 and Me 163," XIXth Symposium, SETP, Beverly Hills, CA, Sept. 27, 1975.

Reynolds, Quentin. *The Amazing Mr. Doolittle: A Biography of Lieutenant General James H. Doolittle.* New York: Appleton-Century, 1953.

Roberts, Joseph B.; and Briand, Paul L. *The Sound of Wings: Readings for the Air Age.* New York: Holt, 1957.

Robinson, Douglas H. *The Dangerous Sky: A History of Aviation Medicine.* Seattle: University of Washington Press, 1973.

———. *Giants in the Sky: A History of the Rigid Airship.* Seattle: University of Washington Press, 1973.

Rodney, George A. "The P6M Seamaster Jet Flying Boat," XIXth Symposium, SETP, Beverly Hills, CA, Sept. 27, 1975.

Roscoe, Theodore. *On the Seas and in the Skies: A History of the U. S. Navy's Air Power.* New York: Hawthorn, 1970.

Roseberry, C. R. *Glenn Curtiss: Pioneer of Flight.* Garden City, NY: Doubleday & Co., 1972.

Rounds, E. W. "Commercial Flight-Testing," XIXth National Aeronautic Meeting, Society of Automotive Engineers, Detroit, Apr. 15–16, 1931.

Rutan, Burt. "Development of a Small High-Aspect Ratio Canard Aircraft," XXth Symposium, SETP, Beverly Hills, CA, Sept. 24, 1976.

Saint Exupéry, Antoine de. *Wind, Sand and Stars.* New York: Harcourt, Brace & Company, 1940.

Salmon, Herman R. "XFV-1," XXth Symposium, SETP, Beverly Hills, CA, Sept. 25, 1976.

Saundby, Robert. *Early Aviation: Man Conquers the Air.* London: Macdonald, 1971.

Scharff, Robert; and Taylor, Walter S. *Over Land and Sea.* New York: David McKay, 1968.

Schlaifer, Robert; and Heron, S. D. *Development of Aircraft Engines and Fuels.* Cambridge, MA: Harvard Business School, 1950.

Scott, David. "Today's Research—Tomorrow's Aircraft," *Aircraft*, Aug. 1974.

Serling, Robert J. *The Electra Story.* Garden City, NY: Doubleday & Co., 1963.

Shortal, Joseph A. *A New Dimension—Wallops Island Flight Test Range: the First Fifteen Years.* Washington, DC: NASA, 1978.

Showalter, N. D. "High Altitude Flight Test Procedures," Boeing High Altitude Flight Symposium, Seattle, Aug. 25–27, 1947.

Shrader, Welman A. *Fifty Years of Flight: A Chronicle of the Aviation Industry in America, 1903–1953.* Cleveland: Eaton, 1953.

Sikorsky, Igor I. *The Story of the Winged-S.* New York: Dodd, Mead, 1938.

Smith, Dean. *By the Seat of My Pants.* Boston: Little, Brown, 1961.

Smith, E. P. "Space Shuttle in Perspective: History in the Making," XIth Annual Meeting of the American Institute of Aeronautics and Astronautics, Washington, DC, Feb. 24–26, 1975.

Smith, R. H. "Antecedents and Analogues: Experimental Aircraft," AIAA Diamond Jubilee of Powered Flight / Evolution of Aircraft Design Meeting, Dayton, OH, Dec. 14–15, 1978.

Smith, Richard K. *The Airships Akron and Macon.* Annapolis: U. S. Naval Institute Press, 1965.

Smyser, Albert T. "Reverse Pitch Props Offer Safety," *Aviation Week,* Dec. 15, 1947.

Society of Experimental Test Pilots. *Report to the Aerospace Profession.* Lancaster, CA, SETP, annually.

——. *The Society of Experimental Test Pilots: History of the First Twenty-Five Years.* Covina, CA: Taylor, 1978.

—— and the American Institute of Aeronautics and Astronautics. *Pilot's Handbook for Critical and Exploratory Flight Testing.* New York: SETP-AIAA, 1972.

Spearman, M. Leroy; and Driver, Cornelius. "Supersonic Flight: Past, Present, and Future," *AIAA Student Journal,* Spring 1980.

Sproule, J. S. "Checking Up on Sir George," *Shell Aviation News,* No. 405, 1972.

Stevens, Albert W. "Man's Farthest Aloft," *The National Geographic Magazine,* Jan. 1936.

Stevenson, James Perry. *Grumman F-14 Tomcat.* Fallbrook, CA: Aero Publishers, 1975.

——. *McDonnell Douglas F-15 Eagle.* Fallbrook, CA: Aero Publishers, 1978.

Stiffler, Ronald. *The Bell X-2 Rocket Research Aircraft: The Flight Test Program.* Edwards, CA: AFFTC, 1957.

Stillwell, Wendell H. *X-15 Research Results.* Washington, DC: NASA, 1965.

Strickland, Zack. "Series of Lunar Landings Simulated," *Aviation Week & Space Technology,* June 30, 1969.

Sturm, Thomas A. *The USAF Scientific Advisory Board: A History of Its First Twenty Years, 1944–1964.* Washington, DC: USAF Historical Division Liaison Office, 1967.

Sugano, M. J.; and Brice, T. R. "The Approach and Landing Test Program of the Space Shuttle Orbiter 101," AIAA Aircraft Systems and Technology Conference, Los Angeles, CA, Aug. 21–23, 1978.

Swanborough, Gordon; and Bowers, Peter M. *United States Military Aircraft Since 1909.* London: Putnam, 1963.

———. *United States Navy Aircraft Since 1911.* New York: Funk & Wagnalls, 1968.

Sweetser, Arthur. *The American Air Service: A Record of Its Problems, Its Difficulties, Its Failures, and Its Final Achievements.* New York: D. Appleton Century Company, 1919.

Swenson, Loyd S.; Grimwood, James M.; and Alexander, Charles C. *This New Ocean: A History of Project Mercury.* Washington, DC: NASA, 1966.

Syvertson, C. A. "Aircraft Without Wings," *Science Journal,* Dec. 1968.

Taylor, C. Fayette. *Aircraft Propulsion: A Review of the Evolution of Aircraft Piston Engines.* Washington, DC: Smithsonian Institution, 1971.

Taylor, H. A. *Test Pilot at War.* London: Ian Allan, 1970.

Taylor, John R.; and Taylor, Michael J. H. *Jane's Pocket Book of Research and Experimental Aircraft.* New York: Collier Books, 1976.

Thomas, Lowell; and Jablonski, Edward. *Doolittle: A Biography.* Garden City, NY: Doubleday & Co., 1976.

Thompson, Milton O. "I Fly Without Wings," *Air Progress,* Dec. 1966.

Thruelsen, Richard. *The Grumman Story.* New York: Praeger Publishers, 1976.

Trapnell, Frederick. "A Test Pilot Looks at the Jets," *Aeronautical Engineering Review,* May 1950.

Twiss, Peter. *Faster than the Sun.* London: Macdonald, 1963.

Ulsamer, Edgar. "On the Threshold of 'Nonclassical' Combat Flying," *Air Force Magazine,* June 1977.

U. S. Air Force. *Air Force Supersonic Research Airplane XS-1 (Report No. 1).* Dayton, OH: AMC, 1948.

———. *Chronology of Significant Aerospace Events, 1903–1971.* Washington, DC: USAF, 1972.

——. *Definitions of Phase Tests Accomplished by the Air Force Flight Test Center*. Edwards AFB, CA: AFFTC, 1954.

——. *Wright Patterson AFB: A Pictorial Review, 1917–1967*. Dayton, OH: WPAFB, 1967.

U. S. Army Air Corps. *Wright Field*. Dayton, OH: AAC Materiel Division, 1938.

U. S. Army Air Service. *A Little Journey to the Home of the Engineering Division*. Dayton, OH: AAS Engineering Division, n.d.

U. S. Army Division of Military Aeronautics. *Test Report on Performance of Le Pere Two-Seater Fighter*. Dayton, OH: DMA Technical Section, 1918.

U. S. Congress, Committee on Government Operations, Senate. *TFX Contract Investigation (Second Series), Part 3*. Washington, DC: GPO, 1970.

U. S. National Advisory Committee for Aeronautics. *Annual Reports of the NACA*. Washington, DC: NACA, 1919–58.

U. S. NACA High-Speed Flight Station. "10th Anniversary Supersonic Flight," *X-Press*, Oct. 14, 1957.

U. S. National Aeronautics and Space Administration. *Fifty Years of Aeronautical Research*. Washington, DC: NASA, 1967.

U. S. Navy. *The U. S. Naval Test Pilot School*. Patuxent River, MD: NATC-TPS, 1975.

Uwins, C. F. "Experimental Test Flying," *The Aeronautical Journal*, May 1929.

Van Deurs, George. *Anchors in the Sky: Spuds Ellyson, the First Naval Aviator*. San Rafael, CA: Presidio Press, 1978.

——. *Wings for the Fleet: A Narrative of Naval Aviation's Early Development, 1910–1916*. Annapolis: U. S. Naval Institute Press, 1966.

Van Vleet, Clarke; Van Wyen, Adrian O.; and Pearson, Lee. *U. S. Naval Aviation, 1910–1970*. Washington, DC: Naval Air Systems Command, 1970.

Villard, Henry Serrano. *Contact! The Story of the Early Birds*. New York: Crowell, 1968.

Von Kármán, Theodore. *Aerodynamics: Selected Topics in Light of Their Historical Development*. New York: McGraw-Hill, 1963.

——, with Edson, Lee. *The Wind and Beyond: Theodore von Kármán, Pioneer in Aviation and Pathfinder in Space*. Boston: Little, Brown, 1967.

Wagner, Ray. *American Combat Planes*. Garden City, NY: Doubleday & Co., 1968.

———. *The North American Sabre*. Garden City, NY: Doubleday & Co., 1963.

Wagner, Wolfgang. *Kurt Tank: Konstrukteur und Testpilot bei Focke-Wulf*. Munich: Bernard & Graefe Verlag, 1980.

Warden, Harold H. "Propeller Considerations for High-Speed Aircraft," *Aeronautical Engineering Review*, Oct. 1948.

Waterton, W. A. *The Quick and the Dead: The Story of a Chief Test Pilot*. London: Frederick Muller, 1956.

Weir, Kenneth W. "The U-2 Story," XXIInd Symposium, SETP, Beverly Hills, CA, Sept. 30, 1978.

Wheeler, Allen. *Building Aeroplanes for "Those Magnificent Men."* London: G. T. Foulis, 1965.

———. *". . . that nothing failed them": Testing Aeroplanes in Wartime*. London: G. T. Foulis, 1963.

White, Lynn, Jr. "Eilmer of Malmesbury: An Eleventh Century Aviator," *Technology and Culture*, Spring 1961.

———. "Medieval Uses of Air," *Scientific American*, Aug. 1970.

Whittle, Frank. *Jet: The Story of a Pioneer*. New York: Philosophical Library, 1954.

Williams, Walter C. "The Role of the Pilot in the Mercury and X-15 Flights," XIVth AGARD-NATO General Assembly, Lisbon, Sept. 16–17, 1964.

———; and Drake, Hubert M. "The Research Airplane: Past, Present, and Future," *Aeronautical Engineering Review*, Jan. 1958.

Wolfe, Tom. *The Right Stuff*. New York: Farrar, Straus & Giroux, 1979.

Wood, Derek. *Project Cancelled: British Aircraft that Never Flew*. Indianapolis, IN: Bobbs-Merrill, 1975.

Woolams, Jack. "How We Are Preparing to Reach Supersonic Speeds," *Aviation*, Sept. 1946.

Wooldridge, E. T. *The P-80 Shooting Star: Evolution of a Jet Fighter*. Washington, DC: Smithsonian Institution, 1979.

Wright, Orville. "How We Made the First Flight," *Flying and The Aero Club of America Bulletin*, Dec. 1913.

Yeager, Charles E. "Operation of the XS-1 Airplane," XIXth Symposium, SETP, Beverly Hills, CA, Sept. 27, 1975.

INDEX